The United States at War

The United States at War

Volume 2

World War II — Post-Cold War Conflicts
Appendices
Indexes

Edited by
John C. Super
West Virginia University

SALEM PRESS, INC.
Pasadena, California   Hackensack, New Jersey

Frontispiece: U.S. Marines patrolling in Afghanistan in April, 2004.
(U.S. Department of Defense)

Some essays originally appeared in *Censorship* (1997), *Encyclopedia of Flight* (2002), *Encyclopedia of the U.S. Supreme Court* (2000), *Great Events, 1990-2001, Revised Edition* (2002), *Great Events from History: North American Series, Revised Edition* (1997), *Human Rights Violations* (2002), *Magill's Guide to Military History* (2001), *Weapons and Warfare* (2001), and *Women's Issues* (1997). New material has been added.

Library of Congress Cataloging-in-Publication Data

The United States at war / edited by John C. Super.
   p. cm.
Essays selected from various publications together with new material.
Includes bibliographical references and indexes.
ISBN-10: 1-58765-236-6 (set: alk. paper)
ISBN-10: 1-58765-237-4 (vol. 1 : alk. paper)
ISBN-10: 1-58765-238-2 (vol. 2 : alk. paper)
ISBN-10: 978-1-58765-236-3 (set 13 digit: alk. paper)
[etc.]
   1. United States—History, Military.   2. United States—History, Military—Chronology.   I. Super, John C., 1944-
E181.U64 2005
355'.00973—dc22

                                                    2005006689

First Printing

PRINTED IN THE UNITED STATES OF AMERICA

Table of Contents

Table of Contents

The
United States
at
War

World War II
1939-1945

World War II

At issue: Democracy and communism vs. fascism; German or Soviet dominance in Eastern Europe; Japanese or American dominance in the Pacific
Date: September 1, 1939-August 14, 1945
Location: Europe, Asia, Africa, Middle East, and Pacific and Atlantic Oceans
Combatants: Allies: Great Britain, France, United States, Soviet Union vs. Axis Powers: Germany, Italy, Japan
Principal commanders: *British*, Bernard Law Montgomery (1887-1976); *French*, Charles de Gaulle (1890-1970); *American*, Dwight D. Eisenhower (1890-1969), Chester W. Nimitz (1885-1966), Douglas MacArthur (1880-1964), George S. Patton (1885-1945); *Soviet*, Georgy Zhukov (1896-1974); *German*, Erwin Rommel (1891-1944), Adolf Hitler (1889-1945); *Japanese*, Isoroku Yamamoto (1884-1943)
Principal battles: France, Britain, Operation Barbarossa, Pearl Harbor, Singapore, Coral Sea, Midway, Guadalcanal, El Alamein, Stalingrad, Kursk, Normandy, the Bulge, Iwo Jima, Okinawa, Berlin
Result: A total Allied victory over the Axis in which Germany lost territory and was occupied and partitioned, the Soviet Union replaced Germany as the dominant power in Eastern Europe, and Japan lost territory and was occupied.

World War II was the largest, most destructive, and most widespread war in history. During the conflict, more than 50 million people died and hundreds of millions were wounded, physically and psychologically. The war, fought on land, sea, and air, was the epic struggle of the twentieth century and was central to the whole century. It was caused in large part by the unresolved issues of World War I (1914-1918), and its aftermath became the Cold War (1945-1991).

Two coalitions of nations, the Axis and the Allies, fought the war. The Axis states were fascist and militaristic. Fascism was an extreme form of racist nationalism under the leadership of dictators who claimed to express the collective will of their peoples. The major powers of the Axis were Germany, Italy, and Japan. The major Allied Powers were Great Britain, France, the United States, and the Soviet Union. Some nations switched allegiances during the war. Italy changed sides in 1943. After 1940, France had forces on both sides, the Free French and Vichy French. The Soviet Union cooperated with Germany until attacked in June, 1941,

(continued on page 386)

Time Line of World War II

Dec., 1937-Jan., 1938	Japanese troops invade China, beginning World War II in East Asia.
Sept. 15-29, 1938	British and German leaders meet in Munich.
Aug., 1939	The possibility of American involvement in the war developing in Europe and East Asia prompts conversion of domestic production to meet military needs.
Sept. 1, 1939	Germany invades Poland, beginning World War II in Europe.
Sept. 3, 1939-May 4, 1945	Battle of North Atlantic: Eventual definitive victory for Allied forces.
Oct., 1939-Dec. 7, 1941	Polish Campaign.
Apr. 9, 1940	Germany invades Norway.
May-June, 1940	Germany occupies France.
May 10, 1940	Germany invades Luxembourg, the Netherlands, and Belgium.
June 10, 1940	Italy declares war on France and Great Britain. Italian forces enter southern France.
July 10-Oct. 31, 1940	Battle of Britain: Germany bombs Great Britain in preparation for a land invasion. Despite great losses on both sides, the British repulse German air power and avoid German occupation.
Sept. 27, 1940	Japan signs the Tripartite Pact with Germany and Italy, becoming a member of the Axis powers.
Oct. 8, 1940	Germany begins occupation of Romania.
Oct. 28, 1940	Italy invades Greece.
Nov. 11, 1940	Battle of Taranto.
Dec. 9-13, 1940	Battle of Sīdī Barrāni.
1941-1942	Battle of Moscow.
1941-1944	Siege of Leningrad.
Mar. 11, 1941	Before the United States becomes formally involved in the war, it uses the Lend-Lease program to support Great Britain's war effort while declaring official neutrality.
May 20-31, 1941	Crete campaign.

July 24, 1941	Japan occupies French Indochina (modern Vietnam). United States halts trade with Japan, sends General Douglas MacArthur to oversee military forces in the Philippines.
Sept. 16-26, 1941	Battle of Kiev.
Nov. 18, 1941- June 21, 1942	Battles of Tobruk.
Dec., 1941-Apr., 1942	Battle of Bataan: A Japanese victory that is a major step in Japan's attainment of the Philippines.
Dec. 7, 1941	Battle of Pearl Harbor: Japanese bomb Pearl Harbor in the Hawaiian Islands, sinking or disabling five of eight U.S. battleships, as well as other ships and airplanes. Nearly 2,500 persons, including 68 civilians are killed. Japan simultaneously attacks Guam, the Philippines, Midway Island, Hong Kong, and the Malay Peninsula.
Dec. 8, 1941	United States declares war on Japan.
Dec. 10, 1941- Feb. 15, 1942	Battle of Singapore.
Dec. 11, 1941	Axis nations declare war on the United States.
1942-1943	Battles of Kharkov.
Feb. 19, 1942	U.S. government begins relocating persons of Japanese descent on the Pacific Coast.
Feb. 27-Mar. 1, 1942	Battle of the Java Sea: Severe U.S. losses; Japan occupies Java.
Mar. 9, 1942	Japan occupies Rangoon, Burma, cutting off Allied access to China.
May 3-8, 1942	Battle of the Coral Sea: For the first time in history, all fighting in a naval battle is conducted by planes launched off aircraft carriers. Japanese advance into Australia is halted.
May 6, 1942	Bataan Peninsula and Corregidor fall to the Japanese.
June 3-21, 1942	Japan bombs Alaska, occupies the Aleutian Islands, and shells the Oregon coast.
June 3-5, 1942	Battle of Midway: Japan's advance across the Pacific is stopped, and Japan suffers severe losses. Turning point in the Pacific war.
June 17, 1942	President Roosevelt approves the Manhattan Project, which is to build an atomic bomb.

continued

TIME LINE OF WORLD WAR II—continued

Aug. 7, 1942- Feb. 9, 1943	Battle of Guadalcanal: United States prevents Japanese from landing reinforcements, ensuring Allied conquest of Guadalcanal. Japanese evacuate Guadalcanal on Feb. 9, 1943.
Aug. 19, 1942	Raid on Dieppe.
Aug. 23, 1942- Feb. 2, 1943	Battle of Stalingrad.
Aug. 23-25, 1942	Battle of Eastern Solomons: United States inflicts severe damage on Japanese ships.
Sept. 13-14, 1942	Battle of Bloody Ridge: Six thousand Japanese troops are routed.
Oct. 23-Nov. 4, 1942	Battle of El Alamein.
Nov. 7-8, 1942	North Africa Invasion: An Allied campaign designed to drive the Germans out of North Africa, this operation provides a training ground for U.S. forces in World War II.
Feb., 1943	Casablanca Conference.
July 5-15, 1943	Battle of Kursk.
July 6, 1943	Battle of Kula Gulf: First U.S. victory in South Pacific.
July 9-Sept. 19, 1943	Italy Invasion: This campaign forces Germany to use troops and resources that might otherwise have been used in northern France.
Aug. 15, 1943	United States regains Aleutian Islands.
Sept. 8, 1943	Italy surrenders unconditionally.
Sept. 9-Oct. 1, 1943	Battle of Salerno: The Allies accomplish their objective, taking the port of Naples.
Nov., 1943- June, 1944	Battle of Monte Cassino.
Nov. 2, 1943	Battle of Empress Augusta Bay: Japanese defeat in South Pacific secures Solomons for the Allies.
Nov. 20-23, 1943	Battle of Tarawa: Costly U.S. victory in which U.S. forces use the captured airstrip to support invasions of the Marshall Islands.
Jan. 22-May 25, 1944	Battle of Anzio.
Jan. 31-Nov. 25, 1944	United States takes Marshall Islands, Mariana Islands, Guam, and the Palaus.
June 6, 1944	D Day: Operation Overlord's Normandy invasion begins.

June 15-July 9, 1944	United States seizes the island of Saipan, headquarters for the Japanese defense of the Central Pacific. Its fall impairs the Japanese defense strategy and gives the Americans an air base from which B-29 Superfortress bombers can reach Tokyo.
June 15, 1944	Superfortress bombing of Japan begins.
June 19-20, 1944	Battle of the Philippine Sea: Inflicts severe losses on Japan, of both sea vessels and airplanes.
June 22-July 11, 1944	Soviets send 166 divisions against German positions in Belorussia in Operation Bagration.
July 20-Aug. 10, 1944	Battle of Guam: United States recaptures a strategic base in the Pacific from the Japanese.
July 24-Aug. 1, 1944	Battle of Tinian: United States swiftly takes Tinian from the Japanese; it becomes the launching site for numerous B-29 bombing raids against the Japanese main islands.
Aug. 25, 1944	Liberation of Paris.
Sept. 11, 1944	Liberation of Luxembourg.
Sept. 17-26, 1944	Battle of Arnhem.
Oct. 23-26, 1944	Battle of Leyte Gulf: In three major naval engagements, United States destroys remaining Japanese naval forces and takes control of Philippines. The largest naval battle of the war.
Dec. 16, 1944-Jan. 25, 1945	Battle of the Bulge: German forces are routed in a desperate campaign to halt advancing Allied armies.
Feb. 4-11, 1945	Yalta Conference: This significant meeting of the "Big Three" Allied powers marks the height of Allied cooperation but also reveals conflicting agendas.
Feb. 19-Mar. 26, 1945	Battle of Iwo Jima: U.S. Marines seize a Japanese island air base located southeast of Japan.
Mar., 1945	Battle of Mandalay.
Mar. 7-May 8, 1945	Rhine Crossings.
Apr. 1-July 2, 1945	Battle of Okinawa: United States invades Okinawa, occupying it by June 21. Japanese suicide flights contribute to making this the costliest battle of the war.
Apr. 19-May 2, 1945	Battle of Berlin.
May 7, 1945	Germany signs surrender documents.
May 8, 1945	V-E Day: President Harry S. Truman declares victory in Europe.

continued

Time Line of World War II—continued

July 17-Aug. 2, 1945   Potsdam Conference: The third and final "Big Three" meeting plans a peace settlement at the end of World War II.

Aug. 6 and 9, 1945   United States drops atomic bombs on Hiroshima and Nagasaki, Japan.

Aug. 14, 1945   V-J Day: Japan accepts terms of surrender and occasion is declared "Victory in Japan" day.

---

and the United States did not officially participate until attacked by Japan on December 7, 1941.

Causes of the War

World War II grew out of grievances produced by the aftermath of World War I. Germans were outraged by the harsh Treaty of Versailles (1919), which had taken away German territory in the east and west, destroyed the Austro-Hungarian Empire, humiliated Germans by including a "war guilt" clause, imposed disarmament, and demanded payments for war damage. Racked by inflation and depression, a substantial minority of Germans voted the extremist Nazi Party into power in 1933. Adolf Hitler, the charismatic and fanatical nationalist, pursued policies of economic control and rearmament. The Nazis were both anticommunist and anti-Semitic, blaming Reds and Jews for Germany's problems. Hitler saw a need for "living space" for "superior" Germans, which was to be carved from lands occupied by "inferior" Slavic peoples living to the east.

Hitler pursued a policy of aggression in foreign policy, with the express aim of bringing all ethnic Germans into the new Reich, or empire. German forces entered the demilitarized German Rhineland in 1936, Austria in 1938, and Czechoslovakia in 1938 and 1939. Meanwhile, Britain and France sought to appease the Nazis by granting concessions in the hope that this would satisfy German ambitions. The height of the policy of appeasement came at the Munich Conference in 1938, which dismembered Czechoslovakia. However, in the eyes of the Western democracies, concessions to Hitler appeared only to encourage more aggression. Britain and France decided to guarantee the integrity of several small states in Europe, including Poland.

Hitler's demands on Poland centered on the surrender of territory that had been shifted from Germany to Poland after World War I, particularly the Polish corridor and the city of Danzig. The Poles resolved to resist dismemberment of their country, and World War II began on September 1, 1939, when Germany attacked Poland. Britain and France honored their commitment to Poland and went to war.

Just before attacking Poland, Hitler made an unexpected agreement, the German-Soviet Pact of 1939, with Soviet leader Joseph Stalin. It called for peace and economic cooperation between Germany and the Soviet Union and divided Poland between them. It was Stalin's hope that Germany and the Western powers would destroy themselves while a neutral Soviet Union would continue to gain strength.

Italy did not join the war on the German side until 1940. Italy had been appeased when it attacked Ethiopia in 1935. Another important fascist state, Spain, whose leader, Francisco Franco, had been aided by the Germans during its civil war of 1936, managed to remain neutral throughout the war.

A major question decided by World War II was whether Germany or the Soviet Union would dominate the lands of Eastern Europe and control the Poles, Czechs, Slovaks, Hungarians, and many South Slavs. Germans had enjoyed economic predominance in this area for centuries, and Russians had long regarded the Slavic peoples as ethnic and cultural relatives who needed their protection. The Russo-German phase of the war, beginning with the sudden German invasion of the Soviet Union in June, 1941,

German chancellor Adolf Hitler receiving an ovation from the Reichstag after announcing his annexation of Austria in March, 1938. (National Archives)

Soviet foreign minister Vyacheslav Molotov signs the German-Soviet nonaggression pact in Moscow on August 23, 1939, while Soviet premier Joseph Stalin (in white jacket) and German foreign minister Joachim von Ribbentrop (behind Molotov) look on. (National Archives)

brought the war's most ferocious fighting and worst attrition to the plains of Eastern Europe. Before the invasion of the Soviet Union, some military leaders had favored a war against the Soviet Union.

The War in Asia

The war in Asia began earlier, in 1931, when Japan moved against the rich Chinese province of Manchuria. Japan had modernized rapidly and wanted the province's raw materials for its industries. Military figures came to dominate Japanese domestic politics as ruthless aggression led to a full-scale war between Japan and China. The United States favored China and began an anti-Japanese foreign policy that ultimately led to the Japanese attack on Pearl Harbor. Both Japan and the United States had large naval forces in the Pacific. One of the great questions to be decided by World War II was which of these nations would dominate the Pacific.

Japan signed a defensive pact with Germany and Italy in 1936. Partly as a result of Germany's success in invading the Soviet Union in 1941, the Japanese decided to strike southward against the European nations' holdings in Asia. By attacking European holdings in Asia, Japan could claim to be freeing Asians from European rule. Southeast Asia would give Japan an abundance of resources, particularly oil and rubber. Japan and the Soviet Union maintained neutrality toward each other until the Soviets attacked the Japanese in 1945.

Only the U.S. Navy stood in the way of Japan. The United States had a large, modern navy, divided between the Atlantic and the Pacific. President Franklin D. Roosevelt sought to curtail Japanese expansion in Asia at the same time that he opposed German advances in Europe. He had the utmost concern for the plight of Britain in 1940, when Britain stood alone in Europe against Hitler. Like many Americans, Roosevelt thought that German victory in Europe would bring tyranny to millions and eventually threaten democracy in the United States as well. What hampered Roosevelt from joining outright in Britain's defense was very strong isolationist sentiment in the United States. Isolationists did not want to support or participate in foreign wars, which they claimed had nothing to do with the United States. Roosevelt could not risk deeply offending the isolationists because he needed their support to be reelected. However, he gave as much aid to Britain as possible under legislative constraints, allowing the U.S. Navy to help protect convoys destined for Britain.

PACIFIC THEATER OF WORLD WAR II

When Japan launched a surprise attack on Pearl Harbor on December 7, 1941, World War II took on its full global dimensions. Shortly afterward, Germany declared war on the United States. As 1942 began, all the major powers were engaged in the conflict. Land, sea, and air forces contended throughout the globe.

The War in Europe

Germany's September 1, 1939 attack on Poland utilized new techniques of air assault and armored breakthrough, called Blitzkrieg, or lightning war. Planes would bomb to disrupt ground operations while tanks, mobile guns, and mechanized infantry would punch through a soft spot and race to surround defending forces. The Germans defeated poorly equipped Polish forces by September 28. The British and French did not attack Germany's lightly defended western border but stayed on the defensive. Meanwhile, a desultory war at sea began, featuring submarine sinkings and sorties by units of the German surface fleet. The calm in the west in the fall and winter of 1939-1940 was called the "Phony War."

The storm broke in the west in April of 1940 when Hitler launched a swift campaign against Denmark and Norway. Naval units, parachute troops, and transport planes boldly carried out the Norwegian invasion. British forces landed in northern Norway but could not prevail without air cover.

The Netherlands fell next as German troops swarmed across the border and planes dropped bombs on the region. Hitler adopted a daring strategy for his western offensive. While the Allies sent their forces north to defend Belgium, just as they had during World War I, German armored units lined up to storm through the rough terrain of the almost undefended Ardennes forest, the least likely access route to France. German tanks broke out and crossed below the Allied armies and raced to the sea.

The Allies had more troops and more tanks than the Germans, but the superior tactics and communication and air power of the Germans soon caused the French and British armies to retreat in panic. Hundreds of thousands of Allied troops were surrounded at Dunkirk, a northern French port. Instead of crushing them with armor, Hitler elected to allow the Luftwaffe (German air force) to destroy these forces from the air. They failed, in part because of the resistance of the Royal Air Force (RAF) and also because a great flotilla of varied ships arrived from Britain to evacuate soldiers. Through these actions, Britain's defeat became a heroic retreat. In May, 1940, the Germans renewed the attack on France, which surrendered in June. Northern France was occupied, and Vichy France, a collaborating fascist state, was established under General Henri-Philippe Pétain in

World War II saw the introduction of paratroops to combat, making it possible for the first time for combatants to place large numbers of troops behind enemy lines quickly. (National Archives)

southern France. General Charles de Gaulle escaped to Britain, where he came to lead the Free French forces worldwide.

As France collapsed, the British government changed hands. Prime Minister Neville Chamberlain was replaced by Winston S. Churchill, who had always opposed appeasing the Germans. Britain stood all alone, except for its overseas empire, and faced a continent dominated by Hitler. In stirring and famous speeches, Churchill vowed to fight to the death. Hitler was not as eager to fight the British as he was to fight the Soviets, who were still helping him, because he saw the British as racially similar to the Germans. Nevertheless, he tried to subdue Britain in the summer of 1940. Before he could mount an invasion, he had to establish German superiority in the air. The Battle of Britain was fought entirely in the air from July to November, 1940. The Luftwaffe could not destroy the RAF and suffered substantial losses in the effort.

Thwarted, Hitler turned his attention to preparing for a land campaign against the Soviet Union. However, German forces continued mass night

EUROPEAN THEATER OF WORLD WAR II

bombings of British cities, a tactic known as the Blitz. London was particularly hard hit, but Londoners showed amazing bravery and determination. Britain was also threatened on the seas by a growing submarine campaign against merchant ships, which provided the imports necessary to sustain industry and feed the nation. The Battle of the North Atlantic, which raged all through the war, destroying many British ships, greatly worried Churchill.

Italy joined the war as France collapsed, hoping to gain more territory in Africa. Italy launched unsuccessful campaigns against British forces in North Africa in the summer of 1940 and against Greece in October, 1940. German forces had to rescue Italian troops in both campaigns. To save the Italians, Hitler had to conquer the Balkans and send the German Afrika Corps to North Africa, led by General Erwin Rommel.

North Africa was only a sideshow for the Axis, however. The great campaign of 1941 was Operation Barbarossa, in which more than three million

German and Axis forces attacked the Soviet Union. Victory followed victory as German forces advanced on a three-pronged front, aiming at Leningrad, Moscow, and Ukraine. Many people thought that the Soviet collapse was near, but despite fearful losses, the Russians held on until mud and cold stalled the German invasion. The Germans had expected victory before winter and were unprepared for Russia's bitter cold.

The United States Enters the War

When Japan attacked Pearl Harbor (December 7, 1941), the Germans were about to be thrown back on the outskirts of Moscow. The brilliant surprise attack sank U.S. battleships but U.S. carriers were at sea. Japanese strategy called for the rapid conquest of Southeast Asia after crippling the U.S. fleet. U.S. forces held out in the Philippines as long as possible, but Japanese forces stormed to victory all through the area, easily conquering the British bastion of Singapore (1941-1942). Nevertheless, American leaders decided that Japan was less of a threat than Nazi Germany and gave the war in Europe first priority for the rapidly expanding U.S. forces.

At the beginning of 1942, the Axis Powers were at the height of their expansion, dominating continental Europe and the western Pacific. The Soviet Union appeared about to collapse, and Britain was being strangled by submarine warfare. The United States was unable to stop the victorious Japanese fleet. Then the course of the war changed through three dramatic turning points: the Battles of Coral Sea (May 3-8, 1942), Midway (June 4, 1942), and Guadalcanal (August 7, 1942-February 9, 1943), when the tide turned against the Japanese in the Pacific; El Alamein (October 23-November 4, 1942) in North Africa, where Rommel was defeated by Bernard Law Montgomery at the outskirts of Egypt; and the most important battle of all, Stalingrad (August 23, 1942-February 2, 1943) along the Volga River, deep in the Soviet Union, which threw the Germans back.

The Russian Front

The hitherto invincible German army was destroyed on the plains of Russia. Four out of five German casualties in the war occurred on this battle site, at the cost of more than twenty million Soviet lives. In 1942, Hitler planned to drive his troops to the southeast to capture oil fields in the Caucasus. When his forces became bogged down in Stalingrad, the campaign foundered. The Soviets launched a counterattack that surrounded the city and eventually forced a stunning German surrender. An even more destructive defeat occurred at Kursk (July, 1943) in the

Ukraine. Until 1943, the Germans had advanced in the summer and the Soviets had pushed them back in the winter. Beginning in 1943, however, Soviet forces advanced westward in the summer and winter, arriving in eastern Europe by 1944 and in Berlin in 1945. The fighting on the eastern front was vicious and included the mass murder of civilians and prisoners by both sides.

Stalin constantly called for a "second front," meaning an Allied invasion in Western Europe. Anglo-American forces were cautious, first invading North Africa in November, 1942, and Italy in 1943. The Italians changed sides and eventually executed Italian leader Benito Mussolini. Meanwhile, the great Allied bombing offensive against German cities intensified, which drew German forces from the critical eastern front. Simultaneously, the convoy system, long-range air power, and new equipment diminished the submarine menace.

U.S. wartime production became phenomenal. Massive numbers of ships, planes, tanks, and guns poured out of factories to equip U.S. and Allied forces. Powerful trucks, landing craft, and rapidly evolving aircraft were particularly important American contributions to the war. Women took jobs hitherto reserved for men in all countries involved in the war.

A more sinister operation gained speed in German-occupied Europe: the deliberate mass killing of Jews and other groups, a well-documented event called the Holocaust. More than eight million Jews and three million others were murdered in concentration camps.

Allied Victory

The long-expected Allied invasion of Europe took place June 6, 1944, at Normandy, long after the Soviets had begun to push back the German armies on the eastern front. Breakout and the liberation of Paris followed, due in large measure to the actions of General George S. Patton. General Montgomery's plan to cross the Rhine via Holland, Operation Market Garden, September, 1944, failed. A surprise German attack in Belgium in December, 1944, the Battle of the Bulge, temporarily caused the Allies concern. Yet by the spring of 1945, they were able to push deep into Germany and link up with Soviet forces, which reached Berlin in April, 1945. The war in Europe came to an end after Hitler committed suicide in a Berlin bunker as Soviet troops conquered the city.

Meanwhile, U.S. forces under Douglas MacArthur in the Pacific liberated the Philippines (October, 1944-July, 1945), and Chester W. Nimitz used the dramatically expanded U.S. Navy in an island-hopping campaign. The Japanese fleet and air forces were virtually wiped out in a series of one-sided battles. When islands close to Japan—Iwo Jima (February-

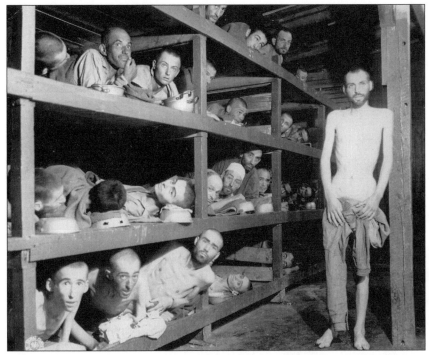

Many of the inmates of Germany's Buchenwald concentration camp were barely alive when Allied troops liberated the camp in April, 1945. (National Archives)

March, 1945) and Okinawa (April-July, 1945)—were seized, the Japanese turned to suicidal kamikaze attacks against U.S. ships. An invasion of Japan was planned, but became unnecessary after the world's first atomic bombs were dropped on Hiroshima and Nagasaki in August, 1945. Japan surrendered but was allowed to keep its emperor.

Aftermath

The results of World War II largely determined the course of the rest of the century. Devastated Germany was shorn of territory to the east, west, and south, and was partitioned and occupied. The Soviet Union replaced Germany as the dominant power in Eastern Europe as communist puppet states emerged in the shadow of the Red Army. Bombed-out Japan was occupied by the now clearly dominant power in the Pacific, the United States.

The postwar world was soon overshadowed by the Cold War, as the Soviet sphere in Europe was delineated by what Churchill came to call the Iron Curtain. Western Europe was uplifted and protected by the United States. The generous Marshall Plan poured millions of dollars into non-

As Supreme Allied Commander in the Pacific, General Douglas MacArthur signs the formal documents recognizing Japan's surrender in the war. The ceremony took place aboard the battleship USS Missouri, *anchored in Tokyo Bay, on September 2, 1945.* (National Archives)

communist countries to bolster their resistance to communism and eventually to make them good business partners for the United States. Observers expected Western Europe to take generations to recuperate, but Europe recovered with surprising rapidity.

The ideology of fascist racism was thoroughly discredited by the war. Communism in the Soviet bloc continued until the Soviet Union's dissolution during the early 1990's. The Cold War's key confrontation was the border between democratic West Germany and communist East Germany.

The United States emerged from the war as a global superpower with its productive capacities hugely expanded by the war. National pride and confidence in democracy and capitalism flourished as wealth and power soared. Overall, Americans and their allies looked back on the war, terrible as it was, as a necessary struggle to preserve freedom.

Henry Weisser

Weapons, Tactics, and Strategies

While World War I was the first global war to employ the advanced destructive capabilities of modern weapons systems and armaments, it was World War II that brought modern tactical and strategic thinking to their application. The result was destruction of human life and property on a scale unprecedented in history.

At the end of World War I, there was no longer a balance of power in Europe. Great Britain and France had been physically devastated and were close to financial bankruptcy; Germany had been defeated and disarmed; Russia, by then the Soviet Union, had been excluded as a result of the Russian Revolution (1918-1921) and the spread of communism. The United States had withdrawn from European affairs, devoting its attention to the Western Hemisphere and the Pacific and leaving Britain and France as the only real powers in an unstable political and military system. France decided to strengthen its border defenses, known as the Maginot line, using the Treaty of Versailles (1919) to prevent the rearmament of Germany and entering into a series of security alliances. Great Britain, perceiving no serious threat, returned to the advancement of its imperial interests, relying upon its navy for defense. Although both Britain and France belonged to the League of Nations created at the end of World War I, neither saw this organization as a credible deterrent to war.

With the exception of the persistent threat of communism, the 1920's witnessed a lessening of international tensions, with the drafting of the Locarno Pact (1925), establishing Germany's western borders; the Kellogg-Briand Pact (1928), renouncing the use of war in settling international disputes; and the entrance of Germany into the League of Nations (1926).

Everything changed, however, after the U.S. stock market collapsed in 1929. Financial and economic crisis brought political instability and a renewal of international tensions. On January 30, 1933, Adolf Hitler came to power in Germany. Italy began to assert its authority under fascist dictator Benito Mussolini, and Fascism spread into Romania and Hungary, as the rest of Eastern Europe began to disintegrate. At the same time, communist activities directed by Communist International (Comintern), the communist organization founded by Vladimir Ilich Lenin, under the control of the Soviet Union increased. Governments were forced to direct all available resources to provide social services for the large numbers of unemployed and destitute.

Germany Rearms

International tensions escalated after Hitler began to rebuild German military power. In 1933, after the League of Nations refused to weaken the restrictions on German rearmament, Hitler's Germany left the organization. In 1935 the Saar was returned to Germany in response to a wave of Nationalist propaganda, and Hitler then attempted to take over Austria. Britain and France were able to thwart Hitler but only with the support of Mussolini, who allied with Hitler two years later when Britain and France refused to support his conquest of Ethiopia.

In 1936 Hitler and Mussolini also sent aid to Nationalist general Francisco Franco in Spain at the beginning of the Spanish Civil War, whereas the West relied on sanctions and weak protests. By 1936 Germany under Hitler and his National Socialist Party (Nazis) had begun to rearm at a frantic pace, whereas Britain, France, and the United States used almost all of their resources to bolster their economies. However, it should be noted that a considerable amount of the Works Progress Administration (WPA) spending in the United States was devoted to military purposes, including the building of two aircraft carriers and several military posts. Britain, in the meantime, had devoted a large portion of its 1936, 1937, and 1938 defense budgets to the building of radar stations and the infrastructure of an early warning system.

In 1936 military-age Germans outnumbered their French counterparts two to one. France, the key to Allied defense against Nazi aggression, realized that it would be unable to match either German manpower or German industrial production. For a short time, the French government actively sought an alliance with the Soviet Union, but this alliance never materialized, due to the purges of Joseph Stalin in the late 1930's. Increasingly forced to rely on a defensive strategy, France became more obvious in its weaknesses, taking no action when Hitler remilitarized the Rhineland in 1937.

British Appeasement

Meanwhile, Britain had decided that some kind of accommodation or appeasement could be reached with Hitler, offering only perfunctory protests when Hitler remilitarized the Rhineland and carried out his Anschluss, or annexation, of Austria in early 1938. When Hitler demanded that something be done about Czechoslovakia, the British, with French acquiescence, decided to appease Nazi Germany rather than risk a war they were not prepared to fight. In September, 1938, the British and French leaders, Neville Chamberlain and Édouard Daladier, allowed Hitler to seize the Sudetenland, which included most of Czechoslovakia's defenses and armament industries, in return for Hitler's promise that he would meet with them to negotiate future problems. In March, 1939, Hitler violated the agreement and seized the rest of Czechoslovakia.

Neither France nor Britain had begun to rearm seriously until the crisis over the Sudetenland, and they thus negotiated from a position of weakness. For example, all the aircraft used by Britain to fight the Battle of Britain (1940) were manufactured after the Czech crisis. Although both France and Britain had begun to rebuild their military forces in early 1939, their action was too little, too late. When the Polish crisis escalated into war with the German invasion of Poland on September 1, 1939, neither France nor Britain was prepared to fight. In actuality, the military weakness of Britain and France encouraged German aggression and added to the crises that led to World War II.

U.S. Preparedness

The United States was even further behind its European allies in military development. Preoccupied with the efforts to deal with the Great Depression and perceiving no immediate external threat to national security, the U.S. Army was less prepared to wage war than it had been at any time since the Civil War. Ranked equally with Britain and Japan in naval power, in 1939 the United States was ranked seventeenth in overall military strength, behind both Spain and Romania. The U.S. armed forces had no tanks, few first-line fighter aircraft, and barely enough rifles for its army.

It should be remembered that the United States, disillusioned by the outcome of World War I, was determined to stay out of World War II. However, as British and French power in the Pacific diminished as a result of the fighting in Europe, the Japanese seized the opportunity to expand their influence in the region. Although the U.S. armed forces were in a weakened state, U.S. interests in the Pacific, mainly China and the Philippines, had to be protected. A series of crises, misunderstandings, and miscalculations on both sides resulted in the Japanese decision to attack the United States Pacific Fleet at Pearl Harbor, Hawaii, on December 7, 1941. Unprepared, the United States suddenly found itself involved in World War II.

Military Achievement

The military role of France during World War II was limited by its early defeat and surrender in 1940. Hampered both by its reliance on the fixed fortifications of the Maginot line and by its refusal to create a modern armored force, the French army was neither doctrinally nor technically capable of defeating the Germans. Later in the war, however, the First French Army, equipped and supplied by the United States and commanded by

One key to Allied success in the war was American industrial might. Here women at Douglas Aircraft's Long Beach, California, plant assemble nose cones for A-20 attack bombers. (National Archives)

General Jean-Marie-Gabriel de Lattre de Tassigny, performed well and helped to liberate France.

The British army did no better than the French. Defeated on the frontier of France in 1940, it was forced to retreat to Dunkirk and had to be evacuated, leaving behind all of its heavy equipment. Only in the initial battles against the Italians in North Africa did the British army emerge victorious. The Royal Air Force did perform better: With their Spitfire and Hurricane fighters, both guided by sophisticated early-warning radar systems, they were able to defeat the German air force, or Luftwaffe, and prevent the invasion of Britain. At the same time the heavy bomber force under British air marshal Arthur T. Harris, after concluding that daylight bombing would be too costly, began the successful development of night bombing operations. Harris developed the concept of "saturation bombing"; in May, 1942, he attacked Cologne with 1,000 planes and destroyed 600 acres of the city. However, high losses of 970 bombers between May and November, 1942, hampered his efforts.

British military performance, even when supported by a large infusion of U.S. aid, improved little in the desert battles against German commander Erwin Rommel's Afrika Korps. Problems with command and control, armor, and leadership led to numerous British defeats. At the same time, the British army in the Far East was outfought and outmaneuvered by the Japanese, resulting in one of the worst defeats in British history, at Singapore (1941-1942). The situation did begin to improve when British generals Harold Alexander and Bernard Law Montgomery reorganized the British Eighth Army and won the Battle of El Alamein (1942). At the same time the British army came increasingly under U.S. control, both logistically and tactically.

U.S. Mobilization

Although the United States had not been prepared to fight a war when the Japanese attacked Pearl Harbor, the nation quickly mobilized its vast resources and was able to launch offenses in both North Africa and the South Pacific within less than a year. Although its initial performance was unimpressive, the U.S. Army was victorious at the Battles of the Kasserine Pass (1943) and New Guinea (1943). Three factors played a major role in early U.S. victories: material superiority, command of the air, and adaptability to changing circumstances.

Due in large measure to the training provided by the government and armed forces service schools, senior officers were intellectually prepared for a global war. The logistical accomplishments of the Army and Navy were formidable. Despite initial problems and some brief shortages of critical supplies, the U.S. servicemen and their allies were amply supplied with everything they needed to fight the war. Another area of exceptional performance was the U.S. artillery, which used forward observers and new operational techniques. The U.S. artillery proved to be the most successful arm of the service, a fact repeatedly remarked upon by captured German soldiers.

The U.S. Army excelled in two other aspects of warfare: air and amphibious operations. In the air, using heavy bombers such as B-17's and B-24's, the U.S. Army Air Corps was able to destroy much of Nazi Germany's infrastructure, making it very difficult to maintain production. In the Pacific the B-29's were even more successful in destroying Japanese industrial production. Although strategic bombing did not win the war, as some prewar theorists had predicted, it did play a significant role in the defeat of the Axis Powers. Amphibious operations were very difficult, and much of the necessary equipment had to be developed during the war. Thanks to U.S. engineering and production genius, the United States was able to carry out successful landings on hostile beaches in both the European and Pacific theaters of operation. The most important amphibious operations were the landings during Operation Overlord on Normandy beaches launched on June 6, 1944 (D day), which marked the start of the final campaign of World War II.

British and American intelligence was able to break the German and Japanese codes during the war, thereby gaining advanced warning of enemy intentions. At Bletchley Park, 50 miles north of London, Britain assembled a large group of cryptologists, who successfully decrypted the German codes throughout the war, providing real-time intelligence to the commanders in the field. The Allied intelligence system was code-named Ultra, and its existence was not revealed until almost twenty years after the war ended. At the same time, U.S. cryptologists broke the Japanese codes. Despite this success, however, the United States was surprised by the Japanese attack on Pearl Harbor, and reliance upon the Ultra codes contributed to the failure of U.S. intelligence to realize the seriousness of the German attack in December, 1944, that resulted in the Battle of the Bulge (1944-1945).

Perhaps the greatest military achievement during World War II was the development and use of the atomic bomb by the United States. Rarely has a single weapon so changed the nature of warfare and the global balance of power. The decision to drop the atomic bomb, though controversial, hastened the end of the war.

Weapons

World War II witnessed the development and deployment of a large number of weapons ranging from the M1 Garand rifle to the atomic bomb. Science and technology played a greater role in the operational aspects of World War II than in those of any other war in history. In fact, a whole new area of military operations, called operational analysis, developed from the application of science to military problems. Operational analysis dealt with everything from the best depth at which to set depth charges to the most efficient force structure for combat divisions.

During the 1920's and 1930's the British experimented with a wide variety of armored vehicles, as well as other weapons systems. However, due to a lack of funding and a perceived lack of a serious military threat, these experiments were carried no further. The British went to war in 1939 with an army that was essentially equipped with slightly upgraded World War I weapons, except for the Spitfire and Hurricane fighters and some heavy bombers, which were developed late in the war. This failure in military modernization resulted in an increasing reliance throughout the war upon U.S. weapons, especially tanks and armored vehicles. After its defeat in 1940, the reconstituted French army that fought alongside the Allies in 1944 and 1945 relied almost entirely upon American weapons.

Within a year after the U.S. entry into the war, it had become the "Arsenal of Democracy," providing weaponry and supplies for all of the Allies, including the Soviet Union. At the same time, it equipped the ninety-division U.S. Army with excellent weapons. The standard infantry weapon was the M1 Garand, which was a gas-operated, clip-fed, semiautomatic rifle that fired eight shots and weighed 9.5 pounds. The artillery, especially the 105-millimeter howitzer and the 155-millimeter gun, used the fire-control system developed early in the war and proved to be the most effective arm of the army.

In the air, the U.S. heavy bombers (B-17's, B-24's, and B-29's) and fighters (P-47's and P-51's) were dependable and proved capable of defeating their adversaries. One of the less well known technical triumphs of American ingenuity was the proximity (V.T.) fuse. Actually a small radar set built into an explosive shell, it was so effective that no one was allowed to fire it over land, for fear the enemy might get their hands on one that did not explode. The greatest success of American technology was the atomic bomb, which hastened the end of the war against Japan and revolutionized warfare.

The greatest failure of American weaponry was the M4 Sherman medium tank. Although the reliable Sherman tank was capable of performing most of the tasks assigned to it, it had not been designed to be an antitank weapon and failed when called upon to engage the German medium or heavy tanks known as Panthers and Tigers. Produced in large numbers, more than 40,000, it provided armor not only for the U.S. Army but also for the British, French, and Polish forces in Europe. The M26 Pershing, which was designed to fight other tanks, was introduced at the end of the war but arrived too late to have any real effect. Only 700 Pershings were shipped to Europe.

Military Organization

At the beginning of World War II, the British Expeditionary Force (BEF) was dispatched to France. While retaining its independence, it served under the French commander General Maurice-Gustave Gamelin and later General Maxime Weygand. Organized into two army groups, the French concentrated the bulk of their mobile forces in the north with the BEF. After the defeat of France and the evacuation of the BEF to Dunkirk, most of the French army became a home-defense force. The remainder, along with Commonwealth forces, were sent to North Africa, whereas the British army stationed in India under separate command was used to reinforce the defenses in the Near East and Asia.

After the United States entered the war, the British army, although more experienced, came under U.S. field command. At the highest levels, the military command structure was the Combined Chiefs of Staff, consisting of the U.S. Joint Chiefs of Staff and the British Imperial General Staff. Although the Combined Chiefs of Staff operated on the principle of unanimity, the United States was decidedly the dominant partner. The staffs of both countries became more elaborate as the war progressed. The U.S. Joint Chiefs of Staff became increasingly involved in the formulation of U.S. foreign policy during the war. When the North African campaign began, the Free French were brought in as a junior partner. However, this relationship remained tenuous throughout the war because of President Franklin D. Roosevelt's personal distrust of the French leader, General Charles de Gaulle. Although the Soviet Union was an ally, it was seldom involved in military decisions at the strategic or tactical level.

The war was fought by the Allies—mainly the United States, Britain, and France—in four theaters of operation. The European theater was commanded by U.S. general Dwight D. Eisenhower, who had taken direct control over the cross-Channel invasion, prompting Field Marshal Alexander to take control of the Italian campaign. In the Pacific theater, the Southeast Pacific was commanded by General Douglas MacArthur, the Central Pacific by Admiral Chester W. Nimitz, and the China-Burma-India theater by Admiral Louis Mountbatten.

For a brief period during the Guadalcanal campaign in the Solomon Islands, there was a further division called the South Pacific theater, commanded by Admiral William F. Halsey. In all of these commands there were joint staffs of U.S., British, and other Allied officers. The Americans were in command and provided most of the forces who fought in all theaters, except the China-Burma-India theater. One major difference in operations should be noted: in the European theater of operation, Commonwealth—mainly Canadian—troops remained as part of the British command, whereas in the Southwest theater of operations, the Australian army served directly under MacArthur.

The reconstituted French army served not as a separate force but rather as one of the armies under U.S. command. One of the primary reasons for this arrangement was U.S. responsibility for logistical support. At the end of the war, the First French Army was separated and given its own sector of Germany to occupy.

Cooperation between the Western Allies and the Soviet Union was difficult at best. At the beginning of the war, due to British resistance to an early cross-Channel invasion, U.S. staff officers had been more favorable to the Soviet Union. However, as the war progressed and Soviet intentions in

Eastern Europe became apparent, the U.S. Joint Chiefs of Staff became increasingly hostile to the Soviets. The resulting mutual suspicion contributed to the beginning of the Cold War.

Doctrine, Strategy, and Tactics

A nation's military doctrine generally determines the nature of its weapons development, strategy, and tactics. During the years immediately following World War I, all the major powers reevaluated their military in the light of lessons learned in that war. The French came to the conclusion that defensive fortifications such as Verdun were their best option along with an infantry force supported by artillery and some armor. They believed that such a force would be able to take the offensive only in a limited way, using armor basically as mobile artillery to support the infantry rather than as an independent force capable of disrupting the enemy's lines.

Britain experimented with a variety of armor operations during the interwar years. For example, General Sir Percy Hobart conducted deep penetration armor maneuvers in 1935. However, the lack of adequate funding and the absence of a clear threat limited any deployment to small units more suitable for use as an empire constabulary rather than a continental army.

Some American planners such as Colonel George Patton did conceive of the use of large armored formations but the absence of any real threat, the financial restraints created by the Great Depression, and the conviction that the United States would not be involved in a European war in the future resulted in inadequately trained and equipped forces. The U.S. Army and many planning staff did develop very extensive plans (the Rainbow Plans) and realized many of the possible difficulties that were found later in the war. For example, under the leadership of Marine major Earl H. Ellis, doctrine and planning for amphibious warfare was developed prior to the war.

By not entering the war until December of 1941, American planners were able to take advantage of the experiences of both the Allies and the Germans. The decision to create only a ninety-division army hampered some operations, especially the large-scale armor attacks favored by the Germans and the Soviets. Much of American doctrinal development during the war centered on the use of the vast material advantage that the United States possessed, especially in artillery and airpower.

In the area of airborne operations, the U.S. Army developed the doctrine, organization, equipment, and tactics during the early part of the war. After basing much of their development on reports of German successes in

1939 and 1940, the U.S. airborne units and their British counterparts proved to be some of the most effective fighting forces in the European theater of operations, despite their limited use. The 82nd and 101st Airborne Divisions were considered two of the best.

Strategies

From the beginning of U.S. involvement in the war, the Allied strategy was "Europe first." Although unable to launch a cross-Channel invasion in 1942, the Allies attacked Germany first in North Africa (Operation Torch) and then in Sicily (Operation Huskey). At the same time priority was given to the heavy bomber offensive against Germany.

After the successful landings at Normandy, Allied strategy in Europe was a broad-front strategy. Rather than concentrate on one or two major thrusts, as the British commander Field Marshal Montgomery advocated, Eisenhower opted to attack along the entire front, forcing the German army to retreat back into Germany and ultimately destroying its ability to fight. Probably the greatest failure of American strategy was Eisenhower's decision to stop his advance at the Elbe River, allowing the Soviets to take Berlin and consequently to occupy all of Eastern Europe.

In the Pacific, General MacArthur directed an island-hopping strategy that avoided Japanese strong points. At the same time, the Japanese were further stretched by the U.S. decision to shift the axis of their attacks along two fronts: the Southwest Pacific from New Guinea through the Philippines and the Central Pacific. The Japanese surrendered before they were actually invaded.

Jachin W. Thacker

The Naval War

On the eve of World War II, the U.S. government began building warships that would dominate both the Atlantic and the Pacific theaters of naval warfare.

The goal of establishing a two-ocean fleet was a powerful, if elusive, force in determining the nature of the United States Navy before the Japanese attack on Pearl Harbor plunged the United States into war in 1941. In the late 1930's, the two-ocean standard became the latest in a succession of rallying cries designed to gain popular support for naval expansion. Its appeal originated in a growing recognition that vital U.S. interests were being threatened simultaneously by Germany and Japan. This two-ocean focus was an extension of threat perceptions and arguments dating back to the 1890's and made more pressing with the Anglo-Japanese alliance of 1902 and Japan's victory over Russia in the 1904-1905 Russo-Japanese War. With the collapse of naval arms limitations in 1936, the rearmament of National Socialist Germany, and the naval buildup and military adventurism of Japan, the necessity of creating fleets capable of fighting independently in widely separated theaters seemed evident. Congress, responding to the change in popular attitude, passed legislation between 1938 and 1941 designed to translate the ideal of a two-ocean fleet into reality.

U.S. Naval Policy

U.S. naval policy has been a mirror of national ambition. During the 1890's, and especially after the Spanish-American War, the horizon of that ambition increased measurably. At a single stroke, the United States became both a Caribbean and a Pacific power. U.S. control of the Philippines was perplexing for many people in the United States but exciting for navalists and imperialists. Together with Hawaii, which was annexed in 1898, the Philippines provided U.S. commerce with a toehold in the fabled China trade. Distant possessions seemed to mandate an increased fleet, and an increased fleet required overseas bases, setting the foundation for a self-perpetuating expansion of the military and naval establishment.

For better or worse, expanded interests called for expanded responsibilities, and President Theodore Roosevelt, an enthusiastic convert to U.S. imperialism, led the movement to secure those interests. Between 1905 and 1909, Congress authorized the construction of sixteen new battleships of the all-big-gun, dreadnought style by which international naval power was measured. Meanwhile, work on the Panama Canal, which was intended to provide much-needed flexibility for the fleet, continued toward its completion in 1914.

By the time of Theodore Roosevelt's presidency, Japan and especially Germany were seen as the most important potential threats to U.S. commerce and possessions. Tension caused by the treatment of Japanese nationals living in the United States was the primary reason for congressional approval of the last six new battleships authorized during Roosevelt's administration. The attention of most U.S. naval experts was fixed on Germany, where an ambitious twenty-year naval construction program had been announced in 1900. While the German fleet law was intended as a challenge to British naval supremacy, it was also perceived as a threat to U.S. interests by a host of U.S. congressmen and naval authorities. That traditional German concerns were continental and that the German navy had a nearer rival in Great Britain seemed to make no difference.

Those guiding U.S. naval policy believed that it would be a mistake for the United States to allow itself to be surpassed in naval power by any na-

Japan planned its attack on Pearl Harbor with the idea of knocking the U.S. Pacific Fleet completely out of action. However, while the damage done to the fleet was temporarily crippling, its effects were not long lasting. This photo shows the USS West Virginia, *one of the battleships most badly damaged at Pearl Harbor.* (National Archives)

tion that also maintained a great standing army. This growing U.S. fear of Germany was also reflected in the concentration of the fleet. Long a dictum of the most distinguished U.S. naval strategic synthesizer, Captain A. T. Mahan, the concentration of naval forces was adopted by Roosevelt as a cardinal principle of fleet deployment. Throughout his presidency, and Taft's as well, the main fleet remained posted in the Atlantic Ocean.

Interwar Developments

After 1914, the prewar desire to improve the United States Navy to second place behind the British fleet was replaced by a determination to build a navy second to none. This challenge to British naval superiority, the first ever by the United States, was engendered by British arrogance toward neutral U.S. shipping and a fear of the naval landscape in the postwar world. President Woodrow Wilson and Congress joined in the $588 million naval construction act of 1916, which mandated ten new superdreadnought battleships and six battle cruisers. Wilson called for a similar program in 1918 to strengthen the U.S. bargaining position at the Versailles Conference.

By 1924, the United States Navy would be the most powerful in the world, a dismaying prospect to the British government. U.S. naval ascension was delayed by the decision to shift battleship construction assets to the production of antisubmarine warships, such as destroyers, and to merchant ships to counter losses to German submarines. In the three years that followed the signing of the armistice ending World War I, the United States built more warships than all the rest of the world combined. In taking dead aim at British naval superiority, the United States also revealed apprehension concerning Japan's being linked to Britain by the ten-year renewal of the Anglo-Japanese alliance in 1911. Between 1917 and 1921, Japanese naval appropriations tripled, undoubtedly affected by the upsurge in U.S. construction. It is not surprising that with the demise of German naval power in 1919, concern in the United States shifted from the Atlantic to the Pacific. In the summer of that year, the battle fleet was divided, with the newer and heavier units being sent to the West Coast.

Fear of a costly, all-out naval race in the immediate postwar period served to induce a certain amount of moderation. In Washington, D.C., in 1921-1922, the five leading naval powers adopted a system of restrictions on individual capital ships (battleships and battle cruisers) and aircraft carriers as well as on the aggregate tonnages of capital war fleets. By the terms of the Five-Power Treaty, Great Britain and the United States were to share the first rank of naval power, Japan was assigned the second rank (approximately 60 percent of capital ship parity with the first-rank powers), while France and Italy were relegated to the third rank. In 1930, this agreement was augmented by the London Treaty, which established similar kinds of restrictions on the noncapital construction (cruisers, destroyers, and submarines) of Great Britain, the United States, and Japan. Thus, from 1922 through 1936, the size and nature of the United States war fleet was restricted by international agreement.

The Japanese Challenge

Domination of the Imperial Japanese Navy by the hardliners of the so-called Fleet Faction, who chafed at Japan's second-rank status under the treaties, resulted in significant pressure on the Japanese government to demand equal status with the United States and Great Britain at the London Naval Conference of 1935. When Great Britain and the United States demurred, the Japanese government provided the requisite notice that it would no longer abide by the naval treaties after December, 1936. Japan's subsequent penetration of China in 1937 and Hitler's annexation of Austria and absorption of the Sudetenland in 1938 seemed to provide ample proof for the proposition that unilateral restraint by the United States was a dangerous policy. The issue of naval preparedness became correspondingly less controversial.

In 1932, U.S. naval officers applauded the election of navalist Franklin D. Roosevelt to the presidency after the lean years of Republican naval and military expenditures. They were not disappointed. On the same day that he signed the National Industrial Recovery Act (NIRA) into law in June, 1933, Roosevelt signed an executive order using $238 million of NIRA public works funds for construction of new warships. This first step in building the U.S. Navy up to "treaty limits" was followed by congressional moves to improve the status of the war fleet. Spearheaded by the navalist chairman of the House Naval Affairs Committee, Carl Vinson, and the aging chairman of the Senate Naval Affairs Committee, Park Trammel, this movement's objective was the replacement of all the fleet's obsolete warships, or "floating coffins," to use Vinson's words. The resulting Vinson-Trammel bill which became law in March of 1934, also known as the Vinson Naval Parity Act, envisioned the replacement of almost a third of the existing tonnage of the Navy, including practically all the destroyers and submarines. The act did not appropriate funds for construction but served as a blueprint for U.S. naval policy. The clear intention of this action was the establishment of a fighting force that would be the equal of any in the world. Both the NIRA-funded ships and the Vinson-Trammel Act exacerbated strategic concerns in Japan, which was approaching its warship treaty limits and now faced new, qualitatively superior, U.S. warships.

The Pacific theater of the war was dominated by naval combat, and most land operations were dependent on naval assistance. Of particular importance in coordinating land and sea operations were amphibious landing craft such as these, which were used to carry large numbers of troops ashore as quickly as possible . (National Archives)

Preparations for War

By 1938, many isolationists, hemispherists, and internationalists were in agreement that a powerful navy was an indispensable adjunct to a free United States. Thus, another authorization bill swiftly passed through Congress. The second Vinson-Trammel bill, the Naval Expansion Act, or Vinson Naval Parity Act, sought the creation of a navy 20 percent larger than that permitted by the former limitation treaties. As Europe plunged into war, the last restraints on full-scale naval construction disappeared. On June 14, 1940, the day that Paris fell to the German Blitzkrieg, President Roosevelt signed into law a naval expansion bill that authorized an 11 percent increase in appropriations. Three days later, Admiral Harold R. Stark, chief of naval operations, asked Congress for an additional four billion dollars in order to bring the fleet up to the two-ocean standard. This bill, which was passed the following month, was the largest single naval construction program ever undertaken by any country. It provided for a 70 percent increase in combat tonnage to be constructed over a period of six years.

An F6F fighter plane preparing to take off from the USS Yorktown *in late 1943. Because of the immense distances between combat zones in the Pacific, air operations played a crucial role in Pacific theater naval operations, and aircraft carriers assumed an importance not matched in any other war.* (National Archives)

Franklin D. Roosevelt acted largely as his own navy secretary and shared most admirals' perception that the battleship defined naval power. While additional aircraft carriers were authorized in the late 1930's, the main focus of the Roosevelt naval buildup was the production of the seventeen new battleships authorized prior to U.S. entry into World War II.

Despite the flurry of construction authorizations, U.S. naval power was insufficient to protect the Atlantic and Pacific interests of the United States in the wake of Pearl Harbor. A full year prior to that catastrophe, the Navy, pressured by the president, had been forced to shift its strategic focus from an offensive action against Japan to a position that in any future war would include both Germany and Japan; the fleet would take the offensive in the Atlantic while assuming a defensive posture in the Pacific. Even this severe modification of the strategy implicit in the two-ocean standard did not achieve satisfactory results for a disconcertingly long period of time. While the success of Japan's surprise attack on Pearl Harbor might well be considered the result of a failure of specific rather than general preparedness, the inability of U.S. naval resources to provide adequate protection against the onslaught of Germany's U-boat attacks during all of 1942 provides convincing evidence that the Atlantic fleet had not achieved even a one-ocean capability at that time. This was an outgrowth of the myopic battleship strategic paradigm that restricted movement toward true capabilities in air, surface, and subsurface warfare. It was not until early 1943 that U.S. naval forces began to gain the upper hand in the Atlantic and Pacific theaters of the war.

Meredith William Berg
updated by William M. McBride

The Air War

The outbreak of World War II marked the beginning of a new era in aerial warfare, speeding up development of piston-engine-driven aircraft leading to the inauguration of the first jet to fly a combat mission, the German Messerschmitt Me-262. Following World War II, fighting jets often determined the outcome of contemporary military confrontations as their speed, maneuverability, and destructive capability rapidly escalated.

World War II began with the 1939 German bombing of major cities in Poland and the rapid destruction of the Polish air fleet by the German air force, called the Luftwaffe. The 1940 German victories over Denmark, Norway, Holland, Belgium, and France were greatly assisted by air support. The Battle of Britain in August and September of 1940 dramatically ended with the Royal Air Force (RAF) Fighter Command's defeat of the Luftwaffe. Later German strategic air bombing efforts, designed to destroy factories and civilian morale, were curtailed from completing their objectives by technically advanced Allied warcraft.

As the European front of the war developed, U.S. president Franklin D. Roosevelt repeatedly proclaimed the neutrality of the United States, thus satisfying the public opinion of the majority of Americans. U.S. neutrality laws forbidding arms sales to warring nations were quickly changed by Congress to assist the aerial warfare efforts of Britain and France.

The U.S. entry into World War II began with the Japanese carrier-borne aircraft attacks on Pearl Harbor, on the island of Oahu, Hawaii, which quickly destroyed or disabled many U.S. land-based combat aircraft in the Pacific. At the time of the December 7, 1941, Pearl Harbor bombing, the U.S. Army Air Force possessed only 1,100 combat-ready planes. Historians of aviation often note that no motivating force speeds up aircraft development and technology more rapidly than war. By 1944, the U.S. Army Air Force had nearly 80,000 planes in sixteen separate air forces stationed around the world.

Aircraft Development

On August 27, 1939, four days before the outbreak of war in Europe, the Heinkel He-178 took off from Germany's Marienhe Airport. The monumental first successful flight of this slender research turbojet aircraft began a new era in aerial warfare and is generally credited to two men: Hans von Ohain of Germany and Sir Frank Whittle of Great Britain. Desperate to curtail Allied bombing offensives, Germany then rapidly developed the

Messerschmitt Me-262 jet, considered a "Nazi wonder-weapon." Following its maiden flight in July, 1942, the Me-262 was regularly utilized by German engineers as a flying laboratory for the testing of new weapons. Among the more successful weapons utilized on the Me-262 were 550-pound bombs installed on the aircraft's wing racks and a row of twelve R4M rockets fitted directly upon each wing. These attached rockets were able to fire in rapid succession and could saturate a target the size of a B-17. In their rush to enhance the capabilities of the Me-262, German scientists initially attempted to attach a 50-millimeter nose cannon, which produced a flash that blinded the pilot when fired. Engineers also experimented with attaching a 2,200-pound bomb in tow, which made the plane functionally unstable during flight.

Allied bomber crews flying over Germany during the summer of 1944 were stunned by their encounters with the Messerschmitt Me-163 Komet, a jet fighter much faster than the jet-propelled Me-262. The Komet carried a

In order to lift American morale after Japan's December, 1941, attack on Pearl Harbor, the United States mounted its first bombing attack on Japan during the following April. Under the command of James Doolittle, sixteen B-25 bombers took off from the aircraft carrier Hornet *off the east coast of Japan and struck Tokyo, Yokohama, and other Japanese cities before continuing west to land in China. The bombing raid inflicted only minor damage on Japan but boosted American morale and forced the Japanese to divert resources to air defense. (National Archives)*

revolutionary 3,750-pound thrust rocket motor, which enabled travel at nearly 600 miles per hour. Called the "powdered egg" by Luftwaffe test pilots, the Komet had a limited radius of action of only 25 miles. It would exhaust its 437-gallon fuel supply within seven minutes of takeoff. The Komet's great effectiveness was due to its ability to climb vertically at 11,810 feet per minute, thus rising quickly above Allied planes. The Komet could then nose over and dive-attack Allied bomber formations and efficiently utilize its twin 30-millimeter cannons.

After the war, historians noted that only a handful of the 279 Komets manufactured during the war actually saw combat, but the fact that the Komets claimed nine monumental victories over Allied forces should not be minimized. The most serious flaw of the Komet was its required fuel mixture of methyl alcohol and concentrated hydrogen peroxide, which proved so volatile that several prototypes exploded on the runway during takeoff. Some Komets suffered engine failures that rapidly filled the cockpit with acrid fumes, literally blinding the crew and dousing them with corrosive chemicals from ruptured fuel lines that rapidly dissolved any exposed flesh. Military analysts later reflected that the Komet was probably

American naval pilots celebrate their success in the November, 1943, Battle of Tarawa in the Marshall Islands, in which they shot down seventeen of the twenty Japanese planes that attacked American forces. (National Archives)

ten years ahead of its time. Despite the flaws consequent to its escalated development, the Komet remained known as the most dangerous warplane in the sky during World War II.

In the summer of 1944, Germany first flew the Blitz, a twin-engine Arado 234B bomber capable of a maximum speed of 461 miles per hour and an elevation of 33,000 feet. Other features attempted on the Blitz included a dramatically reduced weight and drag, a trolley that was jettisoned after takeoff, skids that allowed grass landings, rocket boosters enabling takeoffs from short runways, a pressurized cabin, four engines, and one of the first crew ejection seats. Although the Blitz was considerably more advanced than any Allied bomber, its implementation came too late to significantly assist Third Reich bombardment strategy.

Major Wolfgang Schenk, a top Luftwaffe pilot, established the Edelweiss Bomber Group of Me-262's, which were originally designed as fighters but later manufactured as fighter-bombers by a late change in orders directly from Adolf Hitler. Schenk's unit of fifteen planes, stationed in Orléans, France, however, was too small to deter significantly the advancing Allies and was pulled back to Germany for the final unsuccessful German defense.

Experimental Planes

Frantically trying to rapidly manufacture a miracle jet that might turn the tide late in the war, German engineers designed three revolutionary planes later considered to be amazingly ahead of their time. The German Gotha 229 Flying Wing, originally designed as a glider, was modified as a high-speed fighter by the attachment of turbojets to its drag-resistant body. One experimental Gotha was clocked at 497 miles per hour while still in its development stage as the war ended.

The German Junkers Ju-287 was designed with forward-swept wings mounted over swept-back wings to delay the onset of air compressibility and establish stability at low speeds. The first Junkers was built in 1944 from sections of other planes, including the nose wheels of a downed U.S. Consolidated B-24. The Junkers made seventeen test flights before it was captured in 1945 by Soviet troops, who experimented extensively with the plane themselves for three years before moving to later designs. Soviet engineers attached tufts of wool to the fuselage and forward-swept wings of the Junkers to study its airflow. The planned design of the first jet attempted with variable-sweep wings, the Messerschmitt P-1101, was probably never flown, but the swing-wing design was later developed on the U.S. F-14 and F-111 fighters of the 1970's, the B-1 bomber of the 1980's, and an entire generation of Soviet fighters.

The first fighting jets had only minimal influence on the outcome of World War II, but they clearly set the stage for the rapid, future evolution of jet warplanes. Great Britain, the United States, and Japan rapidly followed Germany by developing and flying jet fighters before the conclusion of the war. Britain's first jet fighters consisted of seven Gloster Meteors, which joined the RAF in July, 1944, after four years of development. With an airspeed of 490 miles per hour, the Gloster Meteors were effective in intercepting German bombers that were daily attacking London at speeds of 400 miles per hour. However, they proved ineffective at downing enemy planes due to faulty guns. The first combat victory for an Allied jet occurred on August 4, 1944, when pilot T. D. Dean's gun failed as he maneuvered alongside the attached missile of a German bomber and used his plane's wing to unbalance and crash the German aircraft.

Other Technological Developments

British air-defense systems were greatly assisted by the development of radar. The development of German night-fighter systems was not prompted until after British night bombers began large-scale raids on Germany, most notably the one-thousand-plane raid over Cologne in May, 1942. Radar enhanced the ability of U.S. bombers to avoid detection and simultaneously to carry out early morning attacks on prominent German industrial and military targets. These Combined Bomber Offensives notably included the Ploesti, Romania, mission of August 1, 1943. The Ploesti raid utilized B-24's of the U.S. Fifteenth Air Force, originally based in Italy but launched from Africa, to bomb the Romanian oil refineries that were Germany's largest supplier of fuel. This costly mission, known as the "graveyard of the Fifteenth," was quickly followed by the Regensburg-Schweinfurt mission of August 17, the first large-scale U.S. attack on Germany launched from English bases. American losses in these offensives were considerable until 1944, when long-range P-47 and P-51 escort fighters enabled the attack of strategic sites deep within German-occupied territories with relative safety. The Allies were then able to establish clear air superiority and hit considerably more German planes and aircraft facilities. A notable example of this timely Allied air supremacy was D day, June 6, 1944, when Allied air forces restricted Germany to only a few Luftwaffe sorties against land invasion forces.

Newer designs of wings and other structural improvements greatly increased the speed and maneuverability of combat jets. By the end of the war, one of the most advanced fighters was the British Spitfire, which achieved a top airspeed of 350 miles per hour and an elevation of 40,000 feet. The United States and the Soviet Union both developed jet bombers that could fly nonstop from their homelands deep into enemy territory anywhere in the world in only a few hours.

Surfaces that deflected radar beams and materials that absorb radar energy and made planes much more difficult to detect, later known as stealth technology, were initially developed during World War II. Modern supersonic wings, which are thinner and flatter for increased speed and range, began to be made with heat-resistant materials. Materials such as titanium later began replacing aluminum, which melts at high speeds, using ideas initiated during World War II.

Other notable German aerial warfare developments included the V-1 buzz bomb, a pilotless jet-propelled plane carrying 2,000 pounds of explosives, which flew against England in June, 1944. The V-2, a true guided missile capable of carrying 1,650 pounds of explosives more than 200 miles, was launched in September, 1944. These technologies arrived too late to have an impact on the final outcome of the war, but their designs set the stage for future military warcraft.

Notable Battles and Flying Groups

Air battles in the Pacific most notably included the June, 1942, Battle of Midway, a crucial victory for the U.S. carrier-based Navy. Battles for the

"Flying Tiger" P-40 fighter planes on an airfield in China in 1942. (National Archives)

Gilbert Islands, the Marshall Islands, and the Mariana Islands were also monumental, as they later provided bases for air attacks upon Japan. Because Japan failed to develop a strong home air defense, the Boeing B-29 Superfortress caught that nation unprepared in late 1944 to detect bombers and coordinate army and navy maneuvers. On March 9, 1945, a massive raid on Tokyo, Japan, torched approximately 25 percent of the city's buildings. On August 6, 1945, the U.S. B-29 *Enola Gay* dropped the first atomic bomb on the city of Hiroshima, three days later a second atomic bomb was dropped on the city of Nagasaki, after which Japan surrendered.

The skills of the Flying Tigers, a United States Volunteer Group, were displayed in the China-Burma-India theater, following the Japanese conquest of Burma, later known as Myanmar. Supply flights from India to China over the Himalayas became as critical as combat flights, with bases in China later used to launch critical bombing operations against Japan.

Casualties and Costs

Advances in air warfare strongly contributed to making World War II the costliest military conflict in history, in terms of both human casualties and resources. An estimated 15 million to 20 million military personnel were killed in action, along with approximately 25 million civilians. Military deaths for the Axis Powers have been estimated at 3.5 million Germans, 1.5 million Japanese, and 200,000 Italians. Of the Allies, the Soviets lost an estimated 7.5 million military personnel, and China lost an estimated 2.2 million combatants from July, 1937, until the war's end. Britain lost 300,000; the United States lost 292,000; and France lost 210,000. In terms of civilian casualties, the Soviet Union lost 10 million; China 6 million; France 400,000; Britain 65,000; and the United States 6,000. Of the Axis Powers, Germany lost 500,000 civilians; Japan lost 600,000; and Italy lost 145,000. Approximately 6 million Jews, most from Eastern Europe, died in Nazi death camps. Total expenditures for war materials is estimated at $1.154 trillion, with the United States spending $300 billion and Germany $231 billion.

Long-Term Effects

The Japanese surrender in 1945, which did not require a land invasion, indicated to many that future military encounters would ultimately be determined by the combatant that controlled the battlefield in the air. The tactical use of fighting aircraft continued to escalate immediately following World War II, with essentially all world governments developing military planes by the early 1950's in response to the Cold War. Military air force strategies have since displayed disturbing trends, from the use of aircraft to prevent enemy movements and destroy enemy communications and supply lines to the doctrine of massive retaliation, whereby a country would not necessarily confine air strikes to local hostilities but would consider bombardment of civilian centers within enemy homelands.

Notable battles in which the ultimate victor was determined by warcraft technology begun during World War II included those of the Korean War, in which American propeller-equipped planes were initially very effective. Later Korean air combats employing the F-80 and F-86 against the Soviet-built MiG-15 were notably the first aerial combats between opposing modern jet fighters. After spending the Korean War dodging the best in Soviet fighter technology in what became known as "MiG Alley," the United States developed the world's first supersonic fighting jet, the F-100 Super Sabre, in 1953.

Another example was the 1967 Six-Day War between Israeli and Palestinian forces, which was essentially decided within the first three hours when Arab forces lost 452 aircraft. Ground warfare was also transformed forever by World War II aircraft developments. The widespread use of helicopters mounted with jet engines enabled enhanced speed and lift capacity to transport troops and supplies efficiently.

Daniel G. Graetzer

U.S. Supreme Court During the War

Many U.S. actions during this war, especially on the home front, were affected by and interpreted by the Supreme Court. These actions include war-making powers, emergency powers, economic controls, and the internment of Japanese Americans, both resident aliens and U.S. citizens of Japanese descent.

Late in the nineteenth century, Justice Stephen J. Field declared, "War seems to create—or leave unresolved—at least as many problems as it settles." Issues are raised when a nation is at war that would never be raised during times of peace. World peace was shattered by the German invasion of Poland in 1939. The Japanese attack on Pearl Harbor in Hawaii, the headquarters of the U.S. Pacific Fleet, on December 7, 1941, thrust the United States into its second world war within twenty-five years.

A major U.S. objective in World War II was to preserve the principle of constitutional government. Ironically, parts of that principle had to be sacrificed in order to preserve the whole. During World War II, the wheels of U.S. government had to be streamlined as part of the war effort. Early in 1942, in a lecture at Cornell University, political scientist Robert Cushman outlined three changes that he believed would result from that streamlining. The first was the relationship between the states and the federal government, in which the states would lose. Second was the relationship between Congress and the president, in which Congress would lose. The last change would be the impact on civil liberties, where individual citizens would lose to strengthen the nation as a whole. Cushman's predictions proved accurate, although surprisingly few of the changes rose to the need of a Supreme Court decision.

War-Making Powers

The Constitution carefully divides the war-making powers of Congress and of the president. Congress has the responsibility for raising and supporting military forces and the sole authority to declare war. The president is the commander in chief of all military forces and therefore has the authority to send them anywhere in the world. After President Franklin D. Roosevelt asked Congress, on December 8, 1941, for a declaration of war against Japan, each branch carried out its constitutional responsibilities.

One major issue involving war-making powers was the raising of military forces by involuntary means. Conscription was used during the Civil War and accepted as constitutional. However, during World War I, conscription was criticized as being involuntary servitude and therefore in violation of the Thirteenth Amendment. The Supreme Court, in *Butler v. Perry* (1916) and in subsequent *Selective Draft Law Cases* (1918), differentiated between involuntary servitude and involuntary duty. In 1939, with war again raging in Europe, the possibility and constitutionality of a peacetime draft was discussed in the United States. By June, 1940, with France on the verge of collapse, eventual U.S. involvement in the war seemed certain.

President Roosevelt did not want the nation caught unprepared as in 1917, but knowing that a peacetime draft would arouse strong opposition, especially with the inborn American fear of a strong government, he appointed a private citizen task force to develop a plan. The group was led by Grenville Clark, a highly respected law partner of Elihu Root (secretary of war, 1901-1904). The plan was implemented with surprisingly little opposition or refusal to register, as in 1917. The Court resolved, in *Falbo v. United States* (1944), an issue involving a conscientious objector who had failed to report for alternate civilian service as ordered. Falbo's claim of ministerial exemption had been rejected by his draft board, but the Court refused to accept his appeal. Other draft-related problems, such as congressional expansion of the draft to include eighteen-year-olds, pre-Pearl Harbor fathers, and some farmworkers, the issue of African American soldiers in combat after D day in 1944, and interpretation of fair deferment standards, were all resolved without further Court action. A related issue of national

President Franklin D. Roosevelt signing the declaration of war against Japan on December 8, 1941.
(National Archives)

civilian service was raised by Clark and Roosevelt in 1944 but was rejected by Congress.

Military courts also became an issue during the war. In *Ex parte Quirin* (1942), the Court ruled that a military commission had the right to try eight German saboteurs who were captured with explosives on beaches in New York and Florida six months after Pearl Harbor. The Court in *In re Yamashita* (1946) upheld the right of the military to condemn a Japanese officer for war crimes. However, in *Duncan v. Kahanamoku* (1946), the Court refused to extend the power of military courts to include civilian crimes not related to the war.

Emergency Powers

The Constitution does not make specific provisions for emergency powers to be used by the executive branch of government. However, an issue that arose during World War II was the presidential use of emergency or discretionary funds. In 1943 Congress passed the Urgent Deficiency Appropriations Act. Section 304 of that act, initiated by the House Committee on Un-American Activities, chaired by Representative Martin Dies (Democrat, Texas), suspended salary or compensation for three federal employees after November 15, 1943, unless by that date they were reappointed by the president with the advice and consent of the Senate. The named employees were Robert Morse Lovett, William E. Dodd, Jr., and Goodwin B. Watson. They were among thirty-nine federal employees attacked in a speech in the House by Representative Dies on February 1, 1943, as being "irresponsible, unrepresentative, crackpot radical bureaucrats" and affiliates of "communist front organizations."

Although the president did not reappoint Lovett, Dodd, and Watson, the agencies for which they worked kept them on the job after November 15, but without their salaries. The men later filed with the Court of Claims to recover their lost salaries on three grounds: that Congress has no power to remove executive employees, that section 304 violated Article I, section 9, clause 3, of the Constitution, which prohibits bills of attainder and *ex post facto* laws, and that it violated the due process clause of the Fifth Amendment. In *United States v. Lovett* (1946), the Court ruled that section 304 was in fact a bill of attainder and thus in violation of the Constitution. Lovett, Dodd, and Watson were entitled to receive their salaries and compensation after November 15, 1943.

Japanese American Internment

After the United States declared war on Japan, President Roosevelt issued several executive orders that seriously affected the rights of any per-

After losing his test case in the Supreme Court in 1944, Fred Korematsu continued to challenge the ruling until 1983, when the Court finally vacated its earlier decision because the government had suppressed evidence. Meanwhile, Korematsu became a prominent spokesperson for civil liberties and remained a sought-after lecturer into the twenty-first century.
(Asia Week)

son of Japanese ancestry living in the United States, especially those living on the West Coast. The orders authorized the secretary of war to designate military areas within the United States and to limit individual rights in those areas. Congress soon ratified the president's action by authorizing curfew orders to protect vital war resources. On March 24, 1942, in accordance with the orders, the military commander of the Western Defense Command, Lieutenant General J. L. DeWitt, proclaimed the entire Pacific coast to be a military area and that all persons of Japanese descent must observe a curfew from 8:00 P.M. to 6:00 A.M.

Gordon Kiyoshi Hirabayashi was an American citizen and a student at the University of Washington in Seattle. After he was convicted of violating the curfew, he appealed on the grounds that the executive orders and the power delegated to military authorities were in violation of the Fifth Amendment. His case, *Hirabayashi v. United States* reached the Court in 1943. The Court, in an opinion written by Chief Justice Harlan Fiske Stone, unanimously upheld both the presidential orders and the curfew, basing the action on the great importance of the military installations on the West Coast and on the close ties that persons of Japanese descent had with their mother country. The decision viewed the curfew as a protective measure but did not answer the constitutional issues involved. Chief Justice Stone went so far as to say that racial discrimination was justified during times of war when applied to those who had ethnic affiliation with an invading enemy.

Military authorities eventually decided that people of Japanese descent must be evacuated from the West Coast. When voluntary evacuation failed, a new presidential order created the War Relocation Authority, which was given the task of relocating one hundred thousand people. Fred Korematsu, from San Leandro, California, was arrested for refusing evacuation. The American Civil Liberties Union chose him as a test case for the constitutionality of the presidential order. Like Hirabayashi, Korematsu was a U.S. citizen. The Court, in an opinion written by Justice Hugo L. Black in 1944, decided *Korematsu v. United States* on the same basis as Hirabayashi's case but this time without a unanimous decision. Justice Black stated that compulsory evacuation was constitutionally suspect but was justified by the national emergency.

In a case related to *Korematsu, Ex parte Endo* (1944), Justice William O. Douglas ordered the release of a Japanese American whose loyalty was never questioned. He argued that congressional approval of the War Relocation Authority was not a blanket approval for every individual case.

The Court treated the internment of people of Japanese ancestry as an exercise of the government's emergency powers and appeared to regard the suspension of civil liberties as necessary in the interest of national security.

Economic Controls

Less than two months after the attack on Pearl Harbor, Congress passed the Emergency Price Control Act in order to prevent inflation that would hinder the war effort. In *Yakus v. United States* (1944), the Court ruled only on the manner in which Congress should achieve its goal, not on the goal itself. The Court upheld the power given by the act to the administrator of the Office of Price Administration to fix maximum prices and rents for a limited period of time, stating that sufficient standards had been established by Congress to ensure the just application of the law. Similar issues relating to economic controls followed the same pattern.

Glenn L. Swygart

Women in the War

World War II provided American women with their first major opportunity to serve their country in a military capacity, paving the way for expanded roles for women in succeeding decades.

Although military service traditionally had been limited to men, the personnel demands of World War II spurred the U.S. military leadership to accept women in significant numbers. By 1943, women's military branches had been established in all the services. A total of 350,000 women served in the U.S. Armed Forces during World War II. Although women were not permitted to serve in combat, many served with distinction, and some were counted among American war casualties. Women's military service during the war altered perceptions about the capabilities of female soldiers and helped bring some specific women's issues to the fore.

The Women's Corps

The impetus for women's corps in the United States began with the extension of the vote to women in 1920. Fearing extreme pacifism among the new female voters, the War Department (the forerunner of the Department of Defense) established a director of women's relations, whose job was to bolster support for the U.S. military among women's groups. Anita Phipps held the position throughout the 1920's, during which time she developed a plan to create a women's corps within the Army. The War Department was not amenable, and it was not until World War II was underway, and with the support of First Lady Eleanor Roosevelt, that such a corps was finally authorized. Edith Nourse Rogers, a member of Congress and a longtime advocate of women's military service, introduced a bill in 1941 to create a women's Army auxiliary corps. The Japanese attack at Pearl Harbor on December 7, 1941, which brought the United States into the war, virtually ensured passage of the bill.

In 1942, the Women's Army Auxiliary Corps (WAAC) was established. The following year, its auxiliary status was dropped, and it was placed under the direction of Oveta Culp Hobby. Members of the Women's Army Corps (WAC) were uniformed servicewomen with full military status. The Navy established a women's reserve and placed as its head Mildred McAfee, the president of Wellesley College; members of the Navy women's reserve would be known as Women Accepted for Voluntary Emergency Service (WAVES). The Coast Guard also established a women's reserve, based on the acronym SPAR, from the Coast Guard motto "Semper Paratus—Always Ready." The Marine Corps was less eager to take on women, but in 1943 it finally established a reserve for women, headed by Ruth Cheney Streeter; members of the Marine Corps Women's Reserve were not given an official acronym, and thus were simply "marines."

Although the women's corps represented a major advancement in the removal of barriers to women's service, most jobs within the corps were clerical and secretarial. In effect, women in the military were taking office jobs from men, who thus were released to serve in combat assignments. Many women also were placed in nursing jobs or other traditional occupations for women.

The most dramatic exception to the tendency of relegating women to office jobs were Women's Airforce Service Pilots (WASPs). A severe shortage of pilots during the war spurred the Air Force to use female pilots in noncombat assignments. Between 1942 and 1944, more than a thousand women ferried warplanes, tested aircraft, and towed practice targets. By all accounts, these women performed exceptionally. Although never involved in battle, thirty-eight WASPs died in the line of duty. The leader of the WASPs, Jacqueline Cochran, resisted integration of her unit with the Women's Army Corps, and thus her pilots retained civilian status. In an ex-

World War II was the first conflict in which women were encouraged to enlist in the military services in large numbers.
(National Archives)

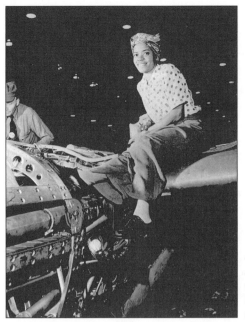

As during World War I, thousands of American women—such as this aircraft riveter—assisted the war cause by working in armament factories. (National Archives)

ample of the changing attitudes that followed the military performance of women during the war, military status was retroactively granted to the WASPs in 1977.

Impact

The employment of women in the U.S. military during World War II was largely driven by need. This situation was not unique to the United States; other countries, notably Great Britain, Japan, and the Soviet Union, pressed women into more integral military assignments. Although women's military assignments in the United States during the war generally were limited to support roles, the very entrance of women into military service had far-reaching effects on the military and society in general.

The widespread inclusion of women forced a number of unspoken gender issues. In many ways, the U.S. military leadership—including its female officers—continued to impose a traditional cultural value system on women, expecting chastity, temperance, and otherwise "ladylike" language and behavior. Meanwhile, women in the military often were subjected to sexual harassment and intimidation. Double standards were evident throughout the armed forces. Pregnancy was frowned on and, if it occurred outside of wedlock, could lead to various official sanctions. At the same time, abortion was discouraged, and an illegal abortion could lead to a dishonorable discharge.

Although the military contributions of women during the war were significant and recognized within the military leadership and society, some people disapproved of, and even actively opposed, women serving in military roles. Among the complaints were that women "feminized" the military, that military service "masculinized" women, and that the presence of women caused morale problems. Some people believed that any woman who would volunteer to serve in the military was a lesbian. These and similar charges reached a peak in a slander campaign against the WAC in late 1943 and early 1944. Charges (later to be deemed unfounded) surfaced that women's official role in the military was primarily to improve troop morale, that the War Department was providing them with contraceptives, and that a high rate of lesbianism existed among female personnel. Many of these stories were traced to servicemen who resented the presence of women in the military.

The friction, double standards, and clashing social conventions caused by the introduction of women into the military were addressed in a variety of ways, including compromises on an individual basis and some policy changes in the services. In the long run, these incidents created an awareness that various social customs were biased and outmoded, eventually leading to their demise. Most directly, women's military service during World War II caused changes in the military itself. Women had proved that they have the strength, courage, and commitment to make tremendous sacrifices in defense of their country, and therefore that the military excluded their contributions to its own detriment. Indeed, by 1945, President Franklin D. Roosevelt was prepared to draft women as nurses, but the war ended before such an action could take place. These developments started a long process of accepting women into all areas of military service. In 1948, the U.S. Congress passed the Women's Armed Services Integration Act, which permanently opened all branches to women. For the next several decades, advancements in women's military service would occur until women were even accepted in some combat roles.

Steve D. Boilard

Censorship During the War

During this conflict censorship was extended beyond military security material to delete, minimize, or classify any news conceivably useful to an enemy or damaging to home front morale.

During World War II, censorship became part of a broader attempt on the part of combatant nations to develop an effective overall news policy that, in addition to protecting military information from the enemy, would also serve to bolster civilian morale. News of military victories, of course, required little censorship, while defeats were normally ignored, then denied, then explained as unimportant. Depressing news was generally taboo in all belligerent, or warring, nations. Beyond such common factors, censorship varied from country to country.

United States

Censorship in the United States during the war avoided the heavy-handed bungling of World War I and caused relatively few media complaints. The war itself enjoyed broad public support, and antifascism was overwhelmingly endorsed by journalists, who wanted to be "on the team." The public was less ideologically oriented, but after Japan's surprise attack on Pearl Harbor, Americans were ready for extensive control of war news, including the Navy's refusal to reveal its losses at Pearl Harbor.

Under the War Powers Act of 1917, President Franklin D. Roosevelt named Byron Price on December 19, 1941, to head an Office of Censorship, which would develop guidelines for voluntary censorship by the producers of newspapers, magazines, radio shows, and films. Military plans, presidential trips overseas, intelligence operations, and new weapons (such as the atomic bomb) were secret, as were statistics concerning war production, shipping losses, and so on. The 1917 Espionage Act and the Trading with the Enemy Act were invoked to restrict use of the mails and to suppress, directly or otherwise, about thirty publications, most notably Father Coughlin's *Social Justice*. An attempt to prosecute the *Chicago Tribune* for revealing intelligence secrets failed to gain a grand jury indictment. The 1940 Smith Act, making it illegal to advocate the overthrow of the American government, was used more to prosecute individuals—mostly communists—than to censor the media. Most of the sixteen thousand employees assigned to censorship-related matters spent their time reading letters to and from servicemen stationed overseas.

A consistent theme in wartime propaganda on the homefront was the need for maintaining secrecy in any and all matters relating to the military and war industries. This 1942 poster suggests that an indiscrete remark by someone could have consequences as dire as the sinking of an Allied ship.
(National Archives)

Broadly speaking, bad news in the media was discouraged, and the government gave the African American press a particularly hard time for its supposed insufficient enthusiasm in support of the war effort. In war reports, censors deleted or minimized news of units refusing to go into combat, officers' cowardice, soldiers panicking or going AWOL, and casualties incurred from friendly fire, as well as of looting, black marketeering, rape, race riots, and mutiny. The tendency to sanitize the news obscured brutality and blunders and encouraged an ongoing tendency to "classify" inconvenient information.

The American Civil Liberties Union reported in 1945 that "wartime censorship raised almost no issues in the United States." Newsmen hailed what was widely called "the best reported war in history," although some admitted that they didn't always write the whole truth. Indeed, a Vietnam-era journalist might well have been surprised at the military misconduct that did not get reported.

United Kingdom

The Emergency Powers (Defence) Bill approved on August 24, 1939, authorized the renewal of the censorship powers contained in the Defence of the Realm Acts of 1914 (DORA), apparently including many of DORA's well remembered faults. A new Ministry of Information provided voluntary censorship guidelines, but, with the outbreak of war, it was not clear who was in charge of releasing news. Ministry of Information censorship was largely entrusted to former navy officers whose instinct was to tell the public nothing and refer all problems to higher authorities, sometimes with incongruous results. American journalist John Gunther, for example, asking for a copy of a propaganda leaflet scattered by the millions in Royal Air Force flights over Germany, was informed that the government was not allowed to disclose information which might be of value to the enemy.

The fall of France in 1940 prompted a new spirit. The British mythologized the "Dunkirk Miracle," deleting from press reports all negative comments by returning troops. The tally of planes downed in the Battle of Britain was reported with a view to impressing public opinion in both Britain and neutral countries such as the United States. Making a favorable impression in America was considered to be worth security risks; Edward R. Murrow, for example, was allowed to do live and unscripted radio broadcasts critical of Britain during London air raids. On the other hand, any British public comments on the 1940 U.S. elections or the 1941 Lend-Lease Act were strictly forbidden. Among other countries, Canada was considered an especially important military and intelligence link with the United States, and the three countries often coordinated censorship operations.

British military censorship was successful in controlling news of advances in radar, details of the Normandy invasion, and the invention of the atomic bomb. It was a remarkable achievement to develop an effective news management system during a period of military defeats. Some confidential material remained classified after 1945, not by wartime censorship but under the Official Secrets Act of 1911.

France

French censorship from 1939 to 1940 by the information ministry under Jean Giraudoux was a model of ineffective news management. Compared to news from Berlin, Paris wartime bulletins were invariably late, vague, and misleading. French censorship did protect military secrets from the enemy, but it also promoted ignorance and complacency about the state of the country's defenses. From the debacle of 1940 to liberation in 1944, censorship in both occupied France, which was administered by Germany, and Vichy France, which was administered by a collaborationist French government, was under direct or indirect German control.

The Soviet Union

Czarist censorship, which ended in 1917, was soon followed by that of the communists, and under the dictatorship of Joseph Stalin there was ample information for the censors to keep from public view—devastating famines, crippling production shortages, the ruthless purge of military and political opponents, and so on. In any case, the purpose of the Soviet news media was less to provide information than to define correct opinions and attitudes. World War II did not constrict the scope of Soviet news but even slightly expanded it.

The major problem facing Soviet news agencies during World War II was explaining why the unpreparedness, defeats, and casualties of 1941-1942 were not the fault of Stalin and the communist leadership. Censoring news about British and American war efforts made more plausible the emerging Stalinist interpretation that the British and Americans were covert partners in Adolf Hitler's treachery—an international conspiracy of fascists and imperialists attacking the Soviet Union again, as it had in 1919. Censorship left Stalin's leadership as the only hope of resistance. For the Soviet people, wanting to believe in victory meant having to believe in Stalin.

China

The struggle against Japanese aggression in World War II was complicated by the intense internal conflict between Chiang Kai-shek's Nationalist party (Guomindang) and a rival offshoot, Mao Zedong's Chinese Communist Party. Between 1927 and 1937, as communist writers called for radical policies, the Guomindang censored or banned their books and articles and bribed, shot, or beheaded their editors. The Sino-Japanese War (1937-1945) produced an official but uneasy truce between the Chinese rivals. In Chiang's wartime capital of Chongqing, the communist activist Zhou Enlai supervised *The New China Daily*'s attacks on the Guomindang, while Nationalist officials tried to prevent the paper from being delivered. Even the Guomindang papers depended on left-wing writers who had to be censored. After 1945 the government's obvious inability to control inflation, corruption, and inefficiency could not be disguised by censorship, and popular support as well as armed force brought the communists to power in 1949.

Germany

In 1933 Adolf Hitler appointed Joseph Goebbels minister of propaganda in order to gain and keep control of German thought and opinion. While it was deemed important to advertise the positive objectives of Nazism, it was also considered essential to conceal a great deal about Hitler's character, associates, goals, and methods. A journalism law of October, 1933, systematized Goebbels's approach.

Censorship of foreign reporters kept the West from realizing the extent of antiwar sentiment in Germany during the West's calamitous appeasement of Hitler at the Munich Conference in 1938. However, newsreels showing Nazi Brownshirts attacking Jewish shops and homes in the 1938 riots known as the Night of Broken Glass were allowed to leave Germany, as was a 1939 film of Hitler rudely mocking Roosevelt in a speech to the Reichstag. Censorship also surrounded the staged incident in 1939 which Hitler used as an excuse to invade Poland and start the war.

German victories in 1939 and 1940 needed little censorship except to delete images of German dead from combat films. However, after the failure to take Moscow in 1941, soldiers' letters home began to be censored, and newspapers were limited to a "quota" of obituaries for local soldiers. As the war progressed, reporting on shortages of food, coal, and other necessities had to be censored, as did accounts of Allied air raids.

It was forbidden to report in the press on the extermination of the Jews and other victims of Nazi death camps. Nazi propaganda attempted to portray Germany's defeat as a tragic misfortune for Hitler and to conceal his indifference to German suffering. After the war ended, many Germans still found it impossible to blame Hitler for the Nazis' unspeakable crimes.

Italy

Statutes passed in 1923, the year after the Fascists seized power, proclaimed that "the press is free, but a law regulates the abuse thereof." In practice, editors applied censorship according to government directives. The primary specific goal was to present dictator Benito Mussolini as a great and infallible leader and conceal his many shortcomings and failures. Censorship helped to glamorize the conquest of Ethiopia in 1935-1936, minimize Italian defeats from 1936 to 1939 in the Spanish Civil War, and conceal Mussolini's mismanagement of the supposed conquest of Albania in 1939. However, after Italy entered World War II, the military's many failures—France in 1940, Greece in 1941, and the campaign against the British and Americans from 1941 to 1943—were impossible to hide from the Italian people. Censorship served only to further weaken confidence in Mussolini, who was ousted from power in 1943, prior to Italy's surrender.

Japan

Imperial Japan's traditionally nationalistic and authoritarian society favored unity rather than the ideological divisions encouraged by a free press. A government agency dictated which news would be available to the press. Censorship in the form of "token suppression" or jailing "token editors" in the 1920's became stricter as Japan's expansion into China became an undeclared war in 1937. The National Mobilization Law of February, 1941, tightened secrecy and censorship rules, assisting preparations for the December 7 attack on the U.S. Navy base at Pearl Harbor.

As war extended the Japanese Empire, propaganda and censorship, usually in English, were aimed at conquered peoples. The main attempts at thought control, however, were directed at the Japanese people themselves. Victory depended on loyalty and obedience to the hierarchy of authority in Japanese life—neighborhood groups, local officials, national leaders, and the emperor. The censors' task was to exclude ideas that might challenge this pattern of united action.

Following the war, Japan eventually lifted censorship on such topics as its wartime biological warfare research program, which was continued as a highly classified project by the U.S. armed forces. As the secret weapon changed hands, it was protected by a new shield of censorship.

K. Fred Gillum

Campaigns, Battles, and Other Events

August, 1939
Mobilization for Possible War

Date: Beginning August, 1939
Location: United States
Principal figures: President Franklin D. Roosevelt (1882-1945); Secretary of the Treasury Henry J. Morgenthau, Jr. (1891-1967); James Francis Byrnes (1879-1972), director of the Office of Economic Stabilization; William Martin Jeffers (1876-1953), head of the Government Rubber Board; William Signius Knudsen (1879-1948), head of the Office of Production Management; Emory Scott Land (1879-1971), head of the U.S. Maritime Commission; Donald Marr Nelson (1888-1959), head of the War Production Board; Senator Harry S. Truman (1884-1972)
Result: The prospect of American involvement in the war developing in Europe and East Asia prompted conversion of domestic production to meet military needs.

In June, 1940, German forces overran France. U.S. industrial mobilization became necessary when large British orders for military supplies were received. European events also aided the Roosevelt administration in passing a number of military appropriations bills. Although more money was becoming available for war production, U.S. industry was reluctant to exploit this market. Conditioned by the static economic situation of the Depression, many capitalists expected such conditions to return after the war.

Expanding plants for wartime production was seen as a risky, short-term investment. The Roosevelt administration tried in various ways to persuade industrialists that this was not true. The federal government offered to finance expansion through low-interest loans from the Reconstruction Finance Corporation. The Revenue Act of 1940 provided an incentive in the form of a 20 percent per year depreciation of new defense plants, instead of the former 5 percent tax write-off. Most important, however, was the "cost-plus" provision incorporated into government defense contracts. Private industry was guaranteed the cost of producing particular military hardware, plus a profit of a certain percentage of the cost. This plan proved lucrative to industry but led to excessive waste in production. Eventually, Senator Harry S. Truman of Missouri led a special investigation into the waste and corruption in defense work, the revelations of which resulted in improved efficiency.

Centralizing Control

Roosevelt wrestled desperately with the problem of centralizing control of industrial mobilization. Drawing upon his experiences during World War I, he first established a War Resources Board (WRB) in August, 1939. The WRB drew up a plan of mobilization providing for rigid government controls. Roosevelt rejected this plan for political and personal reasons and permitted the WRB to be dissolved in October, 1939, after organized labor accused it of being prejudiced in favor of big business. A pattern of establishing an agency with a vague mandate and then reorganizing it when its attempts to operate provoked criticism was repeated during succeeding years.

The next attempt at central direction was the establishment of the National Defense Advisory Commission on May 28, 1940. Composed of representatives of labor, industry, the armed services, and the consuming public, the commission was under the direction of a former General Motors executive, William S. Knudsen. Knudsen was expected to balance these various interests. The most vexing problem was the assignment of priorities to the various manufacturers for the acquisition of scarce materials. Ideally, such materials ought to have gone to factories in proportion to the relative importance of their finished products to the health of the economy as a whole. Knudsen never solved this problem but permitted the Army-Navy Munitions Board to gain great power in acquiring scarce materials.

On January 7, 1941, Roosevelt tried another reorganization. The Office of Production Management (OPM) was set up, with Knudsen and Sidney Hillman of the Congress of Industrial Organizations (CIO) as joint directors. The OPM did succeed in beginning the shift toward a war economy, but it placed strains on domestic needs and shortages developed in the electric power, aluminum, steel, and railroad equipment industries. By August 28, 1941, Roosevelt was ready for another change. At first, a slight adjustment was made by creating a Supplies Priorities and Allocation Board headed by Sears Roebuck executive Donald M. Nelson. Within a few months, the OPM had gone the way of the WRB, and Nelson was called to the White House to head an entirely new organization, the War Production Board (WPB).

The War Production Board

Established on January 16, 1942, the WPB was to have supreme command over the entire economy. Nelson, however, proved inadequate for the job; he permitted the military to regain control over priorities and seemed to favor big corporations in the allocation of contracts. He also permitted the economy to develop unevenly. Ship factories were built at a pace far exceeding the ability of the steel industry to supply material for ship construction. Nelson remained as head of the WPB until 1944, but long before then control of economic mobilization had been assigned to yet another agency.

Recognizing that problems were developing under the WPB, Roosevelt asked Supreme Court associate justice James F. Byrnes to head the new Office of Economic Stabilization (OES). This new office replaced the WPB as supreme arbiter of the economy. Byrnes did solve the problems of priorities and brought order to the entire mobilization scheme. He seemed to have the political astuteness required to make the OES work. In May, 1943, his agency's official title was changed to Office of War Mobilization, and in October, 1944, it became the Office of War Mobilization and Reconversion.

Despite such frequent reorganization of the government's regulatory bodies, U.S. industry performed fantastic feats of production during the war years. Statistics tell part of the story. In 1941, the United States produced approximately eight and one-half billion dollars' worth of military equipment. Using the same dollar value, in 1944 the sum was sixty billion dollars. Included in these gross figures was an increase in the annual production of planes from 5,865 in 1939 to almost 100,000 in 1944. Ship tonnage rose from one million tons in 1941 to nineteen million in 1943. Certain parts of the economy performed miracles. As public director of WPB, William M. Jeffers, president of the Union Pacific Railroad, directed the creation of a great synthetic rubber industry; Admiral Emory S. Land, head of the United States Maritime Commission, prodded the shipping industry into building ships in fewer than ten days; comparable production feats were achieved by other industries.

Economic Impact

Probably most significant in the long run was the fact that this remarkable production was accomplished with little effect on the basic corporate structure of the economy. Shortages existed in the civilian community during World War II, and rationing was introduced for foodstuffs, including meat and sugar. While restraints were imposed on free enterprise, outright government seizure of private industry was never attempted. For the most

A young boy presents his family's ration book while making a grocery purchase. Individual consumer goods were assigned point values, and the books were used to keep track of the points that each family expended. (National Archives)

part, government gave businessmen exceptional latitude in what they could produce and how, as long as it met national goals. The government let contracts for a wide variety of experimental or unusual projects, such as the famous *Spruce Goose* developed by Howard Hughes's engineers. Government allowed exceptional industrialists, such as Andrew Jackson Higgins, Preston Tucker, and Henry Kaiser, to mass-produce patrol torpedo (PT) boats and landing craft, gun turrets, and ships with little interference and with almost no concern for cost. Kaiser, for example, cut the production time of a Liberty Ship (a basic freighter crucial to the war effort) from 120 days to 4.5 days. As British historian Paul Johnson observed, the war "put back on his pedestal the American capitalist folk-hero."

The efforts of the War Production Board also involved businesses in planning future economic activities more than ever before, and persuaded many that government could and should play a role in that planning. The size of government has never returned to its pre-Depression levels, and only in the administration of Ronald Reagan did the military share of the gross national product remain at less than 6 percent for more than a year.

Ironically, many business leaders took from the war the exact opposite message from what it had taught. Rather than reaffirming the phenomenal productive capacity of the United States, business left the war expecting special favors and government considerations.

George Q. Flynn
updated by Larry Schweikart

September, 1939-May, 1945
Battle of the North Atlantic

Date: September 3, 1939-May 4, 1945
Location: North Atlantic ocean
Combatants: Primarily German submarines vs. Allied surface vessels and aircraft
Principal commanders: *German*, Admiral Karl Dönitz (1891-1980); *American*, Ernest King (1878-1956)
Result: Eventual decisive victory for Allied forces.

The Battle of the North Atlantic began on September 3, 1939, with the sinking of the British liner *Athenia* by the German submarine U-30. At the time, neither side was prepared for what was to follow. Germany had only fifty-six operational submarines of which only twenty-two were suited for service in the Atlantic Ocean. The British did not attach a high priority to planning and equipment for antisubmarine warfare, thinking that they could improvise at the outbreak of hostilities.

At the outset of the war, the Germans sought to impose a submarine blockade of all British ports. This proved not to be the best strategy. The commander of U-boats, Admiral Karl Dönitz, was soon convinced that operating in coastal waters made the U-boats too vulnerable to land-based aircraft and that they should instead concentrate in the mid-Atlantic, which was out of reach for most aircraft at that time. In this first phase, U-boats operated singly rather than as a group. However, the Allies, including the U.S. Navy under Ernest King, soon organized a convoy system, and the Germans adapted by attacking in groups called wolfpacks.

Dönitz calculated that sinking a monthly average of 800,000 tons of shipping would cripple the British war effort and bring about its capitulation. Without merchant shipping, the British could neither eat, run their industries, nor continue fighting. In the early years of the war, losses of merchant ships exceeded the rate of ship production by a 2-1 margin. It was not until August, 1942, that ship production balanced the losses.

By April, 1943, more than 400 U-boats were in service, and victory in the Atlantic was almost achieved by the Germans. Abruptly, however, the tide of battle turned. The Allies were able to close the gap and provide air cover the entire width of the Atlantic. Improved radar enabled the Allies to pinpoint the location of German submarines after only a brief radio transmission. The United States was constructing merchant ships at a rate far exceeding losses. More than 2,500 of these wartime merchant vessels known as Liberty ships were built in American shipyards.

In May, 1943, the Germans lost thirty-five submarines with only 96,000 tons of shipping to show for it. It was now clear that it was pointless to send submarines into the North Atlantic to attack shipping as the losses would exceed any reasonable return. Dönitz temporarily withdrew U-boats from the North Atlantic and used them in other locations where they would not be so vulnerable. The U-boats were returned to the Atlantic, but their main function became to slow and harass Allied shipping and force the Allies to continue devoting resources to an antisubmarine campaign, thus preventing these resources from being used elsewhere. The end came on May 4, 1945, when Dönitz sent a radio signal to all U-boats to stop all hostile action against Allied shipping.

The battle was costly to both sides. During the course of the war, the Allies lost more than 2,600 ships. More than 30,000 merchant seaman and supporting naval personnel lost their lives. The Germans lost more than 750 U-boats, which amounted to more than 85 percent of all operational boats. Of the approximate 40,000 who served as U-boat crewmen, 27,491 died in action.

Winning the Battle of the North Atlantic was essential for an Allied victory. Britain could not be sustained nor could offensive operations be undertaken on the European continent without control of the North Atlantic.

Gilbert T. Cave

March, 1941
Lend-Lease Act

Date: March 11, 1941
Location: Washington, D.C.
Principal figures: Prime Minister Winston S. Churchill (1874-1965), President Franklin D. Roosevelt (1882-1945)

Result: Before the United States became formally involved in the war, it used the lend-lease program to support Great Britain's war effort while maintaining official neutrality.

Germany's invasion of Poland on September 1, 1939, plunged Europe into a second major war within twenty-five years—a war that would prove to be the worst in human history. As in the beginning of World War I, the United States hoped to remain neutral, although popular sentiment weighed heavily toward Great Britain and France. With memories of World War I still fresh in the minds of most Americans, isolationist views prevailed. For six years prior to Germany's move against Poland, the United States watched developments in Europe with concern. Adolf Hitler, whose Nazi Party governed Germany, made no attempt to conceal his intentions to break with the Treaty of Versailles, rearm Germany, and expand Nazi control throughout Europe. At the same time, Italy's Benito Mussolini advanced aggressively against Ethiopia, and Japan continued military operations in China.

Neutrality Laws

Keenly aware of these developments, the U.S. Congress in 1935 legislated the first in a series of neutrality laws. A six-month renewable act, the legislation prohibited the United States from selling arms or transporting munitions to belligerent (warring) nations. When it was renewed, a ban against making loans to warring nations was included. Congress and the president believed such a foreign policy would prevent the United States from slipping into another European war, should one arise.

The following year, developments in Europe proved peace to be but an illusion. Hitler's forces moved unopposed into the Rhineland, a French territory; in 1937, Germany involved itself in the Spanish Civil War and sealed the Rome-Berlin alliance. The United States responded with the Neutrality Act of 1937, which retained the principal features of the 1935 act but, at Roosevelt's urging, allowed presidential discretion to sell military goods to belligerents on a "cash and carry" basis, provided the material was not transported on U.S. ships. The altered policy pleased manufacturers who wanted to profit while the nation remained officially neutral and apart from the European crisis. The new policy also pleased those in the United States who thought it essential to aid the country's traditional allies.

Germany's expansion continued, and in his state of the union address, on January 4, 1939, President Roosevelt announced his dismay over the course of European affairs and his dissatisfaction with existing neutrality laws. He believed that the 1937 act benefited Hitler more than it did France or Great Britain. If Hitler's enemies were unable to acquire sufficient material for defense, Germany would find the Western nations unable to halt German aggression. Surely, the president hinted, the United States could devise methods short of war to aid British and French military defense preparations.

Answering Britain's Appeal

Early that summer, the British government made a direct appeal to Roosevelt for military supplies, and in June, the president suggested revision of the Neutrality Act of 1937 to broaden the cash-and-carry provision. Fearful that such a program of support for Great Britain would cast the United States in an image of cobelligerent, isolationists in Congress blocked Roosevelt's efforts. Germany's invasion of Poland on September 1, and the British-French declaration of war that followed, changed the congressional mood. By year's end, revisions to the 1937 act were sanctioned, making it easier for Britain to obtain needed supplies.

France fell to the Germans in June, 1940. Great Britain was the sole surviving power in Europe. Many thought that the United States should provide direct military aid to the British, the U.S. front line against Germany. If Britain collapsed, the United States would become Hitler's next target. Others contended that the United States needed to strengthen its own defenses in preparation for German actions in the Western Hemisphere. Roosevelt chose to follow both courses. He gained approval from Congress to appropriate funds for U.S. rearmament and for a peacetime compulsory military training law. In June, using executive authority, Roosevelt authorized the supply of outdated aircraft and rifles to Great Britain; in September, he arranged with Britain the exchange of fifty U.S. naval destroyers for leases of British naval bases.

Great Britain's financial reserves dwindled as autumn faded. In December, Prime Minister Winston S. Churchill informed Roosevelt that the cash-and-carry system needed modification. Roosevelt understood that Great Britain could not withstand further German attacks without direct U.S. aid and that the security of the United States was largely dependent on British resistance to Hitler. In mid-December, Roosevelt conceived the idea of lend-lease: War goods would be provided to Allied nations and either returned or paid for at war's end.

In both a press conference and a radio "fireside chat," Roosevelt stated that the best defense for the United States was a strong Great Britain. Every step short of war should be taken to help the British Empire defend itself. Great Britain's inability to pay cash for U.S. supplies should not relegate the empire to German conquest. To lend or lease the necessary goods would provide for Great Britain's immediate war needs and indirectly benefit the United States by making Great Britain the U.S. front line of defense. Roosevelt presented an analogy to clarify the proposal: "Suppose my neighbor's home catches fire, and I have a length of garden hose four hundred or five hundred feet away. If he can take my garden hose and connect it up with his hydrant, I may help him to put out his fire." If the hose survived the fire, it would be returned. Should it be damaged, the neighbor would replace it. Military aid would be treated in the same way. The United States must become the "arsenal of democracy" and provide the goods necessary to halt German expansion.

The Lend-Lease Bill

To secure permission and funding to aid Great Britain, Roosevelt introduced into the House of Representatives the lend-lease bill. The bill generated intense debate. Opponents said the measure would move the United States from neutrality to the status of active nonbelligerent and risk war with Germany. They believed that it would be more logical to plan to build up the U.S. defenses. Supporters argued that Hitler posed a real, direct threat to the United States, and that aiding Great Britain would make U.S. entry into the war less likely. Public opinion favored the president. Although 82 percent of Americans believed war was inevitable, nearly 80 percent opposed entry unless the nation were directly attacked.

After two months of congressional debate, the Lend-Lease Act was passed on March 11, 1941. It permitted the president to lend or lease war materiel to any nation whose defense was deemed critical to the United States, and it authorized an immediate appropriation of seven billion dollars for Great Britain. In June, following Germany's invasion of the Soviet Union, Roosevelt extended lend-lease to the Soviet Union. The Lend-Lease Act retained official U.S. neutrality, but the measure also placed the United States more squarely in opposition to Nazi Germany. In March, 1941, the United States teetered on the brink of war.

By war's end, in 1945, the United States appropriated slightly more than fifty billion dollars under the lend-lease program. Great Britain received twenty-seven billion dollars in aid, the Soviet Union was provided ten billion dollars, and the remaining funds supplied goods to other Allied nations.

Roosevelt's contemporaries and postwar scholars have questioned the president's prewar direction of U.S. policy, particularly with regard to lend-lease. Some have argued that Roosevelt desperately wanted U.S. entry into the war long before Pearl Harbor but was restrained by popular opinion and political realities. Therefore, they argue, Roosevelt worked within the system to place the United States on an ever-advancing course toward war by molding public opinion, relaxing neutrality laws, and securing lend-lease. Others contend the president hoped to avoid intervention in Europe's war. Lend-lease thus was a practical method for the United States to aid the Allies while remaining a nonbelligerent. Regardless of Roosevelt's motives, Japan's attack on Pearl Harbor on December 7, 1941, sealed U.S. fate. War came to the United States.

Kenneth William Townsend

December, 1941
Battle of Pearl Harbor

Date: December 7, 1941
Location: Pearl Harbor, Oahu, Hawaiian Islands
Combatants: Japanese First Air Fleet vs. U.S. Pacific Fleet and U.S. Army, Hawaiian Department
Principal commanders: *U.S. Navy*, Admiral Husband Edward Kimmel (1882-1968); *U.S. Army*, Lieutenant General Walter C. Short (1880-1949); *Japan*, Vice Admiral Chuichi Nagumo (1886-1944), Admiral Isoroku Yamamoto (1884-1943)
Result: Japan's surprise attack on the U.S. Pacific Fleet forced U.S. entry into World War II.

The surprise attack by Japanese naval air forces upon the huge United States naval base at Pearl Harbor, Hawaii, has become synonymous with duplicity and cunning. Nevertheless, the circumstances of the attack engendered bitter controversy over the reasons for the failure of U.S. leaders to anticipate and to defend themselves against this devastating blow.

Background

In retrospect, Pearl Harbor can be explained without recourse to a "devil theory of war"—that Japan, unprovoked by the United States, deliberately and wantonly struck the Navy's Pacific command center. Given the Japanese military and political situation and the dictates of Japanese strategic thinking, the attack was the logical result of a series of confrontations between Japan and the United States. Although U.S. interest was focused primarily on Europe between 1939 and 1941, events in the Far East aroused increasing concern in Washington, D.C., as Japan carried forth its ambitious creation of a Japanese-dominated Greater East Asia Co-Prosperity Sphere, which championed "Asia for Asians." Much of China had fallen under Japanese control by 1939. Japan officially became an Axis Power in September, 1940, with the signing of the Tripartite Pact—a "defensive" alliance among Germany, Italy, and Japan. By the summer of 1941, Japan had gained concessions in Indochina and was threatening to engulf Thailand, the Soviet Union's Siberian provinces, the British bastion of Singapore, Burma, the Dutch East Indies, and the Philippines.

The United States opposed this Japanese expansion primarily with economic sanctions. Throughout the 1930's, as Japan seized Manchuria and moved against China, the United States proved unable or unwilling to oppose Japan by force. Although sympathetic toward China, President Franklin D. Roosevelt was more concerned about Germany than about Japan. Supported by Navy spokesmen who feared that a two-ocean war would lead the United States to disaster, Roosevelt adopted a policy of caution toward Japanese expansion in the hope that liberal Japanese leaders would wrest power from the more militant imperialists and reverse Japan's course. Despite British and Dutch pressure, the United States was slow to accept the necessity of economic sanctions until August, 1940, when Roosevelt imposed an embargo on aviation gasoline. Restrictions on the export of scrap iron and steel followed in September, 1940, and Japanese assets in the United States were frozen in July, 1941.

Japanese leaders, almost all of whom supported the program of expansion and differed only on how it should be accomplished, came to believe that Japan was being encircled by the Western powers. If Japanese demands were not achieved by diplomacy, military force would become necessary. Economic sanctions by the United States, Great Britain, and the Netherlands—especially the embargo—meant that Japan had to choose between peace and war within a year, before its oil reserves were exhausted. In July, 1941, an advance into Southeast Asia for oil and other resources was approved by the Japanese Imperial Council, even if it meant war with the United States. On September 6, an Imperial Conference set what amounted to a time limit on diplomatic efforts for the settlement of negotiations with the United States. Negotiations continued, with neither side offering concessions. Roosevelt and Secretary of State Cordell Hull were pessimistic but believed that discussions should continue, in order that the United States might gain time for defense preparations.

Meanwhile, Army and Navy intelligence at Pearl Harbor and in Washington, D.C., learned that Japan might be planning to mount a surprise attack, but the evidence was fragmentary. U.S. military planners knew from intercepted messages that things would happen automatically if the U.S. rejected a final Japanese proposal, but most indications pointed to an attack somewhere in Southeast Asia. Ambassador Kichisaburo Nomura of Japan presented to Hull what was to be the final Japanese proposal for peace on November 10. Hull declared it unacceptable and on November 26 made a counteroffer, which he knew from intercepted Japanese messages would be rejected. Diplomacy proved futile. On Sunday, December 7, while Japanese planes were making their bomb runs over Pearl Harbor, a Japanese diplomatic note was handed to the secretary of state; it implied disruption of relations, but it was not a declaration of war.

Japanese Preparations

Japan's preparations for the attack on Pearl Harbor had begun with tactical planning in the early months of 1941. Japanese strategists recognized that an advance into Southeast Asia would likely generate a U.S. military response. Destruction of the United States Pacific Fleet based in Hawaii was essential if Japan's move into the region was to succeed. A daring plan by Admiral Isoroku Yamamoto to destroy or cripple the fleet at anchor in Pearl Harbor was at first considered impractical, if not suicidal, but the proposal was later accepted when table-top games proved it workable and Yamamoto exerted his powerful influence in favor of it. Pilots began training in September, and all objections were overcome. To cope with the shallow waters of Pearl Harbor, wooden-finned torpedoes were devised, together with a new method of delivering them on target; elaborate precautions were undertaken to preserve secrecy; and abundant intelligence was gathered concerning the movements of the U.S. Pacific Fleet.

Under the command of Vice Admiral Chuichi Nagumo, a special task force of thirty-one vessels, including six aircraft carriers that carried 432 airplanes—fighters, dive-bombers, high-level attack bombers, and torpedo planes—left Japanese ports in early November. On November 22, this force gathered in the Southern Kuriles. Four days later, it headed out to sea for a run of 3,500 miles to a rendezvous point 275 miles north of Pearl Harbor. The strike force was not to attack until final clearance for action was issued from the Japanese high command. On December 2, the signal "Climb Mount Niitaka" was received by Nagumo and the date of attack confirmed. Early on December 7, the strike force reached position, so that the first Japanese planes were flying over Pearl Harbor by 7:55 A.M., local time.

The Attack

The weather was ideal for an attack, and Pearl Harbor was caught totally unprepared. The blow was deliberately planned for Sunday morning,

Japanese sailors give an enthusiastic sendoff to planes taking off from an aircraft carrier before the attack on Pearl Harbor. (National Archives)

when the ships of the Pacific Fleet were moored in perfect alignment and their crews were ashore, having breakfast, or relaxing on board ship. There was no advance warning in Hawaii. An operator at a temporary U.S. radar post observed the oncoming Japanese squadrons at 7:02 A.M.; he reported the blips shown on the radar screen, but the watch officer did not pass on the information, thinking they were a group of U.S. bombers expected to arrive that morning from the West Coast.

The Japanese planes swooped to the attack. Fighters and dive-bombers strafed and bombed the neat rows of aircraft at Wheeler Field and the Naval Air Station. Torpedo planes and dive-bombers also attacked Battleship Row in the devastating first phase, which lasted thirty minutes. After a fifteen-minute lull, the Japanese launched high-level bombing attacks on the harbor, airfields, and shore installations, followed by more attacks by dive-bombers, which pressed through mounting antiaircraft fire. The last planes withdrew at 9:45 A.M., less than two hours after the attack had begun.

They left behind a scene of destruction and carnage without parallel in U.S. history. Casualties were 2,403 dead and 1,178 wounded. Three battleships—the *West Virginia*, *Arizona*, and *California*—were sunk; the *Oklahoma* lay capsized; and the *Tennessee*, *Nevada*, *Maryland*, and *Pennsylvania* suffered varying degrees of damage. Several smaller warships were sunk, and

The destroyer USS Shaw *explodes after its forward magazines are hit by bombs. Although the ship sustained heavy fire damage and lost its entire bow, it remained afloat the next day.* (National Archives)

others were seriously crippled. Almost all combat aircraft on the islands were damaged or destroyed. Twenty-nine Japanese airplanes were lost, along with one full-sized submarine and five midget submarines.

Recovery

The U.S. forces in Hawaii fought courageously and recovered quickly from their initial shock. However, they were tragically unprepared to repel the skillful blows rained down by the Japanese strike force. The Japanese were successful far beyond the expectations of their high command; the United States Pacific Fleet lay grievously wounded and would not, Japan believed, be able to undertake offensive operations for months. The attack failed, however, in two particulars. First, the Japanese missed their prime targets: the aircraft carriers *Lexington* and *Enterprise* (both of which were at sea), and *Saratoga* (which was in dry dock on the West Coast). Second, the Japanese failed to destroy the huge oil storage facilities, without which the Pacific Fleet would have been forced to retire to the West Coast. While historical debate continues regarding the necessity of the attack for Japan and the lack of U.S. preparedness, the Pearl Harbor attack unified the U.S. people and eliminated whatever isolationist sentiment still existed in 1941. Within a few days, the United States was at war with Japan, and, because of the Tripartite Pact, with Germany as well.

Theodore A. Wilson
updated by Kenneth William Townsend

December, 1941
Axis Declaration of War on the United States

Date: December 11, 1941
Location: Berlin, Rome, and Washington, D.C.
Principal figures: Chancellor Adolf Hitler (1889-1945), Benito Mussolini (1883-1945), President Franklin D. Roosevelt (1882-1945)
Result: By declaring war on the United States, Germany and Italy transformed the Pacific and European conflicts into a single global war.

On December 11, 1941, four days after the Japanese attack on Pearl Harbor, the governments of Germany and Italy issued declarations of war against the United States of America. Although both the Germans and the Italians had pledged Japan their aid in the event of a conflict between Japan and the United States, their declarations cited President Franklin D. Roosevelt's anti-Axis attitude and hostile U.S. actions as reasons for their decision to declare war. In response, Congress passed two joint resolutions affirming a state of war against Germany and Italy. With these events, the war in Europe and the war in the Far East merged to become World War II.

American Neutrality

That the United States would become involved in a war in Europe seemed highly unlikely from 1936 to 1940, because during these years, the U.S. government and people were strongly isolationist. Moreover, Nazi Germany was preoccupied in Europe and not primarily interested in the Western Hemisphere. Although most Americans were opposed to Benito Mussolini's invasion of Ethiopia, the United States government did no more than invoke the first Neutrality Act, which included an arms embargo designed to weaken Italy. By 1936, it became clear that Germany and Italy were bent on territorial revisions. The Rome-Berlin Axis was formed in 1936, and Japan joined Germany and Italy in the Anti-Comintern Pact in

1937. In response, the United States government extended the Neutrality Act in 1937.

Despite their desire to stay out of war, President Roosevelt and his advisers grew increasingly concerned about the dangers of foreign aggression and human rights violations in both Europe and the Far East during the last years of the 1930's. In November, 1938, Roosevelt responded to the German riots against Jews during *Kristallnacht* (literally, "night of broken glass") by replacing the U.S. ambassador in Berlin with a chargé d'affaires; in April, 1939, the president sent letters to Adolf Hitler and Mussolini asking for assurances that they would refrain from aggression and suggesting discussions on armaments reductions. Hitler's invasion of Poland on September 1, 1939, increased the Roosevelt administration's belief that Germany posed a real threat to U.S. security.

France's Fall

The year 1940 marked a turning point in U.S. foreign policy. The fall of France seriously alerted people in the United States to the might of Nazi Germany, while England's dogged resistance to Hitler, exemplified in the Battle of Britain, resulted in increased U.S. aid to the English. During the last six months of 1940, the United States responded to the German Blitz-

Benito Mussolini (left) and Adolf Hitler in Munich in 1940. (National Archives)

German troops marching through Warsaw shortly after invading Poland in September, 1939. (National Archives)

krieg in Europe with billions of dollars for defense, destroyers for England, and the first peacetime Selective Service Act in U.S. history. In addition, Roosevelt, after winning an unprecedented third term in office in November, 1940, proclaimed the United States "the great arsenal of democracy" and announced his intention to secure congressional approval of a Lend-Lease Act to aid all countries fighting to preserve freedom.

During 1941, the United States inched ever closer to war with Germany. In January, the Joint Chiefs of Staff of the U.S. armed forces met with their British counterparts and discussed how to coordinate military actions in the event of U.S. entry into the war. It was decided that the defeat of Germany should be given top priority. On March 11, the U.S. Congress passed the Lend-Lease Act, authorizing Roosevelt to provide arms, equipment, and supplies to "any country whose defense the President deems vital to the defense of the United States." In a speech on May 27, Roosevelt stressed the German danger to the Western Hemisphere and declared a state of national emergency. In August, Roosevelt and British prime minister Winston S. Churchill issued the Atlantic Charter against the Axis Powers. Serious naval incidents occurred in September and October, when German submarines torpedoed the U.S. destroyer *Greer* and sank the *Reuben James*. In November, the president extended lend-lease to the Soviet Union, which had been attacked by Germany on June 22, while Congress modified the Neutrality Act to permit the arming of U.S. merchant ships. It is clear that by the fall of 1941, Roosevelt believed Germany was bent on world domination, was a great threat to the Western Hemisphere, and that war was a strong possibility.

German Intentions

In spite of the increased U.S. presence in the European conflict, the ultimate initiative for war lay with Germany and its ally Japan. By 1941, Hitler, who had first mentioned the possibility of a conflict with the United States in his 1928 unpublished sequel to *Mein Kampf* (1925-1927), clearly intended to wage war against the United States at some undetermined point in the future. Hitler believed the United States was culturally and racially decadent and underestimated its industrial capacity and willingness and ability to fight a war. In this connection, he was impressed by the strength of U.S. isolationism. Thus, unlike many German diplomats, Hitler failed to grasp the implications of U.S. power. Hitler's contempt for the United States turned to hostility when Roosevelt expressed his opposition to Nazi totalitarianism and aided Great Britain and the Soviet Union.

Despite Hitler's intention to fight, Germany developed no military plans. The Nazi dictator wanted to postpone war with Washington until Germany could construct a navy large enough to win what would certainly be a naval conflict. Consequently, Hitler ordered the German navy to avoid any incidents with U.S. ships in the Atlantic that might bring on war sooner than desired. Nevertheless, incidents did occur, the result being that an undeclared, limited naval war between the United States and Germany existed by the autumn of 1941.

Germany's caution in the Atlantic was offset by a reckless support of Japanese ambitions in the Far East. Hoping that the Japanese would exacerbate Great Britain's already difficult position and help check the United States commitment to Europe, Hitler began in 1940 to urge Tokyo to expand into southeast Asia. To encourage the Japanese, the Nazi dictator and Mussolini entered into a defense mutual assistance agreement, the Tripartite Pact, with Japan on September 27, 1940. Six months later, on April 4, 1941, the Nazi dictator went further, assuring Japan of his full support in the event of a Japanese-American war, no matter who was the aggressor.

Pearl Harbor

The Japanese attack on Pearl Harbor came as a surprise to both Hitler and Mussolini. Believing that Japan would weaken the British, Soviet, and U.S. war efforts, the Nazi dictator decided the time had come for war with the United States. Hitler took the initiative for this conflict, ordering all-out submarine attacks on U.S. ships and, along with his Italian ally, declaring war on the United States.

In declaring war on the United States at a time when Axis military forces found themselves bogged down in the Soviet Union and under attack by the British in North Africa, Hitler and Mussolini may have made the worst blunder of their careers. When the Nazi dictator said that his declaration of war on the United States would be "decisive not only for the history of Germany, but for the whole of Europe and indeed for the world," he was right. With their declaration of war, Germany and Italy not only unleashed a global war but also went a long way toward guaranteeing their own ultimate defeat and the postwar superpower ascendancy of the United States.

Leon Stein
updated by Bruce J. DeHart

December, 1941-April, 1942
Battle of Bataan

Date: December, 1941-April, 1942
Location: Bataan Peninsula in Luzon, Philippines
Combatants: 80,000 American and Filipino troops vs. 43,000 Japanese troops
Principal commanders: *American-Filipino*, General Douglas MacArthur (1880-1964); *Japanese*, General Masaharu Homma (1887-1946)
Result: A Japanese victory that was a major step in Japan's conquest of the Philippines.

Japanese landings on Luzon in late December, 1941, forced General Douglas MacArthur to withdraw to Bataan and Corregidor Island. By January 6, 1942, more than 80,000 Americans and Filipinos had retreated to the jungles and mountains of the rugged peninsula.

Fierce Japanese attacks, amphibious assaults along the west coast, and numerous infiltration operations pushed the defenders back until they es-

American prisoners carrying their disabled comrades on the "Death March" from Bataan in May, 1942. (National Archives)

tablished a solid defensive line on January 26. With both armies exhausted, a two-month stalemate developed. Severe shortages of all supplies, especially food and medicine, progressively weakened MacArthur's men. Even though their effectiveness deteriorated daily, "the battling bastards of Bataan" believed they might be rescued. MacArthur's departure from the Philippines on March 11 dashed those hopes.

The heavily reinforced Japanese, led by General Masaharu Homma, resumed their offensive in early April and steadily drove the sick and starving defenders down the peninsula until April 9, when all troops on Bataan were unconditionally surrendered. Corregidor would hold out for almost a month, but Japan won the Philippines with its victory on Bataan.

The tragedy of Bataan—beyond the death and suffering of those who fought there—was the fate that befell the 75,000 surviving American and Filipino soldiers immediately after surrender. On the Bataan Death March, a grueling, six-day, sixty-mile march to prison camps, thousands of prisoners died.

Ralph L. Eckert

February, 1942
Japanese American Internment

Date: February 19, 1942
Location: Pacific coast states
Principal figures: *Military,* Major General Allen W. Gullion (1880-1946), Lieutenant General John L. DeWitt; *Government,* Karl R. Bendetsen (c. 1908-1989), Assistant Secretary of War John J. McCloy, Secretary of War Henry L. Stimson, President Franklin D. Roosevelt, California state attorney general Earl Warren (1891-1974)
Result: The forced removal and internment of approximately 110,000 Japanese Americans was one of the gravest violations of civil liberties in United States history.

At the time of the Japanese attack on Pearl Harbor, December 7, 1941, approximately 110,000 Japanese Americans lived on the Pacific coast of the United States. Roughly one-third of those were known as issei—foreign-born Japanese who had migrated before the exclusion of Japanese immigrants in 1924 and were barred from United States citizenship. The rest were nisei—their United States-born children who were U.S. citizens and for the most part strongly American-oriented. The government had in place plans for the arrest of enemy aliens whose loyalty was suspect in the event of war.

Attack on Pearl Harbor

In the immediate aftermath of Pearl Harbor, approximately fifteen hundred suspect Japanese aliens were rounded up. Those not regarded as security risks were, along with German and Italian aliens, restricted from traveling without permission, barred from areas near strategic installations, and forbidden to possess arms, shortwave radios, or maps. The attack on Pearl Harbor, however, gave new impetus to the long-standing anti-Japanese sentiment held by many in the Pacific coast states. The result was loud demands from local patriotic groups, newspapers, and politicians for removal of all Japanese Americans. Leading the clamor was California State attorney general Earl Warren, who warned that their race made all Japanese Americans security risks.

Within the military, the lead in pushing for the roundup of Japanese Americans on the Pacific coast was taken by Major General Allen W. Gullion, the Army's chief law enforcement officer as provost marshal general, in a bid at bureaucratic empire building. His key lieutenant in pushing this program was his ambitious aide, Major (later Colonel) Karl R.

Bendetsen, chief of the Aliens Division of the provost marshal general's office. Lieutenant General John L. DeWitt, the commander of the Army's Western Defense Command, was an indecisive and easily pressured man with a history of anti-Japanese prejudice. At first, DeWitt opposed total removal of the Japanese Americans. By early February, 1942, however, he added his voice to the calls for such action. "In the war in which we are now engaged," DeWitt would rationalize, "racial affinities are not severed by migration. The Japanese race is an enemy race." He warned in apocalyptic terms about the dangers raised by the "continued presence of a large, unassimilated, tightly knit racial group, bound to an enemy nation by strong ties of race, culture, custom, and religion along a frontier vulnerable to attack."

Those views were shared by his civilian superiors. The decisive figure was Assistant Secretary of War John J. McCloy, who in turn brought Secretary of War Henry L. Stimson to support total removal. Attorney General Francis Biddle and most Justice Department officials saw no necessity for mass evacuation, but Biddle yielded to the War Department on the issue. Most important, President Franklin D. Roosevelt, from motives of political expediency as much as from any anxiety over possible sabotage, gave his full backing to the military program.

On February 19, 1942, Roosevelt issued Executive Order 9066, authorizing the military to designate "military areas" from which "any or all persons may be excluded." Congress followed by adopting legislation in March making it a criminal offense for anyone excluded from a military area to remain there.

The Internment Camps

No one appeared to have given much thought to what would be done with the evacuees. At first, the military simply called upon the Japanese Americans living in the western parts of California, Oregon, and Washington, and in the strip of Arizona along the Mexican border, to leave voluntarily for the interior of the country. Resistance by interior communities to the newcomers led the Army to issue, on March 27, 1942, a freeze order requiring Japanese Americans to remain where they were. The next step was the issuance of orders requiring Japanese Americans to report to makeshift assembly centers pending transfer to more permanent facilities. By June, 1942, more than one hundred thousand Japanese Americans had been evacuated. The evacuees were transferred from the assembly centers to ten permanent relocation camps in the interior, each holding between ten and eleven thousand persons, administered by the newly established War Relocation Authority (WRA).

Internees lining up at a Southern California assembly center in April, 1942, awaiting transportation to inland camps, where most of them would live through the duration of the war. (National Archives)

The camps were surrounded by barbed wire and patrolled by armed military guards. The typical camp consisted of wooden barracks covered with tar paper, and each barrack was subdivided into one-room apartments—each furnished with army cots, blankets, and a light bulb—to which a family or unrelated group of individuals was assigned. Toilets and bathing, laundry, and dining facilities were communal. Religious worship (except for the practice of Shinto) was allowed. Schools were later opened for the young people. Although the evacuees grew some of their own food and even undertook small-scale manufacturing projects, most found no productive outlets in the camps for their energies and talents. The WRA promoted the formation of camp governments to administer the day-to-day life of the camps, but those governments lacked meaningful power and rapidly lost the respect of camp populations.

Conditions in the Camps

Conditions were at their worst, and the resulting tensions at their height, at the Tule Lake, California, relocation center, which became a dumping ground for those from other camps regarded as troublemakers.

The upshot was terror-enforced domination of the camp by a secret group of pro-Japan militants.

A nisei recalled poignantly the scene of the evacuees being taken off to a camp: "The sight of hundreds of people assembled with assorted baggage, lined up to board the buses at the embarkation point, with rifle-bearing soldiers standing around as guards, is still imprinted in memory. And I can still remember the acute sense of embitterment. . . ." Life in the camps, said another, held evils that "lie in something more subtle than physical privations. It lies more in that something essential [is] missing from our lives. . . . The most devastating effect upon a human soul is not hatred but being considered not human."

At first, Dillon S. Myer, the director of the WRA from June, 1942, on, regarded the relocation centers as simply "temporary wayside stations." In 1943, the WRA instituted a program of releasing evacuees against whom there was no evidence of disloyalty, who had jobs waiting away from the Pacific coast, and who could show local community acceptance. By the end of 1944, approximately thirty-five thousand evacuees had left the camps under this release program. The Roosevelt administration had, by the spring of 1944, recognized that there was no longer any possible military

A dust storm envelopes the Manzanar, California, internment camp in the eastern Sierras, where internees had to endure harsh weather conditions. (National Archives)

justification for the continued exclusion of Japanese Americans from the Pacific coast. To avoid any possible political backlash, however, the Roosevelt administration waited until after the 1944 presidential election to announce the termination of the exclusion order and allow nearly all of those still in the relocation centers to leave at will. Many of the evacuees, fearful of a hostile reception on the outside, continued to cling to the camps. In June, 1945, the WRA decided to terminate the camps by the end of the year and later imposed weekly quotas for departure, to be filled by compulsion if required.

Aftermath

The evacuation and internment was a traumatic blow to the Japanese American population. Since evacuees were allowed to bring with them only clothes, bedding, and utensils, most sold their possessions for whatever they could get. Only slightly more than half of the evacuees returned to the Pacific coast, and most found their homes, businesses, and jobs lost. Japanese Americans suffered income and property losses estimated at $350 million. Of even longer-lasting impact were the psychological wounds. Internment dealt a heavy blow to the traditional Japanese family structure by undermining the authority of the father. Many nisei, eager to show their patriotism, volunteered for service in the United States military. The Japanese American One Hundredth Infantry Battalion and 422d Regimental Combat Team were among the Army's most-decorated units. On the other hand, more than five thousand nisei were so embittered by their experiences that they renounced their U.S. citizenship. Thousands more would carry throughout their lives painful, even shameful, memories from the years spent behind the barbed wire.

Defenders of civil liberties were appalled at how weak a reed the U.S. Supreme Court proved to be in the war crisis. The first challenge to the treatment suffered by the Japanese Americans to reach the Court involved Gordon Hirabayashi, a student at the University of Washington who had been imprisoned for refusing to obey a curfew imposed by General DeWitt and then failing to report to an assembly center for evacuation. Dodging the removal issue, the Court on June 21, 1943, unanimously upheld the curfew. Refusing to second-guess the military, the Court found reasonable the conclusion by the military authorities that "residents having ethnic affiliations with an invading enemy may be a greater source of danger than those of a different ancestry." On December 18, 1944, a six-to-three majority in *Korematsu v. United States* upheld the exclusion of the Japanese from the Pacific coast as a similarly reasonable military precaution. The Court, in the companion case of *Ex parte Endo* handed down the same day, however, barred continued detention of citizens whose loyalty had been established. The ruling's substantive importance was nil, because it was handed down one day after the announcement of the termination of the order barring Japanese Americans from the Pacific coast.

The Supreme Court never formally overruled its Hirabayashi and Korematsu rulings. Later decisions, however, transmuted Korematsu into a precedent for applying so-called "strict scrutiny" to classifications based upon race or national origin—that is, that such classifications can be upheld only if required by a compelling governmental interest. Pressure from the Japanese-American community led Congress in 1981 to establish a special Commission on Wartime Relocation and Internment to review the internment program. The commission report concluded that the internment was not justified by military necessity, but had resulted from race prejudice, war hysteria, and a failure of political leadership. At the same time, petitions were filed in federal courts to vacate the criminal convictions of resisters to the evacuation. The climax was the unanimous decision by a three-judge panel of the Ninth Circuit Court of Appeals in 1987—which the government declined to appeal to the Supreme Court—vacating Gordon Hirabayashi's curfew violation conviction on the ground that the order had been "based upon racism rather than military necessity." In 1988, Congress voted a formal apology along with $1.25 billion in compensation to surviving internment victims.

John Braeman

May, 1942
Battle of the Coral Sea

Date: May 3-8, 1942
Location: Coral Sea, southwest of New Guinea
Combatants: U.S. Navy vs. Japanese navy
Principal commanders: *Japanese*, Vice Admiral Shigeyoshi Inouye (1889-1980); *American*, Rear Admiral Frank Fletcher (1885-1973)
Result: The U.S. victory halted the Japanese advance in the Pacific, creating an important precedent for the Battle of Midway.

Until this battle, the Japanese advance into the Pacific had continued unabated. Japanese forces sought to take Port Moresby on the southern side of the large island of New Guinea. It was essential for the Japanese to control the approaches to Australia and thereby protect the large base that they had recently established at Rabaul on New Britain. Japanese strategy called for the establishment of a large defensive perimeter far out from the home islands. Eventually, Japan hoped to lure the remnants of the U.S. fleet into a climactic battle somewhere along its defensive ring of bases, where the Japanese fleet could rely on the additional impact of land-based aircraft.

Japanese forces under the command of Vice Admiral Shigeyoshi Inouye launched an end run around western New Guinea by sending invasion forces to Port Moresby by sea. Some invasion forces were also intended to establish a seaplane base in the nearby Solomon Islands, and they took Tulagi in the Solomons on May 3. However, they ran into a U.S. naval ambush in the Coral Sea. ULTRA, the U.S. code-breaking operation, had deciphered most of the Japanese naval code, and U.S. intelligence had learned of Japan's invasion plans. For the first time in naval history, surface ships from both fleets never saw each other during the battle. Fighting was carried out entirely by aircraft flying from three Japanese and two U.S. carri-

The U.S. aircraft carrier Lexington *explodes after being hit by Japanese bombs during the Battle of the Coral Sea. The other large U.S. carrier in the battle, the* Yorktown, *was so badly damaged that it had to return to port for repairs.* (AP/Wide World Photos)

ers that were approximately 175 miles apart. During the exchange of attacks on May 7 and 8, the Japanese lost one light carrier, the *Shoho*, and suffered damage on the larger *Shokaku*. The Americans, under the command of Rear Admiral Frank Fletcher, lost one of their two large carriers, the *Lexington*. The other carrier, the *Yorktown*, was damaged and had to limp to Pearl Harbor for repairs. Several other ships were sunk on both sides.

Which side gained the victory was not clear at first. The Japanese had exchanged a small carrier for a large one, and when other losses are calculated, they won the tactical victory in terms of tonnage sunk. At the time, Japanese leaders boasted of having won a great victory, convinced that they had sunk both U.S. carriers. However, the battle was really a strategic victory for the United States. The Japanese invasion fleet, which had been steaming toward Port Moresby, turned back. This was the first time that a Japanese advance in the Pacific was prevented. Checked in the Battle of the Coral Sea, the Japanese began a campaign to take Port Moresby over land, which necessitated going up and over the spine of New Guinea, the Owen Stanley Range. The Australians were able to hold them back in a struggle fought in miserable terrain.

The U.S. Navy gained vital combat experience and a boost in morale from the battle, which demonstrated that the Japanese advance could be held up and turned back. The battle set the stage for the long series of land, sea, and air battles centering on the island of Guadalcanal in the Solomons. These battles were part of the Japanese plan to threaten Australia, an extension of Japanese power that met considerable resistance from the U.S. Navy. The battle also reduced Japanese strength available for the Battle of Midway: Two Japanese carriers were not available for the battle so American carriers could confront the Japanese fleet outnumbered by only four to three instead of six to three.

Henry Weisser

June, 1942
Battle of Midway

Date: June 3-5, 1942
Location: Pacific Ocean near Midway Island
Combatants: Four Japanese carriers vs. three American carriers and defenders

Principal commanders: *Japanese,* Admiral Chuichi Nagumo (1886-1944), Isoroku Yamamoto (1884-1943); *American,* Frank Fletcher (1885-1973), Chester W. Nimitz (1885-1966), Admiral Raymond A. Spruance (1886-1969)
Result: The U.S. naval victory ended Japanese dominance in the Pacific theater of the war.

From December, 1941, until the spring of 1942, Japanese forces conquered British, Dutch, and U.S. possessions in East Asia and the Pacific Ocean. Fast aircraft carriers enabled them to project their power far into the Pacific, and the December 7 strike by their carrier-based aircraft on the U.S. naval base at Pearl Harbor, Hawaii, had crippled the United States Pacific Fleet. Six months later, Japanese planners prepared for another strike toward Hawaii. They intended to neutralize the remaining vessels in the U.S. fleet and occupy Midway, an island located a thousand miles east of Hawaii that could serve as the springboard for future operations in the Hawaiian chain proper. With Midway and Hawaii in their hands, the Japanese believed they could force the United States to retreat to California.

The commander in chief of the Japanese Combined Fleet, Admiral Isoroku Yamamoto, sought to initiate the operation before the overwhelming U.S. industrial capacity began to play a decisive role in the conflict. Yamamoto put together the largest fleet the Japanese ever had assembled; it included eleven battleships, headed by the *Yamato,* Japan's newest and the world's largest battleship; four heavy and four light carriers; twenty-one cruisers; sixty-five destroyers; more than fifty support and smaller craft; and nineteen submarines. In a serious strategic error, Yamamoto dispersed these vessels in many groups so widely scattered that they could not be mutually supporting. The Northern Force—comprising two light carriers, eight cruisers, thirteen destroyers, and six submarines—sped toward the Aleutian Islands of Alaska in order to divert the U.S. forces and capture Kiska and Attu, which might be used as the springboards for future operations. The islands were successfully occupied, but the operation was secondary in nature, and the ships could have been used more effectively for the main thrust toward Midway.

Japanese forces were badly divided within the main strike force, as well. From the southwest came Japan's Midway Occupation Group, supported by the Second Fleet with two battleships, eight cruisers, a light carrier, and a dozen destroyers. Approaching Midway from the northwest was Yamamoto with the Main Body and the Carrier Striking Force. His main force was organized around three battleships and a light carrier. Split off to the north in order to move either to the Aleutians or to Midway, but in ac-

U.S. Navy fighter planes flying over a burning Japanese ship during the Battle of Midway. (National Archives)

tuality too far from either, was the Guard Force of four battleships and a screen of cruisers and destroyers. In the vanguard was the First Carrier Striking Force under Vice Admiral Chuichi Nagumo, with four heavy carriers, *Akagi*, *Kaga*, *Soryu*, and *Hiryu*, and their screen and support vessels.

Japanese Plan of Attack

Nagumo's carriers were to attack Midway on June 4 and destroy the U.S. airfields and planes preparatory to the landings; when the Americans sortied from Pearl Harbor, the Main Body would move in and destroy them. Previous successes had made Japanese planners arrogant. They made no plans for what to do if the U.S. response unfolded in a different manner from the one they anticipated.

United States naval intelligence teams had advance warning of Japanese plans from official Japanese navy messages that had been intercepted. The intelligence unit at Pearl Harbor, under Commander Joseph J. Rochefort, Jr., decided, on the basis of incomplete information and brilliant analysis, that Midway was the primary target. Admiral Chester W. Nimitz, commander in chief of the Pacific Fleet, called in all of his available carriers and could come up with only three: the *Enterprise* and the *Hornet*, commanded by Rear Admiral Raymond A. Spruance, and the wounded *Yorktown*, commanded by Rear Admiral Frank Jack Fletcher. The carriers were screened by a total of eight cruisers and fourteen destroyers. Nimitz ordered the extensive reinforcement of Midway to a total of 120 planes, antiaircraft guns, and 3,632 defenders. The three carriers lay in wait for the Japanese, northeast of Midway, as ready as forewarning could make them.

Confirmation that the intelligence guesses were correct came early on June 3, when a scout plane sighted the invasion force six hundred miles to the southwest. Army and Marine pilots attacking from Midway scored no significant hits. Unaware that U.S. ships were anywhere nearby, Nagumo launched an attack with half of his planes (108) before dawn on June 4; the other half he held back, in case the United States fleet threatened. Searches by Nagumo's own planes were inadequate.

The Midway defenders put all of their planes in the air and took heavy punishment, but were not knocked out. Defending planes were totally outclassed, but they and the antiaircraft guns still inflicted losses on the Japanese Zeros. By 7:00 A.M., the first raid was over and the Japanese flight leader radioed Nagumo that another attack was required.

Before the second attack could be launched, the Japanese carriers were scattered repeatedly by Marine and Army pilots from Midway, none of whom scored hits and nearly all of whom died trying. In the midst of these attacks, a Japanese scout plane reported a U.S. carrier within range. Rather than immediately launching the second wave of planes that were being rearmed for another attack on Midway, Nagumo decided to recover his first

Ships Sunk at Midway, June 4, 1942

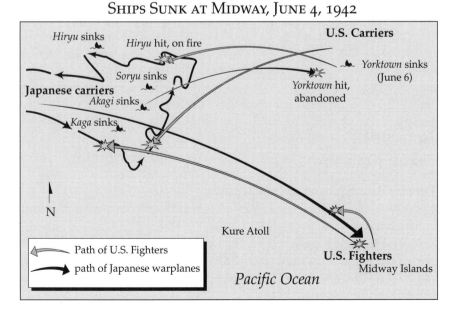

Hiryu sinks

Hiryu hit, on fire

U.S. Carriers

Yorktown sinks (June 6)

Soryu sinks

Yorktown hit, abandoned

Japanese carriers

Akagi sinks

Kaga sinks

N

Kure Atoll

Path of U.S. Fighters

path of Japanese warplanes

U.S. Fighters
Midway Islands

Pacific Ocean

wave and rearm the second for fleet action. By 9:18, all was ready, although the haste meant that bombs and torpedoes were piled around the carrier decks.

U.S. Bombers

At that point, forty-two slow-moving, low-level U.S. torpedo bombers arrived unescorted by fighters and began nearly suicidal attacks, in which thirty-eight planes were lost. None scored hits, but the defending Zeros were drawn down to low levels to attack them. At the end of these attacks, thirty-three high-altitude SBD Dauntless dive bombers, led by Lieutenant Commander C. Wade McCluskey, by chance managed to locate the *Kaga*, *Akagi*, and *Soryu*. McCluskey's planes soon were joined by another group of dive bombers, led by Lieutenant Commander Maxwell Leslie. The Zeros were flying too low to intercept the U.S. planes before the damage was done. In only five minutes, U.S. pilots made fatal hits on the three Japanese carriers. With poor fire management policies on their ships, the Japanese were unable to prevent the sinking of the carriers. Later the same day, the *Hiryu* was also fatally hit and sunk by U.S. pilots. While Yamamoto wanted to engage the U.S. surface fleet in a nighttime battle, a U.S. course change prevented him from doing so.

The Japanese lost 275 planes, about three thousand military personnel, and their four largest carriers in the Battle of Midway. The United States, by contrast, lost one carrier (the *Yorktown*), one destroyer, 150 planes, and 307 personnel. Many of Japan's best pilots were lost in the battle, and the balance of power in the Pacific soon shifted in favor of the United States.

Charles W. Johnson
updated by William E. Watson

June, 1942
Manhattan Project

Date: Project approved on June 17, 1942
Location: Los Alamos, New Mexico; Oak Ridge, Tennessee; Hanford, Washington
Principal figures: Physicist Albert Einstein (1879-1955), Carnegie Institute president Vannevar Bush (1890-1974), Harvard president James Conant (1893-1978), General Leslie R. Groves (1896-1970), U.S. president Franklin D. Roosevelt (1882-1945)

Result: Under the looming threat of German scientists' developing an atomic bomb that would advance the Nazi regime's plans for conquest, a U.S.-government supported team of scientists developed the world's first nuclear weapon.

The building by the United States of an atomic bomb was not the result of a single decision, but of a series of decisions taken over more than two years. Although President Franklin D. Roosevelt held the ultimate responsibility, his attitudes were shaped by scientific advisers whose reasoned conclusions and best guesses persuaded him that it was possible to construct a nuclear fission device "of superlatively destructive powers," as a 1941 report termed it.

Research had begun during the 1920's and 1930's, primarily by European physicists, including James Chadwick in Great Britain, Enrico Fermi and Emilio Segrè in Italy, Lise Meitner and Otto Frisch, who in 1938 fled Austria for Denmark, (where Niels Bohr was working), Hungarians such as Leo Szilard, the Frenchman Frédéric Joliot-Curie, and Otto Hahn and Fritz Strassmann at the Kaiser Wilhelm Institute in Berlin. Their research indicated the possibility of bombarding the nucleus of the uranium atom, splitting it into lighter fragments, and releasing tremendous amounts of energy. A significant number of these scientists fled fascism for the United States or England. Many of them gathered with U.S. physicists in January, 1939, at the fifth Washington Conference on Theoretical Physics to hear Bohr recount the exciting atomic discoveries. Within the year, nearly one hundred papers had been published in scholarly journals expanding on and confirming this new work.

In March, 1939, Fermi, Szilard, and a number of other émigré physicists who feared that the Germans were developing an atomic bomb began a lengthy effort to arouse in both their U.S. colleagues and the United States government some sense of their own urgent concern. After Fermi's direct approach to the U.S. Navy on March 17 failed to generate any active interest, and after the Germans forbade further export of uranium ore from the Joachimstal mines in recently conquered Czechoslovakia, Szilard became convinced that Albert Einstein was the only scientist in the United States with enough fame and prestige to garner a sympathetic hearing from the U.S. government. During a visit to Einstein on Long Island in mid-July, 1940, Szilard exacted from his old friend a promise to write, or at least sign, any letter or letters that might be needed to attract the attention of the U.S. government. With Einstein's promise in hand, Szilard and fellow émigré physicist Eugene Wigner wrote a letter addressed to President Roosevelt. Dated August 2, 1939, and signed "A. Einstein," this letter, detailing the dangers and possibilities of atomic energy, was presented to Roosevelt on October 11 by Alexander Sachs, an occasional presidential adviser who had eagerly agreed to serve as the intermediary for Szilard.

Roosevelt Becomes Involved

Sachs and the Einstein letter convinced the president that the situation should be explored. Accordingly, he established the Advisory Committee on Uranium. Headed by Lyman Briggs, director of the National Bureau of Standards, and including representatives from the Army, the Navy, and the scientific community, this attempt to draw federal support into scientific research for the national defense produced few early results. The committee met infrequently, and its financial support involved only a six-thousand-dollar research grant.

Research on the explosive potential of uranium, which was being conducted at university laboratories scattered across the country, pointed in two main directions. One involved the separation of the fissionable isotope U-235 from the much more common U-238 by a variety of methods, including gaseous or thermal diffusion, electromagnetic separation, and the centrifuge. The other sought to transmute uranium into a new fissionable element, plutonium (U-239), through a controlled chain reaction in an atomic pile. It was not until 1942 that either a chain reaction or the separation of more than a few micrograms of U-235 would be accomplished.

As the Germans drove into France in May and June, 1940, others in the scientific community, including Hungarian-born émigré physicist Edward Teller, grew increasingly concerned. Responding to that concern, on June 15, President Roosevelt established the National Defense Research Council (NDRC) under the leadership of Vannevar Bush, president of the Carnegie Institute. Creative and highly capable, Bush and his able deputy, Harvard president James Conant, played key roles in the decision to make the bomb.

While support for the Advisory Committee on Uranium and other scientific defense research grew during the next year, Bush believed that the work lacked the necessary urgency. On June 28, 1941, acting on Bush's advice, Roosevelt created the stronger Office of Scientific Research and Development (OSRD), with Bush as the head. Conant moved up to head the NDRC, and the Uranium Committee, strengthened and enlarged, became the S-1 Section of OSRD.

The Decision to Make the Bomb

Although the establishment of OSRD represented a significant organizational step, it did not signify a decisive commitment to the building of an

Oak Ridge National Laboratory in Tennessee in 1944, a year after it was built. The lab's contribution to the Manhattan Project was production of the plutonium needed to produce atomic bombs. (Martin Marietta)

atomic bomb. Key figures in the U.S. government—Roosevelt, Vice President Henry Wallace, Secretary of War Henry L. Stimson, and Army Chief of Staff George C. Marshall—members of the OSRD, and members of the U.S. scientific community remained skeptical about both the cost and feasibility of developing an atomic weapon. This skepticism, however, began to give way during the second half of 1941. At that time, the British government, based on the recent ideas of Otto Frisch and Rudolf Peierls, refugee physicists working at Cambridge, reported to the OSRD its belief that an atomic bomb could be developed within two years. Another push to the U.S. atomic effort was provided by Mark Oliphant, the Australian-born head of the physics department at the University of Birmingham. During a visit to the United States in August, 1941, Oliphant pressed upon Bush the British conviction that a bomb really could be made.

With the Japanese attack on Pearl Harbor and the German and Italian declarations of war on the United States in December, 1941, Roosevelt had to choose between committing to the construction of a weapon that might win the war in the long run or cutting back on an unproven program to concentrate valuable resources to the more immediate goal of not losing the war in the short run. On March 9, 1942, Bush informed the president that a major industrial effort might produce an atomic weapon in 1944, but that a decision had to be made soon. After receiving additional encouraging news, Roosevelt decided on June 17, 1942, that the United States would build an atomic bomb.

Having committed itself to the construction of an atomic weapon, the U.S. government had to determine how to produce sufficient quantities of fissionable materials. After learning from S-1 Section researchers that four methods—gaseous diffusion, the centrifuge, electromagnetic separation, and controlled chain reactions in uranium piles—were at comparable stages of development, it was decided to make an all-out effort on all four fronts, rather than explore a single method that might prove a dead end.

The U.S. atomic bomb program—code-named the Manhattan Project and headed by General Leslie R. Groves (appointed September 17, 1942)—involved highly secret research at Los Alamos, New Mexico, where basic bomb development took place; Oak Ridge, Tennessee, where U-235 was separated from U-238 by gaseous diffusion and electromagnetic techniques; and Hanford, Washington, where plutonium was produced in graphite piles. At a cost of nearly two billion dollars, the Manhattan Project ultimately paid dividends: The first bomb was successfully detonated on July 16 at Alamogordo, New Mexico, and there followed production of the weapons that ended World War II in August, 1945, and that enabled the United States to lead the world into the Atomic Age.

Charles W. Johnson
updated by Bruce J. DeHart

August, 1942-February, 1943
Battle of Guadalcanal

Date: August 7, 1942-February 9, 1943
Location: Solomon Islands
Combatants: Americans vs. Japanese
Principal commanders: *Japanese*, Admiral Hiroaki Abe (1879-1953), General Harukichi Hyakutake (1888-1947), General Kiyotake Kawaguchi, Admiral Gunichi Mikawa; *American*, Admiral Frank Fletcher (1885-1973), Admiral Ernest Joseph King (1878-1956), Admiral Robert Lee Ghormley (1883-1958), Admiral William Frederick Halsey (1882-1959), General Douglas MacArthur (1880-1964), Chester W. Nimitz (1885-

1966), Rear Admiral Richmond Kelly Turner (1885-1961), General Alexander Archer Vandegrift (1887-1973)
Result: One of the first military campaigns to use air, land, sea, subsurface, and amphibious forces together, this conflict turned the tide in the Asian-Pacific war.

During the first half of 1942, the Japanese achieved spectacular expansion and the Allies were in desperate straits in all theaters of World War II. The global strategic priority was Germany first, so resources were scarce. The Guadalcanal and larger Solomon Islands campaigns were fought under these challenging circumstances, and the Allied situation was reversed.

The Battle of Midway set the stage for the Battle of Guadalcanal, one of the most important struggles during the war in the Pacific. The engagement at Midway had taken place in early June, 1942. It was a spectacular air engagement, in which the Japanese lost 4 aircraft carriers, 275 planes, and one hundred first-line pilots. Land-based Army Air Force planes also participated, although they achieved little. This stunning defeat forced Japan onto the defensive and gave the Allied powers a badly needed reprieve. As a result of the Battle of Midway, U.S. planners soon decided to launch a limited offensive in the area of the Pacific Ocean where the Central Pacific and Southwest Pacific commands overlapped.

U.S. Objectives

The logical initial objective was the Solomon Islands. This chain of islands was located within easy bombing range of the great Japanese air base at Rabaul on New Britain Island and the important Allied base of Port Moresby in southern New Guinea. Furthermore, the Japanese had begun construction of a bomber field on Guadalcanal—one of the southernmost islands in the Solomons. Whoever controlled Guadalcanal and finished the airfield would hold an important advantage in the Pacific war.

Acting from the initiative of Admiral Ernest King, chief of naval operations, the Joint Chiefs of Staff ordered Admiral Chester Nimitz and General Douglas MacArthur, theater commanders, to gather all available forces and equipment for an amphibious operation in the Solomon Islands against the adjoining islands of Guadalcanal and Tulagi. The invasion, planned in conjunction with a renewed attack in New Guinea and an attempt to seize Rabaul, was to begin on August 1, but delays and a lack of supplies dictated that the Solomons operation be postponed until August 7. The Allied forces included U.S. air, marine, army, naval, and submarine units, and various other forces from Australia and New Zealand, native coastwatcher units coordinated by the Royal Australian Navy, and

Battle of Guadalcanal

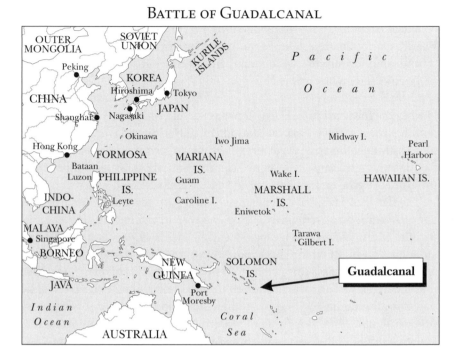

intelligence agencies modeled on British methods. The U.S. forces were largely ignorant of the islands that they were to invade and had little time to work out plans for the landings. The combined force, consisting of eighty-two ships carrying the First Marine Division, elements of the Second Marine Division, and other contingents, met near the Fiji Islands in late July.

The Campaign Begins

Early on August 7, a U.S. carrier task force took position south of Guadalcanal. Under its protection, the first support ships and landing force, commanded by Rear Admiral Richmond K. Turner, slipped along the west coast of Guadalcanal. After a heavy shore bombardment, Major General Alexander A. Vandegrift's Marines waded ashore. The landings were practically unopposed on Guadalcanal, although strong resistance was encountered on Tulagi. On August 8, the Marines seized their primary objective, the unfinished airfield soon to be named Henderson Field. Japanese forces on Guadalcanal were fewer than twenty-five hundred, and within a few days there were approximately sixteen thousand Marines on the island. Other factors, however, intervened to prevent a swift Allied victory.

The Japanese were able to respond quickly to the attack by dispatching reinforcements to Guadalcanal and initiating steps designed to gain naval superiority in the area. They were assisted by U.S. timidity regarding the safety of the carrier task force. Vice Admiral Frank J. Fletcher, commander of the invasion, withdrew his carriers on August 8. Thereafter, the beachhead received almost no air protection, and heavy Japanese bombing attacks began. The withdrawal of the carriers emboldened the Japanese to send a strong surface force, in the hope of destroying U.S. warships and transports and thereby isolating the Marines. The Japanese striking force of five heavy cruisers, two light cruisers, and a destroyer slipped past Allied patrol vessels and entered Iron Bottom Sound at 1:00 A.M. on August 9. Carefully trained for night action, the Japanese sank four Allied cruisers and won a tremendous victory, although their commander, Vice Admiral Gunichi Mikawa, erred in not attacking the unprotected support ships and the beachhead itself. The defeat caused Rear Admiral Turner to withdraw his amphibious force, leaving behind sixteen thousand Marines who were insufficiently supplied for the task of maintaining their positions on Guadalcanal. However, their enemy had even more serious logistical problems.

War of Attrition

From mid-August, 1942, until early February, 1943, when Allied forces finally cleared the entire island, Japanese and Allied forces were locked in bitter conflict. Both sides made desperate efforts to reinforce their numbers in this struggle of attrition and to deny supplies and reinforcements to the other. After initial success, the Marines encountered stubborn resistance and made little progress for several months. The Japanese launched several offensives, but inaccurate information about the strength of the Allied forces caused them to fail. The most notable engagements were the Battle of the Tenaru River, in which one thousand Japanese were virtually wiped out, and the Battle of Bloody Ridge on September 13 and 14, at which a Japanese force of six thousand troops under Major General Kiyotake Kawaguchi was cut to pieces. By the time the Japanese high command realized that large reinforcements were required, Allied naval and air defenses were much improved. After mid-September, the Marine foothold was secure, and reinforcements and supplies were coming in on a continual basis.

Final victory could not be won, however, until one side achieved naval dominance in the area. The struggle between Allied and Japanese naval forces continued through the autumn, with the Imperial Navy controlling the waters around Guadalcanal at night and the Allies—because of Henderson Field's aircraft, mostly with Marine pilots—commanding the area during the day. A number of important but indecisive carrier and ship-to-ship engagements occurred, such as the Battle of the Eastern Solomons and the Battle of Cape Esperance. The latter was the result of a desperate Japanese effort to reinforce Guadalcanal. Although it was considered an Allied victory, the Japanese moved ahead, bombing Henderson Field and dispatching a battleship force to bombard Allied positions. On October 15, forty-five hundred Japanese soldiers were landed, raising their total on the island to twenty thousand, and the Imperial Army prepared for a victorious offensive.

The Marines suffered from low morale, malaria and other diseases, and exhaustion. With more than half the planes on Henderson Field rendered nonoperational, a defeatist feeling spread throughout the chain of command. On October 16, Vice Admiral William F. Halsey replaced Vice Admiral Robert L. Ghormley as commander of the Southwest Pacific forces. Halsey was convinced that control of Guadalcanal was essential, and the Joint Chiefs had reached the same conclusion.

Escalation of Fighting

The main Japanese attacks came on October 24 and 25, but these frontal assaults against fortified U.S. positions resulted in costly defeats. In November, both sides attempted to bring in reinforcements. The Allies were successful, but the Japanese, having lost a crucial naval engagement in the middle of the month, were able to land only about four thousand soldiers, who were badly equipped and poorly supplied.

In December, U.S. Army units replaced the exhausted Marines, and these fresh forces soon launched a powerful attack, assisted by air strikes from Henderson Field and from aircraft carriers. The Japanese held on grimly until January 4, 1943, when Tokyo ordered the evacuation of Guadalcanal within thirty days. Operating brilliantly under constant pressure from the Allies, the Imperial Army command evacuated more than eleven thousand troops by destroyers February 9. The bitter six-month struggle for Guadalcanal ended on this note of indecisiveness. Allied casualties were sixteen hundred killed and forty-two hundred wounded. Fourteen thousand Japanese were killed or missing, nine thousand dead from disease, and approximately one thousand captured.

Later disclosures concerning intelligence, communications, and reconnaissance have shed additional light on events. The coastwatchers rightly have received major credit. One reason the Japanese cruisers that annihilated the Allied naval forces at Savo Island were a surprise was a communication breakdown between regional commands. An Australian reconnaissance aircraft sighted and reported the Japanese, but the message was lost between command centers. The Allies benefited frequently from intercepts and analysis of signals intelligence. The Japanese achieved complete surprise when they withdrew more than ten thousand troops at the end. Indeed, the Allies were expecting a Japanese offensive.

Guadalcanal received much interest on the home front, and a new vocabulary arose: Guadalcanal, Henderson Field, the Tokyo Express (Japanese reinforcements), Iron Bottom Sound (a bay north of Guadalcanal, where naval and air forces were destroyed and sunk), the Long Lance torpedo (a superior Japanese weapon), and Starvation Island (the Japanese name for Guadalcanal). The fiftieth anniversary commemorations of events of World War II paid tribute to Guadalcanal through several publications, a reenactment, an entire summer of events involving underwater searches and the discovery of wrecks, and a symposium.

Theodore A. Wilson
updated by Eugene L. Rasor

November, 1942
North Africa Invasion

Date: November 7-8, 1942
Location: French North Africa
Combatants: Allies vs. Germans
Principal figures: *British*, Prime Minister Winston S. Churchill (1874-1965); Bernard Law Montgomery (1887-1976), commander of the Eighth Army in North Africa; *Allied*, Dwight D. Eisenhower (1890-1969); *French*, General Henri-Honoré Giraud (1879-1949), Jean Louis Darlan (1881-1942), Henri-Philippe Pétain (1856-1951); *American*, George C. Marshall (1880-1959), George S. Patton (1885-1945), President Franklin D. Roosevelt (1882-1945); *German*, Field Marshal Erwin Rommel (1891-1944)
Result: An Allied campaign designed to force the Germans out of North Africa, this operation provided a training ground for U.S. forces in World War II.

On December 11, 1941, Germany and Italy declared war on the United States. Thereafter, the United States devoted its chief efforts to defeating its European enemies. Officers of the U.S. Army, however, disagreed with their British counterparts about how this aim should be accomplished. General George C. Marshall, chief of staff of the U.S. Army, wanted to build

German field marshal Erwin Rommel in Libya. (National Archives)

up air and ground forces in the British Isles and then launch a cross-channel invasion into France, aimed ultimately at Berlin. He hoped to be ready to invade late in 1942 and certainly by early 1943. The British leaders, especially Prime Minister Winston S. Churchill, favored a peripheral strategy designed to wear down Germany and Italy through air attacks and by striking at weak points on the frontiers of their empires. Churchill argued that only when the enemy was exhausted should the Allies cross the English Channel and confront the German army directly.

President Franklin D. Roosevelt and Marshall also believed that by concentrating on a cross-channel operation, they could achieve several objectives. First, the operation would satisfy the Soviet Union's Joseph Stalin, who was pressuring the Allies for a second front in Europe, which would take pressure off the beleaguered Soviets. Second, such an attack would take the Germans by surprise and stimulate French resistance. In the long run, it was unrealistic to attack the powerful Germans on their home ground without preparation. The dangers of defeat were great, but it was imperative that the United States show its colors somewhere.

Roosevelt insisted that U.S. troops be in action against the Germans somewhere before the end of 1942. Invasion of France was not possible in 1942 because of a lack of landing craft and trained troops to staff them, so the Allies had to find an easier target. Churchill won the argument when the Allies decided that French North Africa was ideal for invasion. There were no German troops in that area, and it was probable that the Vichy

French forces (set up as part of the French puppet state after France had surrendered to the Germans in June, 1940) would put up only token resistance against British and U.S. invaders.

At the other end of the North African landmass, the British Eighth Army was fighting General Erwin Rommel's Afrika Korps. An Allied landing in French North Africa would relieve the pressure on the British in Egypt and, it was hoped, make it possible to force the Germans out of North Africa altogether. Allied possession of North Africa would free the Mediterranean Sea for British shipping, so that oil from the Near East and supplies from India could come to the British Isles by the most direct route. Marshall argued that a landing in North Africa would delay an invasion of northern France by two years because of the drain on supplies, but Roosevelt overruled him.

Preparations

The planning for the invasion, called Operation Torch, proved to be difficult. The United States preferred simultaneous landings in Morocco and Algeria, while the British wanted the operation to focus on the Algerian coastline alone. Both sides had good reasons. The United States wanted a foothold in Morocco, near Casablanca, if things went poorly in Algeria. Casablanca also would give the Allies a port that would not be subject to Axis air attacks. On the other hand, the British argued that if the landings did not include eastern Algeria, the Germans and Italians could quickly occupy all of Tunisia, using it as a base for air attacks and for a solid defensive position that would take many Allied lives to reduce.

By the end of August, the plans were in place, and General Dwight D. Eisenhower was firmly entrenched as the overall commander of the operation. In October, 1942, Major General Mark Clark and diplomat Robert Murphy were sent on a secret mission into North Africa to gauge the sentiments of the French forces there. Clark and Murphy ran head-on into French politics in North Africa. One problem was deciding which French general would lead the defection from Vichy and from collaboration with the Axis. It was clear that the maverick French general Charles de Gaulle would be unacceptable to French military leadership in North Africa. Admiral Jean Darlan, commander in chief of Vichy forces, was suspect because of his previous support for Vichy. It was agreed that General Henri-Honoré Giraud would announce the landings and order Vichy troops not to resist the Allies. In another undercover operation, Giraud was brought to Gibraltar to confer with Eisenhower on the eve of the invasion. In the long run, Giraud's selection did not settle French political problems in North Africa.

First Landings

In the early morning of November 8, 1942, Eisenhower's troops landed at Casablanca, Oran, and Algiers. General Giraud's orders not to resist too often were ignored by French officers unaware of Giraud's new role in French North Africa, and the aged Marshal Henri-Philippe Pétain, head of the Vichy government, ordered his forces to resist. Eisenhower, contacting Admiral Darlan, arranged for Darlan to assume control of French North Africa and then order his troops to cease fire preparatory to a later attack on the Germans. The U.S. press criticized Eisenhower for coming to terms with a pro-Fascist, but Churchill and Roosevelt supported him, especially when Eisenhower explained that the deal was necessary to avoid fighting the French and to begin the real job of fighting the Germans.

In November and early December, Eisenhower made a dash for Tunis, hoping to seize that port before the Germans could pour troops into Tunisia. Rain, superior German tank tactics, and German air superiority stalled his offensive before it reached its objective. The British Eighth Army, under General Bernard L. Montgomery, was driving Rommel back. By February, 1943, Rommel had crossed Libya and reached southern Tunisia. He then turned against Eisenhower's troops and inflicted a sharp blow on them at Kasserine Pass. The Allies, however, were building up their forces, while the Germans received no significant reinforcements. By May 13, the last resistance had ended, and Eisenhower had captured nearly three hundred thousand prisoners in Tunisia.

Despite his lack of combat experience, General Dwight D. Eisenhower was made overall commander of the Allied invasion of North Africa and he was later elevated to supreme commander of all Allied forces in the European theater of the war.
(National Archives)

British field marshal Bernard Montgomery. (National Archives)

As Marshall had feared, the large troop commitment to North Africa made a cross-channel invasion in 1943 impossible. Because the troops and landing craft were already in the Mediterranean, they had to be used there. Despite Marshall's concerns, Operation Torch did have a number of beneficial results. First, it established Eisenhower as a military planner and as an officer who could be diplomat as well as warrior. Second, it gave Eisenhower's staff valuable training in planning and executing a complex mission that involved air, land, and sea components. Third, Operation Torch and subsequent fighting in North Africa allowed U.S. Army troops to train in realistic conditions. Fourth, Operation Torch was carried out successfully less than one year after the attack on Pearl Harbor, thereby showing the U.S. resilience, resolve, and combat potential.

On July 10, 1943, Anglo-American forces invaded Sicily, and the Allies soon captured the island. The fall of Sicily and the Allied bombing of Rome led to the downfall of the Italian head of government, Benito Mussolini, on July 25, 1943, and ultimately to an Italian surrender. Before the negotiations could be planned, however, the Germans had occupied the country. In September, U.S. troops invaded Italy. The progress of the Allied forces up the peninsula was slow; not until June 4, 1944, did the U.S. Fifth Army liberate Rome. The campaign that began with the invasion of North Africa had accomplished much, principally the freeing of the Mediterranean Sea and the elimination of Italy from the war.

Stephen E. Ambrose
updated by James J. Cooke

July-September, 1943
Italy Invasion

Date: July 9-September 19, 1943
Location: Sicily and the Italian mainland
Combatants: c. 170,000 Allied troops vs. smaller number of German troops
Principal figures: *Americans,* General Harold R. L. George Alexander (1891-1969), commander of the Fifteenth Army Group; Mark W. Clark (1896-1984), commander of the U.S. Fifth Army; General Dwight D. Eisenhower (1890-1969), supreme commander of the Allied Expeditionary Force; General George S. Patton, Jr. (1885-1945), commander of the U.S. Seventh Army; *British,* Field Marshal Bernard Law Montgomery (1887-1976), commander of the British Eighth Army; *Italian,* Benito Mussolini (1883-1945), prime minister of Italy, 1922-1943; Pietro Badoglio (1871-1956), prime minister of Italy, 1943-1944; *German,* Albert Kesselring (1885-1960), German commander in chief, South
Result: This campaign forced Germany to use troops and resources that might otherwise have been used in northern France.

One of the decisions made by President Franklin D. Roosevelt and Prime Minister Winston S. Churchill at the Casablanca Conference in February of 1943 was to occupy the island of Sicily in order to assure the safety of Allied shipping lines in the Mediterranean. At the time, no decision was made as to an invasion of the Italian mainland. General Dwight Eisenhower was given overall military command of the Mediterranean theater, while General Harold R. L. George Alexander was in command of the invasion force, the Fifteenth Army Group.

The invasion of Sicily was preceded by the capture of a small garrison on the nearby island of Pantelleria on June 11, 1943. The Germans were not convinced that the capture of this island pointed to an invasion of Sicily, but were tricked by a British ruse that suggested that an Allied invasion of Sardinia was forthcoming.

Following a monthlong bombardment of Axis air bases, the Fifteenth Army Group, consisting of the British Eighth Army under General Bernard Law Montgomery and the U.S. Seventh Army commanded by General George S. Patton, carried out two separate landings on the southern coast of Sicily on July 9 and July 10, 1943. Supported by naval gunfire and airborne operations, the Allies landed 160,000 men on the island. The Allies benefited greatly from superior air power, having thirty-seven hundred planes as opposed to sixteen hundred Axis aircraft. Although the landing itself went relatively smoothly, tragedy struck when U.S. airborne drops encountered friendly fire. Montgomery's forces ran into some stubborn German resistance south of Catania, while Patton, whose forces had landed on the left flank, first moved through western Sicily and later assisted the British. On August 17, both forces arrived in Messina, on the northern tip of the island. In spite of complete Allied air superiority, the Germans had managed to evacuate more than a hundred thousand troops and a considerable number of vehicles to the Italian mainland.

Fall of Mussolini

The fall of Sicily was a major factor in the collapse of Benito Mussolini's government. The Fascist leadership had become increasingly disenchanted with Mussolini, in particular with his alliance with Adolf Hitler. A meeting between Mussolini and Hitler, in which Mussolini requested the transfer of Italian divisions from the Russian front to be used in the defense of Italy, had brought no results. During a subsequent meeting of the Fascist Grand Council on July 24, Mussolini was handed a vote of no confidence. On the following day, he was dismissed from office by the king of Italy, Victor Emmanuel III, arrested, and spirited away to a hotel on the Gran Sasso in the Abbruzzi Mountains.

Mussolini was succeeded as prime minister by Marshal Pietro Badoglio, a former Fascist leader whose emissaries had negotiated secretly with the Allies in Lisbon and Madrid. Badoglio's problem was to make peace with the Allies and extricate Italy from the war, while preventing the Germans from defending Italy against an expected Allied invasion.

The collapse of the Fascist government in Italy brought to the fore the still unresolved issue of the entire purpose of the Italian campaign. U.S. military planners had insisted all along that the Italian campaign was to be no more than a secondary effort, insisting that the primary Allied effort had to be Operation Overlord, the Normandy invasion. In their view, the purpose of the Italian campaign was merely to force the Germans to commit troops and resources in the Italian theater to prevent their use on the eastern front and, more important, against an Allied invasion in Normandy. On the other hand, British military planners—perhaps with an eye toward postwar settlements in the Balkans—assigned far greater importance to the Italian theater. The conflict of opinion was reflected in the fact that it took until the end of July to authorize an invasion of the Italian peninsula.

On September 3, 1943, an armistice was signed between Italy and the Allies. By mid-October, the Badoglio government had declared war on Germany and was recognized by the Allies as a cobelligerent. Although the announcement of the Italian capitulation took many Germans by surprise, Hitler had prepared for such an eventuality ever since Mussolini's overthrow by ordering troops to assemble for possible entry into Italy. Thus, by the beginning of September, the Germans had eight divisions in readiness in the north of Italy, in addition to Field Marshall Albert Kesselring's forces in southern Italy.

The Invasion

The invasion of the Italian mainland began on September 3. It involved the movement of two British divisions under General Montgomery across the narrow Straits of Messina into Calabria. On September 9, another British division landed at Taranto. The Italians were unprepared for the invasions, but the Germans reacted quickly, occupying Rome and airfields in the vicinity, thereby putting an end to any hopes for a possible Allied airborne operation in the area.

Unlike the invasions in Calabria and Taranto, which met with virtually no resistance, Allied landings at Salerno (Operation Avalanche) on September 9 met with stiff resistance. An invasion force of 55,000 troops for the initial landings, with another 115,000 to follow, was confronted by a much smaller contingent of German defenders. Lieutenant General Mark Clark, who had intended to surprise the defenders by forgoing preparatory naval bombardment, was faced with counterattacks from the Germans that almost turned the entire invasion into a disaster. Only with the help of skillful naval gunnery, artillery, and considerable air support could the invasion force maintain its precarious positions on the beach. By September 18, the beachhead was at last secured and the German offensive could be checked. Montgomery, after some prompting to accelerate, at last had managed to make contact with the beachhead on September 16.

The Germans realized that their failure to drive the Allies back into the sea left them only one option: a gradual withdrawal northward beyond Naples, where they had established a strong defensive zone, the so-called Winter Line or Gustav Line. The Allied campaign to penetrate this line met with little success. In an effort to break the stalemate, the Allies, on January

22, 1944, resorted to a landing behind the German lines on the beaches at Anzio. In spite of initial successes, the effort bogged down, and during four months on the beachhead, the Allies had to evacuate more than thirty thousand casualties. Following a combined air-ground offensive, a breakthrough was at last effected, and Allied troops entered Rome on June 4, 1944, two days before the Normandy invasion.

The Allied drive toward the new German defensive positions south of Bologna—the so-called Gothic Line—again bogged down, and the offensive could not be resumed until the spring of 1945. Bologna fell on April 21, only a few days before Mussolini was captured and executed by partisans. In fact, since March, 1945, SS General Karl Wolff secretly had been negotiating surrender terms for the German forces in Italy with Allen Dulles, the chief of the American Office of Strategic Services in Switzerland. Fighting in Italy ceased on May 2, 1945, five days before the final capitulation of Germany.

Helmut J. Schmeller

September-October, 1943
Battle of Salerno

Date: September 9-October 1, 1943
Location: Gulf of Salerno off the southwest coast of Italy
Combatants: United States Fifth Army (British Tenth and American Sixth Corps) vs. German Tenth Army
Principal commanders: *American*, General Mark Clark (1896-1984); *German*, General Heinrich von Vietinghoff (1887-1952)
Result: The Allies achieved their objective, taking the port of Naples.

With Sicily secured and Benito Mussolini's Fascist government collapsing, the Allies decided to invade Italy rather than attempt a 1943 cross-channel invasion of northern France. On September 9, 1943, a combined British and American amphibious assault (Operation Avalanche) led by General Mark Clark took place at Salerno, with the intent of drawing German troops to Italy and away from more potentially active and important invasion possibilities elsewhere.

Although the Allies anticipated little or no resistance, German troops, led by Heinrich von Vietinghoff, put up a strong defense from positions in the mountains from which they could fire down on the attacking troops.

After Allied troops drove the German occupation forces out of Salerno, some of the towns-people waded out into the surf to get closer looks at the unusual Allied landing craft. (AP/Wide World Photos)

Nonetheless, Allied progress was slow but steady until September 12, when the Germans unleashed a furious counterattack. However, necessary Allied assistance arrived, including two battalions of the Eighty-second Airborne, additional firepower provided by two British battleships, two thousand air sorties, and fifteen hundred additional troops from North Africa. The Germans retreated, and on October 1, Allied troops entered Naples.

British and American losses exceeded 15,000 men, German losses were estimated at 8,000. About 175,000 Allied troops, more than two-thirds of whom were British, and about 60,000 Germans and Italians participated in the battle.

Both Salerno in the southwest and General Bernard Law Montgomery's invasion of Southeast Italy were the beginning of the Allied effort to drive the Germans out of Italy. A less than well-planned strategy engendered a great deal of controversy both at the time and later.

John Quinn Imholte

November, 1943
Battle of Tarawa

Date: November 20-23, 1943
Location: Tarawa Atoll, Gilbert Islands
Combatants: 35,000 Americans vs. 4,700 Japanese and Koreans
Principal commanders: *American*, Rear Admiral Harry W. Hill, Major General Holland M. "Howlin' Mad" Smith (1882-1967); *Japanese and Korean*, Rear Admiral Keiji Shibasaki
Result: A costly U.S. victory.

Admiral Raymond A. Spruance launched Operation Galvanic in November, 1943, to gain air bases in the Gilbert Islands to support the push toward Japan. The first objective was the airstrip on 300-acre Betio Island in Tarawa Atoll.

Rear Admiral Harry W. Hill's naval and air bombardment (November 17-20) had little effect. Rear Admiral Keiji Shibasaki had boasted that a million Americans could not take Tarawa in a hundred years. Major General

U.S. infantry troops wade ashore during the Battle of Tarawa. (National Archives)

Holland M. Smith's Second Marine Division began landing at dawn on November 20. Shallow reefs, unpredictable tides, and Japanese obstacles frustrated landing craft. Marines had to wade hundreds of yards to shore under the fire of more than five hundred Japanese pillboxes. The first wave had 75 percent casualties. Smith ordered reinforcements from Makin Atoll. The Americans advanced inland on the second day and secured the island after seventy-six hours of tenacious, inch-by-inch fighting, including desperate suicide charges by the Japanese on the third day.

Tarawa was the bloodiest battle that the U.S. Marine Corps had experienced up until its time. U.S. losses were 1,057 killed, 2,351 wounded, and 88 missing in action. All except 17 of the Japanese and 129 of the Koreans died. The Americans used the captured airstrip to support invasions of the Marshall Islands.

Eric v.d. Luft

June, 1944
Operation Overlord

Date: June 6, 1944
Location: Normandy, France
Combatants: Allies vs. Germans
Principal commanders: *Allied*, Omar Bradley (1893-1981), Dwight D. Eisenhower (1890-1969), Bernard Law Montgomery (1887-1976); *German*, Chancellor Adolf Hitler (1889-1945), Erwin Rommel (1891-1944), Karl Rudolf Gerd von Rundstedt (1875-1953)
Result: This amphibious invasion of northern France began the final liberation of Western Europe from German control.

The Allied invasion of German-occupied France in June, 1944, remains one of the most famous events in World War II history. Crossing the English Channel from England to the French coast of Normandy, the forces waging the attack constituted the largest amphibious operation undertaken in military history.

To command this challenging effort, Western Allied leaders appointed General Dwight D. Eisenhower as commander in chief of Allied Forces in Western Europe. Arriving in England in January, 1944, to oversee the complicated project, he spent many months directing the planning for the cross-channel invasion. Excellent cooperation between the Western Allies

General Dwight D. Eisenhower gives encouragement to American paratroopers preparing to join the assault on German positions in Europe in June, 1944. (Library of Congress)

was essential for successfully planning and implementing the attack. The second highest military appointment was, therefore, assigned to a prominent British general, Bernard Montgomery.

Allied Planning

Defining the attack's size, scope, and location required careful consideration. Normandy was selected because of its proximity to Great Britain. German defenses in Normandy were weaker than elsewhere on France's northern coast, although Field Marshal Erwin Rommel had strengthened his fortified positions in early 1944. Beach and tide characteristics also made Normandy a likely choice. The original plan for "Overlord," the operation's code name, designated three army divisions for the initial invasion. Eisenhower and Montgomery expanded the size of the target area and increased the divisions to five for the coastal attack: two U.S. divisions, two British, and one Canadian.

Allied deception played an important role before the attack. Adolf Hitler and most German military leaders predicted an invasion would occur in the Pas de Calais region to the northeast. Significant German forces therefore were positioned there, and did not play a role when the actual invasion began. Allied schemes increased Hitler's belief that the Pas de Calais was the intended target. Phantom armies were "located" in eastern England and fake radio transmissions misled the Germans. Eisenhower

Normandy Invasion, 1944

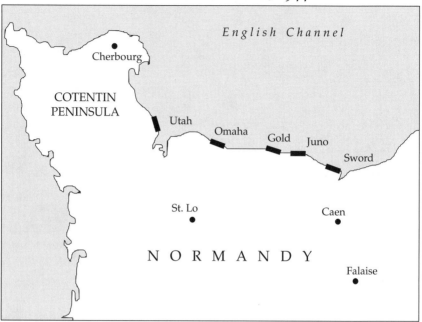

also ordered widespread air attacks on railroad centers, bridges, and other transportation targets within France to hinder German reinforcements from reaching the coast when the invasion eventually began. The Normandy attack was therefore nearly a complete surprise.

The plan required the landings to begin at dawn, so troops would have a full day to establish a beachhead and begin to move inland. Other requirements included a full moon the night before, so parachute forces could be dropped in predawn hours behind enemy lines to cut communication lines and control key bridges and road junctions; a low tide at dawn, so beach obstacles could be cleared; and a fairly calm sea, as soldiers had to land from small assault craft. Early June would meet these requirements, assuming favorable weather. General Eisenhower selected June 5 as D day for the attack. The right combination of tide and moon would not occur again for several weeks, and planners did not wish to postpone the invasion.

The Invasion

In early June, soldiers boarded ships in English embarkation ports, but bad weather on June 3 and June 4 made the scheduled June 5 invasion impossible. An updated weather forecast indicated a break in the storm might occur the night of June 5-6. Eisenhower decided on June 5 to take the risk. The weather improved, and more than five thousand ships, carrying more than a hundred thousand troops, headed for the continent. Paratroopers dropped inland during the night, the first Allied soldiers to land in occupied France. By daylight on June 6, bombers and fighter planes were flying overhead, as ground forces moved toward the beaches. Warships pounded German fortifications with heavy artillery from the sea. Each of the five army divisions had an assigned coastal sector (identified by a code name) to attack and secure: "Utah" and "Omaha" were assigned to the United States, "Gold" and "Sword" to the British, and "Juno" to the Canadians. The landings succeeded in the face of heavy German resistance, although the United States troops at "Omaha Beach" had the greatest difficulty and highest casualties. By the end of the first day, approximately 150,000 soldiers had landed in Normandy.

The invasion forces gradually consolidated and expanded their positions. By the end of June, more than 850,000 Allied troops were in France.

American soldiers pour ashore at Normandy under heavy German machine fire. Most of the landing craft in such amphibious operations were operated by Coast Guard sailors, who suffered among the highest casualties of any branch of the service. (National Archives)

The Germans, because of the disruption of their transportation systems from air attacks, could not bring sufficient units to launch effective and sustained counterattacks. Rommel's preferred strategy favored using all available German forces to drive the Allies into the sea. However, Hitler in Berlin and Field Marshal Gerd von Rundstedt adopted a policy of using their forces on a more selective basis. Thus, the German defense was not well coordinated at the highest levels.

German forces occasionally succeeded in blocking Allied advances from the beachhead. British and Canadian troops on Montgomery's left flank were unable to capture the city of Caen, a D day objective, until mid-July. On the right flank, General Omar Bradley's U.S. First Army finally succeeded in capturing the port of Cherbourg on June 27 but was unable to break out of the Cotentin Peninsula quickly.

Greater Allied firepower, both on the ground and in the air, finally broke the impasse. By August 1, Bradley's troops were in open country, and General George Patton's U.S. Third Army headed to the south and east. The German Seventh Army, nearly cut off in the "Falaise pocket," sustained major losses of troops and equipment by mid-August. U.S. and French forces liberated Paris on August 25.

Aftermath

Casualty figures for Operation Overlord vary, in part because of incomplete data. Considering the large numbers of troops in the operation, contradictory totals seem inevitable. Tallies of battle losses also differ according to the period included in any tabulation. Descriptions of the Normandy campaign often cover the weeks between June 6 and the Allied breakout into the French interior by the end of July. Some figures include the liberation of Paris in late August. Casualties on D day (June 6) alone are estimated to be between 10,000 and 10,500 for the Allies and 6,500 for the Germans. Eisenhower referred to 60,000 casualties in three weeks. Another source placed casualties from June 6 to the end of August at approximately 84,000 British and Canadian, 126,000 U.S., and 200,000 German.

Relations between Eisenhower and Montgomery eroded during the campaign. Eisenhower believed the British commander was overly cautious in advancing toward Caen. Montgomery favored holding German forces there while urging Bradley to break out to the west. Eisenhower was displeased when Montgomery did not push his British forces toward Falaise, where, if they had linked with U.S. forces advancing from the west, they would have cut off an entire German army. In both cases, Montgomery believed he had acted correctly and resented Eisenhower's assessment.

Western scholars emphasize the significance of the Normandy invasion in the overall history of World War II. Veterans and the general public correctly interpret Operation Overlord as a major step toward the ultimate defeat of Nazi Germany. In June, 1994, on the fiftieth anniversary of the battle, an elaborate commemoration of the campaign was held in the locale where this dramatic and violent conflict had occurred.

Stephen E. Ambrose
updated by Taylor Stults

June-July, 1944
Battle for Saipan

Date: June 15-July 9, 1944
Location: Saipan, one of the Mariana Islands in the Central Pacific
Combatants: 66,779 Americans vs. 31,650 Japanese
Principal commanders: *American*, Lieutenant General Holland M. Smith (1882-1967); *Japanese*, Lieutenant General Yoshitsugo Saito
Result: U.S. capture of the island from Japan.

U.S. troops cross a coral reef to reach Saipan from their landing craft. (National Archives)

At 8:00 A.M. on June 15, 1944, 40,000 marines of the Second and Fourth Marine Divisions, led by Lieutenant General Holland M. Smith, began amphibious landings on beaches around Garapan, Saipan's principal city, with the Army's Twenty-seventh Division in reserve. The landing followed four days of bombardment from the invasion fleet, during which U.S. forces won air superiority.

Awaiting the marines were 31,650 Japanese, many of them untested and led by overconfident commanders. Despite heavy small-arms and artillery fire, both U.S. marine divisions were ashore by nightfall. They pushed through the thin beach defenses during the next day and crushed sporadic Japanese counterattacks. By the end of June 17, Japanese forces, led by Lieutenant General Yoshitsugo Saito, were in hasty retreat inland. A mass suicide attack on July 7 failed to check U.S. advances, and Saipan was declared secured on July 9, although small groups continued resistance until the end of the war. The Japanese sustained 28,500 killed in action; 3,471 Americans died, and another 13,160 were wounded.

Saipan was headquarters for the Japanese defense of the Central Pacific, a vital shield for the Japanese homeland. Its fall crippled the Japanese defense strategy and gave the Americans an airbase from which B-29 Superfortress bombers could reach Tokyo.

Roger Smith

June, 1944
Superfortress Bombing of Japan

Date: June 15, 1944
Location: Chengtu, China; and Yawata, Japan
Principal figures: *American*, Henry Harley "Hap" Arnold (1886-1950), President Franklin D. Roosevelt (1882-1945), LaVerne "Blondie" Saunders (1903-   ), Kenneth B. Wolfe (1886-1971)
Result: A raid on Yawata marked the beginning of the American strategic bombing campaign against the Japanese home islands.

The Doolittle raid against Tokyo on April 18, 1942, was the first air raid by United States bombers on the Japanese home islands and the only one for the next two years. The rapid Japanese advance in the Pacific and the Japanese hold on the Asian mainland drove U.S. forces from any bases close enough to carry out air raids on Japan. The available heavy bombers,

B-29's on a bombing run over Yokohama, Japan. (National Archives)

the B-17 Flying Fortress and the B-24 Liberator, did not have adequate range. The B-29 Superfortress, however, brought to bear new technology that made possible a devastating strategic bombing campaign against the Japanese home islands.

The B-29 Bomber

The Army had shown interest in the new long-range, high-altitude bomber that the Boeing Company had begun to develop in 1938. Although the prototype, the XB-29, was not test-flown until September 21, 1942, the Air Corps had already ordered 250 planes from Boeing, which built an entire new plant to produce the new bomber exclusively. Far larger than the B-17, the Superfortress measured 99 feet in length, with a wing span of 141 feet. It weighed more than sixty tons fully loaded and had a top speed of up to 375 miles per hour. Powered by four twenty-two-hundred-horsepower Wright Duplex Cyclone engines, it had a combat radius of sixteen hundred miles fully loaded. Three separate pressurized compartments meant that its crew of eleven could cruise at the plane's service ceiling of 31,800 feet without needing oxygen masks. The aircraft was armed with twelve .50-caliber machine guns, or ten machine guns and a 20-millimeter cannon, all mounted in power-driven turrets. Under ideal conditions, it could carry a bomb load of ten tons.

Plans by the Air Force for the plane's use had taken various forms, including its commitment in Europe. By the time significant numbers of the planes could be ready, however, British and U.S. bombers flying from England had made the B-29 less than essential for the war against Germany. By the end of 1943, Air Force chief General H. "Hap" Arnold, was committed to its use against Japan. United States air bases in the Aleutian Islands, however, were too far from Japan. The islands in the Mariana group that could provide bases (Saipan, Tinian, and Guam) were not projected to be in U.S. hands until the winter of 1944. Thus, Air Force planners, wanting to get the new Superfortresses into operation as soon as possible, looked to China.

The U.S. Plan

On Arnold's orders, Brigadier General Kenneth B. Wolfe drew up a plan. Submitted to the Air Force chief on October 11, 1943, Wolfe's plan called for basing the new B-29's in India and staging them through fields in China. Approved by Arnold, the plan then went to President Franklin D. Roosevelt. Desiring to do something for China and fearing that China's leader, Chiang Kai-shek, might quit the war if he did not receive some tangible help against the Japanese, Roosevelt proved a receptive audience and approved the plan, known as Operation Matterhorn, in November, 1943.

The idea of an independent, powerful, strategic bombing force had long been a dream of U.S. flyers. Supplying itself with all the necessities of war, this command could, it was believed, bludgeon any enemy into surrender by strategic bombing without the necessity of invasion. Perhaps the Superfortress was the weapon.

While the Superfortress bombing raids were being conducted, the United States attacked Japanese cities with smaller planes launched from aircraft carriers. Here, gunners on the carrier USS Hornet *shell Japanese positions from the sea, while their own aircraft are bombing Tokyo, in February, 1945.*
(National Archives)

Having committed itself to a strategic bombing campaign against the Japanese home islands, in April, 1944, the United States Joint Chiefs of Staff established a special organization, the Twentieth Air Force, to direct all B-29 operations. General Arnold, acting as executive agent of the Joint Chiefs of Staff, was selected to command this new force and given control over the deployment of the Superfortresses. Neither the British commander in the area, Lord Louis Mountbatten, nor U.S. Army commander Lieutenant General Joseph W. Stilwell exercised any authority over the deployment and use of the B-29's in the China-Burma-India theater of operations, except in an emergency. However, they would see a significant amount of the very limited tonnage that was flown over the Hump into China diverted to the B-29 bases at Chengtu.

Implementation of Operation Matterhorn was entrusted to Wolfe's Twentieth Bomber Command, which originally was made up of the Fifty-eighth and the Seventy-third Bombardment Wings. The Seventy-third was detached in April, 1944, to go to the Mariana Islands, whose date of capture had been advanced to June, 1944. A wing contained 112 bombers plus replacement ships, and slightly more than three thousand officers and eight thousand enlisted men. Support, service, and engineering personnel brought the total strength of the Twentieth Bomber Command to approximately twenty thousand troops.

Because all supplies for Chinese bases had to be flown in, stockpiling was difficult. B-29s from India had to fly seven round trips to bring enough gasoline and other necessities to make possible one mission over Japan. With the loss of the Seventy-third Wing, the Fifty-eighth Wing could not supply itself for raids of one hundred planes or more, the hoped-for number, more than a few times each month. This, combined with the high rate of engine failure, the loss of planes because of inexperienced crews, and the other faults to be expected in a new weapon meant that the first raid on Japan could not be launched until June 15, 1944.

The Army Air Force's (AAF) Committee of Operations analysts had suggested that an appropriate strategic target for B-29s would be the coke ovens that supplied Japan's steel mills. Consequently, the first strike was directed against the coke ovens of the Imperial Iron and Steel Works at Yawata. Located on the island of Kyushu, at the edge of the bomber's combat range, the Yawata plant produced 24 percent of Japan's rolled steel and was considered the most important target in the Japanese steel industry.

The Raids Begin

Beginning on June 13, ninety-two planes left the Bengal fields in India, seventy-nine of which reached the Chengtu bases. Each came loaded with two tons of five-hundred-pound bombs and needed only to refuel in China. Commanders in Washington, D.C., who had picked the target, ordered a night mission with bombs to be dropped from between eight thousand and eighteen thousand feet. On June 15, the same day that Marines went ashore on Saipan, sixty-eight planes, led by Wing Commander Brigadier General LaVerne "Blondie" Saunders, left the fields. Four were forced back by engine trouble, and one crashed immediately after take-off. Forty-seven Superfortresses bombed Yawata that night, thirty-two using radar because of an effective blackout of the city compounded by haze and smoke. The other planes did not make it over Yawata for a variety of reasons, most of them mechanical. Six planes were lost, one to enemy fighters on the return trip. Fighter opposition over the target and antiaircraft fire had been light.

Photo reconnaissance showed little damage, the only significant hit being on a power station thirty-seven hundred feet from the coke ovens. This was not a massive fire-bomb raid of the type that would begin in March, 1945, from the Mariana Islands. The AAF was still concentrating on high-altitude, precision bombing. The Fifty-eighth Wing averaged two raids a month until March, 1945, when it was moved to Saipan. Operating under a very difficult logistical situation, Operation Matterhorn had been a stimulant for Chinese morale and had provided a necessary shakedown for the new bombers and crews. Matterhorn was not a success, nor was the first raid on Japan; but both presaged a more destructive future for the Superfortress.

Charles W. Johnson
updated by Bruce J. DeHart

July-August, 1944
Battle of Guam

Date: July 21-August 10, 1944
Location: Guam, the largest island of the Mariana Islands in the Pacific
Combatants: Third U.S. Marine, First Marine Brigade, and Seventy-seventh Army divisions vs. 19,000 Japanese
Principal commanders: *American,* Admiral Chester W. Nimitz (1885-1966), Admiral Marc Mitscher (1887-1947); *Japanese,* Admiral Jisaburo Ozawa (1886-1966)
Result: The United States recaptured from the Japanese a strategic base in the Pacific.

The first Marines to land on Guam plant a U.S. flag on the beach. (National Archives)

On June 15, 1944, U.S. Army and U.S. Marine divisions under Admiral Chester W. Nimitz landed on Saipan, beginning a bloody three-week battle. Then, on July 21, Army and Marine units invaded Guam, one hundred miles south of Saipan, and three days later, Marines attacked Tinian Island. Guam fell to the Third Marine, Seventy-seventh Army divisions, and First Marine Brigade on August 10, after a difficult struggle. Admiral Marc Mitscher's Fast Carrier Task Force (which included six heavy and six light carriers, escorted by fast battleships, cruisers, and destroyers) used bombers to strafe Guam, neutralizing the Japanese airfield.

The United States had 1,400 fatalities and 5,600 wounded. The Japanese, led by Jisaburo Ozawa, had 10,000 fatalities, and several hundred more died when they refused to surrender during the mopping-up operations.

The Battle of Guam was an important turning point of the Pacific war because the U.S. seizure of the Marianas placed the U.S. Army Air Force's B-29 bombers in easy reach of Japanese islands, enabling the United States to fly missions against Japan in late November and destroying Japan's objective of controlling the Pacific.

Keith Garebian

July-August, 1944
Battle of Tinian

Date: July 24-August 1, 1944
Location: Mariana Islands, 1,250 miles southeast of Tokyo
Combatants: 40,000 Americans vs. 9,000 Japanese
Principal commanders: *American*, Major General Harry Schmidt; *Japanese*, Colonel Kiyochi Ogata
Result: American forces swiftly took Tinian from the Japanese.

After the fall of the Marshall Islands in January, 1944, the next phase of the American Central Pacific Campaign focused on the taking of the Marianas from Japanese forces, led by Colonel Kiyochi Ogata. Saipan fell in early July; American designs then turned to Tinian, only three miles south of Saipan.

American landings on July 24, led by Major General Harry Schmidt, surprised the Japanese because they arrived on the small beaches to the

An amphibious vehicle known as a "Water Buffalo" carries Marines to the beaches of Tinian Island during the Battle of Tinian. (National Archives)

north of the island rather than on the large beaches to the south. Taken by surprise, unable to make effective use of gun emplacements directed toward the southern beaches, greatly outnumbered, and hampered by poor communication between military units, Japanese resistance was quickly overcome. The island was declared secure on August 1, though small pockets of Japanese troops held out in caves for nearly three more months.

The Americans suffered 389 dead and 1,816 wounded compared with more than 5,000 Japanese dead and 252 prisoners. The unaccounted-for Japanese most likely perished in their cavernous hiding places.

The world's longest runways were built on Tinian and became the launching sites of numerous B-29 bombing raids against the Japanese main islands, including the planes that dropped the atomic bombs against Hiroshima and Nagasaki.

Paul John Chara, Jr.

October, 1944
Battle for Leyte Gulf

Date: October 23-26, 1944
Location: Leyte Gulf, Surigao Strait, San Bernardino Strait, and Cape Engaño in the Philippines
Combatants: U.S. Navy vs. Imperial Japanese Navy
Principal commanders: *American*, Admiral William F. Halsey (1882-1959), Admiral Thomas C. Kinkaid (1888-1972), General Douglas MacArthur (1880-1964), Admiral Chester W. Nimitz (1885-1966), Rear Admiral Jesse Oldendorf (1887-1974), Rear Admiral Clifton A. F. Sprague (1896-1955); *Japanese*, Vice Admiral Jisaburo Ozawa (1886-1966), Admiral Takeo Kurita (1889-1977)
Result: This largest naval engagement of the war secured Allied control of the seas surrounding the Philippine Islands and broke Japanese naval power.

The Battle for Leyte Gulf, October 23- 26, 1944, was history's largest naval engagement. Its 282 vessels (216 U.S., 2 Australian, and 64 Japanese) outnumbered the ships of the 1916 Battle of Jutland. The battle in Leyte Gulf involved almost 200,000 men and encompassed an area of more than 100,000 square miles. It saw all aspects of naval warfare—air, surface, submarine, and amphibious—as well as the use of the largest guns ever at sea, the last clash of the dreadnoughts, and the introduction of kamikazes. The battle was also distinguished by fine planning and leadership, brilliant deception, failed intelligence, and great controversies.

Allied Objectives

The invasion of Leyte Island, beginning on October 20, 1944, was the first phase of an Allied campaign to liberate the Philippine Islands from the Japanese. The Philippines occupied a strategically important position between Japan and its important resources base of the East Indies. Leyte is in the middle of the Philippine archipelago.

The Japanese anticipated a U.S. offensive and had plans to combat it; Shō Ichi Go (Operation Victory One) covered defense of the Philippines, to which the Japanese decided to commit the entire Combined Fleet. The Combined Fleet commander, Admiral Soemu Toyoda, knew the operation would be a gamble. He said after the war,

> If things went well, we might obtain unexpectedly good results; but if the worst should happen, there was a chance that we would lose the entire fleet. But I felt that chance had to be taken.

Toyoda knew that should the Americans retake the Philippines, even with the fleet left, the shipping lane to the south would be completely cut off, so that if the fleet came back to Japanese waters, it could not obtain fuel. If the fleet remained in southern waters, it could not receive supplies of ammunition and arms. In Toyoda's opinion, there would be no reason to save the fleet at the expense of the Philippines.

The Allied armada that advanced toward Leyte in mid-October comprised more than seven hundred ships. The U.S. Third Fleet also was available for strategic support of the operation. Under the command of Admiral William F. Halsey, the Third Fleet was given two tasks: to cover the Leyte landings and, if the opportunity arose, to destroy the Japanese fleet.

Japanese Forces

Opposing the Allied forces were four Japanese naval forces. The Northern Force, commanded by Vice Admiral Jisaburo Ozawa, consisted of one heavy carrier, three light carriers, two hybrid battleship-carriers, three cruisers, and eight destroyers. It was to serve as a decoy, drawing Halsey's Third Fleet toward the north and away from the beaches. The most powerful of the Japanese units was Central Force (First Division Attack Force), commanded by Admiral Takeo Kurita. It included the two super battleships, *Musashi* and *Yamato*. With their 18.1-inch guns, these 862-foot long, 70,000-ton behemoths were, at the time, the largest warships ever built. Kurita also had three older battleships, twelve cruisers, and fifteen destroyers. Kurita's ships were to slip through San Bernardino Strait. Meanwhile, Southern Force (C Force)—comprising two battleships, one heavy cruiser, and four destroyers, commanded by Vice Admiral Shoji Nishimura—would strike eastward through the Sulu Sea in an effort to force its way through Surigao Strait between the islands of Leyte and Mindanao. It was trailed by the Second Division Attack Force, commanded by Vice Admiral Kiyohide Shima, which had one light and two heavy cruisers and four destroyers. These two prongs would then converge simultaneously on the landing area in the Leyte Gulf and destroy Allied shipping there. At the same time, Japanese shore-based aircraft were to inflict maximum damage on U.S. forces assisting the landings. The main strength of the Japanese fleet lay in its naval gunnery, because its carrier- and land-based aircraft had largely been destroyed in earlier battles and by U.S. Army and Navy air raids during September and early October. Any chance the Japanese had for success lay in using their huge battleships to shell the Leyte beaches. Shō Ichi Go was, at best, a long shot.

U.S. Forces

Opposing the Japanese were two U.S. fleets: the Seventh Fleet, commanded by Admiral Thomas C. Kinkaid and operating under General Douglas MacArthur's Southwest Pacific Command, and Admiral Halsey's Third Fleet, under Admiral Chester Nimitz at Pearl Harbor. Leyte was the first landing to involve two entire U.S. fleets and the first landing without unified command. Divided command had unfortunate consequences.

The Seventh Fleet was divided into three task groups. The first consisted of Rear Admiral Jesse Oldendorf's six old battleships, sixteen escort carriers, four heavy cruisers, four light cruisers, thirty destroyers, and ten destroyer escorts. The other two elements were amphibious task groups carrying out the actual invasion. Seventh Fleet had escorted the invasion force to Leyte and now provided broad protection for the entire landing area. As most of Halsey's amphibious assets had been loaned to Kinkaid, Third Fleet consisted almost entirely of Admiral Marc Mitscher's Task Force (TF) 38: fourteen fast carriers (with more than one thousand aircraft) organized into four task groups containing six battleships, eight heavy cruisers, thirteen light cruisers, and fifty-seven destroyers. Third Fleet's orders called for it to secure air superiority over the Philippines, protect the landings, and maintain pressure on the Japanese. If the opportunity to destroy a major part of the Japanese fleet presented itself or could be created, that destruction was to be Third Fleet's primary task.

The Battle Begins

First contact between the rival forces was made on October 23. In the Battle of the Sibuyan Sea, U.S. submarines sighted the Central Force and sank two Japanese heavy cruisers, one of which was Kurita's flagship, *Atago*. When reports of Nishimura's Southern Force reached Admiral Halsey, he issued a preliminary order detailing a battle line of battleships known as Task Force 34, to be commanded by Vice Admiral Willis A. Lee. Admiral Kinkaid was aware of that signal and assumed TF 34 had been established. Kinkaid ordered the fire-support portion of Seventh Fleet, commanded by Rear Admiral Jesse Oldendorf, to assume a blocking position at the lower end of Leyte Gulf to halt any Japanese attempt to force Surigao Strait; Seventh Fleet escort carriers guarded the eastern entrance to Leyte Gulf.

Halsey, meanwhile, ordered his own fleet carriers to launch air strikes against enemy units then steaming through San Bernardino Strait. These planes concentrated on the *Musashi*. She took nineteen torpedoes and nearly as many bombs before finally succumbing. Half of her nearly 2,200-man crew perished with her. Several other Japanese ships were damaged. On the afternoon of October 25, U.S. pilots reported that Kurita had reversed course and was heading west; Halsey incorrectly assumed that this part of the battle was over.

Meanwhile, Japanese land-based planes from the Second Air Fleet attacked U.S. ships supporting the land invasion. Most were shot down, but they sank the light carrier *Princeton* and damaged the cruiser *Birmingham*. Unknown to Halsey, after nightfall Kurita's force changed course and resumed heading for San Bernardino Strait.

Halsey broke off the engagement in order to pursue what appeared to be a more tempting target. U.S. scout planes had sighted the Northern Force, and Halsey, believing it to be the most powerful Japanese threat, turned his carrier task forces northward. Several of Halsey's subordinates registered reservations about his decision, but the admiral would not be deterred. Compounding the error, Halsey failed to inform Admiral Kinkaid, who still assumed that TF 34 was protecting the strait. Halsey's decision left the landing beaches guarded only by Seventh Fleet's Taffy 3 escort carrier group commanded by Rear Admiral Clifton A. F. Sprague. Taffy 3 was one of three such support groups operating off Samar. Sprague had six light escort carriers, three destroyers, and four destroyer escorts. This was precisely what the Japanese had intended; for the U.S. forces, it was a grave tactical error, because it enabled the Japanese Central Force to sail undisturbed through the San Bernardino Strait toward the landing area.

Leading the U.S. landing at Leyte Island, General Douglas MacArthur makes his trium-phal return to the Philippines, to which he had vowed to return two and one-half years earlier. (National Archives)

Late on the evening of October 24, battleships and cruisers of the Seventh Fleet engaged the Southern Force. The October 24-25 Battle of Surigao Strait was a classic example of "crossing the T" in naval warfare. The PT boats discovered the Japanese moving in line-ahead formation, but Nishimura's force easily forced the PT boats back. While the battleships often get the credit for the Surigao Strait victory, it was U.S. destroyers that inflicted most of the damage. Two converging torpedo attacks sank a battleship and three destroyers. The Japanese then ran into the line of Oldendorf's battleships. The Allies won a great victory at little cost to themselves; when it was over, the sole survivors of the Southern Force and Second Division Attack Force were five destroyers and a heavy cruiser.

The U.S. escort carriers operating north of Leyte were not as fortunate. Early on October 25, the Central Force emerged from San Bernardino Strait, headed for Leyte Gulf, and surprised the U.S. ships. Crew members of the U.S. destroyers and pilots of escort carriers of Taffy 3, brilliantly commanded by Admiral Sprague, fought a courageous but apparently hopeless battle. The Japanese sank the *Gambier Bay*, the only U.S. carrier ever lost to gunfire, and also sank the destroyers *Hoel* and *Johnston*, and the de-

Giant landing ships (LSTs) open their jaws in the surf, as American soldiers build sand-bag piers to facilitate the unloading of the supplies and equipment to be used in the Philippine campaign. (National Archives)

stroyer escort *Samuel B. Roberts.* Although Japanese guns were registering repeated hits and Kurita was in position to secure a crushing victory, he abruptly broke all contact and retired north toward the San Bernardino Strait. This puzzling action allowed the transports and troops at the beachhead to escape certain destruction.

Kurita believed he was under attack by aircraft from Halsey's fleet carriers. Kurita's decision was strengthened by the fact that the southern attacking force had been destroyed. After the war, Kurita said, "The conclusion from our gunfire and antiaircraft fire during the day had led me to believe in my uselessness, my ineffectual position, if I proceeded into Leyte Gulf where I would come under even heavier air attack." Several days of nearly incessant attacks may also have frayed Kurita's nerves. Kurita hoped to join Ozawa's force to the north but changed his mind and exited through San Bernardino Strait. Sprague later noted that the failure of Kurita's force "to completely wipe out all vessels of this Task Unit can be attributed to our successful smoke screen, our torpedo counterattack, continuous harassment of the enemy by bomb, torpedo, and strafing air attacks, timely maneuvers, and the definite partiality of Almighty God." The four ships lost by Taffy 3 were the only U.S. warships sunk by Japanese surface ships in the Battle for Leyte Gulf.

Meanwhile, Admiral Sprague's escort carriers and Oldendorf's force returning from the Battle of Surigao Strait came under attack from land-based kamikaze aircraft, the first such attacks of the war. These sank the escort carrier *St. Lô* and damaged several other ships.

Aftermath

After the major issues of the battle had been decided, Halsey's Third Fleet caught the Japanese Northern Force off Cape Engaño. By nightfall, U.S. aircraft, a submarine, and surface ships had sunk all four Japanese carriers of Ozawa's force as well as five other ships. This blow ended Japanese carrier aviation. Ironically, the entire Northern Force would have been destroyed if Halsey had not yielded to urgent appeals to turn back to intercept the Central Force. The Third Fleet failed to catch up with Kurita and the remainder of Northern Force was able to get away.

Including retiring vessels sunk on October 26 and 27, Japanese losses in the battle were twenty-nine warships (four carriers, three battleships, six heavy and four light cruisers, eleven destroyers, and a submarine) and more than five hundred aircraft. Japanese personnel losses amounted to some 10,500 seamen and aviators dead. The U.S. Navy lost only six ships (one light carrier, two escort carriers, two destroyers, and a destroyer escort) and more than two hundred aircraft. About twenty-eight hundred Americans were killed and another one thousand wounded. The Battle for Leyte Gulf ended the Japanese fleet as an organized fighting force.

Theodore A. Wilson
Revised by Spencer C. Tucker

December, 1944
Battle of the Bulge

Date: December 16-26, 1944
Location: Belgium and Luxembourg
Combatants: 500,000 Germans vs. 600,000 Americans and 55,000 British
Principal commanders: *American*, General Dwight D. Eisenhower (1890-1969), General George S. Patton, Jr. (1885-1945), General Omar Bradley

(1893-1981); *British*, Field Marshal Sir Bernard Law Montgomery (1887-1976); *German*, Field Marshal Gerd von Rundstedt (1875-1953)
Result: German forces were defeated in a desperate campaign to halt advancing Allied armies.

In December, 1944, six months after the successful landing at Normandy, Allied forces were closing in on Germany's western frontier. The advance across France was so rapid as to overstretch the Allied supply lines that ran five hundred miles back to Normandy and the English Channel. Faced with growing fuel shortages, the supreme Allied commander, General Dwight D. Eisenhower, gave fuel supply priority to the advancing British forces under Field Marshal Sir Bernard Law Montgomery as they drove toward the Low Countries and the port city of Antwerp. The U.S. advance farther south ground to a halt as a result of the lack of fuel. As the Allied assault on Germany stalled, Adolf Hitler saw a chance to alter the course of the war by launching a great counteroffensive against the Western Allies. He announced his intentions on September 16 at a conference held at his East Prussian headquarters, the Wolf's Lair.

Hilter's Plan

Hitler's plan was bold and desperate. It called for an attack against the rugged Ardennes sector, thinly held by U.S. forces. Hoping for a repeat of the highly successful 1940 campaign that led to the fall of France, Hitler aimed at splitting the Allied forces—U.S. troops to the south and the British and Canadians to the north. The German thrust first would obtain the Meuse River and then advance on the strategically important city of Antwerp. Speed and the ability of the advancing German forces to capture key road junctions in the Ardennes were critical ingredients for success. Once this was achieved, the Allied forces (chiefly British and Canadian), north of a line running from Antwerp to the Ardennes, would be destroyed. Hitler hoped that, if the plan worked, the Allied coalition would fall apart, leading to a negotiated peace. It might at least be possible to transfer troops to the Eastern Front to meet the Soviet threat.

Hitler's generals were less confident of success. They argued that Germany did not have sufficient resources in troops and materiel to carry out such an attack. Nevertheless, by tremendous exertion, two new Panzer armies, the Sixth SS Panzer and Fifth Panzer, were assembled. More than twenty-five German divisions were gathered for the attack along a fifty-mile front opposite five U.S. divisions. Two largely infantry armies, the Fifteenth and Seventh, were to provide support on the right and left flanks, respectively, of advancing Panzer armies. Two hundred thousand troops

Battle of the Bulge, 1944-1945

were mustered, along with six hundred tanks and nineteen hundred guns. Opposite, the U.S. front was held by eighty thousand troops, supported by four hundred tanks and four hundred guns. Special commando units composed of English-speaking Germans dressed in U.S. uniforms were assembled to spread chaos behind the U.S. lines.

As the Germans marshaled their forces for the attack, strict secrecy was imposed on all involved. Poor weather and the rugged territory of the Eifel region opposite the U.S. sector covered German preparations. Radio traffic directly mentioning the impending counteroffensive was banned. Although the Allies had various clues that something was being planned, underestimation of German potential led Allied intelligence to disregard the accumulating evidence of a possible enemy winter offensive. Allied intelligence considered the broken terrain of the Ardennes region unsuitable and therefore unlikely to be attacked. Intercepted German radio traffic that mentioned fuel shortages was interpreted as a positive indicator that the Germans were incapable of launching an attack. In reality, fuel was being prioritized for the assembled German forces in the Eifel.

The Offensive Begins

On the morning of December 16, advancing out of the winter gloom, the German forces under General Karl Gerd von Rundstedt obtained complete

An American soldier guards some of the fifty thousand Germans captured at the Battle of the Bulge. (National Archives)

tactical surprise as the great offensive began. Two U.S. divisions, depleted by earlier fighting, were shattered by the initial blow. Rapid gains were made by the attacking Germans, as they drove on the key road junctions at St. Vith and Bastogne. Yet the German advance immediately ran into difficulty. Even cut-off and surrounded U.S. units continued to fight with a ferocity unanticipated by the Germans. If the Allies underestimated the German ability to launch a great counteroffensive, Hitler also seriously erred by underestimating the fighting abilities of the U.S. troops.

For six days, U.S. troops at St. Vith held the critical road junction against German attacks. The 101st Airborne Division encircled at Bastogne held on in the face of tremendous pressure from the Fifth Panzer Army. The commander of the division responded to a surrender demand from the Germans with the famous reply, "Nuts!" To the north, the Eighty-second Airborne Division held on to the shoulder of the bulge. The Germans were unable to widen their initial breech in the Allied line. In the most infamous moment of the battle, on December 17, elements of the First SS Panzer Division participated in the murder of eighty-six U.S. prisoners at Malmedy. A number of the German officers and men involved were later charged with war crimes. The German attack was canalized and proved unable to widen the initial breakthrough that had managed to create only a bulge in the Allied line, from which the famous battle receives its name.

The Allied Response

The Allied response to the German attack was swift. Eisenhower halted all offensive operations along the front and concentrated all available Allied forces to stop the German advance. With communications sliced, Lieutenant General Omar Bradley's troops north of the salient were put under the command of Field Marshal Montgomery. In a remarkable feat, Lieutenant General George S. Patton's Third Army halted the Germans' advance into the Saar and, after a ninety-degree turn north, moved to relieve Bastogne.

By Christmas Day, staunch U.S. resistance and critical fuel shortages had stopped the German momentum more than five miles short of the Meuse River, the first objective of Hitler's battle plan, and one hundred miles from the primary objective of Antwerp. A long but narrow bulge had been created in the Allied lines that was forty miles at the base and nearly sixty miles in depth. The clearing of the skies over the battlefield opened the way for massive Allied air attacks on the German forces. More than five thousand planes moved to cut off the German supply line and support the hard-pressed Allied ground forces. Not until January 21, 1945, did the Allies manage to retake the lost ground.

American casualties of the Battle of the Bulge. (National Archives)

Aftermath

The Battle of the Bulge, perhaps the greatest battle in the history of the U.S. Army, took staggering tolls: The Germans lost 120,000 men either killed, wounded, or missing, along with six hundred tanks and assault guns. Air strikes to cover the retreating German forces had cost the Luftwaffe (the German air force) more than fifteen hundred aircraft. Allied casualties, chiefly from the United States, totaled 8,000 killed, 48,000 wounded, and 21,000 captured or missing. Nearly 740 tanks and tank destroyers were lost. Among the soldiers, 4,500 African Americans saw action.

Hitler's great gamble had failed without achieving any of its objectives. The Germans, using up their strategic reserves, lost irreplaceable men and equipment, hastening the end of the war. At most, the Germans had merely slowed the Allied advance by weeks. With the destruction of Germany's reserves, little was left to stop the Soviet New Year offensive on the Eastern Front and the Allied advance across the Rhine into the heart of Germany.

Van M. Leslie

February, 1945
Yalta Conference

Date: February 4-11, 1945
Location: Livadia Palace, Yalta, Crimea, Soviet Union
Principal participants: *British*, Prime Minister Winston S. Churchill (1874-1965); *American*, President Franklin D. Roosevelt (1882-1945); *Soviet*, Premier Joseph Stalin (Joseph Vissarionovich Dzhugashvili, 1879-1953)
Result: This most important meeting of the "Big Three" Allied Powers marked the height of Allied cooperation but also revealed conflicting agendas.

In February, 1945, the armies of the Soviet Union moved rapidly toward Berlin with the Germans in full retreat. In the West, British and U.S. forces, commanded by General Dwight D. Eisenhower, prepared to invade Germany. The unconditional surrender of Germany was expected in a matter of weeks. In the Far East, U.S. forces moved steadily from island to island across the Pacific toward a final invasion of the Japanese home islands. The possibility of using an atomic bomb to end the war remained questionable.

Military experts did not believe the bomb could be made ready before the end of the year.

With the defeats of Germany and Japan a certainty, the Big Three Allied leaders—Prime Minister Winston S. Churchill of Great Britain, Communist Party secretary Joseph Stalin of the Soviet Union, and President Franklin D. Roosevelt of the United States—met to plan the postwar world. It was the last time the three would see one another, for Roosevelt died on April 12, 1945, just two months after the conference ended and less than a month before Germany surrendered. At Stalin's request, the Allies gathered at Livadia Palace (once a summer home of Czar Nicholas II) at Yalta on the Crimean Peninsula of the Black Sea. The conference lasted from February 4 to February 11, 1945.

Allied Issues

Yalta represented the height of Allied cooperation. The Big Three spoke happily of the end of the fighting, but conflicting aims and conflicting personalities led to compromises in the spirit of cooperation that failed to satisfy any of them. Four major issues were discussed, and in spite of much talk of cooperation, no comprehensive settlement proved possible. The future of Germany, the future of Poland, the nature of a world organization to replace the discredited League of Nations, and the Soviet Union's formal entrance into the war against Japan were all highly controversial issues that needed to be settled by the Big Three.

Upon the defeat of Germany, Stalin wanted to divide that country into permanent zones of occupation; he also wanted reparations in kind (food and industry) to compensate for the nearly twenty million Soviet dead and the German destruction of one thousand Soviet towns and cities. Stalin demanded a harsh policy to prevent Germany from ever making war again. Churchill agreed to divide Germany, but not permanently. He insisted that a healthy Europe depended upon a prosperous Germany. Roosevelt's position was somewhere between these two views. Stalin's reparations demands were incorporated into the conference's final protocol, and the three powers called for Germany's "dismemberment" into occupation zones during the period following surrender. A U.S. proposal granting France the status of an occupying power gained Stalin's reluctant approval. The details of Allied occupation policy, however, as well as the precise amount of reparations, were deferred to a later meeting.

In addition to a neutralized Germany, Stalin wanted the security of a friendly Polish government. He sought boundaries giving the Soviet Union territory from eastern Poland, while compensating the Poles with part of eastern Germany. The Soviet Union recognized the provisional Pol-

British prime minister Winston S. Churchill (left), U.S. president Franklin D. Roosevelt (center), and Soviet premier Joseph Stalin at Yalta. (National Archives)

ish government in Warsaw (the so-called Lublin Poles), but both Great Britain and the United States insisted that the Polish government-in-exile in London also participate in the political rebuilding of Poland after the war. The Big Three agreed on a formula calling for the reorganization of the Lublin government with open elections, worded in such a way that both sides could see their respective interests maintained. The question of Poland's postwar boundaries also found a compromise solution. Ignoring the protests of the London Poles, the Big Three set the Curzon Line as the basis for Poland's eastern border, thereby sanctioning Soviet reacquisition of areas lost in the fighting during the Russian Civil War of 1918-1921. As compensation, the Poles would receive substantial accessions of territory in the north and west, but the precise delineation of the new German frontier was left to the peace conference.

The United Nations

Primarily at U.S. insistence, discussion of a world organization to maintain the postwar peace enjoyed a high priority at Yalta. The Big Three planned an international conference to be held in San Francisco in April, at which the United Nations would be formed. Stalin, Roosevelt, and Churchill reached agreements on several points concerning membership and voting in the new body. Churchill resented U.S. proposals for United Nations trusteeships of colonial territories, which the British prime minister interpreted as an attempt by Roosevelt to dismantle the British Empire. Stalin exploited the disagreement over trusteeships between the Western Allies to gain Churchill's support for his own plan to have two Soviet republics recognized as independent voting members of the new United Nations. The atomic bomb was still a somewhat vague conception at Yalta, and so it was assumed that the Soviets would be needed to defeat Japan. Stalin promised that in return for Russian territory ceded to Japan under Russia's czarist imperial government, he would declare war on Japan within three months of Germany's surrender. The agreement on the Far East was not made public in February, 1945.

The agreements at Yalta could have become the basis for an amicable peace, for the spirit of the conference was one of hope and trust. In the spring and summer, however, charges of bad faith and double-dealing began to replace the spirit of compromise. Serious disagreements that heralded the Cold War to come were soon in evidence, and within a short time, the good will that marked the Yalta Conference had vanished.

Burton Kaufman
updated by William Allison

February-March, 1945
Battle for Iwo Jima

Date: February 19-March 26, 1945
Location: Volcano Islands, south of the Bonin Island chain (six hundred miles southeast of Japan)
Combatants: 250,000 Americans vs. 22,000 Japanese
Principal commanders: *American*, Admiral Raymond A. Spruance (1886-1969); *Japanese*, Lieutenant General Tadamichi Kuribayashi (1891-1945)
Result: American forces captured a Japanese island air base located southeast of Japan.

The eight square miles of Iwo Jima, defended by Tadamichi Kuribayashi, served as the most important Japanese base in the Bonin-Volcano chain because its defenders could provide Japan with a two-hour advance warning

One of the most dramatic photographs to come out of any war shows soldiers raising an American flag on Iwo Jima after U.S. troops captured the island. (National Archives)

of impending U.S. air attacks from the Marianas, and fighters from its air-fields could intercept oncoming U.S. planes. Following a heavy but ineffective naval bombardment, U.S. Marines landed on Iwo Jima on February 19, 1945. The U.S. advance was hampered by volcanic sand and enemy defenses including miles of underground tunnels and trenches.

Combat focal points were at Mount Suribachi (taken February 23), the airfields (taken February 24-28), and a central area of the island called "the Meatgrinder" (pacified in early March). Fighting ended with a futile night-time Japanese *banzai* charge on March 26. The assault on the island, led by Admiral Raymond A. Spruance, killed 5,400 Americans and wounded 17,400 others. Admiral Chester W. Nimitz summed up the fight with the statement "Uncommon valor was a common virtue." Only 216 Japanese surrendered.

Control of Iwo Jima provided U.S. bombers with fighter escorts to accompany them on their missions to Japan and gave crippled planes access to Allied airfields. Nimitz stated that more U.S. military personnel were thus saved than were lost in the island's capture.

William E. Watson

April-July, 1945
Battle of Okinawa

Date: April 1-July 2, 1945
Location: Okinawa, 350 miles southwest of Japanese main islands
Combatants: 208,750 Americans vs. 77,199 Japanese and 40,000 Okinawans
Principal commanders: *American*, Admiral Chester W. Nimitz (1885-1966);
  Japanese, Lieutenant General Mitsuru Ushijima (1887-1945)
Result: The United States took Okinawa from the Japanese.

On April 1, some 60,000 U.S. troops landed, largely unopposed, on Okinawa. Intense fighting began a few days later when the Americans reached the strong, inland Japanese fortifications. Grueling ground combat raged throughout the spring until the last line of significant Japanese defenses, led by General Mitsuru Ushijima, was overcome on June 22.

The naval portion of the war was similarly bloody and drawn out. The Japanese launched several thousand aircraft and one naval task force against the Americans, led by Admiral Chester W. Nimitz. The task force was intercepted and routed, and the largest battleship in the world, the *Yamato*, was sunk on April 7. However, nearly 2,000 missiles and kamikaze (suicide planes) helped cause the worst U.S. naval losses in history.

An American Corsair fighter plane unloads a volley of rockets against a Japanese position on Okinawa. At ground level, smoke can be seen rising from a battle in which U.S. Marines are fighting.
(National Archives)

By the time the battle was officially declared over on July 2, the United States had suffered 12,281 dead, more than 50,000 wounded and other casualties, 763 planes lost, and 36 ships sunk and 368 damaged. Japanese losses included 110,071 killed, 7,401 captured, 7,830 planes lost, and 16 ships sunk and 4 damaged. Okinawa was the bloodiest campaign of the Pacific war, and the high casualty rate was influential in the decision to drop the atomic bomb on Japan.

Paul John Chara, Jr.

May, 1945
V-E Day

Date: May 8, 1945
Location: Rheims, France
Principal figures: *American*, General Omar Bradley (1893-1981), General Dwight D. Eisenhower (1890-1969), President Franklin D. Roosevelt (1882-1945), President Harry S. Truman (1884-1972); *British*, Prime Minister Winston S. Churchill (1874-1965), Field Marshall Bernard Law Montgomery, first Viscount Montgomery of Alamein (1887-1976); *Soviet*, General Secretary Joseph Stalin (1879-1953); *German*, Chancellor Adolf Hitler (1889-1945)
Result: The defeat of Nazi Germany marked the transfer of international power from the center of the European continent to two world powers at Europe's flanks.

After repelling the German counterattack in the Ardennes during the Battle of the Bulge in December, 1944, the commander in chief of Allied forces in Western Europe, General Dwight D. Eisenhower, prepared for the final offensive into the heart of Germany. He planned two major crossings of the Rhine in the spring of 1945—one on the north by Field Marshal Bernard Law Montgomery's Twenty-first Army Group, consisting mainly of British and Canadian troops, and the U.S. Ninth Army; another in the center by General Omar N. Bradley's Twelfth Army Group; and a third in the south by the U.S. Third and Seventh Armies. Adolf Hitler, the führer of Germany, had ordered his commanders to defend every inch of ground, and as a result of this directive, Eisenhower was able to destroy much of the German army in battles west of the Rhine in February, 1945. He also was able to capture the Ludendorff railroad bridge over the Rhine at Remagen

American troops advancing into war-torn Germany. (National Archives)

on March 7, so that he had a bridgehead in the center; consequently, he abandoned plans to cross the river on his left and right flanks, and instead he rushed troops across the Rhine at Remagen.

The Campaign

By March 28, Bradley's forces had passed through Remagen and reached Marburg, where they were ready to swing northward to link up with Montgomery's Twenty-first Army Group, which also had crossed the Rhine and had cut off German Army Group B, assigned to defend Germany's main industrial area, the Ruhr Valley. Eisenhower informed Montgomery that once the latter's encirclement of German units had been completed, the U.S. Ninth Army (which had been fighting with Montgomery's Twenty-first Army Group) would revert to General Bradley's Twelfth Army Group for the final thrust into Germany.

This administrative shift was a major change in Eisenhower's overall strategy. Before the capture of the railroad bridge at Remagen, he had intended that Montgomery should spearhead the major military effort east of the Rhine, with Berlin as the primary target; now he was shifting the emphasis to General Bradley's Twelfth Army Group headed for Dresden. On March 28, Eisenhower informed Soviet dictator Joseph Stalin of his intentions, implying that he would leave capture of the German capital to the Soviet armies advancing from the East.

Allied Disagreements

The prime minister of Great Britain, Winston S. Churchill, was furious. He considered Eisenhower's shift in emphasis uncalled-for from the military point of view and held that Berlin should remain the prime objective for both the British and U.S. forces. Eisenhower insisted that Berlin was no longer important, because no German armies or government agencies of any significance remained in the capital. The Supreme Allied Commander wanted to end the war as soon as possible; to do so he had to destroy the remaining armed forces of Germany, which were concentrated in southern Germany. Churchill insisted that politically it was essential for the British and Americans to capture Berlin, for if the Soviets were allowed to capture the capital, they would gain an exaggerated opinion of their contribution to the common victory. Churchill also implied that if the British-U.S. forces took Berlin, they could hold the city for the purpose of making postwar deals with the Soviets.

The division of Germany into zones of occupation already had been decided, and Berlin was located within the territory allotted to the Soviet zone. Berlin itself was to be divided into sectors among the Allies. Eisenhower held that it would be foolish to waste U.S. and British lives in taking a city that would have to be handed over by prior agreement to the Soviets

After Germany's capitulation, Generals Dwight D. Eisenhower (right), Omar N. Bradley (left) and George S. Patton (behind Eisenhower) inspect art treasures stolen by German forces and hidden in a salt mine in Germany.
(National Archives)

because it was to be allocated to their zone. At no time did Churchill advocate repudiating earlier agreements with the Soviets concerning the division of Germany, although he did want "to shake hands as far east as possible" with the Red Army.

Churchill could not give orders to Eisenhower; that prerogative was reserved for the combined chiefs of staff of the United States and Great Britain, or the president of the United States. The chief of staff of the U.S. Army, General George C. Marshall, saw to it that Eisenhower was given a free hand in field operations. Churchill appealed to President Roosevelt, but Roosevelt's foreign policy was to make every effort to attain good relations with Stalin, and he refused to order Eisenhower to race the Soviet army to Berlin. After Roosevelt's death on April 12, 1945, the new president, Harry S. Truman, adopted the same policy. Eisenhower was free to do as he thought fit, and he sent his armies into central and southern Germany, avoiding Berlin. The Soviets captured the German capital in late April. Eisenhower's forces reached the Elbe River in central Germany between April 19 and May 2.

Partition of Germany

On April 25, U.S. and Soviet patrols met near Torgau and cut Germany in half. Hitler committed suicide on April 30; his successor, Admiral Karl Dönitz, began negotiations for surrender on May 4. Dönitz wanted to hand over German forces to the Western Allies, hoping thereby to avoid punishment from the Soviets for German crimes in the east, but Eisenhower refused to comply. Dönitz, his country in ruin, agreed to the immediate unconditional surrender of all Germany's armed forces. German and Allied representatives met at Eisenhower's headquarters in Rheims, France, on May 7, 1945, and signed the necessary documents that made the surrender effective the following day. Truman declared that day, May 8, to be V-E Day (victory in Europe day).

It soon became evident that the documents signed at Reims were not the correct versions previously agreed upon by the Allies. Confusion reigned. The documents had not been approved formally by the Soviets, did not make provisions for authoritative Russian translations, and were signed by an obscure Soviet general without Stalin's knowledge. Although the United States tried to downplay the mistake, the Soviets insisted upon a second surrender ceremony with the proper documents and different representatives in Berlin. That ceremony took place on May 9, a date that Soviets subsequently commemorated as the "true" V-E Day. The Soviets had achieved a symbolic victory over the United States, as the second signing ceremony bolstered Moscow's dark intimations that the Western Allies sought to marginalize the Soviet Union in the postwar order. As much as marking the end of the war against Germany, V-E Day also can be seen as the opening of the Cold War.

Stephen E. Ambrose
updated by Steve D. Boilard

July-August, 1945
Potsdam Conference

Date: July 17-August 2, 1945
Location: Potsdam, near Berlin, Germany
Principal participants: *British,* Clement Richard Attlee (1883-1967), Winston S. Churchill (1874-1965); *American,* Harry S. Truman (1884-1972); *Soviet Union,* Joseph Stalin (Iosif Vissarionovich Dzhugashvili, 1879-1953)
Result: The third and final "Big Three" meeting planned a peace settlement at the conclusion of World War II.

There were only three occasions when all three Allied heads of state met face to face: Teheran, November-December, 1943; Yalta, February, 1945; and the Potsdam Conference, July 17-August 2, 1945. At the Potsdam Conference—the third and last Big Three summit conference during World War II—the Allied leaders attempted, but failed, to resolve outstanding disagreements and to conclude a final peace settlement of the war. In addition to peace, the disposition of Germany, Eastern Europe, and the Japanese surrender were on the agenda.

The personalities involved at the first two conferences were U.S. president Franklin D. Roosevelt, British prime minister Winston S. Churchill, and Soviet premier Joseph Stalin. Roosevelt died in April, 1945, and was succeeded by Vice President Harry S. Truman. The results of the general election of Great Britain were announced on July 26, after the Potsdam Conference began. Churchill, head of the Conservative Party, and Clement Attlee, head of the Labour Party, both attended the conference until the announcement was made that the Labour Party had won. Only Attlee returned. Stalin was the only Big Three leader in power before, during, and after the war. Thus, at Potsdam, Stalin enjoyed some advantage because of his experience and the enormous power he wielded as dictator of the Soviet Union.

The End of the War

The war in Europe had ended with the unconditional surrender of Germany in May, 1945, the Italians having previously surrendered in 1943. The war in the Pacific, to which the Soviet Union was not a party, continued, and at the time of the Potsdam Conference there appeared to be no immediate prospect for ending it. At the Yalta Conference, Stalin had promised to break the Soviet-Japanese neutrality pact concluded earlier and enter the Pacific war within two or three months after the Germans surrendered.

The strategic bombing campaign against Japan, and its ultimate dimension, the use of the atomic bomb, was being developed by the United States, with important British contributions. This effort involved massive resources and enormous costs, however. By the summer of 1945, sufficient materials for a small number of bombs were ready for use. Testing occurred successfully in New Mexico on July 15. President Truman was informed of this while en route to Potsdam. Materials for at least two additional bombs were assembled and rushed to Tinian in the Mariana Islands, from where superbombers could reach Japan. Much has been made of the fact that Truman, in an almost casual manner, informed Stalin of the fact that a bomb with massive destructive potential had been developed. Stalin urged him to use it against Japan. The British, who already knew of the project and its results, also urged the bomb's use.

The Conference

The Big Three leaders assembled at Potsdam, south of war-torn Berlin, where the extensive palace complex of the former Hohenzollern rulers of Prussia was located. The official conference took place at the Cecilienhof Palace on the shores of Lake Griebnitz. At the time, the Soviet Union occupied all of Germany east of the Elbe River, including Berlin and its environs. Stalin and the Soviets therefore acted as host of the conference and made all the arrangements.

At the first of thirteen plenary sessions, Stalin nominated Truman as chairman. Truman was pleased to serve and had already prepared an agenda. The Yalta agreements were reaffirmed and elaborated upon. Previously, the European Advisory Committee had overseen Allied international issues in the European war. At Potsdam, the decision was made to replace that committee with the Council of Foreign Ministers, charged with preparation for peace terms in Europe, initially for Italy, Romania, Bulgaria, Austria, Hungary, and Finland. Other items included the political and economic principles that would govern Germany, continued discussion of the question of German reparations, German disarmament and military occupation, provisions for punishment of war criminals, and the disposition of Poland and other Eastern European states.

Plans for Germany

The disposition of Germany was perhaps the most important, pressing, and controversial issue on the table of the Big Three. At Yalta, a general agreement had been reached that Germany would be occupied by Allied forces. After much deliberation and debate, the Attlee Plan, named for the then vice prime minister of Great Britain, was accepted. Germany was to be divided temporarily into three zones—the Northwest, the Southwest, and the East—to be militarily occupied by Great Britain, the United States, and the Soviet Union respectively. Berlin, the old capital, located about one hundred miles inside the Soviet zone, was also to be divided into three zones.

Originally, there were to be three occupiers, and zones of occupation were drawn up. However, at the Yalta Conference, after much persuasion, Stalin reluctantly had agreed with the Roosevelt-Churchill recommendation that France participate. Subsequently, the French did participate and a French zone was carved out contiguous to the French border. However, the French were bitter and disappointed because they were not a party to the arrangements, and they had not been invited to Potsdam.

Reparations

War reparations was another sensitive issue harking back to the previous treaties at Vienna and Versailles. Stalin consistently pressured for huge amounts to be extracted from Germany, rightly pointing out that the Soviet Union, more than any other power, deserved to be compensated for massive destruction of its homeland caused by the Germans. Roosevelt and Churchill acknowledged that, but also recalled the imbroglio caused by the reparations question after World War I. They effectively renounced all claims on Germany.

A tentative arrangement was initialed stating that the Soviet Union was eligible for the equivalent of ten billion dollars worth of reparations from Germany. Further discussion and much debate ensued on how, and especially from which zones of occupation, in-kind reparations could be obtained. Anglo-American leaders insisted that the future health of the German economy must be considered. Reparations remained a contentious issue between the Soviet Union and the Anglo-Americans, and final amounts and other details were not decided until later.

The central authority that was to administer occupied Germany was the Allied Control Council. Its objective was to disarm, demobilize, demilitarize, de-Nazify, and democratize Germany. Trials of Nazi war criminals were prepared and conducted at Nuremberg. Certain limits were placed on reparations if a threat to the future of the German economy was indicated.

Complications abounded. The Potsdam Declaration came out of the Potsdam Conference and was published on July 26. This was a joint statement to Japan calling for immediate surrender, signed by Truman, Churchill, and a representative of Chiang Kai-shek, the Chinese head of state. Since the Soviet Union was not, at that time, an official belligerent in the Pacific war, it was not a signatory.

Eugene L. Rasor

August, 1945
Atomic Bombing of Japan

Date: August 6 and 9, 1945
Location: Hiroshima and Nagasaki, Japan
Principal figures: *American*, James Francis Byrnes (1879-1972), Leslie R. Groves (1896-1970), Henry L. Stimson (1867-1950), Harry S. Truman (1884-1972)
Result: The use of powerful new weapons against civilian populations accelerated the end of World War II and unleashed a new age of nuclear weapons.

At 2:45 A.M. on August 6, 1945, a U.S. B-29 bomber, the *Enola Gay*, took off from the island of Tinian in the Mariana Islands, carrying an atomic bomb. Shortly after 8:15 A.M., from an altitude of about 31,600 feet, the bomb was released over Hiroshima, Japan. It exploded with terrible fury over the center of the city, immediately killing more than eighty thousand people and maiming thousands more. The searing heat that resulted from the explosion set the city afire and utterly destroyed it. Two days later, on August 8, the Soviet Union declared war on Japan. On August 9, over Nagasaki, Japan, at 11:00 A.M., the United States dropped a second atomic bomb, which killed more than forty thousand of the city's inhabitants.

The destruction of Hiroshima and Nagasaki was a shock to the Japanese, but the Soviet Union's declaration of war was devastating, for it removed all hope of Soviet mediation with the West to end the war. Moreover, it necessitated that the Kwangtung Army—the force that Japanese

Colonel Paul W. Tibbets, the pilot of the B-29 bomber Enola Gay, waves a farewell before taking off to drop the atomic bomb destined to destroy Hiroshima.
(National Archives)

extremists were hoping to bring home to face the anticipated Allied invasions—remain in Manchuria to protect the region from Soviet invasion. Throughout the day and into the night of August 9, the Japanese Supreme War Council met in grim deliberation. At 2:00 A.M., on August 10, the Japanese prime minister asked Emperor Hirohito to decide Japan's future. Speaking softly, the emperor told his ministers that he wished the war brought to an end. That day, Japan announced that it would accept the terms of surrender that the Allies had demanded in the Potsdam Declaration, with the addition of a sole condition not contained therein: that the position of the emperor be protected. The Japanese accepted the Allies' terms on August 14, 1945, now known as V-J (for "victory in Japan") day.

Background

The dropping of the atomic bomb by the United States was one of the most portentous events in history. Development of the bomb had begun in 1939, after a small group of scientists persuaded the U.S. government that such a weapon was feasible and that Germany was already conducting experiments in atomic energy. The research program that began in October, 1939, ultimately developed into the two-billion-dollar Manhattan Project, which was headed by Leslie R. Groves. The project's goal was to produce a bomb before the Germans did. Few U.S. political or military officials ever doubted that such a bomb, if produced, would be used. Yet before the first bomb was perfected and tested, Germany surrendered. Only Japan remained at war with the Allies.

Early in 1945, as the first bomb neared completion, some scientists began to have doubts about using it. The wave of horror that might follow its use and the moral burden of unleashing such an awesome weapon might, they thought, offset any immediate advantage the bomb could provide. Several options were possible: The United States might demonstrate the new weapon on a barren island before representatives of the United Nations, who could then warn the Japanese of its destructive power; the bomb might be dropped on a military target in Japan after giving a preliminary warning; or the United States could refuse to drop it at all.

While the scientists pondered such choices, military officials prepared to use the bomb. By the end of 1944, possible targets in Japan had been selected, and a B-29 squadron had begun training for the bomb's delivery. Two weeks after President Roosevelt died in 1945, Secretary of War Henry L. Stimson, on April 25, met with the new president, Harry S. Truman, informed him about the bomb, and predicted that in four months it would be available for use. Upon Stimson's recommendation, Truman appointed a special Interim Committee on Atomic Policy to consider use of the bomb. On June 1, 1945, the committee recommended to the president that the bomb be used against Japan as soon as possible, be used against a military

The mushroom cloud rising from the atomic bomb dropped on Nagasaki.
(National Archives)

President Harry S. Truman announces Japan's surrender on August 14, 1945—five days after the second atomic bomb was dropped on Japan. (National Archives)

target, and be dropped without prior warning. By early July, 1945, as Truman left for the Potsdam Conference in Germany to discuss postwar settlements with Great Britain and the Soviet Union, he had decided to use the bomb once it was perfected.

On July 16, in the Trinity Flats near Alamogordo, New Mexico, the first atomic bomb was successfully tested. The United States now had its weapon, although the war in the Pacific had already driven Japan to the brink of surrender. As early as September, 1944, the Japanese had sought to sound out the Allies concerning peace terms. On the eve of the Potsdam Conference, the Japanese ambassador in Moscow asked the Soviet government to mediate with the Allies to end the war. Japan could not accept unconditional surrender, but the Japanese appeared ready to surrender under terms that would allow them to preserve the position of the emperor in the Japanese system. This the Allies would not accept.

Truman's Dilemma

The Truman administration faced difficult problems. Total defeat and unconditional surrender of Japan might require a costly and prolonged invasion of the Japanese home islands. The Soviets, as they had promised at

Yalta in February, 1945, were scheduled to enter the Pacific war in early August. Although their support had been eagerly sought until the spring of 1945, it now appeared less vital; indeed, Truman now hoped to defeat Japan before the Soviet Union could effectively enter the war and gain any control over the postwar settlement with Japan. Also, use of the atomic bomb in Japan would indicate to the Soviets just how powerful the United States was. On July 26, from Potsdam, the Allies called upon Japan to surrender unconditionally or suffer "the utter devastation of the Japanese homeland," a veiled reference the significance of which only the Allies fully understood. The Potsdam Declaration did not mention the atomic bomb and did not offer Japan any terms. The Japanese government chose not to reply to the declaration, while it waited for a reply to the peace overtures it had made through the Soviet government. For home consumption, the Japanese government called the Potsdam Declaration "unworthy of public notice."

In the Mariana Islands, two bombs had been readied for use, and the B-29 crews were standing by. Truman ordered the U.S. Air Corps to drop them. When they were dropped, the age of atomic warfare and the Cold War began.

Aftermath

During the fiftieth anniversary of the dropping of the bomb on Hiroshima, in 1995, there was considerable controversy in the United States concerning why the first bomb over Hiroshima was dropped. The Smithsonian Institution first proposed an exhibit that would have the *Enola Gay* as its centerpiece with four side displays, two of which would depict the devastation of the Japanese cities of Hiroshima and Nagasaki. With these displays, it intended to depict the Japanese as victims. Veterans' groups and Congress complained, pointing out that the bomb was dropped not only to end the war but also to retaliate for the Japanese attack on Pearl Harbor, which produced U.S. victims. In spite of the efforts of various scholars, the exhibit ultimately simply contained the *Enola Gay*. Thus, the significance of dropping the bomb on Hiroshima, the start of the Cold War and the atomic age, is by no means uncontroverted. The question still remains: Was it necessary to drop the bomb on population centers in the first place?

Burl L. Noggle
updated by Jennifer Eastman

Further Reading

Alexander, Joseph H. *Storm Landings: Epic Amphibious Battles in the Central Pacific.* Annapolis, Md.: Naval Institute Press, 1997.

_____. *Utmost Savagery: The Three Days of Tarawa.* Annapolis, Md.: Naval Institute Press, 1995.

Alexander, Joseph H., with Don Horan and Norman C. Stahl. *A Fellowship of Valor: The Battle History of the United States Marines.* Foreword by Edwin H. Simmons. New York: HarperCollins, 1997.

Ambrose, Stephen E. *Citizen Soldiers: The U.S. Army from the Normandy Beaches to the Bulge to the Surrender of Germany, June 7, 1944-May 7, 1945.* New York: Simon & Schuster, 1997.

_____. *D-Day, June 6, 1944: The Climactic Battle of World War II.* New York: Simon & Schuster, 1994.

_____. *Eisenhower and His Boys: The Men of World War II.* New York: Simon & Schuster, 1998.

Astor, Gerald. *A Blood-Dimmed Tide: The Battle of the Bulge by the Men Who Fought It.* New York: Donald I. Fine, 1992.

_____. *Operation Iceberg: The Invasion and Conquest of Okinawa in World War II.* New York: D. I. Fine, 1995.

_____. *Wings of Gold: The U.S. Naval Air Campaign in World War II.* New York: Presidio Press/Ballantine Books, 2004.

Atkinson, Rick. *An Army at Dawn: The War in North Africa, 1942-1943.* New York: Henry Holt, 2002.

Badsey, Stephen. *Modern Air Power: Fighters.* New York: Gallery Books, 1990.

Baird, Jay W. *The Mythical World of Nazi War Propaganda, 1939-1945.* Minneapolis: University of Minnesota Press, 1974.

Balfour, Michael. *Propaganda in War, 1939-1945.* London: Routledge & Kegan Paul, 1979.

Balkoski, Joseph. *Beyond the Beachhead: The Twenty-ninth Infantry Division in Normandy.* Foreword by Stephen E. Ambrose. Mechanicsburg, Pa.: Stackpole Books, 1999.

_____. *Omaha Beach: D-Day, June 6, 1944.* Mechanicsburg, Pa.: Stackpole Books, 2004.

Beach, Edward L. *Scapegoats: A Defense of Kimmel and Short at Pearl Harbor.* Annapolis, Md.: Naval Institute Press, 1995.

Beck, John J. *MacArthur and Wainwright: Sacrifice of the Philippines.* Albuquerque: University of New Mexico Press, 1974.

Beschloss, Michael. *The Conquerors: Roosevelt, Truman, and the Destruction of Hitler's Germany, 1941-1945.* New York: Simon & Schuster, 2002.

Bicheno, Hugh. *Midway.* London: Cassell, 2001.

Bishop, Chris, and Chris McNab, eds. *Campaigns of World War II Day by Day.* Hauppauge, N.Y.: Barron's, 2003.

Blair, Clay. *Hitler's U-Boat War.* 2 vols. New York: Random House, 1996-1998.

——————. *Silent Victory: The U.S. Submarine War Against Japan.* Annapolis, Md.: Naval Institute Press, 2001.

Blumenson, Martin. *The Battle of the Generals: The Untold Story of the Falaise Pocket—the Campaign That Should Have Won World War II.* New York: William Morrow, 1993.

——————. *Mark Clark.* New York: Congdon & Weed, 1984.

——————. *Salerno to Cassino.* Washington, D.C.: Center of Military History, 1969.

Breuer, William B. *The Great Raid on Cabanatuan: Rescuing the Doomed Ghosts of Bataan and Corregidor.* New York: J. Wiley & Sons, 1994.

——————. *They Jumped at Midnight: The "Crash" Parachute Missions That Turned the Tide at Salerno.* New York: Jove Books, 1990.

Buchheim, Lothar-Gunther. *U-Boat War.* New York: Bonanza Books, 1986.

Buckner, Simon Bolivar. *Seven Stars: The Okinawa Battle Diaries of Simon Bolivar Buckner, Jr. and Joseph Stilwell.* Edited by Nicholas Evan Sarantakes. College Station: Texas A&M University Press, 2004.

Burgett, Donald R. *Seven Roads to Hell: A Screaming Eagle at Bastogne.* Novato, Calif.: Presidio Press, 1999.

Chamberlain, Peter, and Charles Ellis. *British and American Tanks of World War II: The Complete Illustrated History of British, American, and Commonwealth Tanks, 1939-1945.* New York: Arco, 1969.

Chandler, David G., and James L. Collins, Jr. *The D-Day Encyclopedia.* New York: Simon & Schuster, 1994.

Chrisman, Catherine Bell. *My War: WW II, as Experienced by One Woman Soldier.* Denver, Colo.: Maverick, 1989.

Christy, Joe. *American Aviation: An Illustrated History.* Blue Ridge Summit, Pa.: Tab Books, 1987.

Clausen, Henry C., and Bruce Lee. *Pearl Harbor: Final Judgment.* New York: Crown, 1992.

Cole, Hugh M. *The Ardennes: Battle of the Bulge.* Washington, D.C.: Center of Military History, 1994.

Cole, Jean Hascall. *Women Pilots of World War II.* Salt Lake City: University of Utah Press, 1992.

Collins, Donald E. *Native American Aliens: Disloyalty and the Renunciation of*

Citizenship by Japanese Americans During World War II. Westport, Conn.: Greenwood Press, 1985.

Condon, John Pomeroy. *Corsairs and Flattops: Marine Carrier Air Warfare, 1944-1945*. Annapolis, Md.: Naval Institute Press, 1997.

Conn, Stetson, Rose C. Engelman, and Byron Fairchild. *The United States Army in World War II: Guarding the United States and Its Outposts*. Washington, D.C.: Office of the Chief of Military History, Department of the Army, 1964.

Conroy, Robert. *The Battle of Bataan: America's Greatest Defeat*. New York: Macmillan, 1969.

Cooksley, Peter G., and Bruce Robertson. *Air Warfare: The Encyclopedia of Twentieth Century Conflict*. London: Arms and Armour Press, 1998.

Coulthard-Clark, C. D. *Action Stations Coral Sea: The Australian Commander's Story*. Sydney: Allen & Unwin, 1991.

Cressman, Robert J., et al. *A Glorious Page in Our History*. Missoula, Mont.: Pictorial Histories, 1990.

Currie, David B. *The Constitution in the Supreme Court: The Second Century—1888-1986*. Chicago: University of Chicago Press, 1990.

Cutler, Thomas J. *The Battle of Leyte Gulf, 23-26 October 1944*. New York: HarperCollins, 1994.

Daniels, Roger. *Concentration Camps U.S.A.: Japanese Americans and World War II*. New York: Holt, Rinehart and Winston, 1972.

_____. *The Decision to Relocate the Japanese Americans*. Philadelphia: J. B. Lippincott, 1975.

Degan, Patrick. *Flattop Fighting in World War II: The Battles Between American and Japanese Aircraft Carriers*. Jefferson, N.C.: McFarland, 2003.

Dencker, Donald O. *Love Company: Infantry Combat Against the Japanese, World War II: Leyte and Okinawa: Company L, 383rd Infantry Regiment, Ninety-sixth Infantry Division*. Manhattan, Kans.: Sunflower University Press, 2002.

Denfeld, D. Colt. *Hold the Marianas: The Japanese Defense of the Mariana Islands*. Shippensburg, Pa.: White Mane, 1997.

Doubler, Michael D. *Closing with the Enemy: How GIs Fought the War in Europe, 1944-1945*. Lawrence: University Press of Kansas, 1994.

Dunmore, Spencer. *In Great Waters: The Epic Story of the Battle of the Atlantic, 1939-1945*. Toronto: McClelland & Stewart, 1999.

Duskin, Gerald, and Ralph Segman. *If the Gods Are Good: The Epic Sacrifice of HMS Jervis Bay*. Annapolis, Md.: Naval Institute Press, 2004.

Dyess, Wm. E. *Bataan Death March: A Survivor's Account*. Edited and with a biographical introduction by Charles Leavelle. Lincoln: University of Nebraska Press, 2002.

Edwards, Bernard. *The Twilight of the U-Boats*. Annapolis, Md.: Naval Institute Press, 2004.

Ellis, John. *Brute Force: Allied Strategy and Tactics in the Second World War*. New York: Viking, 1990.

Falk, Stanley L. *Decision at Leyte*. Norwalk, Conn.: Easton Press, 1989.

Foster, Barry J. *The Last Destroyer: The Story of the USS Callaghan*. Haverford, Pa.: Infinity, 2002.

Frank, Richard B. *Guadalcanal*. New York: Random House, 1990.

Fremon, David K. *Japanese-American Internment in American History*. Springfield, N.J.: Enslow, 1996.

Friedman, Kenneth I. *Afternoon of the Rising Sun: The Battle of Leyte Gulf*. Novato, Calif.: Presidio, 2001.

Fuchida, Mitsuo, and Masatake Okumiya. *Midway*. Annapolis, Md.: Naval Institutes Press, 1955.

Gannon, Michael. *Black May*. New York: HarperCollins, 1998.

_____. *Operation Drumbeat: The Dramatic True Story of Germany's First U-Boat Attacks Along the American Coast in World War II*. New York: Harper & Row, 1990.

Giangreco, D. M., with Kathryn Moore. *Eyewitness D-Day: Firsthand Accounts from the Landing at Normandy to the Liberation of Paris*. Edited and with a foreword by Norman Polmar. New York: Barnes & Noble Books, 2004.

Gilbert, Martin. *D-Day*. Hoboken, N.J.: J. Wiley & Sons, 2004.

Gilbert, Oscar E. *Marine Tank Battles in the Pacific*. Conshohocken, Pa.: Combined Publishing, 2001.

Grace, James W. *The Naval Battle of Guadalcanal: Night Action, 13 November 1942*. Annapolis, Md.: Naval Institute Press, 1999.

Graham, Michael B. *Mantle of Heroism: Tarawa and the Struggle for the Gilberts, November 1943*. Novato, Calif.: Presidio, 1997.

Grahlfs, F. Lincoln. *Undaunted: The Story of a United States Navy Tug and Her Crew in World War II*. St. Louis, Mo.: Author, 2002.

Gregg, Charles T. *Tarawa*. New York: Stein and Day, 1984.

Hallas, James H. *Killing Ground on Okinawa: The Battle for Sugar Loaf Hill*. Westport, Conn.: Praeger, 1996.

Hammel, Eric M. *Guadalcanal—Decision at Sea: The Naval Battle of Guadalcanal, November 13-15, 1942*. Pacifica, Calif.: Pacifica Press, 1999.

Hammel, Eric M., and John E. Lane. *Bloody Tarawa*. Pacifica, Calif.: Pacifica Military History, 1998.

Hart, Russell A. *Clash of Arms: How the Allies Won in Normandy*. Boulder, Colo.: Lynne Rienner, 2001.

Hart, Stephen A. *Montgomery and Colossal Cracks: The Twenty-first Army Group in Northwest Europe, 1944-1945.* New York: Praeger, 2000.

Harvey, Robert. *Amache: The Story of Japanese Internment in Colorado During World War II.* Dallas, Tex.: Taylor Trade Publishing, 2003.

Harwood, Richard. *A Close Encounter: The Marine Landing on Tinian.* Washington, D.C.: U.S. Marine Corps, U.S. Government Printing Office, 1994.

Hastings, Max. *Overlord: D-Day and the Battle for Normandy.* New York: Simon & Schuster, 1984.

Hayashi, Brian Masaru. *Democratizing the Enemy: The Japanese American Internment.* Princeton, N.J.: Princeton University Press, 2004.

Henry, Chris. *The Battle of the Coral Sea.* Annapolis, Md.: Naval Institute Press, 2003.

Herken, Gregg. *Brotherhood of the Bomb: The Tangled Lives and Loyalties of Robert Oppenheimer, Ernest Lawrence, and Edward Teller.* New York: Henry Holt, 2002.

Hess, Gary. *The United States at War: 1941-1945.* Arlington Heights, Ill.: Harlan Davidson, 1986.

Hoffman, Carl W. *The Seizure of Tinian.* Washington, D.C.: U.S. Marine Corps, U.S. Government Printing Office, 1951.

Holt, Thaddeus. *The Deceivers: Allied Military Deception in the Second World War.* New York: Scribner, 2004.

Hornfischer, James D. *The Last Stand of the Tin Can Sailors.* New York: Bantam Books, 2004.

Hoyt, Edwin Palmer. *The Men of the Gambier Bay.* Introduction by Thomas H. Moorer. Guilford, Conn.: Lyons Press, 2002.

The Impact of the War on America: Six Lectures by Members of the Faculty of Cornell University. Ithaca, N.Y.: Cornell University Press, 1942.

Inada, Lawson Fusao, ed. *Only What We Could Carry: The Japanese American Internment Experience.* Berkeley, Calif.: Heyday Books, 2000.

Jasper, Joy Waldron, James P. Delgado, and Jim Adams. *The USS Arizona: The Ship, the Men, and Pearl Harbor Attack, and the Symbol That Aroused America.* New York: St. Martin's Press, 2001.

Josephy, Alvin M. *The Long and the Short and the Tall: The Story of a Marine Combat Unit in the Pacific.* New York: Alfred A. Knopf, 1946.

Kaminski, Theresa. *Prisoners in Paradise: American Women in the Wartime South Pacific.* Lawrence: University Press of Kansas, 2000.

Kaplan, Philip, and Jack Currie. *Convoy: Merchant Sailors at War, 1939-1945.* Annapolis, Md.: Naval Institute Press, 1998.

_____. *Wolfpack: U-Boats at War, 1939-1945.* Annapolis, Md.: Naval Institute Press, 1997.

Katz, Robert. *The Battle for Rome: The Germans, the Allies, the Partisans and the Pope, September 1943-June 1944*. New York: Simon & Schuster, 2003.

Keegan, John. *The Second World War*. London: Penguin Books, 1989.

Kelly, Orr. *Meeting the Fox: The Allied Invasion of Africa, from Operation Torch to Kasserine Pass to Victory in Tunisia*. New York: J. Wiley, 2002.

Kitano, Harry H. L. *Japanese Americans: The Evolution of a Subculture*. Englewood Cliffs, N.J.: Prentice-Hall, 1976.

Knightley, Phillip. *The First Casualty*. New York: Harcourt Brace Jovanovich, 1975.

Knox, Donald. *Death March: The Survivors of Bataan*. New York: Harcourt Brace Jovanovich, 1981.

Kutler, Stanley, ed. *The Supreme Court and the Constitution: Readings in American Constitutional History*. 2d ed. New York: W. W. Norton, 1977.

Leckie, Robert. *Okinawa: The Last Battle of World War II*. New York: Viking, 1995.

Lee, Robert Edward. *Victory at Guadalcanal*. Novato, Calif.: Presido Press, 1981.

Lord, Walter. *Day of Infamy*. 60th anniversary ed. New York: H. Holt, 2001.

Lorelli, John A. *To Foreign Shores: U.S. Amphibious Operations in World War II*. Annapolis, Md.: Naval Institute Press, 1995.

Lowry, Thomas P., and John Wellham. *The Attack on Taranto: Blueprint for Pearl Harbor*. Mechanicsburg, Pa.: Stackpole Books, 1995.

Loza, D. F. *Attack of the Airacobras: Soviet Aces, American P-39s, and the Air War Against Germany*. Translated and edited by James F. Gebhardt. Introduction by Von Hardesty. Lawrence: University Press of Kansas, 2002.

Lundstrom, John B. *The First South Pacific Campaign*. Annapolis, Md.: Naval Institute Press, 1976.

_____. *The First Team and the Guadalcanal Campaign: Naval Fighter Combat from August to November 1942*. Annapolis, Md.: Naval Institute Press, 1994.

Lyne, Mary C., and Kay Arthur. *Three Years Behind the Mast: The Story of the United States Coast Guard, SPARS*. Washington, D.C.: U.S. Coast Guard, 1946.

MacDonald, Charles B. *A Time for Trumpets: The Untold Story of the Battle of the Bulge*. New York: Morrow, 1985.

McIntosh, Elizabeth P. *Sisterhood of Spies: The Women of the OSS*. Annapolis, Md.: Naval Institute Press, 1998.

Macintyre, Donald. *U-Boat Killer: Fighting the U-Boats in the Battle of the Atlantic*. London: Cassell, 1999.

McManus, John C. *The Americans at D-Day: The American Experience at the Normandy Invasion*. New York: Forge, 2004.

——————. *The Americans at Normandy: The Summer of 1944—the American War from the Normandy Beaches to Falaise*. New York: Forge, 2004.

——————. *Deadly Sky: The American Combat Airman in World War II*. Novato, Calif.: Presidio, 2000.

Mann, B. David. *Avenging Bataan: The Battle of Zigzag Pass*. Raleigh, N.C.: Pentland Press, 2001.

Mansoor, Peter R. *The GI Offensive in Europe: The Triumph of American Infantry Divisions, 1941-1945*. Lawrence: University Press of Kansas, 1999.

Marion, Ore J., with Thomas Cuddihy and Edward Cuddihy. *On the Canal: The Marines of L-3-5 on Guadalcanal, 1942*. Mechanicsburg, Pa.: Stackpole Books, 2004.

Mathews, Joseph J. *Reporting the Wars*. Minneapolis: University of Minnesota Press, 1957.

Monahan, Evelyn M., and Rosemary Neidel-Greenlee. *All This Hell: U.S. Nurses Imprisoned by the Japanese*. Lexington: University Press of Kentucky, 2000.

——————. *And If I Perish: Frontline U.S. Army Nurses in World War II*. New York: Knopf, 2003.

Morris, Eric. *Salerno: A Military Fiasco*. New York: Stein and Day, 1983.

Morrison, Samuel Eliot. *Coral Sea, Midway, and Submarine Actions*. Vol. 4 in *History of United States Naval Operations in World War II*. New York: Little, Brown, 1964.

——————. *The Struggle for Guadalcanal*. Vol. 5 in *History of United States Naval Operations in World War II*. New York: Little, Brown, 1964.

Morrison, Wilbur H. *Birds from Hell: History of the B-29*. Central Point, Oreg.: Hellgate Press, 2001.

Morton, Louis. *The Fall of the Philippines: History of the United States Army in World War II—the War in the Pacific*. Washington, D.C.: Center of Military History, United States Army, 1953.

Muller, Eric L. *Free to Die for Their Country: The Story of the Japanese American Draft Resisters in World War II*. Foreword by Daniel K. Inouye. Chicago: University of Chicago Press, 2001.

Murray, Williamson, and Allan R. Millett. *A War to Be Won: Fighting the Second World War*. Cambridge, Mass.: Belknap Press of Harvard University Press, 2000.

Neill, George W. *Infantry Soldier: Holding the Line at the Battle of the Bulge*. Norman: University of Oklahoma Press, 2000.

Nesmith, Jeff. *No Higher Honor: The U.S.S. Yorktown at the Battle of Midway*. Atlanta, Ga.: Longstreet, 1999.

Newcomb, Richard F. *Iwo Jima*. 2d rev ed. New York: Bantam Books, 2002.

Nieva, Antonio A. *The Fight for Freedom: Remembering Bataan and Corregidor*. Quezon City, Philippines: New Day, 1997.

Norman, Elizabeth M. *We Band of Angels: The Untold Story of American Nurses Trapped on Bataan by the Japanese*. New York: Random House, 1999.

Norris, Robert S. *Racing for the Bomb: General Leslie R. Groves, the Manhattan Project's Indispensable Man*. South Royalton, Vt.: Steerforth Press, 2002.

O'Brien, Francis. *Battling for Saipan*. New York: Ballantine Books, 2003.

O'Donnell, Patrick K. *Into the Rising Sun: In Their Own Words, World War II's Pacific Veterans Reveal the Heart of Combat*. New York: Free Press, 2002.

O'Neill, William L. *A Democracy at War*. New York: Free Press, 1993. Discusses many economic issues relating to World War II.

Overy, Richard. *Why the Allies Won*. New York: W. W. Norton, 1995.

Owens, William J. *Green Hell: The Battle for Guadalcanal*. Central Point, Oreg.: Hellgate Press, 1999.

Parker, Danny S., ed. *Hitler's Ardennes Offensive: The German View of the Battle of the Bulge*. London: Greenhill Press, 1997.

Petty, Bruce M. *Voices from the Pacific War: Bluejackets Remember*. Annapolis, Md.: Naval Institute Press, 2004.

Pitt, Barrie. "Italy's Pearl Harbor." *Military History Quarterly* 3 (Spring, 1991): 50-57.

Prange, Gordon W. *At Dawn We Slept: The Untold Story of Pearl Harbor*. New York: Viking, 1991.

_____. *Miracle at Midway*. New York: McGraw Hill, 1982.

Prange, Gordon W., with Donald M. Goldstein and Katherine V. Dillon. *Pearl Harbor: The Verdict of History*. 1991. Reprint. New York: Penguin Books, 2001.

Rhodes, Richard. *The Making of the Atomic Bomb*. New York: Simon & Schuster, 1986.

Robinson, Greg. *By Order of the President: FDR and the Internment of Japanese Americans*. Cambridge, Mass.: Harvard University Press, 2001.

Ross, Bill D. *Iwo Jima*. New York: Vintage, 1986.

Ryan, Cornelius. *The Longest Day*. New York: Simon & Schuster, 1959.

Schom, Alan. *The Eagle and the Rising Sun: The Japanese-American War, 1941-1943, Pearl Harbor Through Guadalcanal*. New York: W. W. Norton, 2004.

Schrijvers, Peter. *The GI War Against Japan: American Soldiers in Asia and the Pacific During World War II*. New York: New York University Press, 2002.

Shaw, Henry I. *Tarawa: A Legend Is Born*. New York: Ballantine, 1969.

Sherrod, Robert Lee. *Tarawa: The Story of a Battle*. New York: Duell, Sloan, and Pearce, 1944.

Short, K. R. M., ed. *Film and Radio Propaganda in World War II*. Knoxville: University of Tennessee Press, 1983.

Shteppa, Konstantin F. *Russian Historians and the Soviet State*. New Brunswick, N.J.: Rutgers University Press, 1962.

Sides, Hampton. *Ghost Soldiers: The Forgotten Epic Story of World War II's Most Dramatic Mission*. New York: Doubleday, 2001.

Sledge, Eugene B. *With the Old Breed at Peleliu and Okinawa*. Annapolis, Md.: Naval Institute Press, 1996.

Sloan, Bill. *Given Up for Dead: America's Heroic Stand at Wake Island*. New York: Bantam Books, 2003.

Smith, Michael S. *Bloody Ridge: The Battle That Saved Guadalcanal*. Novato, Calif.: Presido Press, 2000.

Smith, Page. *Democracy on Trial*. New York: Simon & Schuster, 1995.

Smithers, A. J. *Taranto, 1940*. Annapolis, Md.: Naval Institute Press, 1995.

Soderbergh, Peter A. *Women Marines: The World War II Era*. Westport, Conn.: Praeger, 1992.

Solberg, Carl. *Decision and Dissent: With Halsey at Leyte Gulf*. Annapolis, Md.: Naval Institute Press, 1995.

Spector, Ronald H. *Eagle Against the Sun: The American War with Japan*. New York: Vintage Books, 1985.

Stinnett, Robert B. *Day of Deceit: The Truth About FDR and Pearl Harbor*. New York: Free Press, 2000.

Stokesbury, James L. *A Short History of World War II*. New York: William Morrow, 1980.

Sweeney, Michael S. *Secrets of Victory: The Office of Censorship and the American Press and Radio in World War II*. Chapel Hill: University of North Carolina Press, 2001.

Taylor, Frederick. *Dresden, Tuesday, February 13, 1945*. New York: HarperCollins, 2004.

Thomas, Dorothy S., and Richard S. Nishimoto. *The Spoilage: Japanese-American Evacuation and Resettlement During World War II*. Berkeley: University of California Press, 1946.

Toland, John. *Battle: The Story of the Bulge*. Introduction by Carlo D'Este. Lincoln: University of Nebraska Press, 1999.

Tomblin, Barbara. *With Utmost Spirit: Allied Naval Operations in the Mediterranean, 1942-1945*. Lexington: University Press of Kentucky, 2004.

Treadwell, Mattie E. *The Women's Army Corps*. Washington, D.C.: Office of the Chief of Military History, Department of the Army, 1954.

Van Creveld, Martin. *Fighting Power: German and U.S. Army Performance, 1939-1995*. Westport, Conn.: Greenwood Press, 1982.

Walker, J. Samuel. *Prompt and Utter Destruction: Truman and the Use of*

Atomic Bombs Against Japan. Chapel Hill: University of North Carolina Press, 1997.

Walling, Michael G. *Bloodstained Sea: The U.S. Coast Guard in the Battle of the Atlantic, 1941-1944*. Camden, Maine: International Marine/McGraw-Hill, 2004.

Watt, Donald Cameron. *Too Serious a Business: European Armored Forces and the Approach to the Second World War*. New York: W. W. Norton, 1975.

Weeks, Albert L. *Russia's Life-Saver: Lend-Lease Aid to the U.S.S.R. in World War II*. Lanham, Md.: Lexington Books, 2004.

Weglyn, Michi Nishiura. *Years of Infamy: The Untold Story of America's Concentration Camps*. Seattle: University of Washington Press, 1996.

Weigley, Russell F. *Eisenhower's Lieutenants: The Campaign of France and Germany, 1944-1945*. Bloomington: Indiana University Press, 1981.

Weinberg, Gerhard L. *A World at Arms*. Cambridge, England: Cambridge University Press, 1994.

Welch, Bob. *American Nightingale: The Story of Frances Slanger, Forgotten Heroine of Normandy*. New York: Atria Books, 2004.

Wells, Mark K. *Courage and Air Warfare: The Allied Aircrew Experience in the Second World War*. London: Frank Cass, 2000.

Wheeler, Richard. *Iwo*. Annapolis, Md.: Naval Institute Press, 1994.

Winchester, Jim, general ed. *Aircraft of World War II*. San Diego, Calif.: Thunder Bay Press, 2004.

Wragg, David W. *Swordfish: The Story of the Taranto Raid*. London: Weidenfeld & Nicolson, 2003.

Yahara, Hiromichi. *The Battle for Okinawa*. New York: John Wiley & Sons, 1997.

Yellin, Emily. *Our Mothers' War: American Women at Home and at the Front During World War II*. New York: Free Press, 2004.

Young, Donald J. *The Battle of Bataan*. Jefferson, N.C.: McFarland, 1992.

Young, Roland. *Congressional Politics in the Second World War*. New York: Columbia University Press, 1956.

Korean War
1950-1953

Korean War

At issue: Reunification of Korea
Date: June 25, 1950-July 27, 1953
Location: Korea
Combatants: North Korea and China vs. South Korea, the United States, and fifteen members of the United Nations
Principal commanders: *North Korean*, Choe Yong Gun (1900-1976); *American*, Douglas MacArthur (1880-1964); *U.N.*, Matthew B. Ridgway (1895-1993)
Principal battles: Kaesong, Seoul (1950), Osan, Taejon, Inchon Landing, Seoul (1951), Bloody Ridge, Heartbreak Ridge, Pork Chop Hill
Result: Military stalemate and restoration of prewar status quo.

The division of Korea in 1945 after World War II at the thirty-eighth parallel into U.S. and Soviet zones of military occupation resulted in the creation of two separate governments. The determination of both the Republic of Korea (ROK) in the south and the Democratic People's Republic of Korea (DPRK) in the north to reunify the country ignited the Korean War.

After its creation in September, 1948, North Korea had focused on supporting southern guerrillas, holding its army in reserve, and allowing South Korea to initiate most of the clashes along the thirty-eighth parallel. Starting in May, 1949, North Korea escalated its retaliation, resulting in major fighting. After Soviet arms deliveries tilted the balance in its favor, North Korea committed its regular army in August, 1949, to a campaign that drove ROK forces from salients north of the parallel. Except for a brief clash on the Ongjin Peninsula, there were few serious border incidents for the next ten months, as South Korea avoided fights it could no longer win. However, the clashes persuaded the United States to limit South Korea's offensive military capability, denying it tanks, planes, and much heavy artillery, while bolstering North Korea's argument to Moscow that only conquest of South Korea would remove future threats to its survival.

The North Korean Invasion

Soviet leader Joseph Stalin gave his reluctant consent to North Korea's invasion plan in April, 1950. At dawn on June 25, 1950, the North Korean People's Army (NKPA), led by Choe Yong Gun, launched assaults at seven points along the parallel, while staging amphibious landings on the east

TIME LINE OF THE KOREAN WAR

June 25, 1950	Korean War begins when North Korean troops cross the thirty-eighth parallel.
June 28, 1950	North Koreans occupy Seoul.
July 1, 1950	First U.S. ground combat troops arrive in Korea.
July 5, 1950	Battle of Osan: North Korean forces, in their first engagement with poorly equipped and ill-trained U.S. forces, easily sweep them aside.
July 16-20, 1950	Taejon falls.
July 29-Sept. 19, 1950	Battle of the Pusan Perimeter: American and South Korean forces effectively defend the Pusan Perimeter, preventing North Korea's military conquest of the entire peninsula.
Sept. 15, 1950	Inchon Landing: A decisive American and United Nations victory.
Sept. 26, 1950	Recapture of Seoul.
Sept. 29, 1950	United Nations forces drive the remainder of the North Korean forces out of South Korea.
Oct. 8, 1950	United Nations and Chinese forces move into North Korea.
Oct. 14, 1950-Apr. 11, 1951	Truman-MacArthur Confrontation: An irreconcilable dispute between General Douglas MacArthur, the head of military forces in Korea, and President Harry S. Truman tests the principle of civil control of the military.
Nov. 24, 1950	MacArthur launches his Home-by-Christmas Offensive to force North Korea to surrender.
Nov. 26, 1950	Chinese forces intervene in the war by crossing the Yalu River and attacking the exposed flanks of MacArthur's forces.
Jan., 1951	Chinese forces recapture Seoul, which they maintain until March, 1951.
Apr. 22-30, 1951	Battle of Imjin River: Communist offensive fails to take Seoul, and the Chinese army fails to sever the primary supply line to U.S. First Corps.
Aug., 1952	Battle of Bloody Ridge.
Sept., 1952	Battle of Heartbreak Ridge.
Mar. 23-July 11, 1953	Battle of Pork Chop Hill: Chinese forces seize Pork Chop Hill near the end of the war.
June 4, 1953	China accepts voluntary repatriation.
July 27, 1953	Armistice ends the fighting.

coast. Composed of roughly 135,000 well-trained troops, it had about 150 Soviet-built T-34 tanks, 110 combat planes, and abundant heavy artillery. The South Korean army consisted of eight combat divisions totaling 65,000 soldiers plus 33,000 support troops, with only flat-trajectory antitank guns and rocket-launching bazookas.

The North Korean army's main offensive thrust sent four of seven infantry divisions and 120 tanks toward Kaesong (June 25, 1950), seizing the city after just three hours. Early the next day, the North Korean forces crushed South Korea's counterattacking Seventh Division, and fleeing South Korean soldiers abandoned countless mortars, howitzers, machine guns, and antitank guns. The North Koreans occupied Seoul on June 28, 1950. Meanwhile, in the center of the peninsula, South Korean forces mounted a spirited defense against two Northern Korean divisions and thirty tanks for five days, then withdrew to avoid being flanked from the west. Isolated on the east coast, the South Korean Eighth Division fought well and delayed the North Korean advance.

The U.S. Reaction

North Korea's attack surprised the United States, although intelligence reports that spring had indicated that North Korea was evacuating civilians and staging a military buildup just north of the parallel. Following existing plans, President Harry S. Truman secured resolutions at the United Nations (U.N.) authorizing military assistance to South Korea. He ordered U.S. naval and air support for South Korean forces on June 25 but did not commit ground troops until five days later, approving the urgent request of General Douglas MacArthur, the occupation commander in Japan.

Reorganized remnants of the South Korean army delayed the North Korean advance south of the Han River until July 3. At the Battle of Osan (July 5, 1950), the North Korean forces, in their first engagement with understrength, poorly equipped, and ill-trained U.S. forces, easily swept aside Task Force Smith. A United Nations resolution created the U.N. Command, and Truman named MacArthur commander. After Taejon fell (July 16-20, 1950), North Korea pushed U.N. forces back to the Pusan Perimeter (July 29-September 19, 1950) in the southeastern corner of Korea. By August, the North Korean army had grown to ten divisions with the addition of South Koreans who either had been impressed into service or had voluntarily enlisted. It faced five reorganized South Korean divisions and the U.S. Twenty-fourth and Twenty-fifth Infantry Divisions and First Cavalry Division.

The Tenth Corps' amphibious assault at the port of Inchon (September

15, 1950), thirty miles west of Seoul, met only slight resistance. The next morning, the U.S. First Marines moved eastward, with the Seventh Infantry Division protecting its right flank. Recapture of Seoul (September 26, 1950) was more difficult even after linking up with the U.S. Eighth Army that had broken out of the Pusan Perimeter, but once accomplished, United Nations forces on September 29 pushed the remnants of the North Korean forces out of South Korea.

China Enters the War

After the United States sent its Seventh Fleet into the Taiwan Strait, the People's Republic of China feared that U.S. destruction of the North Korean army would threaten not only its own security, but its image as the leader in Asia. In July, China reorganized its Thirteenth Army Corps into the Northeastern Border Forces and deployed it along the Yalu River. On October 2, Mao Zedong persuaded his reluctant colleagues to approve sending troops to fight in Korea as "volunteers." Beijing made a final effort to avoid entry when on October 3, Premier Zhou Enlai told India's ambas-

General Douglas MacArthur (right) visiting the front lines, accompanied by his military secretary, Major General Courtney Whitney (second from left) and Lieutenant General Matthew B. Ridgway (center), who was later to replace him as commander of the United Nations ground forces. (National Archives)

KOREAN WAR, 1950-1953

sador that if U.S. forces crossed the parallel, China would react. Most U.S. officials thought Beijing was bluffing.

In fact, the Truman administration had decided in August to invade North Korea, finalizing plans for forcible reunification on September 11 and giving MacArthur almost a free hand in advancing to the Yalu River. On October 8, both United Nations and Chinese forces moved into North Korea. Major engagements early in November confirmed China's intervention, but MacArthur viewed full Chinese participation as unlikely. He launched his Home-by-Christmas Offensive on November 24 to force North Korea to capitulate. The Eighth Army and the Tenth Corps were to strike northward separately before linking to crush the North Korean forces.

The U.N. forces encountered little resistance initially, then China counterattacked in force, sending its enemy into rapid retreat. Only a harrowing withdrawal from the Chongjin Reservoir and a miraculous evacuation at Hungnam rescued the Tenth Corps from annihilation. MacArthur pressed for a naval blockade and military attacks against China, but Truman refused to widen the war, despite publicly hinting in December that he was considering using atomic weapons.

Allied Counteroffensive

General Matthew B. Ridgway, who became commander of U.N. ground forces in December, halted the retreat after Chinese forces recaptured Seoul early in January, 1951. He then implemented a strategy to inflict maximum casualties on the enemy, providing for the use of long-range artillery coupled with air attacks using napalm and rockets before ground troops with support of tanks advanced with heavy machine-gun and mortar fire. Beginning in February, Ridgway employed this "meat-grinder" strategy in Operation Killer and then in Operations Ripper and Courageous. Within three months, the U.N. forces had returned to the parallel. However, on April 22, the Chinese initiated a final effort to destroy the U.N. forces and reunite Korea. The primary target of this offensive was Seoul, with a secondary thrust at Kapyong to the east. The Chinese assault, relying as before on night attacks and superior numbers to overwhelm the enemy, was costly and ineffective against well-prepared U.N. forces, although the South Korean Sixth Division collapsed.

Despite suffering huge casualties, the Chinese redeployed eastward in May and sent thirty divisions against U.N. lines. South Korean units again broke under pressure, but reinforcements blocked a breakthrough. A U.N. counteroffensive soon threatened Chinese forces with envelopment, forcing them to retreat in disarray. China's Fifth Phase Offensive gained nothing, and its forces sustained the worst losses of the war. By confirming the U.N. forces' ability, through superior organization and firepower, to overcome tactics relying on massed manpower, the offensive hastened a military stalemate, thus opening the way to truce talks on July 10. By then, smaller contingents of military forces from Australia, Belgium, Canada, Colombia, Ethiopia, France, Greece, Luxembourg, the Netherlands, New Zealand, Philippines, Thailand, Turkey, South Africa, and Great Britain had joined South Korea and the United States. However, to maintain the multinational character of the U.N. forces, the United States had to comply when its allies opposed military escalation.

Cease-fire

U.N. forces maintained battlefield pressure to achieve a quick armistice, seizing key positions north of the parallel in the Battles of Bloody Ridge (August, 1952) and Heartbreak Ridge (September, 1952). To force concessions, the United States dropped dummy atomic bombs and intensified B-29 bombing raids on North Korea, but communist MiG fighters, often with Soviet pilots, inflicted heavy damage, climaxing in the Battle of Namsi (1952). When negotiators agreed to a cease-fire line in November, the U.N. forces adopted active defense as the basis for ground strategy. The

A U.S. gunnery squadron led by an African American sergeant holds a position north of North Korea's Chongchon River in late November 20, 1950. The Korean War was the first U.S. conflict in which the armed services were racially integrated. (National Archives)

Eighth Army would undertake no major offensives and limit the scope of operations to capturing outposts in terrain suitable for temporary defense. Thereafter, a pattern emerged of patrolling and small-scale fighting with U.N. forces merely reacting to enemy contacts. Peng Dehuai, commander of Chinese forces, followed suit, causing Korea to develop into a war of attrition resembling World War I, with a static battlefield and armies depending on barbed wire, trenches, artillery, and mortars. Because both sides placed a priority on achieving an early armistice, they emphasized gaining and maintaining defense in depth, increasing troops, and stockpiling equipment behind the front line.

U.S. military leaders proposed plans for offensive action but were unable to gain approval for implementation from either the Truman or Dwight D. Eisenhower administration. However, the United States did expand the air war in the spring of 1952, attacking North Korean targets of economic importance to China and the Soviet Union. That summer, the U.N. forces bombed power installations along the Yalu and Tumen Rivers, such as the huge Suiho plant. This strategy extended to attacking targets of political significance, especially Pyongyang, using napalm as well as high explosives, with the aim of undermining enemy

U.S. Marines negotiating Korea's rugged mountain terrain while closing with the enemy. (U.S. Marine Corps)

morale and raising to an unacceptable level the costs of stalling the truce talks.

Despite the raids, the North Koreans remained inflexible, resulting in suspension of the talks in October. Both sides continued to sustain huge losses in protracted ground engagements in the spring of 1953 at Triangle, Whitehorse, and Pork Chop Hill. By then, U.S. planners had gained approval for attacks against the dams supplying water for rice cultivation in North Korea, the first attacks taking place in May.

Armistice

President Eisenhower later credited the armistice ending the Korean War to success in convincing the North Koreans and Chinese that the alternative was a wider war, employing atomic weapons. Atomic coercion may have played a role in China's accepting voluntary repatriation on June 4, 1953, thus opening the way to an armistice, but domestic economic pressures in the communist states, the Soviet bloc's growing desire for peaceful coexistence, and the death of Joseph Stalin were more important. The communists then launched new military thrusts to gain the propaganda value of a symbolic military victory at the end of the war. China also focused attacks on South Korean forces to persuade South Korea's government to endorse and respect the armistice agreement. Despite more than a year of U.S. effort to train and equip an enlarged South Korean army capable of postwar self-defense, only U.S. troops from the Third and Twenty-fourth Divisions, and commitment of the 187th Regimental Combat Team from Japan, halted the offensive. A U.N. counteroffensive on July 17 restored a position six miles south of the original battle line. On July 27, 1953, signing of an armistice ended fighting in the Korean War. More than 2 million Koreans died during the war, and China sustained an estimated 360,000 casualties. U.N. casualties totaled 159,000, which included 33,629 U.S. combat deaths.

Aftermath

Conflict between South Korea and North Korea continued into the twenty-first century, making the demilitarized zone that separates the two Koreas one of the world's most heavily fortified and dangerous boundaries. Chinese forces withdrew, but the United States retained troops in South Korea. Periodic incidents kept alive fears of renewed war.

James I. Matray

The Air War

As the first jet-age war, the Korean conflict affirmed air power's decisive importance in modern warfare, but its conditions undermined some air power expectations.

After World War II, the Korean Peninsula was divided into two countries, the Republic of Korea (ROK), supported by the United States, in the south, and the Democratic People's Republic of Korea (DPRK), with Soviet and Chinese backing, in the north. After communist North Korea invaded South Korea on June 25, 1950, the United States led a U.N. effort to help South Korea repel the assault, supplying the vast majority of U.N. forces. At first, neither the United Nations nor the South Koreans were prepared for the North Korean onslaught, but desperate fighting enabled them to retain some of the southeastern peninsula near Pusan during the summer of 1950. The Americans' September 15, 1950, Inchon Landing, combined with a breakout from Pusan, helped the South Koreans to rout the North Koreans that autumn.

The United Nations then resolved to destroy the North Korean Army and to reunite Korea under its sponsorship. However, China, threatened by U.S. aggression in Asia, attacked U.N. forces in late autumn, 1950, forcing their lengthy retreat back into South Korea. The United Nations counterattacked in early spring, 1951, and had stabilized the lines near the prewar boundary by summer. The two sides entered protracted negotiations as their forces fought for limited advantage. The July 27, 1953, armistice terminated active hostilities.

Air Forces

Both sides in the Korean War fought for limited objectives, and the superpowers were concerned with defense needs elsewhere in their worldwide face-off. Thus, neither side fully committed its air forces to this fight. Also, the war occurred during a transition period in air warfare technology.

Thus, World War II-vintage, propeller-driven fighters, such as the Soviet Yak-9 and U.S. P-51 Mustang, did much of the early fighting for the respective sides. Other propeller planes, such as the A-1, Corsair, and British Sea Fury, also provided excellent service as attack planes throughout the war. Because the Americans did not commit their frontline strategic bombers to Korea, World War II-era B-29's accomplished most of the United Nations' long-range heavy bombing tasks. U.S. transport planes were mostly propeller-driven holdovers from the last war. The communists even used P0-2 biplanes to fly nighttime nuisance attacks, nicknamed "Bedcheck Charlies," against U.N. forces.

Simultaneously, the Korean War introduced jets to air combat. U.S. F-80's and F-9F Panthers were among the straight-wing, subsonic jets that flew attack missions. The most noteworthy jet development occurred with the appearance of the Soviet-built Mikoyan-Gurevich MiG-15. This swept-wing, transonic fighter seriously threatened the U.N. air effort until the Americans quickly fielded a counterpart, the F-86 Sabre jet. Jets such as the U.S. F-94 Starfire and F-3D Skyknight also served as radar-equipped night fighters.

The Korean War also witnessed the first extensive use of helicopters. These early, underpowered, piston-engine models flew light logistics missions. However, they also demonstrated impressive utility for rescue missions and covert operations.

An important contribution of the Korean War to aerial warfare was the first extensive use of helicopters, which made it possible to move materials and personnel in and out of areas inaccessible to other aircraft. Helicopters were particularly useful for evacuating wounded soldiers, as in this Marine photograph, and helped enable the Mobile Army Surgical Hospitals later made famous by the film and television series titled M*A*S*H— in both of which helicopters figured prominently. (U.S. Marine Corps)

Air War Conduct

The war's limited scope precluded nuclear weapons usage by both sides. Also, the combatant air arms attacked targets only in Korea, not communist targets in the Soviet Union and China, or U.S. targets in Japan. Both sides thus emphasized tactical air combat, though each remained wary of the other's capacity to escalate the air war, and with it, the war itself.

At the war's start, U.S. fighters quickly vanquished the inexperienced North Korean Air Force, thus allowing attack planes to maul the North Korean Army's supply lines. These interdiction air raids, along with close air support (CAS) missions against frontline troops, were major factors in repelling the communist invasion.

U.N. air forces pulverized North Korean transportation links during the autumn, 1950, U.N. advance. As they entered the war, the Chinese introduced the MiG-15, flown by Chinese and Soviet pilots, to check this effort. They failed partly because of the MiG's short range and partly because F-86 pilots were better trained. Although U.N. air raids destroyed communist air bases in North Korea, MiG-15's could still fly from their safe havens in China and harrass U.N. planes in far northeast Korea, nicknamed "MiG Alley." The Chinese did have bombers, but they kept them only as an in-place air raid threat.

Air power was important in stopping the late-1950 Chinese advance. On two occasions, U.N. CAS and air supply saved large units surrounded by communist armies. As the battle lines stabilized and truce talks stalemated, U.N. leaders approved several U.S. Air Force-led attempts to interdict the communist supply lines. These interdictions inflicted serious damage and kept many troops and supplies from the front, but they did not compel capitulation or even perceptibly affect the truce talks. The communists were masters of primitive improvisation, and because both sides attempted no major offensives, interdiction's true effect could not be assessed. More dramatic were the MiG Alley air battles between F-86's and MiG-15's, in which U.S. pilots increasingly dominated their opponents.

Air War Results

The Korean War ended after the death of Soviet dictator Joseph Stalin and a veiled American threat to use nuclear weapons. U.N. aerial successes probably helped convince the communists of the war's futility, but the later interdiction campaigns remained controversial because they did not meet their proponents' claims. Indeed, the war demonstrated that not all post-World War II conflicts would be decided exclusively by nuclear bombing campaigns by or conventional interdiction, as some air power advocates asserted.

Instead, the Korean War revealed an ever-widening air warfare spectrum. Per the air power ideal, jet fighters remained necessary to achieve air superiority, and heavy bombers and attack planes remained decisive with behind-the-lines attacks. However, in Korea, tactical missions such as CAS rose in importance. Aircraft carrier-based planes were especially valuable early in the war, when battle conditions eliminated land bases. The performance of helicopters did not match that of airplanes, but their utility showed great promise for future conflicts. Although U.S. leaders saw Korea as an aberration, they encountered similar conditions in the Vietnam War.

Douglas Campbell

Censorship During the War

During this U.S.-led war against North Korea's invasion of South Korea, U.S. government efforts to constrain negative media coverage contrasted sharply with World War II censorship policies, foreshadowing an even more adversarial government-media relationship during the later Vietnam War.

North Korea's invasion of South Korea in June, 1950, triggered a renewal of American military operations barely five years after the end of World War II. American press coverage of the Korean War represented a sharp departure from the role the media had played in the earlier conflict. Whereas the media generally accepted the need to support the Allied effort against the Axis powers, American involvement in the Korean War was controversial and less generally accepted.

General Douglas MacArthur, the supreme commander in Korea, initially instituted a system of voluntary censorship resembling the system used in the world war. However, as it became evident that journalists were less willing to toe Washington's official line, MacArthur instituted a system of formal, prepublication review for all dispatches from the war zone. As a consequence, many press reports were heavily censored, fostering resentment among members of the press corps. This further weakened the shared sense of mission that had characterized military-press relations in the previous war. Moreover, the increasingly critical perspective of press reports in turn fostered the belief among military leaders that the press was handicapping the war effort.

More than practicing simple censorship, MacArthur's headquarters has been accused of deliberately disseminating misinformation during the Korean War. Press conferences, communiqués, and other official statements from the military headquarters in Tokyo, Japan, were frequently challenged by journalists and columnists in the United States and Britain. The official exaggerations of foreign threats and the downplaying of national casualties might partly be explained as owing to the Cold War climate that permeated virtually all aspects of international relations. However, some critics attributed the high command's thoroughgoing control and manipulation of war information to be a function of the supreme commander's personal hubris. Against this interpretation, the fact that press censorship and media manipulation did not significantly ease after President Harry S. Truman's dismissal of MacArthur in April, 1951, suggests that there was a driving force larger than MacArthur's ego behind military censorship. Indeed, censorship was significantly strengthened after the United States began committing troops to the Vietnam War during the 1960's.

Meanwhile, as late as 1996 investigations were continuing into charges that the U.S. government had deliberately hidden embarrassing information about the Korean War effort. U.S. Senate hearings and Pentagon investigations uncovered documents revealing that up to a thousand American prisoners of war (POWs) remained in North Korea after the July, 1953, armistice and prisoner exchange. The possibility that POWs had been left behind has often been raised, but it has repeatedly been discounted by U.S. authorities. Recently discovered evidence indicates, however, that President Dwight D. Eisenhower himself may have been aware that some POWs remained behind in North Korea.

Campaigns, Battles, and Other Events

July-September, 1950
Battle of the Pusan Perimeter

Date: July 29-September 19, 1950
Location: Southeast corner of Korea
Combatants: United States, South Korean, and United Nations forces vs. North Korea and China
Principal commanders: *American and U.N.*, Lieutenant General Walton Walker (1889-1950); *North Korean*, Choe Yong Gun (1900-1976)
Result: American and South Korean forces successfully defended the Pusan Perimeter, preventing North Korea's military conquest of the entire peninsula.

North Korean forces invaded South Korea on June 25, 1950, advancing southward quickly despite U.S. military intervention. After defeats at Osan, the Kum River, and Taejon, the U.S. Eighth Army established in late July a defensive position in the southeast corner of the peninsula. A rectangular area, the Pusan Perimeter was about eighty miles from north to south along the Naktong River and fifty miles east to west to just north of Yongdok on the Sea of Japan. Defending it was the U.S. Twenty-fourth and Twenty-fifth Infantry and First Cavalry Divisions together with the First, Third, Sixth, Eighth, and Capital Divisions of the Republic of Korea (ROK), guided by General Walton Walker.

North Korea's Third, Fourth, Sixth, Eighteenth, and Twelfth Guards and elements of its Thirteenth and Fifteenth Infantry and 105th Armored Divisions, though exhausted and understrength, initiated fierce fighting for over a month. No longer able to use previously devastating flanking and rear attacks and subject to constant U.S. air and naval bombardment, the North Korean forces, under Choe Yong Gun, battered but did not destroy the Pusan Perimeter.

The South Korean forces successfully defended Taegu, allowing supplies and reinforcements to arrive at Pusan behind shorter logistics lines.

U.S. Marines marching through Pusan on their way to the front. (U.S. Marine Corps)

The amphibious landing assault at Inchon on September 15, 1950, and then interdiction of North Korea's extended logistics lines enabled U.S. and South Korean forces to break out of the Pusan Perimeter and move northward swiftly after September 19.

James I. Matray

September, 1950
Inchon Landing

Date: September 15-25, 1950
Location: West-central Korea
Combatants: United States vs. Korean People's Army
Principal commanders: *American*, Major General Edward M. Almond; *North Korean*, unknown
Result: A decisive American and United Nations victory.

As the Battle of the Pusan Perimeter raged, United Nations commander General Douglas MacArthur prepared an amphibious assault behind Korean People's Army (KPA) lines to cut its communications south and open a two-front war. Confident that Lieutenant General Walton Walker's Eighth Army could hold Pusan, MacArthur built up another force for Operation Chromite.

Although there was agreement on a landing, only MacArthur wanted the landing to be at Inchon. Korea's second largest port, Inchon was fifteen miles from the capital city and the main KPA supply line south; cutting it would starve KPA troops on the Pusan Perimeter. However, Inchon's tidal range, strong currents, and narrow channel all made a landing there extremely hazardous. MacArthur overrode all opposition, however.

On September 15, Lieutenant General Edward M. Almond's Tenth Corps (First Marine Division and Seventh Army Division) carried out the landing. Destroyers and U.S. Marine and British aircraft provided support. The operation went off in textbook fashion, and Inchon was taken with light United Nations forces casualties. MacArthur's timing was fortunate; Soviet mines were stacked ashore waiting to be laid.

U.S. Marines (in foreground) commandeer defensive trenches abandoned by North Korean troops as supplies are landed at Inchon. (U.S. Marine Corps)

The Eighth Army shortly broke out on the Pusan Perimeter and drove north. Seoul fell on September 26, and only some one-third of the KPA escaped across the thirty-eighth parallel. MacArthur was convinced the war was won.

Spencer C. Tucker

October, 1950-April, 1951
Truman-MacArthur Confrontation

Date: October 14, 1950-April 11, 1951
Location: Korea, Tokyo, and Washington, D.C.
Principal figures: Douglas MacArthur (1880-1964), President Harry S. Truman (1884-1972)
Result: An irreconcilable disagreement between the head of military forces in Korea and the U.S. commander in chief tested the principle of civil control of the military.

General Douglas MacArthur of the U.S. Army was a powerful military leader and a highly controversial politician, having been a Republican Party contender in the presidential campaigns of 1944, 1948, and 1952. As the overseer of the occupation of Japan, he was the obvious choice as commander of all United Nations forces when the Korean War broke out in June, 1950.

The Korean War challenged the willingness of the U.S. people to accept the burden of a discouraging and dirty struggle to check communist aggression. It was a war being fought for limited ends, without hope of a decisive victory. This was the first war to be carried forward under the policy of containment initiated by President Harry S. Truman. A cause of serious dispute was whether the brand of military strategy dictated by the containment policy would prove workable or would be tolerable to the public and to Congress. In the first year of the Korean War, the question of how communist expansion should be met found expression in a personal, political, and constitutional struggle between President Truman and General MacArthur. MacArthur's flouting of a strategy that had presidential approval resulted in his dismissal. A public outcry ensued. The MacArthur-Truman confrontation was one of the most serious threats in the nation's history to the basic principles of civilian control over the military.

The circumstances in which the Korean War began guaranteed that

President Harry S. Truman greets General Douglas MacArthur at the latter's arrival on Wake Island on October 14, 1950. (AP/Wide World Photos)

MacArthur would have a commanding role. In June, 1950, MacArthur, after a long and illustrious military career, was serving as Supreme Commander for the Allied Powers (SCAP). Since September, 1945, MacArthur had governed Japan, exercising the functions and enjoying much of the prestige of a head of state. For some time, MacArthur had disapproved of the Far Eastern policy of the Truman administration. MacArthur believed that Asia would be the supreme test of communist expansion, not Europe.

When North Korea invaded South Korea in June, 1950, President Truman responded and gained United Nations' sanction. MacArthur was appointed supreme commander of U.N. forces in Korea. Operating out of his headquarters in Tokyo and using staff officers who were personally devoted to him, MacArthur began to plan a bold offensive counterstrike that would place the United Nations on the way to a complete victory. This plan called for amphibious landings at Inchon, the port on Korea's west coast a few miles from Seoul, and was carried forward against strong opposition from some military and naval leaders. MacArthur dismissed all objections, revealing a pattern of authoritarianism that was to become clearer as the weeks and months passed. He believed that Korea provided a priceless opportunity for the United States to recoup lost prestige and to stop Asian communism once and for all. He also saw this war as an outstanding opportunity to conclude a brilliant military career.

China Enters the War

As the U.N. forces approached China in the north, rumors of Chinese intervention abounded. MacArthur downplayed them. He advocated, if necessary, a preventive war against China, including the dropping of twenty or thirty atomic bombs on Chinese cities. He supported a policy of encouraging the Chiang Kai-shek regime on Formosa and employing part of Chiang's army in Korea. This was in direct opposition to Truman's aim of preventing any widening of the war. MacArthur's outspokenness about Formosa caused the first dispute with Truman, and apparently led the president to give serious thought to firing the general. Instead, Truman ordered MacArthur to withdraw the statement, which MacArthur did.

President Truman was forced to move carefully in his relations with MacArthur because of MacArthur's great popularity and the power of his political supporters. The stunning success of the Inchon landings added to the general's reputation. Military success also allowed the Truman administration to expand its political goals in Korea. For a time, Truman and MacArthur worked toward the same ends. The administration's initial aim had been the restoration of the thirty-eighth parallel as the boundary between North and South Korea, but in September, Truman approved MacArthur's proposal that United Nations and South Korean forces move into North Korea and occupy the entire country. This action followed a National Security Council recommendation that all North Korea be occupied, unless Soviet or Chinese troops were encountered. The thirty-eighth parallel was crossed on October 7, and the campaign proceeded without difficulty. By mid-November, advance units were nearing the Yalu River. MacArthur's headquarters was supremely confident that complete victory was assured and discounted growing rumors of military intervention by the Chinese communists.

At that point, an extraordinary conference took place. Truman flew to remote Wake Island for a meeting with MacArthur on October 14. The fact that the president would travel so far to meet with a subordinate was evidence of the delicacy of the relationship between the two men. The Wake Island conference glossed over the differences between them. MacArthur provided assurances that the Chinese would not intervene, but was in error. On November 26, Chinese forces crossed the Yalu River and attacked the exposed flanks of MacArthur's forces. There followed a numbing retreat, and by Christmas, 1950, United Nations forces were once again fighting below the thirty-eighth parallel.

Truman and MacArthur now took opposing positions. The Truman administration, alarmed by China's action, moved to limit the war. MacArthur pressed for attacks against the Chinese troops and supplies in Manchuria and, implicitly, for expansion of the war into China proper. The president refused and decided to allow only the Korean side of the Yalu River bridges to be bombed. This was a compromise that infuriated MacArthur.

MacArthur's Intransigence

MacArthur became increasingly belligerent. In January, 1951, he recommended a naval blockade of China, air attacks to destroy Chinese military and industrial capabilities, and the use of Nationalist Chinese forces in Korea. The president again restrained him, arguing that the worldwide threat of the Soviet Union made a war of containment necessary in Korea. The fact that Lieutenant General Matthew Ridgway, MacArthur's deputy in Korea, was dealing directly with the White House and the Pentagon, and was making a success of limited war, made MacArthur's position more difficult.

The final phase of the MacArthur-Truman confrontation began when the general attempted to bypass the president in order to gain support for his program from Congress and the U.S. people. MacArthur's practice of making public his differences with the president and Washington policymakers angered and embarrassed Truman on several occasions. The break came in late March, 1951. When MacArthur learned that President Truman planned to issue a peace offer, he released a military appraisal, a document that amounted to an ultimatum to the Chinese. It destroyed any hope of a negotiated settlement and precipitated Truman's decision to dismiss MacArthur. "By this act," Truman stated, "MacArthur left me no choice—I could no longer tolerate his insubordination."

After making his decision, Truman was concerned only about the timing of the act, but the timing was to be decided by MacArthur and his allies in Congress. On April 5, Representative Joseph Martin read a letter from MacArthur on the floor of the House of Representatives. MacArthur again rejected the limited war policy and called for total victory in Asia. A series of meetings began in the White House the following day. On April 11, President Truman cabled MacArthur in Tokyo and, at the same time, informed the press that the general was being relieved of his command because he was unable to give wholehearted support to the president's policies.

Aftermath

General MacArthur returned to the United States a triumphant hero. He addressed a joint session of Congress. Across the nation, there was a tremendous surge of support for him. A joint Senate committee conducted hearings during the rest of the summer. Truman rode out the emotional reaction, secure in the conviction that his decision had been correct. He was supported openly by his military advisers. Powerful foreign leaders praised his courage. After two months of hearings, the committee issued no report.

Theodore A. Wilson
updated by Eugene L. Rasor

April, 1951
Battle of Imjin River

Date: April 22-30, 1951
Location: Along the Imjin River, north of Seoul, Korea
Combatants: United Nations (U.N.) forces, mostly U.S. and British vs. Chinese forces
Principal commanders: *U.N.*, Lieutenant General James Van Fleet (1892-1992); *Chinese*, General Peng Dehuai (1898-1974)
Result: Communist offensive failed to take Seoul, and the Chinese army failed to cut the main supply line to U.S. First Corps.

Having failed to maintain their hold on Seoul during the first offensive of 1951 (January through March), Chinese communist forces, under by General Peng Dehuai, launched a second offensive in April against the United Nations forces, under Lieutenant General James Van Fleet. The main goal of the Chinese Sixty-third Army, about 27,000 strong, had been to recapture the South Korean capital. The British Twenty-ninth Brigade Group, including a Belgian infantry battalion, held the ground north of the Imjin River. Only 63 men from the Belgian battalion reached safety, the unit having run out of ammunition, food, and water. Although the brigade group was forced to fall back, they inflicted such heavy casualties on the Chinese army that it was no longer capable of recapturing Seoul.

Chinese casualties were estimated at 11,000; U.N. casualties at about 1,000. The fighting resulted in a U.S. Presidential Unit Citation and the awarding of Victoria Crosses to Lieutenant Colonel J. P. Carne and Lieutenant P. K. E. Curtis. By mid-May, communist forces were forced to withdraw to the north, and by July 1, they had agreed to discuss a possible cease-fire.

John Powell

March-July, 1953
Battle of Pork Chop Hill

Date: March 23-July 11, 1953
Location: East-central Korea
Combatants: United Nations Command vs. Chinese communist forces
Principal commanders: *U.N.*, General Maxwell Taylor (1901-1987); *China,* Commander in Chief Peng Dehuai (1898-1974)
Result: Chinese forces took Pork Chop Hill near the conclusion of the war.

Soldiers wounded in the Battle of Pork Chop Hill are evacuated from the combat zone. (U.S. Department of Defense)

Named because of its shape, Pork Chop Hill became a test of endurance for U.S. and Chinese military forces during the last five months of the Korean War. Located less than sixty miles north of Seoul, Pork Chop possessed little strategic value. However, the Chinese, led by Peng Dehuai, wanted to take possession of the hill before the conclusion of the Panmunjon Peace Talks to demonstrate China's will to continue fighting if necessary.

The Chinese mounted three attacks on Pork Chop Hill between March 23 and July 11, 1953. The first two attempts were unsuccessful, although on March 26, the Chinese did secure Old Baldy, a hill near Pork Chop. In mid-April, a second attack took and held Pork Chop for two days but then lost it to U.S. counterattacks on April 18, thanks to help from an allied artillery barrage of more than 77,000 rounds during the two-day battle.

The third and final Chinese attack began on July 6, just three weeks before the end of the war. For three days, there were U.S. counterattacks, until General Maxwell Taylor decided that increasing the number of casualties was not commensurate to the strategic value of the hill. Pork Chop was evacuated on July 11, 1953. After the armistice on July 27, Pork Chop became a part of both North Korea and the demilitarized zone.

John Quinn Imholte

Further Reading

Appleman, Roy S. *South to the Naktong, North to the Yalu: The U.S. Army in the Korean War.* Washington, D.C.: U.S. Government Printing Office, 1961.

Bateman, Robert L. *No Gun Ri: A Military History of the Korean War Incident.* Mechanicsburg, Pa.: Stackpole Books, 2002.

Blair, Clay. *The Forgotten War: America in Korea, 1950-1953.* New York: Times Books, 1987.

Cagle, Malcolm W., and Frank A. Manson *The Sea War in Korea.* 1957. Reprint. New York: Arno Press, 1980.

Chen, Jian. *China's Road to the Korean War: The Making of the Sino-American Confrontation.* New York: Columbia University Press, 1994.

Clark, Eugene Franklin. *The Secrets of Inchon: The Untold Story of the Most Daring Covert Mission of the Korean War.* Introduction by Thomas Fleming. New York: Putnam's, 2002.

Crane, Conrad. *American Airpower Strategy in Korea, 1950-1953.* Lawrence: University Press of Kansas, 2000.

Cumings, Bruce. *The Origins of the Korean War.* 2 vols. Princeton, N.J.: Princeton University Press, 1990.

Ent, Uzal W. *Fighting on the Brink: Defense of the Pusan Perimeter.* Paducah, Ky.: Turner Publishing, 1996.

Fehrenbach, T. R. *This Kind of War: The Classic Korean War History.* 50th anniversary ed. Foreword by Gordon Sullivan. Washington, D.C.: Brassey's 2000.

Field, James A. *History of United States Naval Operations: Korea.* Washington, D.C.: U.S. Navy, Naval History Division, 1962.

Foot, Rosemary. *The Wrong War: American Policy and the Dimensions of the Korean Conflict, 1950-1953.* Ithaca, N.Y.: Cornell University Press, 1985.

Futrell, Robert. *The United States Air Force in Korea, 1950-1953.* Reprint. Washington, D.C.: Office of Air Force History, 1996.

Goncharov, Sergei, John W. Lewis, and Xue Litai. *Uncertain Partners: Stalin, Mao, and the Korean War.* Stanford, Calif.: Stanford University Press, 1993.

Green, David. *Captured at the Imjin River: The Korean War Memories of a Gloster, 1950-1953.* Barnsley, South Yorkshire: Leo Cooper, 2003.

Haas, Michael E. *In the Devil's Shadow: UN Special Operations During the Korean War.* Annapolis, Md.: Naval Institute Press, 2000.

Hallion, Richard. *The Naval Air War in Korea.* Baltimore: Nautical & Aviation Publishing Company of America, 1986.

Hamburger, Kenneth E. *Leadership in the Crucible: The Korean War Battles of Twin Tunnels and Chipyong-ni*. College Station: Texas A&M University Press, 2003.

Hanley, Charles J., Sang-Hun Choe, and Martha Mendoza. *The Bridge at No Gun Ri: A Hidden Nightmare from the Korean War*. New York: Henry Holt, 2001.

Hermes, Walter G. *Truce Tent and Fighting Front*. Washington, D.C.: Government Printing Office, 1966.

James, D. Clayton. *Refighting the Last War: Command and Crisis in Korea, 1950-1953*. New York: Free Press, 1993.

Kaufman, Burton I. *The Korean War: Challenges in Crisis, Credibility, and Command, 1950-1953*. Philadelphia: Alfred A. Knopf, 1986.

Knox, Donald. *The Korean War: Uncertain Victory*. New York: Harcourt Brace Jovanovich, 1988.

Langley, Michael. *Inchon Landing: MacArthur's Last Triumph*. New York: Times Books, 1979.

Lowe, Peter. *The Korean War*. Basingstoke, England: Macmillan, 2000.

MacDonald, Callum A. *Korea: The War Before Vietnam*. New York: Free Press, 1986.

McLaren, David R. *Mustangs over Korea: The North American F-51 at War, 1950-1953*. Atglen, Pa.: Schiffer Publishers, 1999.

McWilliams, Bill. *On Hallowed Ground: The Last Battle for Pork Chop Hill*. Annapolis, Md.: Naval Institute Press, 2004.

Marshall, S. L. A. *Pork Chop Hill: The American Fighting Man in Action, Korea, Spring, 1953*. 1956. Reprint. Norwalk, Conn.: Easton Press, 1993.

Matray, James I., ed. *Historical Dictionary of the Korean War*. Westport, Conn.: Greenwood Press, 1991.

Merrill, John. *Korea: The Peninsular Origins of the War*. Newark: University of Delaware Press, 1989.

Montross, Lyn, and Nicholas Canzona. *The Inchon-Seoul Operation*. Vol. 2 in *U.S. Marine Operations in Korea*. Washington, D.C.: Historical Branch, United States Marine Corps, 1954-1957.

Owen, Joseph R. *Colder Than Hell: A Marine Rifle Company at Chosin Reservoir*. Annapolis, Md.: Naval Institute Press, 1996.

Rees, David. *Korea: The Limited War*. New York: St. Martin's Press, 1964.

Rottman, Gordon L. *Korean War Order of Battle: United States, United Nations, and Communist Ground, Naval, and Air Forces, 1950-1953*. Foreword by Ed Evanhoe. Westport, Conn.: Praeger, 2002.

Russ, Martin. *Breakout: The Chosin Reservoir Campaign, Korea 1950*. New York: Fromm International, 1999.

Sandler, Stanley. *The Korean War: No Victors, No Vanquished*. Lexington: University Press of Kentucky, 1999.

_____, ed. *The Korean War: An Encyclopedia*. New York: Garland, 1995.

Stueck, William W., Jr. *The Korean War: An International History*. Princeton, N.J.: Princeton University Press, 1995.

_____. *Rethinking the Korean War: A New Diplomatic and Strategic History*. Princeton, N.J.: Princeton University Press, 2002.

Thompson, Warren E., and David R. McLaren. *MIG Alley: Sabres vs. MIGs over Korea: Pilot Accounts and the Complete Combat Record of the F-86 Sabre*. North Branch, Minn.: Specialty Press, 2002.

Toland, John. *In Mortal Combat: Korea, 1950-1953*. New York: Quill, 1991.

Varhola, Michael J. *Fire and Ice: The Korean War, 1950-1953*. Mason City, Iowa: Savas, 2000.

Whiting, Charles. *Battleground Korea: The British in the Korean War*. London: Sutton, 1999.

Zhang, Shu Guang. *Mao's Military Romanticism: China and the Korean War, 1950-1953*. Lawrence: University of Kansas Press, 1995.

Zhang, Xiaoming. *Red Wings over the Yalu: China, the Soviet Union, and the Air War in Korea*. College Station: Texas A&M University Press, 2002.

Vietnam War
1960's-1975

Vietnam War

At issue: Control of South Vietnam
Date: 1961-1975
Location: North and South Vietnam
Combatants: United States, South Vietnam vs. North Vietnam
Principal commanders: *American*, Paul Harkins (1904-1984), William West-moreland (1914-   ), Creighton Williams Abrams, Jr. (1914-1974); *North Vietnam*, Vo Nguyen Giap (1911-   )
Principal battles: Ia Drang Valley (1965), Siege of Khe Sanh (1968), Hue (1968)
Result: After a decades-long struggle, the communist regime of North Vietnam achieved a complete victory and reunited Vietnam under a single government.

The Vietminh victory over the French at Dien Bien Phu in 1954 led to the withdrawal of the French from Vietnam, which they had colonized and controlled for more than a century except for a brief period during World War II. The 1954 Geneva Conference split Vietnam into North and South and recommended elections be held within two years. However, South Vietnamese leader Ngo Dinh Diem rejected the Geneva agreement, proclaiming himself president of the Republic of Vietnam. The United States, which refused to sign the Geneva agreement, supported the Diem regime with funds and, by 1960, with 900 American military personnel.

U.S. Involvement

The incoming presidential administration of John F. Kennedy approved a counterinsurgency plan for Vietnam early in 1961. The Kennedy White House likewise sought a cease-fire in Laos, where communists also sought to gain a foothold. South Vietnamese President Diem requested an increase in the U.S. presence in his country, which rose to 3,205 advisers by the end of the year.

In 1962, the United States established the Military Assistance Command, Vietnam (MACV), under the authority of General Paul Harkins. Changes were also made in the army's joint chiefs and chief of staff positions. In order to gain the support of the South Vietnamese people against communist invaders, the United States assisted South Vietnam with the strategic hamlet program, whereby rural communities were organized and fortified against attacks. American military personnel increased to 11,300 by the conclusion of 1962.

TIME LINE OF THE VIETNAM WAR

Aug. 18, 1945	Indochinese Communist Party leader Ho Chi Minh proclaims a Democratic Republic of Vietnam, and France begins reasserting its colonial rule in Indochina.
Mar. 13-May 7, 1954	Battle of Dien Bien Phu: Viet Minh victory over the French, leads to withdrawal of the French from Vietnam.
July 21, 1954	The Geneva Conference calls for a partition of Indochina into four countries—North Vietnam, South Vietnam, Laos, and Cambodia—and for an election within two years to unify North and South Vietnam.
Aug. 11, 1954	Formal peace treaty partitions the country into North and South Vietnam.
1955	United States assumes political control of South Vietnam from the French.
1956	United States and the U.S.-backed South Vietnamese president, Ngo Dinh Diem, reject the Geneva-mandated reunification elections, knowing that the popular Ho Chi Minh would win.
1961	North Vietnam seeks to absorb South Vietnam; United States gradually becomes involved.
Aug., 1964	Gulf of Tonkin incident: Facts pertaining to this event, which is used to justify empowering the president of the United States to conduct warfare without Senate approval, are suppressed by the U.S. government in order to rally popular support for the Vietnam War.
Nov. 14-16, 1965	Battle of Ia Drang Valley: U.S. disturbance of a planned North Vietnamese offensive.
Jan. 21-Apr. 6, 1968	Siege of Khe Sanh: Although U.S. firepower clearly overwhelmed the North Vietnamese, General Vo Nguyen Giap refuses to admit defeat, claiming that the battle is a calculated diversionary tactic.
Jan. 30-Feb. 25, 1968	Tet Offensive: North Vietnamese and Viet Cong launch the Tet Offensive, which, although unsuccessful, provides a political and psychological victory.
Jan. 31-Feb. 25, 1968	Battle of Hue: The battle signals the beginning of the end of U.S. involvement in the war.
Mar. 16, 1968	My Lai Massacre.
Apr. 29-June, 1970	U.S. troops invade Cambodia.

Nov. 17, 1970- Mar. 29, 1971	Lieutenant William L. Calley is tried and convicted of killing twenty-two Vietnamese civilians.
Jan. 31, 1973	Peace accord is signed; North Vietnam begins releasing U.S. prisoners.
Mar. 29, 1973	Last U.S. troops leave Vietnam.
Apr. 30, 1975	North Vietnam occupies Saigon, ending the civil war, and last U.S. advisers leave the country.
July 2, 1976	North and South Vietnam are formally united.

The following year witnessed several violent demonstrations against the Diem government, which was accused of progressing too slowly on reforms and stifling dissent. After the U.S. ambassador to South Vietnam was replaced, the Kennedy administration gave tacit support to a coup by some of Diem's military commanders. The coup succeeded, and Diem and his brother were subsequently executed. Less than three weeks after the change in the South Vietnamese government, President Kennedy was assassinated. Vice President Lyndon B. Johnson became president, promising no major changes in Vietnam policy. By the end of the year, 16,300 U.S. military advisers were stationed in South Vietnam.

General William Westmoreland replaced General Harkins as head of the MACV, while General Maxwell Taylor replaced Henry Cabot Lodge as U.S. ambassador to South Vietnam in 1964. In August of that year, allegations of two separate attacks by the North Vietnamese on U.S. destroyers in the region led the Johnson administration to request that Congress approve the Gulf of Tonkin resolution, which would permit the United States to suppress communist attacks by any means necessary. The latter legislation was approved unanimously in the U.S. House of Representatives, and it received only two negative votes in the Senate. On November 1, two days before Johnson was elected president in his own right, an attack by communist supporters in South Vietnam (Viet Cong) resulted in the deaths of five U.S. servicemen. Two more Americans were killed by a Viet Cong attack on Christmas Eve. By the end of 1964, 23,300 U.S. soldiers were stationed in Vietnam.

Escalation of the Conflict

After widespread attacks by Viet Cong on U.S. military installations in South Vietnam during early 1965, President Johnson ordered the first large-scale ground troops to the embattled nation. He likewise authorized the beginning of an air-bombing campaign, known as Operation Rolling

*Although American military involve-
ment in Vietnam began long before
Lyndon B. Johnson became president
and did not end until more than six
years after he left office, the war is
associated more closely with his
administration than with that of any
other president, and it ultimately
doomed his presidency.*
(Library of Congress)

Thunder, which would continue on and off until the end of 1972. Lodge returned as U.S. ambassador to South Vietnam in July of 1965. In November,
with American troop strength at 184,300, the first major battle between
American and North Vietnamese soldiers occurred in the Ia Drang Valley
(1965) region. American deaths totaled 636 by the end of the year.

The United States rapidly escalated its military presence in South Vietnam over the next two years. In 1966, Americans bombed oil deposits in
Hanoi and Haiphong. Troop strength increased to 385,300 by the end of
1966. During 1967, Nguyen Van Thieu was elected president of South Vietnam, ending a period of instability in which a series of South Vietnamese
leaders served for a short duration, and Ellsworth Bunker became the new
U.S. ambassador there. By the end of 1967, 485,600 U.S. military personnel
were present in South Vietnam, with a total of 16,021 U.S. servicemen
killed to date in the conflict.

For several reasons, 1968 proved to be a pivotal period in the Vietnam
War. First, the North Vietnamese and Viet Cong engaged Americans in
costly battles at Khe Sanh and Hue. Second, the Viet Cong, led by Vo
Nguyen Giap, used the lunar new year known as Tet to simultaneously attack military, diplomatic, and civilian sites throughout South Vietnam.

Third, General Creighton William Abrams, Jr., replaced General West-moreland as head of MACV. Fourth, President Johnson announced in March that he would not run for reelection as president. Republican Rich-ard Nixon narrowly defeated Democrat Hubert H. Humphrey for the pres-idency in the November election, promising to enact a plan to end the war. Finally, after several years of backing U.S. participation in the Vietnam War, a majority of American citizens expressed opposition to it. By the end of 1968, with the war looking like a stalemate at best, 536,000 U.S. soldiers were stationed in South Vietnam. A total of 30,610 U.S. troops had perished in hostilities to date.

Nixon's Strategy

The incoming Nixon administration implemented a multifaceted strat-egy pertaining to the Vietnam War in 1969. First, in June, President Nixon announced the initial withdrawal of American ground troops, which num-bered about 25,000. Second, Nixon promulgated the Nixon Doctrine in July, which established the policy of Vietnamization. By that policy, the United States would furnish the funds and equipment necessary to permit the South Vietnamese military to defend the country against the commu-nist North. Third, the Nixon White House initiated secret talks with the North Vietnamese aimed at ending the U.S. role in the conflict, which would continue through 1972. Fourth, the Nixon administration enacted a pacification policy, which involved coordinating military, intelligence, and civilian operations in order to take the offensive in the war. Although U.S. troop strength decreased to 475,200 by the end of 1969, the number of American deaths climbed to a cumulative total of 40,024.

Frustrated by the communist tendency to use neighboring Cambodia as a sanctuary from which attacks were mounted against South Vietnam, the Nixon administration sought the assistance of Cambodian leader Prince Norodom Sihanouk. When Sihanouk insisted on remaining neutral, the U.S. supported a coup to topple him from power. The replacement of Sihanouk with General Lon Nol, in March, 1970, led directly to the U.S. oc-cupation of the nation a month later in order to ferret out communist troops. The operation, though approved by General Nol, was viewed by many Americans as an invasion. Subsequent protests at home, many on college campuses, precipitated the killing of four students at Kent State University, in Ohio, and two students at Jackson State University, in Mis-sissippi. The Cambodian mission ended after two months. The reaction by the U.S. Congress was swift: In July, the Senate unanimously repealed the Gulf of Tonkin resolution, and in December, Congress banned both Ameri-can combat forces and advisers from Cambodia and Laos. By the end of

1970, with U.S. troop strength reduced to 334,600, a total of 44,245 Americans had died in the conflict.

In 1971, the Nixon administration faced the release of the Pentagon Papers—the secret history of the Vietnam War as compiled by the Department of Defense—when the U.S. Supreme Court rejected their suppression. Though the mission of U.S. ground troops changed from an offensive to a defensive role, Nixon ordered a resumption of bombing of North Vietnam. By the end of the year, 156,800 American troops were still present in South Vietnam, with 45,626 U.S. soldiers killed in fighting to date.

Turning Point

Other than 1968, the year 1972 was the most eventful of the war. First, the South Vietnamese military, with American logistical support, successfully repelled an Easter offensive by North Vietnam. Second, Nixon's dual visits to China and the Soviet Union resulted in slowing support for North Vietnam by both the Chinese and the Soviets. Third, Americans renewed bombing of Hanoi in March and mined several North Vietnamese ports in April. The combination of the latter factors hastened a peace agreement between the United States and North Vietnam. Announced in October, less than a month from the presidential election, it no doubt contributed to Nixon's overwhelming victory against Democratic candidate George McGovern. The agreement, hammered out by Nixon's national security adviser, Henry A. Kissinger, later appeared to be in jeopardy.

In response, Nixon ordered widespread bombing of North Vietnam, including civilian targets. The massive bombing continued over the Christmas holiday but caused Hanoi to request renewed negotiations on December 26. At the end of 1972, for the first time during the conflict, cumulative American deaths (45,926) outnumbered the remaining troops stationed in South Vietnam (24,200).

The peace agreement ending direct U.S. participation in the Vietnam War was signed in Paris on January 27, 1973. It called for withdrawal of all but a few U.S. troops from South Vietnam along with a return of all U.S. prisoners of war. However, because it also provided for a cease-fire, allowing the North Vietnamese and Viet Cong to remain in South Vietnam, the South Vietnamese government opposed the arrangement.

Aftermath

Though South Vietnamese leaders remained adamantly against the aforementioned peace agreement, they assumed that the United States would fulfill Nixon's pledge to furnish the material and fiscal resources necessary to protect their nation. However, the Watergate scandal, com-

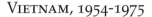

VIETNAM, 1954-1975

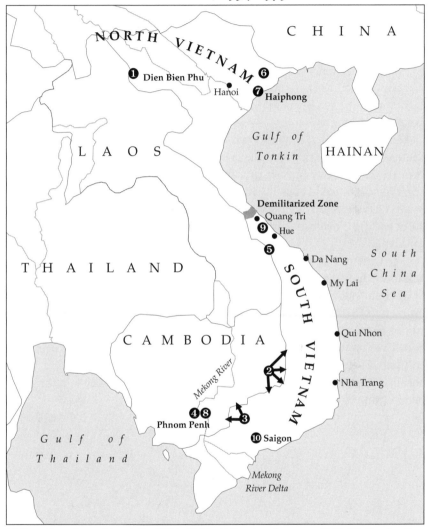

(1) Last French position falls, 1954. (2) Tet Offensive, January, 1968. (3) Cambodian invasion, April-May, 1970. (4) Sihanouk falls, April, 1970. (5) Laotian incursian, February, 1971. (6) Areas of U.S. bombing, 1972. (7) Mining of Haiphong Harbor, May, 1972. (8) Lon Nol falls, April, 1975. (9) North Vietnamese offensive, spring, 1975. (10) South Vietnam surrenders, April 20, 1975.

bined with a newly assertive Congress, compromised the U.S. promise to guard South Vietnam against further communist aggression. In August, 1973, direct U.S. military operations ended in all of Indochina. In November, the U.S. Congress prohibited funds from being expended for military actions in any part of Southeast Asia and passed the War Powers Act over Nixon's veto. In April, 1974, as he faced impeachment, Nixon requested an additional $474 million to assist South Vietnam and was denied it.

After Nixon resigned on August 9, 1974, Vice President Gerald R. Ford became president. He reaffirmed to South Vietnamese President Thieu the U.S. commitment to furnish funds and equipment, but his subsequent proposals in that regard were rejected by Congress. Although they assumed in December, 1974, that it would take two years to conquer the South, North Vietnamese military leaders planned a winter, 1975, offensive. The strategy proved enormously successful, as South Vietnamese troop morale and supplies diminished rapidly. Just two weeks after Cambodia fell to communist forces, North Vietnamese soldiers marched on Saigon on April 30, 1975, ending the decades-long conflict and unifying the nation under communism.

The United States spent over $140 billion in its longest war, which most acknowledge to be the first military defeat suffered by the nation. The United States lost more than money; it lost a generation of its youth, with more than 58,000 killed in fighting or as a result of the war. Some 2,000 U.S. troops missing in action remain unaccounted for and are presumed dead. South Vietnam lost more than one million soldiers and citizens during the conflict, as did North Vietnam. In 1995, twenty years after the end of the conflict, the United States and Vietnam renewed diplomatic relations and began trading with each other.

Samuel B. Hoff

Weapons, Tactics, and Strategies

Although the United States had an overwhelming superiority in weapons through-out its military involvement in Vietnam, it ultimately lost the war because of its failure to find a strategy suitable for the political and geographical conditions of the conflict.

As the conclusion of World War II liberated Southeast Asia from Japanese domination, Indochinese Communist Party leader Ho Chi Minh swiftly moved ahead with his political goal of a unified and independent Vietnam, proclaiming a Democratic Republic of Vietnam on September 2, 1945. At the same time, however, France began reasserting its colonial rule in Indochina. Ho, previously allied with the United States—especially through its Office of Strategic Services (OSS), the forerunner of the Central Intelligence Agency (CIA), against the Japanese, looked for support in his goal from the United States.

Political Considerations

With a Cold War developing between the United States and the Soviet Union, U.S. president Harry S. Truman chose not to risk a break with France and adopted a policy of what has been called "guarded neutrality." The United States accepted France's return to Indochina but required that aid to France not be used in Vietnam. As war in Korea threatened in 1950, the United States recognized the French-supported government of Emperor Bao Dai, the last emperor of the Nguyen Dynasty, and made available both economic aid and military supplies.

The 1954 Geneva Conference, which ended the war between France and Ho's Viet Minh, called for a partition of Indochina into four countries—North Vietnam, South Vietnam, Laos, and Cambodia—and for an election no later than 1956 to unify the two Vietnams. The United States, however, assumed political control of South Vietnam from the French in 1955, when the American choice for president, Ngo Dinh Diem, replaced Bao Dai. Diem proclaimed the Republic of Vietnam in the south, and both he and the United States refused to be bound by the call for a reunification election, knowing that the North's popular Ho Chi Minh would win.

North Vietnam, determined to conquer the South, had the political, financial, and technological support of the Soviet Union and China. The South Vietnamese government sought, with the support of the United States, to maintain its rule in the South. The United States government feared a so-called domino effect; if South Vietnam fell to communism, it reasoned, so would other nations in Asia, including India. Both North and South Vietnam were now markers in the Cold War conflict between the three superpowers—the United States, the Soviet Union, and China. During its long struggle in Vietnam, the United States remained hampered by Cold War concerns and the desire to avoid pushing either of the other superpowers into active engagement in the fighting.

Military Achievement

The crushing defeat of the French at Dien Bien Phu in northern Vietnam in 1954 essentially brought the First Indochina War (1946-1954) to an end. However, Ho Chi Minh controlled only the northern half of Vietnam, and although the French had been forced out, the Americans had replaced them. Now the North Vietnamese turned their attention to undermining the South Vietnamese government and extracting such a high price for American involvement that the United States would withdraw.

The date often given for the beginning of the Second Indochina War, or what Americans call the Vietnam War, is 1956, the year in which the United States and Diem rejected the Geneva-mandated reunification elections. In 1959, North Vietnam's Central Executive Committee formally changed the country's approach from political to armed struggle. Remnants of the Viet Minh who had stayed in the South (the Viet Cong) were activated by the North Vietnamese Politburo.

The Viet Cong specialized in terrorist warfare against U.S. soldiers and South Vietnamese loyal to the Diem government. Their largest campaign was the Tet Offensive of 1968, which ended in the almost complete destruction of the Viet Cong infrastructure and the end of the Viet Cong as a significant military threat. From that point on, the war to unify the country was carried out primarily by traditionally organized North Vietnamese military forces.

U.S. president Richard M. Nixon, taking office in 1969, implemented the policy of Vietnamization, whereby the war effort would be turned over gradually to the South Vietnamese. The final American fighting forces withdrew from Vietnam in late March, 1973, following a January 27 peace agreement. The South Vietnamese were given some breathing room by many American victories, including the decimation of the Viet Cong forces and the disruption of communist staging areas and transportation routes in Cambodia by means of a 1969 bombing (Operation Menu) and a 1970 invasion. Nonetheless, the fall of Saigon eventually occurred, on April 30, 1975.

Weapons, Uniforms, and Armor

The French army in the First Indochina War was highly mechanized and had the support of such artillery pieces as 105-millimeter howitzers, 75-millimeter recoilless rifles, and heavy mortars. Quad-50 machine guns, consisting of four .50-caliber machine guns mounted together, were capable of great destruction. France also had fighters, fighter-bombers, and bombers, but only about one hundred planes altogether. The Viet Minh began its military efforts against the French with a ragtag collection of arms given them by the United States during World War II or captured from the French. Land mines proved useful against the French, as they would later against the Americans.

As the Korean War (1950-1953) neared its end, arms and other equipment began to flow into North Vietnam from the Soviets and Chinese. Soviet heavy-duty Molotova trucks proved invaluable for transporting arms and supplies. The Soviet Union provided rifles, machine guns, and a variety of heavier weapons, including 120-millimeter mortars, recoilless cannons, and bazookas.

Effective additions to Viet Minh uniforms were two large wire-mesh disks, one over the helmet, the other hanging from the back. The wire mesh was filled with foliage to hide the troops from both aerial and ground observation.

In the Second Indochina War, or the Vietnam War, the most powerful aerial weapon for the United States was the Strategic Air Force B-52 Stratofortress bomber, modified to carry thirty tons of conventional bombs and with a range of 7,500 miles. Leading fighter-bombers were the Air Force F-105 Thunderchief and the Navy and Marine Corps A-4 Skyhawk. The top fighter plane was the F-4 Phantom, flown by the Air Force, Navy, and Marines. Napalm, a jellied gasoline, was widely employed by the United States and South Vietnam in aerial bombs. The South Vietnamese Air Force, trained and supplied by the U.S., flew F-5 Freedom Fighters and A-37 Dragonfly fighter-bombers.

The North Vietnamese essentially had no air force until the mid-1960's when China and the Soviet Union started supplying the North with MiG-15, MiG-17, MiG-19, and MiG-21 jet fighters.

The United States relied heavily on helicopters. The Huey utility helicopter (UH-1) was used to transport troops and supplies, evacuate wounded, and even attack the enemy when modified with heavy armaments. The primary attack helicopter was the AH-1 Cobra gunship, armed with a grenade launcher, machine guns, and rockets.

The U.S. Navy's Seventh Fleet deployed attack carrier strike forces consisting of carriers, cruisers, destroyers, and other vessels. American forces

*Vo Nguyen Giap, the chief
Viet Cong commander.*
(Library of Congress)

also had access to amphibious ships, swift inland boats to patrol rivers, and air-cushioned hovercraft (PACVs) and airboats for marshy areas.

U.S. artillery included 105-millimeter towed artillery, 105-millimeter and 155-millimeter self-propelled howitzers, 175-millimeter guns, and 8-inch howitzers. The portable, shoulder-fired M72 Light Antitank Weapon (LAW) was used by Americans and South Vietnamese against tanks and bunkers. North Vietnam began to use medium and heavy artillery in the South during the 1970's. Their artillery pieces ultimately included 76-millimeter, 85-millimeter, 100-millimeter, 122-millimeter, and 130-millimeter guns and howitzers.

Communist forces in the South had only machine guns and rifles to use against planes early in the war but near the end had Soviet SA-7 antiaircraft missiles and Soviet SA-2 surface-to-air missiles (SAMs), the latter able to reach 85,000 feet. Another SAM, the Soviet SA-7, could be shoulder-fired.

Americans switched in 1967 from the heavy M-14 rifle to the lighter and shorter M-16, which used a smaller, 5.56-millimeter cartridge and could be fired either one shot at a time or fully automatically. The United States also armed the South Vietnamese with the new rifle. The most effective sniper weapon was a carefully modified version of the M-14, the M-14 National

Match rifle (M-14NM) with the Limited War Laboratory's adjustable ranging telescope (ART), possessing a range of more than 1,000 yards. North Vietnamese and Viet Cong used the Soviet AK-47 rifle, which was similar to the M-16.

Less conventional weapons included mines and booby traps. The United States and its allies used the antipersonnel Claymore mine, which could be detonated at a distance by closing an electrical circuit, and also did extensive mining from the air. The Viet Cong made widespread use of booby traps, ranging from sharpened bamboo stakes called pungi stakes to a variety of mines including the Bouncing Betty, which would bounce into the air when triggered and explode around waist height.

Military uniforms of generally standard types were worn by the regular forces. Although Viet Cong are associated with the black pajamas and sandals they sometimes wore in combat, they often mingled during the day with other South Vietnamese, wearing no uniform or other clothing that would set them apart.

Despite the often inhospitable terrain, the United States and South Vietnamese troops used tanks throughout the war, including the diesel-powered M48A3 Patton tank and the M42 Duster tank. The North Vietnamese, beginning in 1968, utilized Soviet-made T-34, T-54, and T-59 medium tanks as well as PT-76 amphibious tanks.

The United States made wide use of armored personnel carriers (APCs), especially the M-113 APC. The APCs were often altered to carry weapons and other cargo as well as troops, and with the addition of gun shields, extra armor, and machine guns, served as attack vehicles.

Military Organization

Both the French and communist forces used traditional patterns of organization such as battalions, regiments, and divisions. However, Viet Minh general Vo Nguyen Giap gave his commanders considerable flexibility regarding strategy and tactics, thus permitting quick decision making. French control remained more centralized along World War II models to coordinate armor, infantry, airpower, and parachute drops.

During the Second Indochina War, or Vietnam War, American decision making was fragmented, split along various vectors that included the president of the United States as commander in chief, the secretary of defense, the joint chiefs of staff, and the commander in chief of the Pacific Command (CINCPAC), the latter stationed in Honolulu and responsible for prosecution of the war.

The United States/Vietnam-based command and control entity after 1962 was MACV (U.S. Military Assistance Command Vietnam). As a "subordinate unified command," MACV was required to seek approval from the Honolulu-based CINCPAC headquarters. Virtually all military control for the North Vietnamese was unified under Giap, who was a member of the ruling Politburo, minister of defense, and commander in chief of the armed forces. The United States divided South Vietnam into four tactical zones numbered, from north to south, I, II, III, and IV Corps. Air Force operations, except for Strategic Air Command B-52 actions, were carried out by the Seventh Air Force, with Naval operations conducted by the Seventh Fleet, both ultimately under CINCPAC.

The basic units of the U.S. Army were the squad, platoon, company, battalion, brigade, division, and corps, with minor differences in the Artillery and Marine Corps. Below the Seventh Air Force in Vietnam was the 834th Air Division, divided into wings, squadrons, and flights. A flight included about five aircraft. Marine and Naval air units were similarly organized.

The South Vietnamese Armed Forces were largely organized in the same manner as those of the United States but under the SVNAF Joint General Staff, which increasingly took direction from MACV. The South Vietnamese Regional Forces and Popular Forces, both civilian militias, also were under the Joint General Staff. The Civilian Irregular Defense Groups (CIDGs), primarily Montagnards, were trained and usually led by U.S. Army Special Forces.

The North Vietnamese and Viet Cong were organized generally along the same lines as the U.S. forces, starting with divisions but including regiments rather than brigades. The Viet Cong had a party secretary and various supply, social welfare, and propaganda units. After Tet, remaining Viet Cong were organized into cadres under North Vietnamese control.

Doctrine, Strategy, and Tactics

The primary doctrines that drove the First and Second Indochina Wars were colonialism, nationalism, communism, and democracy. At the conclusion of World War II, France sought to reestablish its colonial rule over Indochina. Ho Chi Minh, widely seen within his country and by the Americans as more of a nationalist than a communist, a perception the validity of which continues to be debated, sought to assert his vision of a unified and independent Vietnam. Ho's triumph over the French in 1954 removed one colonial ruler but failed to unite all of Vietnam.

The Second Indochina War, or the Vietnam War, achieved Ho's nationalist goal of unifying all of Vietnam, but as a communist nation. The United States throughout adopted the position of eschewing colonial domination while attempting to help South Vietnam secure permanent freedom as a democratic state, thus containing the spread of communism. These basic tenants led, affected by a variety of misconceptions, to the strategies and tactics adopted by the various warring parties.

The French tried to fight a war of attrition, believing they could wear down the Viet Minh. The French implemented this strategy by constructing hundreds of forts and pillboxes in northern Vietnam, which the Viet Minh simply went around whenever they chose. The French finally decided to adopt a more active strategy, which included cutting supply lines and luring the enemy into face-to-face battles. In the climactic manifestation of this policy, the French began in November, 1953, to establish a "mooring point" for French troops in a valley in northwestern Vietnam near the village of Dien Bien Phu. There the French established a defense perimeter, built two landing strips, and sent out patrols to cut supply lines to the enemy forces in Laos and engage the enemy in direct combat. Giap used Soviet-supplied trucks and large numbers of construction workers to enlarge a winding mountain road to permit transportation of heavy artillery into the surrounding mountains and began his assault on March 13, 1954. The battle, and effectively the war, ended on May 7.

The United States, during its Vietnam War, fused a war of attrition with both a limited war to contain communism and a misjudgment that the Viet Cong were engaged in an insurgency that could be opposed with counterinsurgency tactics. Because the United States never fully recognized that North Vietnam was the true enemy and that the Viet Cong were an arm of the North, its primary goals, which included supporting the South Vietnamese government and rooting out insurgent elements in the South, at best addressed only parts of the problem.

President Lyndon B. Johnson, given a free hand by the Gulf of Tonkin resolution (1964), began a steady buildup of American forces in Vietnam that numbered about 550,000 by 1968. The United States had thus abandoned its earlier advisory role and taken over primary direction and prosecution of the war.

To weaken the enemy's resolve, the United States bombed the North in a campaign called Operation Rolling Thunder that lasted from 1965 until 1968. The bombing stopped in 1968 to encourage peace discussions but resumed in 1972 to push the communists toward serious negotiations. The United States also steadily bombed the Ho Chi Minh Trail in fruitless efforts to halt infiltration of men and materials into the South.

Airpower never achieved the major goals the United States set for it, but it did help win many battles in the South with bombing and close support for ground operations. Helicopters proved extremely effective in transporting men and supplies and evacuating the wounded. In addition, the bombing of Cambodia in 1969 and 1970 bought time for the South Vietnamese armed forces to try to improve their war capabilities.

On the ground, American forces attempted to engage the enemy in direct combat operations, which first occurred in the fall of 1965 in the Ia Drang Valley. Like most such encounters, the short-term effect was a victory for the Americans.

Counterinsurgency tactics included such pacification efforts as educational, medical, and economic-development programs and search-and-destroy operations such as Cedar Falls (1967) and Junction City (1967) to deny the Viet Cong access to the countryside and its people. The hammer-and-anvil tactic caught Viet Cong between forces already in place (the anvil) and forces sweeping in from the sides (the hammer). These operations cleared the land for a time, but the Viet Cong inevitably moved back in.

As a guerrilla force, the Viet Cong used such tactics as mines and booby traps with deadly effectiveness. They dug elaborate tunnel complexes that served as supply depots, hiding areas for troops, even field hospitals.

The Tet Offensive of 1968 was the result of the change in strategy on the part of the North Vietnamese to a wider armed struggle. In cities, towns, and hamlets, North Vietnamese and Viet Cong launched attacks on January 31, during the Vietnamese Tet holiday. In all locations, the communist forces were ultimately driven back. Although the Viet Cong suffered massive losses and ceased to be a major player in the war, Americans were unaware of the magnitude of their defeat. Instead, seeing attacks all across South Vietnam convinced Americans that the war was going badly. In 1969 President Nixon instituted a new strategy called Vietnamization, which meant getting the United States out of the war and turning the fighting over to the South Vietnamese.

With a plan to capture as much territory as possible before a final peace agreement, the North Vietnamese army launched attacks against provincial and district capitals throughout much of South Vietnam in the spring of 1972. Like Tet, the offensive was a military defeat for the North but a psychological victory, demonstrating how dependent the South Vietnamese were on U.S. support.

By 1975 the North Vietnamese army had twice as many tanks as the South Vietnamese, and the more than 25,000 North Vietnamese troops in the Central Highlands were easily reinforced from the North. The U.S. failure to recognize North Vietnam as the central enemy had led to peace with the supply lines along the Ho Chi Minh Trail still functioning and the war production effort in the North unimpeded after 1973. The strategic definition of the war as counterinsurgency and the principle of containment, along with fear that movement of U.S. forces into the North might trigger a war between superpowers, meant there would be no invasion by U.S. forces. The United States had by neither force nor negotiation been able to drive the communists out of the South. The United States had the military might but not the strategy, and therefore not the tactics, to defeat the enemy.

With the expectation that the March, 1975, offensive would be both a prelude to a final triumph the following year and a test to see whether the United States would intervene, the North began its military push on March 11 with a victory at Ban Me Thuot in the Central Highlands. South Vietnamese president Nguyen Van Thieu decided to abandon the Central Highlands, and the North Vietnamese drove to the sea, cutting South Vietnam in half. The northern provinces fell, Thieu resigned on April 21, and on April 30, the new president, General Duong Van Minh surrendered.

Edward J. Rielly

The Peace Movement

While the U.S. government sought a military solution in Vietnam and mechanisms to contain dissent at home, the peace movement criticized U.S. domestic and foreign policies in social, political, and cultural terms.

The peace movement in the United States was influenced heavily by the Civil Rights movement of the early 1960's. Especially influential was the Student Nonviolent Coordinating Committee (SNCC), which worked to oppose racial segregation in the southern states. Students of all races who had been active in the Civil Rights movement through freedom rides, boycotts, and voter-registration projects learned to demonstrate their discontent through nonviolent protest.

Students for a Democratic Society (SDS) became one of the largest organizations associated with the peace movement during the late 1960's. In 1962, leaders of SDS drafted the Port Huron statement, which called for nonexclusion of socialist and communist groups and for participatory, grass-roots democracy. The rejection of "red-baiting" and promotion of democratic decision making and nonexclusion by SDS became hallmarks of the peace movement and were used to define a "New Left," which rejected dogma and the fragmentation of the "Old Left." The prominence of SDS dramatically increased as a result of its decision to protest the U.S. intervention in Vietnam by sponsoring the first national demonstration against the war in Washington, D.C., and by organizing teach-ins, at which people would hear the SDS perspective on Vietnam and U.S. policy. By June, 1969, however, SDS had become factionalized to the point that it dissolved.

Supporters of the Movement

Despite popular perceptions, the peace movement had a broader base than student organizations. Groups of African Americans protested U.S. involvement in Vietnam as well. Since the combat soldiers who were sent to Vietnam were disproportionately black, and since many blacks were upset at the federal government for not protecting their rights while it was using rhetoric that the United States was defending the rights of Vietnamese, many blacks (especially the youths involved with the SNCC) were strongly involved in the antiwar movement. Martin Luther King, Jr., became an active leader in the peace movement in 1967, stressing that the importance of his emphasis on promoting nonviolence in the Civil Rights movement paled when compared to the level of violence the United States was using in Vietnam.

Prominent Hollywood personalities also became involved with activities in support of the peace movement. In 1970 and 1971, actor Jane Fonda and other entertainers toured under the name "Free the Army Antiwar Troupe" in areas around U.S. military bases in order to encourage military personnel to protest U.S. policies. When Fonda visited Hanoi in 1972, she made numerous antiwar radio broadcasts to U.S. troops. Although Fonda had seen POWs, upon returning to the U.S. she did not defend them. In reaction to her trip and reports, leaders in Colorado and Maryland tried to ban Fonda from entering their states.

An intellectual wing, embodied in the Community of Concerned Asian Scholars (CCAS), became a large factor in the peace movement. Consisting of academics and graduate students who had been trained in various aspects of Asian studies, the CCAS broke from the larger academic community (particularly the Association for Asian Studies), which refused to take an official stand on the war. Seeing complicity in silence, CCAS members were determined to take responsibility for the results of their research. Once organized, the CCAS became a source for vital information on Vietnam for a movement (and a society) that had little understanding of the country or its people. Through books, lectures, periodicals, and conferences, the CCAS served as a counter to the governmental disinformation about Vietnam and U.S. policy.

Utilizing many different tactics, the peace movement was able to exert considerable influence on public opinion. Large marches became a major way in which the movement was able to show its strength and gain media attention. On April 24, 1971, one million protesters crowded Washington, D.C., in the largest demonstration in U.S. history. Parts of the movement also used direct action, especially targeting the draft. Youths burned their draft cards at the risk of imprisonment, and priests destroyed draft boards' records in symbolic protest. The use of teach-ins to spread information about Vietnam spread to college campuses across the United States. On October 15, 1969, millions of people participated in a day of moratorium by not working.

Government Response

The governmental response to the peace movement was multifaceted. Most visibly, the U.S. government, especially under President Richard Nixon, countered demonstrators with strong rhetoric, painting the demonstrators as unpatriotic radicals. This rhetoric sprang from the attitude that protesters were students who were self-indulgent and morally rudderless, allowing officials to discredit their actions. In addition to this criticism, the government instituted harsh policies against the peace movement. More than three thousand draft resisters were imprisoned for burning draft cards or tampering with draft records. Further, the Nixon administration established domestic espionage and infiltration programs, using both the Federal Bureau of Investigation (FBI) and the Central Intelligence Agency (CIA). The FBI and CIA systematically spied on and attempted to subvert activist organizations by planting agents. The information gathered or created was then used to blacklist antiwar activists and, in some instances, was used to bring charges against organizations, diverting their resources from opposing the war. A major target was the Committee of Concerned Asian Scholars. Evidence suggests that the agencies used provocateurs to participate in illegal activities, thereby entrapping activists.

Part of the Nixon administration's response to defuse public opinion was to open public negotiations and to implement "Vietnamization," which called for an increased reliance on Vietnamese troops and a reduction in the number of U.S. troops deployed in Vietnam. The chief proponent of Vietnamization, Melvin Laird, also recommended that the administration make the prisoners of war a public issue, breaking the silence on the issue that had prevailed during the Lyndon Johnson administration. The United States intended to use the POW issue "to bring world opinion to bear on the North Vietnamese" by charging that the Vietnamese had maltreated and tortured prisoners. In accordance with this goal, in 1969 and 1970 the United States brought up the issue with the International Red Cross and the United Nations. Finally, some prisoners who were released early were used to broadcast charges of maltreatment by their captors. Making the POWs a public issue in tandem with negotiations also allowed the administration to dismiss immediate withdrawal plans as unrealistic, since they did not resolve the issue of the POWs.

Critics of the administration's policy charged that the rhetoric used against the Vietnamese merely increased the value of the prisoners as hostages. Another charge of the peace movement was that the Nixon administration manipulated the issue of the prisoners to expand the war and to continue to keep U.S. forces in Vietnam.

Both sides in the war violated international standards for treatment of prisoners. The recounting of torture by U.S. prisoners, the early parading of prisoners as "war criminals" in Hanoi, and the lack of information given about the prisoners by the government of North Vietnam all were clear violations of international conventions. In South Vietnam, however, treatment was as harsh if not harsher. It was revealed that prisoners were kept in "tiger cages" on Con Son island. Guerrillas who were captured were classified as political dissidents, not prisoners of war (and thus were not protected by international conventions). Aside from the evidence of torture of prisoners, there was strong evidence showing that U.S. forces often killed prisoners in the battlefield in order to raise body-count figures.

On January 27, 1973, the Paris Agreement on Ending the War and Restoring Peace in Vietnam and a protocol on prisoners of war were signed by the United States, the Democratic Republic of Vietnam (North Vietnam), the Provisional Revolutionary Government of South Vietnam (National Liberation Front), and the Republic of Vietnam (South Vietnam). When the POWs were returned to the United States, the treatment they received was less than honorable. They were not allowed to speak freely for a period after their return, and when they were allowed to speak it was in controlled press conferences. Some prisoners who had made statements against the war while captives were charged with aiding the enemy. These charges were dismissed after one of the accused shot himself to death. Since there no longer existed any clear issue around which the peace movement could organize, the diverse groups had no reason to continue to work together and returned to separate domestic concerns.

Impact

The peace movement in the Vietnam era changed the way people in the United States thought about government and politics. Foremost among these changes was that a large segment of the population grew to distrust the federal government, especially the presidency. A direct result of this sentiment was the War Powers Act of 1973, which was intended to curb the power of the president to commit U.S. troops abroad.

For the first time since the founding of a bipartisan consensus on foreign policy after World War II, the public grew to challenge the assumptions that underlay U.S. policy. The congressional consensus broke down, resulting in the U.S. decision not to send troops to Angola. The change in perspective about the public's right to debate foreign policy also led to a larger segment active in challenging presidential and State Department decisions.

The methods of the peace movement in the Vietnam era permeated society to such an extent that the ideals of nonviolent resistance and grassroots organizing became mainstays of social movements. Not only did progressive organizations continue to use these protest tactics, but conservative organizations, notably antiabortion groups, also adopted similar strategies in pursuit of their goals.

Scholars who were blacklisted for their antiwar activities in the Vietnam era continued to feel the war's impact, as some still were unable to get jobs within the field of Asian studies. In large part, these scholars' input on governmental decisions was limited, as was their access to research and grant money. Their prolific output of information during the war changed the context of academic debate, however, and helped to encourage a strain of activist scholar.

The division in society did not end with the war but continued to manifest itself in various ways in the United States. Conflict continued over the issue of whether there were any living prisoners of war or soldiers missing in action (MIA) remaining in Indochina. In large part, however, the numbers of MIA included a significant number of people known to have been killed in action. Still, some organizations such as the National League of Families of American Prisoners and Missing In Southeast Asia continued to demand a full accounting of every MIA.

Strongly related to the issue of MIAs was the dispute over whether and when the United States should normalize relations with Vietnam. By the early 1990's, the United States was relaxing its trade embargo on Vietnam, and there were calls to normalize relations with the country. In January, 1994, the Senate approved a nonbinding resolution urging President Bill Clinton to lift the trade embargo completely, in the hope of persuading the Vietnamese government to provide a full accounting of Americans still listed as missing during the war. The president complied with the resolution, and U.S.-Vietnamese relations grew steadily warmer. In May, 1995, Vietnam began giving the United States documents on missing Americans. In July, President Clinton announced that relations with Vietnam would be normalized, and during the following month the first U.S. embassy was opened in Hanoi. High-level dignitaries of the two countries began exchanging visits, and President Clinton himself visited Hanoi with his family in November, 2000.

Richard C. Kagan
updated by the editors

Justice During the War

The war in Vietnam raised significant political and social justice issues, including the constitutional powers of the presidency, free speech, the composition of the armed forces, and the reintegration of veterans into society.

American involvement in the war in Vietnam was the result of Cold War politics. After World War II the United States supported its ally France in French attempts to regain former colonial possessions in Indochina. In 1954, when the French left Indochina after the siege at Dien Bien Phu, the Eisenhower administration gave full backing to a pro-American South Vietnamese dictatorship. Subsequent administrations increased American commitment in Vietnam.

The Powers of the Presidency

On August 7, 1964, Congress approved the so-called Gulf of Tonkin Resolution, the U.S. government's response to an alleged attack by North Vietnamese patrol boats on U.S. naval vessels in the Gulf of Tonkin, off the coast of North Vietnam. The resolution authorized President Lyndon B. Johnson to take "all necessary measures to repel any armed attacks against the forces of the United States and to prevent further aggression" and to "promote the maintenance of international peace and security in Southeast Asia."

Johnson used the resolution as a blank check to expand American involvement in the conflict. By essentially forfeiting its constitutional right to declare war, Congress had made it possible for Johnson and, later, Richard Nixon to expand the U.S. commitment of equipment and troops. In the spring of 1970, the Nixon administration went so far as to bomb two neutral countries, Cambodia and Laos, because the Viet Cong were transporting arms through both countries into South Vietnam and maintained supply bases within their borders. At that point, the Senate repealed the 1964 resolution. On January 27, 1973, the United States and North Vietnam signed a cease-fire agreement, mandating the withdrawal of all remaining U.S. troops within sixty days.

Reacting to the Vietnam experience, Congress passed the War Powers Act on November 7, 1973, which limited deployment of troops without notification of Congress to sixty days. The act was intended to define and circumscribe the powers of the president when acting as the commander in chief of the armed forces.

Opposition to the War

Demonstrations against the war began in earnest in 1965, along with the first burning of a draft card in protest of the war. Many of the early demonstrations against the war were organized by Students for a Democratic Society (SDS), and opponents of the war were generally dismissed as leftists and college radicals. As American involvement in Southeast Asia increased, however, opposition to the war drew wider and wider circles, until it involved people of all ages and walks of life. The war began to polarize American society. Riots occurred in Chicago in 1968 during the Democratic presidential convention; the rioting was later determined to have been provoked by the local police in a "police riot." Nevertheless, the U.S. Department of Justice leveled conspiracy charges against Rennie Davis, Dave Dellinger, Tom Hayden, Abbie Hoffman, Jerry Rubin, John Froines, Lee Weiner, and Bobby Seale, dubbed the "Chicago eight." (The "Chicago seven" trial did not include Bobby Seale, who was tried separately.)

Drawing on his fame as the author of Dr. Spock's Baby and Child Care, *Dr. Benjamin Spock (center front) led many demonstrations to protest American involvement in Vietnam and was frequently arrested. Here, he leads a march in New York City in April, 1965, at a time when the war was starting to be noticed by the average American.* (Library of Congress)

Particular events in the war, as they were reported in the press, fueled antiwar protests and increased the ranks of protesters. One such event was the March, 1968, massacre of civilians at the village of My Lai, which became public knowledge in the fall of 1969 when Lieutenant William Calley was charged with murdering more than a hundred Vietnamese civilians; photographs of the atrocity were printed in *Life* magazine. Another was the American bombing of Cambodia and Laos in 1970. In May, 1970, protests against the bombing were disrupting classes at Kent State University in Ohio, and Governor James Rhodes ordered the state's national guard to patrol the Kent State campus. On May 4, National Guardsmen opened fire, killing four students. In response to the Kent State deaths, five hundred college campuses and four million students across the nation went on strike.

The Draft

Conscription (the draft) and the Selective Service system were among the main targets of the war's opponents. The most attention-getting way to show opposition to the war and the draft was the burning of draft cards. Prosecution of draft card burners was inconsistent. While during the height of resistance hundreds of men burned their cards publicly, the Justice Department brought action against fewer than fifty draft card burners, and only forty were actually convicted. Many observers expected the courts to overturn those convictions. In the 1968 case *United States v. O'Brien*, however, the Supreme Court upheld the law against draft card burning even though the decision seemed to run counter to decisions in other freedom of speech cases.

Among opponents of the draft, conscientious objectors (COs) created the most sustained legal problems. The Selective Service system tended to treat conscientious objectors—individuals who are excused from combatant military service, traditionally for religious reasons—inconsistently, often failing to follow due process of law. Many COs were Jehovah's Witnesses, Quakers, Mennonites, and others whose religious beliefs included strict pacifism. As the war progressed and the death toll rose, interest in becoming a CO rose drastically. In the mid-1960's, the military approved fewer than 30 percent of the several hundred applications for CO status it received. By the late 1960's, CO applicants attempted to take advantage of existing case law pertaining to civilian COs. The military, however, continued to reject CO applications, overlooking precedents in the case law. In 1970, the Supreme Court ruled in *Welsh v. United States* and two other cases that its 1965 decision in *United States v. Seeger* applied to members of the military as well as civilians. The Supreme Court had ruled in *Seeger* that sincere pacifists were entitled to CO status even if their motivation had no foundation in religious beliefs. The courts further ruled that the military could not reject the CO application of a person who was already a member of the service unless the military could point to factual evidence in his or her military record to support the conclusion that the applicant did not have sincere motives. Soon the number of successful CO applications rose, and the military faced a growing number of lawsuits. In 1971 and 1972, two-thirds of CO applications were successful.

Whether draft evaders (as well as soldiers who went AWOL, or "absent without leave") should be prosecuted or given clemency became a growing debate as American involvement in the war came to an end. After 1973, when the United States signed a cease-fire agreement with North Vietnam, the call for clemency no longer fell on deaf ears. In 1974, President Gerald R. Ford created a President's Clemency Board. Considering the generally lenient treatment of draft offenders by then, the Ford program actually offered little improvement; only 2,600 people applied. Another 265,650 received pardons from President Jimmy Carter in 1977.

Military Service and Social Justice

The administration of the draft itself raised issues of social justice. Of 26,800,000 men of draft age, 15,980,000 never served. Of these, 15,410,000 were deferred, exempted, or disqualified. Of 570,000 draft offenders, 209,517 were accused; 197,750 cases were dropped, 3,250 people were imprisoned, and 5,500 received probation or a suspended sentence. Among those who escaped the draft were recipients of deferments (mostly student deferments), draft evaders, nonregistrants, and conscientious objectors. The fact that potential draftees could receive student deferments while attending college struck many observers as unfair, given that the young people likely to be in college were disproportionately white and middle- or upper-class.

For those who served, issues of social and racial justice played a significant role. Among the American forces stationed in Vietnam, fewer than 1 percent were ever needed for combat missions, but that 1 percent was most likely to consist of minorities from disadvantaged backgrounds. Front-line combat personnel were, on average, a cross section of American minorities. In addition, soldiers of low-income background were about twice as likely to serve in Vietnam and about twice as likely to end up in combat service than soldiers from high-income backgrounds.

Agent Orange

Many of the soldiers who went to Vietnam came home with new problems, such as drug dependencies and posttraumatic stress disorder

(PTSD). Those afflicted with PTSD had extraordinary difficulties reintegrating into civilian life. In addition, severe health problems were experienced by those soldiers who had been exposed to an herbicide called Agent Orange, which contained the highly toxic chemical dioxin. During the war, American planes sprayed nearly thirteen million gallons of Agent Orange. The herbicide created health problems for those with significant exposure to it, and it caused birth defects in their children.

The government, Dow Chemical (the principal supplier of Agent Orange), and other companies involved were aware of the possibly fatal consequences of exposure to dioxin but ignored or publicly denied them. The Veterans Administration downplayed the effects of Agent Orange and dismissed veterans' complaints for many years. Veterans had little legal recourse against the Veterans Administration, since federal law barred them from taking Veterans Administration benefit decisions to court.

In 1983, veterans and their families brought a class action suit. Long Island U.S. circuit court judge Jack Weinstein decided against Dow and a number of other makers of Agent Orange, forcing the companies to release crucial documents proving that Dow and others acted in full knowledge of the possible health consequences of the substance. In May, 1984, the involved parties reached a settlement which created a $184 million fund. Dow and the other companies involved appealed the case. In 1989, the U.S. Agent Orange Settlement Fund finally began distributing funds. On average, single lump-sum benefits ranged between $340 and $3,400. By 1993, about sixty-five thousand claims had been filed. By December 29, $22 million was left in the fund, and the claim deadline was extended from December 31, 1994, to January 17, 1995.

In February, 1994, events took another turn when the Supreme Court in *Ivy v. Diamond Shamrock* and *Hartman v. Diamond Shamrock* denied review of cases requesting reopening litigation by two groups of Vietnam veterans and their families. In both cases, the veterans had received benefits but in amounts considered insufficient. On the other hand, the Court has agreed to hear arguments by Hercules and William T. Thompson, two companies that made the herbicide, who were seeking $30 million in costs in relation to the 1984 class action suit. The companies claim that it was not their fault that the government used the defoliant in Vietnam, thereby exposing humans to the toxic chemical dioxin.

Thomas Winter

U.S. Supreme Court During the War

The Supreme Court's actions on Vietnam War-related cases established major precedents regarding the freedoms of speech, press, and religion and the powers of Congress and the president to conduct foreign and defense policies.

The Vietnam War's length and controversial nature raised various constitutional questions. Appeals to the Supreme Court included cases pertaining to the freedom of speech, the relationship between the free exercise clause and military conscription, freedom of the press, and the constitutionality of the U.S. military effort in Vietnam. In some cases, the Court established new precedents and in others, refused to accept a case, often citing the doctrine of political questions.

Freedom of Speech

The Court decisions about the Vietnam War that had the broadest, most long-term effects were those that pertained to the freedom of speech. During antiwar demonstrations obscenities and symbolic actions were sometimes used to communicate opposition to the Vietnam War. In *United States v. O'Brien* (1968), the Court, by a vote of seven to one, ruled against David O'Brien, who had been convicted of violating a federal conscript law by burning his draft card in a symbolic protest. O'Brien claimed that his conviction violated his freedom of speech. The majority opinion, written by Chief Justice Earl Warren, stated that Congress has broad constitutional powers to raise and maintain armed forces, including the process of conscription, which encompasses draft cards. More significantly, *O'Brien's* long-term impact was to place certain restrictions on the freedom of speech, especially when litigants claimed that their symbolic actions were protected by the freedom of speech.

One year later, however, the Court ruled in favor of high school and junior high school students who used symbolism to protest against the Vietnam War in *Tinker v. Des Moines Independent Community School District* (1969). The Tinker children and other students wore arm bands with peace symbols to silently protest the Vietnam War despite the fact that school officials had previously forbidden them to do so. These students were suspended unless they returned to school without the arm bands. The students asserted that this punishment and policy violated their freedom of speech. By a vote of seven to two, the Court ruled in favor of the protesting students. The Court stated that public school students retained their freedom of speech rights as long as their use of speech did not prove to be disruptive. Also, the majority opinion noted that school officials in this district had previously allowed other forms of symbolic political expressions, such as campaign buttons. Therefore, the disciplinary action against students wearing antiwar arm bands seemed to be directed against symbolic protest against the Vietnam War rather than against any student's use of any symbol of political speech.

What was somewhat surprising in the *Tinker* case was the dissenting opinion of Justice Hugo L. Black. Earlier in his career on the Court, Black was often identified as an absolutist in his support of the freedom of speech; that is, he took the view that government policies should not limit "balanced" speech, at least oral speech, in any way. In *Tinker*, however, Black asserted that symbolic actions such as this had less protection under the First Amendment and that school officials needed to have broad discretionary authority to prevent, prohibit, and punish expressions that they believed could be disruptive.

In *Cohen v. California* (1971), the Court had to address Paul Cohen's symbolic protest against the Vietnam War in general and the draft in particular, in which he printed the words "F—k the draft" on his jacket. The state of California convicted him for violating a state law prohibiting "disturbing the peace . . . by offensive conduct." The long-term significance of this decision was the definition of obscenity concerning First Amendment protection. The Court ruled in favor of Cohen, stating that Cohen's profanity was "vulgar" but not obscene because its purpose was to convey a political message. Asserting the value of political speech for constitutional protest,

Chief Justice Earl Warren.
(Supreme Court Historical Society)

the Court ruled that states cannot prohibit and punish such provocative speech and that such speech should not be perceived and punished as an incitement to possible future violent actions. The Court further expanded the freedom of speech-related antiwar expressions by ruling in *Flower v. United States* (1972) that the military could not prohibit antiwar activists from accessing military bases that are open to the public.

The Draft

Although the Court, with the prominent exception of the O'Brien decision, generally ruled in favor of expressions of antiwar opinions, it also expanded and diversified military draft exemptions based on the free exercise and establishment clauses of the First Amendment. Before the Vietnam War, the Court had generally deferred to and closely adhered to the few, limited, specific religious reasons why a person would be designated as a conscientious objector, and therefore, exempted from being drafted into the armed forces.

Although Congress had apparently intended conscientious objector exemptions to be primarily applied to members of pacifistic denominations, such as the Quaker and Amish churches, the Court ruled in *United States v. Seeger* (1965) and *Welsh v. United States* (1970) that agnostics who demonstrated a sincere, consistent philosophy of opposition to war should also be granted conscientious objector status. In its most famous Vietnam War-era draft case, the Court ruled in favor of the famous professional boxer Muhammad Ali, formerly known as Cassius Clay. Ali claimed that he should be exempt from the draft as a conscientious objector because of his Nation of Islam (Black Muslim) beliefs. In *Clay v. United States* (1971), the Court ruled in his favor.

After expanding and diversifying legitimate grounds for conscientious objector status, the Court further clarified, and then limited this expansion in *Gillette v. United States* (1971). In *Gillette*, the Court rejected the claim of conscientious objector status for a man who cited the Roman Catholic doctrine of the just-war theory, that is, that a Catholic should refuse to participate in unjust wars. Gillette asserted his belief that the Vietnam War was an unjust war. The Court concluded that Congress did not violate the establishment clause or Gillette's free exercise rights by refusing to allow draft-eligible men to choose which wars they would participate in according to their professed religious or philosophical beliefs.

Other Issues

The most significant Court decision about the relationship between the Vietnam War and freedom of speech was *New York Times Co. v. United States*

(1971), commonly known as the Pentagon Papers case. Daniel Ellsberg, an antiwar former employee of the Pentagon (the Department of Defense), provided several newspapers, including *The New York Times*, with copies of the documentary history of U.S. foreign and defense policy toward Vietnam. The administration of Richard M. Nixon tried to prevent the publication of the Pentagon Papers, but the Court allowed their publication. The Court concluded that the Nixon administration failed to prove that publishing such papers would endanger current or future national security.

Although the Court generally strengthened the protection of First Amendment freedoms in the cases related to the Vietnam War, it repeatedly refused to rule on the war's constitutionality. Although Congress had never declared war against North Vietnam, it did adopt the Gulf of Tonkin Resolution of 1964, a joint resolution that gave the president broad, discretionary power to conduct war in Southeast Asia. The Court refused to grant writs of certiorari and review the lower court cases of *Holtzman v. Schlesinger* (1973), *Orlando v. Laird* (1971), *Mora v. McNamara* (1967), and *Massachusetts v. Laird* (1970), all of which challenged the constitutionality of the Vietnam War.

Associate Justice William O. Douglas was the most emphatic, determined justice who wanted the Court to grant certiorari and rule on the constitutionality of the Vietnam War. He took the unusual action of writing an opinion criticizing the Court's denial of certiorari in *Massachusetts v. Laird*. However, most justices believed that the existence and conduct of the war were political questions, that is, specific policies and political issues that were not justiciable by the courts because they should be resolved within and between the other two branches of the national government.

The constitutional legacy of major Court decisions related to the Vietnam War is that they provided important, influential precedents for future cases, especially for freedom of speech cases that did not pertain to expressions of protest over foreign and defense policy. For example, the Court partially relied on the *O'Brien* precedent to uphold a public indecency and nudity law in *Barnes v. Glen Theatre* (1991). In *Barnes*, the majority opinion concluded that the *O'Brien* precedent for limiting First Amendment protection of expressive conduct justified state laws prohibiting entirely nude exotic dancing in bars, just as the Court had ruled in *Cohen* that Cohen's use of an expletive to criticize the Vietnam War era draft was not an incitement. According to the *Chaplinsky v. New Hampshire* (1942) "fighting words" precedent, the Court ruled in *Texas v. Johnson* (1989) that burning or desecrating the U.S. flag did not represent an incitement either.

Regarding the more specific issues of whether public or congressional acts of opposition to certain U.S. foreign policy decisions are unconstitutional, the Court has generally followed the Vietnam War-era practice of holding such disputes to be nonjusticiable political questions. In *Goldwater v. Carter* (1979), several members of Congress unsuccessfully challenged the constitutionality of President Jimmy Carter's decision to terminate a treaty with Taiwan without obtaining the advice or consent of the Senate.

Sean J. Savage

Women in the War

American military and civilian women served in a wide variety of primarily sex-specific roles during the Vietnam War and shared the same danger as male support personnel with whom they worked.

Between April, 1956, when the first U.S. Army nurses arrived in South Vietnam to train Vietnamese nurses, and April, 1975, when Americans fled South Vietnam as the North Vietnamese army rapidly advanced on the capital city of Saigon, an estimated 33,000 to 55,000 American civilian and military women served in a variety of roles in the war. There is no reliable count of these women because few organizations recorded personnel by sex. The Department of Defense does not even know exactly how many military women served. Most of the estimated 7,500 servicewomen in Vietnam were members of the Army, Air Force, or Navy nurse corps. Only 1,300 women in the line and staff corps of the armed forces (the non-medical components of the female military) served in Vietnam. Civilians account for the remainder of the 33,000 to 55,000 women.

Servicewomen

About 6,000 military nurses served in more than thirty hospitals throughout the country. Army nurses worked in field, surgical, and evacuation hospitals. Navy nurses staffed two hospital ships, the USS *Repose* and the USS *Sanctuary*, and naval hospitals in Danang and Saigon. Air Force nurses served at casualty staging facilities or evacuation hospitals and as flight nurses on evacuation flights. These women witnessed the worst of the war as they cared for a constant stream of badly injured young servicemen.

The thirteen hundred servicewomen of the line and staff included about seven hundred members of the Women's Army Corps (WAC), five hundred to six hundred Women in the Air Force (WAF), thirty-nine members of the Women's Reserve in the Marine Corps, and nine Women Accepted for Voluntary Emergency Service (WAVES). Members of the WAC, WAF, WAVES, and the Women's Reserve volunteered for the Vietnam War in far larger numbers than were accepted; cultural attitudes toward women kept a majority of them from serving. Military leaders expressed concern about the need to provide guards to protect women in Vietnam. Some women feared that deploying women to a war zone would detract from the feminine image that they wished to maintain. Therefore, servicewomen were requested for duty in Vietnam in a narrow range of sex-specific specialties.

These three U.S. Navy nurses in Saigon became the first American women to win purple heart medals for service in Vietnam in January, 1965. All three were wounded by an explosion in a Saigon hotel. (AP/Wide World Photos)

Civilians

Civilian women who served in the Vietnam War can be roughly divided into three groups: those who provided humanitarian aid to the Vietnamese people; those who provided recreation, entertainment, or social services to the troops; and those who provided secretarial and administrative support. A few groups of women—journalists, flight attendants, and wives who came to Vietnam with their husbands—do not fit neatly into any one of these categories.

Women provided humanitarian aid to the Vietnamese as part of what became known as "the other war in Vietnam," the battle to win the hearts and minds of the people. Aware that military force alone could not win the war, some sought to increase the quality of life for the Vietnamese people to help them resist communism. More than forty nonprofit voluntary organizations worked in Vietnam and cooperated with the United States Agency for International Development (USAID), which was sponsored by the State Department. Many of these organizations recruited women to work as doctors, nurses, teachers, social workers, and home economists in a vast number of projects. USAID and organizations such as Catholic Relief Services, the American Friends Service Committee, and International Voluntary Services helped the Vietnamese establish hospitals, orphanages, day care centers, recreation programs, rehabilitation centers, agricultural projects, refugee centers, and training programs of all kinds.

The American Red Cross, Army Special Services, and United Services Organization (USO) hired women to work as social workers, librarians, entertainers, and craft and recreation specialists. They recruited primarily young, single, college-educated women, though supervisors were often older and sometimes male. The Red Cross provided both social services and recreation programs through Service to Military Installations (SMI), Service to Military Hospitals (SMH), and Supplemental Recreation Activities Overseas (SRAO). SMI, which employed both men and women, received and delivered emergency messages for military personnel and provided emergency loans. SMH women worked as hospital case workers or recreation specialists. SRAO women (nicknamed "donut dollies" after the Red Cross women who served during World War II) provided recreation for able-bodied enlisted men through the club mobile program or at recreation centers. Recreation centers, found at most military bases and operated by SRAO, Army Special Services, or USO women, provided a place where soldiers could relax, listen to music, write letters, play pool, or talk to an American woman. Army Special Services also provided libraries and craft shops at many of the bases. USO-sponsored shows, often featuring female entertainers, regularly toured the military bases for a month or two at a time to entertain the troops.

Women in secretarial or administrative positions worked for the Department of Defense serving under the Army, Navy, or Air Force; for the State Department in the American Embassy or consulates, with United States Information Services, or Joint U.S. Public Affairs Office; or with the Central Intelligence Agency (CIA). They also worked for private companies under contract to the government. Some were well-seasoned civil service career women, while others were young women with little experience.

Risks and Aftermath

Although most men treated these women with respect, some men believed that the real reason for the presence of women in Vietnam was to provide sexual favors. This misperception led to sexual harassment, innuendoes, propositions, sexual assault, and rape. One young Red Cross woman was murdered by an American serviceman.

Most women who came to Vietnam expected to work "behind the lines" in areas of safety. In Vietnam, however, no area was impervious to rocket and mortar attacks, sniper fire, and terrorist bombings. Sixty-five American women are known to have died in Vietnam: eight military women, whose names are inscribed on the Vietnam Veterans Memorial, and fifty-seven civilian women.

Women came home to a nation bitterly divided by the war and experienced the same feelings of alienation as male veterans. No one could understand what they had seen and done, and no one wanted to hear about their experiences. Some women repressed their emotions, only to have them surface later as posttraumatic stress disorder. By the 1980's, some female veterans began to talk and search for others like themselves. Reunions and the dedication of the Vietnam Veterans Memorial and the Vietnam Women's Memorial began to unite many of the women who had for so long been silent and isolated. Talking about their experiences with others who had served in Vietnam began the process of healing.

Lenna H. Allred

Ethics of the War

The morality of U.S. participation in the Vietnam War was questioned by many at the time it occurred and has been questioned ever since. The war's greatest legacy has arguably come in the form of its effects upon U.S. foreign policy, U.S. self-perception, and the world's perception of the United States. It was as a direct result of the Vietnam War that both the moral purity of U.S. interests and the invincibility of the U.S. military came to be questioned on a significant scale, both at home and abroad.

The question of when a powerful nation should intervene militarily in the affairs of a small country is not susceptible to a simple answer. Failure to intervene can mean that a small country will be subjected to tyranny, anarchy, or even genocide. Yet a military intervention that is bloody and inconclusive can also wreak havoc on a small country; furthermore, sending troops into a combat situation abroad means that some people will be killed or wounded. The unsuccessful end of the costly and controversial American intervention in Vietnam by no means ensured that policymakers would be spared similar dilemmas in the future.

The United States had been involved in the affairs of Vietnam ever since that country was divided, in 1954, into a communist North and an anti-communist South. As long as the American military mission in South Vietnam was small-scale, it aroused little opposition in the United States. Between 1965 and 1968, however, the number of American combat troops in Vietnam rose from 50,000 to 500,000; the casualties suffered by the troops and the monthly draft calls soared; and the loud debate at home reached an unprecedented level.

Religious Opposition to the War and the Just War Tradition

Although at least one theologian, R. Paul Ramsey, did support the American military intervention in Vietnam, members of the clergy and theologians were conspicuous in the movement against such intervention. In 1966, the organization Clergy and Laymen Concerned About Vietnam was formed. Vocal opponents of the American war effort included the Protestant theologian Robert McAfee Brown; Yale University's Protestant chaplain, William Sloane Coffin; and two Roman Catholic priests, Daniel Berrigan and Philip Berrigan.

The just war tradition was first elaborated by the theologians of Christian Europe during the late Middle Ages. After centuries of indifference by peoples and governments, this tradition was revived by the Nuremberg Trials of 1946, which followed the defeat of Nazi Germany in World War II.

The just war tradition sets forth six criteria for determining whether a particular war is just. The war must be waged for a just cause; it must be waged as a last resort; the intent behind the war must be right; there must be a reasonable hope of success; the war must be waged by a legitimate, duly constituted authority; and the harm inflicted by the war must not be disproportionate to the good that one hopes to achieve. During the Vietnam War, America's clergy, theologians, and laypersons questioned whether American military intervention in Vietnam met all or even most of these criteria for a just war.

Opposition to the War

The U.S. Constitution, while making the president commander in chief of the armed forces, gives Congress the right to declare war. Yet the massive war effort in Vietnam, dissenters pointed out, had come about through presidential orders alone. The first substantial increase in troop levels in Vietnam had been announced on July 28, 1965, at a little-publicized presidential news conference. The dissenters did not have an airtight case, however: The Korean War (1950-1953) had also started without a congressional declaration.

The official justification for the war, given by presidents Lyndon Baines Johnson and Richard M. Nixon, was that the American military was in South Vietnam to repel aggression launched from communist North Vietnam. Defenders of the war viewed the conflict through an ideological lens, as an assault by international communism against those who loved freedom. The moral and material support that the world's major communist states, China and the Soviet Union, gave to North Vietnam was cited as evidence for this interpretation.

The opponents of the war, by contrast, stressed the facts that both sides of the conflict were ethnic Vietnamese and that Vietnam had been a single country until 1954. Dissenters viewed the United States as meddling in another country's civil war and thus committing aggression itself, rather than nobly defending a victim of unprovoked aggression; hence, the war did not meet the "just cause" criterion.

The dissenters' localized view of the Vietnam War led them to scorn the notion that defeating the communists in South Vietnam was necessary to protect the United States itself. The dissenters saw the Vietnamese communists as nationalist defenders of Vietnamese independence, not as the Southeast Asian arm of a worldwide conspiracy against American democracy. Hence, the war, dissenters believed, did not meet the "last resort" criterion.

Concerned about the Johnson administration's continued escalation of the war, the Senate held hearings on the war in March, 1968, and subjected Secretary of State Dean Rusk (right foreground) to a two-day cross-examination on live television. (Library of Congress)

War Crimes

Until the early 1970's, the spearhead of the communist assault on the South Vietnamese government was not the North Vietnamese Army, but the so-called National Liberation Front, or Viet Cong. The Viet Cong, drawn from communist sympathizers in the South, were not regular troops in uniform; instead, they were guerrillas who wore peasant clothing and blended in with the villagers after conducting hit-and-run raids against American or South Vietnamese troops.

It was nearly impossible for American troops to fight such an enemy without hurting some innocent civilians. The American military attacked villages from which sniper fire had come (one officer declared that he had had to destroy a village in order to save it) and decreed whole areas to be free-fire zones, where anybody who moved was assumed to be the enemy. The chemical Agent Orange was used to defoliate certain areas, in order to deprive the Viet Cong of food. Napalm, a burning jelly, was dropped on centers of enemy fire; inevitably, some children were hurt. In the My Lai massacre of March, 1968 (made public in 1969), all the people in a village were killed by American troops under the command of Lieutenant William Calley.

Such suffering led all dissenters to question whether the war met the "proportionality" criterion; some dissenters even condemned the war as genocidal. Defenders of the war effort pointed out that the Viet Cong also committed atrocities and that the perpetrators of My Lai were finally subjected to American military justice.

The Debate After the War's End

In April, 1975, the North Vietnamese, having signed a peace agreement with the United States in January, 1973, overran and conquered South Vietnam. As a result, the United States admitted, by airlift, a wave of refugees. Contrary to the fears of earlier American administrations, the loss of South Vietnam did not lead to a communist advance to Hawaii or even to the fall of all of eastern Asia; the only other Asian countries to become communist were Vietnam's neighbors, Laos and Cambodia. By 1979, however, the repressiveness of the communist regime led to another massive flight of refugees, this time by boat; ironically, at least a few of the new refugees were former Viet Cong. The results of defeat started a new debate in America.

In 1978, historian Guenter Lewy published a history of the Vietnam War, defending American intervention in that conflict; in 1982, magazine editor Norman Podhoretz did the same thing. Both looked back on the Vietnam War as a noble effort to defend a free people against communism; so also did the president of the United States during the 1980's, Ronald Reagan. Political philosopher Michael Walzer, in *Just and Unjust Wars* (1977), condemned the means used in the Vietnam War without thoroughly discussing the issue of the war's rationale. In 1985, former president Richard M. Nixon published *No More Vietnams* defending his administration's Vietnam policy. Podhoretz's view, that post-1975 communist repression provided a retrospective justification for the American war effort of 1965 to 1973, never won a great following among academics or the general public. By the end of the 1980's, as the Cold War ended, the question of the morality of the war was still controversial among historians and journalists.

Paul D. Mageli

Censorship During the War

The Vietnam War was the first large-scale military conflict closely covered on television; the relative absence of censorship controls was blamed by many for contributing to the failure of the U.S. military effort.

After the U.S. defeat in the Vietnam War, a debate arose over the role played by newspaper and television reporters in that war. Censorship of the media by the United States government was undoubtedly less strict than in some earlier wars. Whether this relative absence of censorship was responsible for the American defeat in Vietnam has, however, been hotly disputed.

Contrasts with World War II

Because World War II began with a formal declaration of war, an Office of Censorship was set up almost immediately after the Japanese bombing of Pearl Harbor in December, 1941. Censors had to approve what appeared concerning the war in print (including combat photographs) and in motion picture newsreels. The American public was spared revelations about bungling or atrocities by the American military, although incidents of both occurred. Government censorship was supplemented by journalists' self-censorship; war correspondents believed it was their patriotic duty to help build up homefront morale. In contrast, the Vietnam War was an undeclared war, in which large numbers of American combat troops did not see action until 1965. Unlike in World War II, there were no war-bond drives, featuring stars of the entertainment world, to arouse homefront enthusiasm for the war and hatred for the enemy; nor was there an Office of Censorship.

During World War II television was not yet a commercial medium; Americans learned about the war through newspapers, radio reports, and motion picture newsreels. Television news broadcasts, which were still in their infancy during the Korean War (1950-1953), had become, by the time of the escalation of the Vietnam War in 1965, the major source of information about the world for most Americans. The existence of communications satellites and regular jet transportation in the early 1960's made the transmission of news faster than it had been in World War II or the Korean War, thereby making any government efforts to manage the news vastly more complicated than it had been in those earlier wars.

Although a ban on journalists' accompanying airmen limited the coverage of the Vietnam air war, efforts by the United States and South Vietnamese governments to control news about the ground war were hampered by the guerrilla nature of much of the conflict, without clear front-lines, as were found in World War II. The military could sometimes keep bad news secret by denying reporters transportation to battlefields; but major battles could—as in 1968—erupt in unexpected places.

The contradictions of fighting a limited war made press self-censorship harder to maintain than in World War II, in which the aim had been the unconditional surrender of the enemy. During World War II journalistic self-censorship, and acceptance of official censorship, were encouraged by a national consensus that the war was necessary and just. The gradual breakdown of national consensus about the Vietnam War set media and government on the road to becoming adversaries rather than allies.

The Early Phase of the Vietnam War

The Geneva Peace Agreements of 1954, under which French colonial forces left Vietnam, divided the country into a communist north and a non-communist south. By the early 1960's South Vietnam was troubled by a communist guerrilla rebellion in the countryside. When the U.S. military buildup was first begun by President John F. Kennedy in late 1961, only several hundred American military advisers were in South Vietnam; by the end of Kennedy's presidency, there were twelve thousand such advisers.

In the spring of 1963, it became clear that the South Vietnamese government of Ngo Dinh Diem had a dangerously narrow base of popular support. On November 1, 1963, after five months of protests by Buddhists angered at what they saw as Diem's favoritism to his fellow Roman Catholics, Diem was overthrown and killed in a military coup. On November 22, 1963, President Kennedy was himself assassinated in Texas.

At first, the Vietnamese developments were overshadowed by other crises around the world, all seen by Americans as part of the Cold War between American democracy and Sino-Soviet communism. Although some American advisers were being killed and wounded in Vietnam in 1963, the relatively low American casualty figures and the fact that all the advisers were volunteers, rather than draftees, kept the Vietnam story from arousing controversy in the United States. Hence, the American media still had only a handful of representatives in South Vietnam. The wire services were represented, but only one newspaper, *The New York Times*. In 1963 there was still no full-time correspondent in Vietnam from any of the three major networks that then dominated television. Network evening newscasts were not even increased from fifteen to thirty minutes until September, 1963.

Meanwhile, three young reporters—Americans David Halberstam and Neil Sheehan and New Zealander Peter Arnett—ran into difficulty with the U.S. military mission in South Vietnam (which wished to minimize publicity for American efforts) because of their frank reporting. Frustrated by the bland optimism of the head of the U.S. military mission, these reporters sought information from lower-level American military advisers working in the field. In October, 1963, President Kennedy himself, unhappy about the pessimism in Halberstam's reporting, secretly—and unsuccessfully—urged *The New York Times* to recall him. Historians who have studied press-military relations for the 1961-1963 period can, however, detect no profound doubts among American reporters about the American goal of preserving a noncommunist South Vietnam.

However much frustration the American military mission caused them, American journalists faced much greater harassment from the South Vietnamese government during the Buddhist crisis of May-November, 1963. Relations became particularly bad after an American reporter photographed a Buddhist monk setting himself on fire in protest. At one point, Arnett was physically beaten by Vietnamese police. To outwit Diem's censors, American reporters sometimes persuaded American military or civilian officials traveling back to the United States to serve as couriers for their film stories.

The Period of Escalation

Following Kennedy's assassination, his successor, President Lyndon Baines Johnson, at first tried to keep the military mission at the level that he had inherited. In the summer of 1964, Johnson won a resolution of support from Congress (the Gulf of Tonkin resolution) after an incident at sea between the U.S. Navy and North Vietnamese forces. Following his election in 1964 to the presidency for a full term, Johnson widened and deepened American involvement, ordering the bombing of North Vietnam in February, 1965, and in July, 1965, for the first time, sending large numbers of American combat troops into South Vietnam. As American casualties and draft calls increased sharply, more and more television reporters were sent to cover Vietnam full-time for the three major television networks.

A controversy that erupted over a single television story in August, 1965, clearly demonstrated both the risks of iconoclastic reporting and the limited ability of the Johnson administration to censor reporters. A correspondent for the Columbia Broadcasting System (CBS) in South Vietnam, Canadian-born Morley Safer, produced a film piece with his own commentary, showing a detachment of American soldiers deliberately setting fire to the huts of a village from which enemy fire was supposed to have originated. After agonizing deliberation by Safer's CBS superior, news division chief Fred Friendly, the decision was made to broadcast the piece on the evening news. After it was aired, Press Secretary Arthur Sylvester wrote an angry letter to Friendly. President Johnson made an angry telephone call to Friendly's superior, CBS network president Frank Stanton, and angry telephone calls and letters poured in from viewers throughout the country. In the end, however, both Friendly and Stanton stood by Safer despite official pressure.

Further examples of dissenting journalism followed. In February, 1966, the voices of dissent from politicians were first heard when the television networks broadcast Arkansas senator J. William Fulbright's Foreign Relations Committee hearings on the war. During World War II no American journalist had reported from an enemy capital; hence, print journalist Harrison Salisbury was harshly criticized when, after returning from a trip to North Vietnam in December, 1966, he reported in *The New York Times* that—contrary to U.S. government statements—American bombing of the north had produced civilian casualties.

As late as 1967 CBS refused to broadcast in full a documentary film on North Vietnam that it had commissioned British journalist Felix Greene to make, when it realized that the film criticized American bombing. Throughout 1966 and 1967, many television reports from South Vietnam still expressed support for the American military effort and hostility toward the North Vietnamese and the Viet Cong.

Reporting on the Tet Offensive of January-March, 1968, in which the Viet Cong launched bold (and ultimately unsuccessful) assaults against South Vietnam's major cities, bred distrust for the press in military circles. Film coverage of the Tet offensive, which was often transmitted by satellite in unedited form, was particularly disturbing to the average American viewer. Especially shocking was a film showing South Vietnam's chief of police, Brigadier General Nguyen Ngoc Loan, shooting a captured Viet Cong insurgent in the head. In his report from the village of Ben Tre, Peter Arnett provided a catchy slogan for the American antiwar movement by simply relaying the conclusion of the American military commander, that American forces had had to destroy the village in order to save it. On February 27, 1968, Walter Cronkite, anchor of the CBS evening news broadcast, departed from his usual impartiality to urge the government to negotiate in good faith with the communist regime in North Vietnam. Shocked by the Tet offensive, Cronkite's defection, and setbacks in the primary elections President Johnson declared, on March 31, 1968, his decision not to run for re-election. Peace talks began in Paris, and Richard Nixon was elected president of the United States later that year.

The Last Years of the War

Under President Richard M. Nixon, the U.S. government tried gradually to shift the burden of fighting to the South Vietnamese. American casualties remained high, however, in 1969 and 1970. Nixon was able to hide enough information from the press so that the American entry into Cambodia in May, 1970, came as a surprise. Throughout his presidency, a markedly adversarial relationship prevailed between the administration and the media over Vietnam, one that contrasted strikingly with the government-media cooperation of the earliest phases of the conflict. There were reports in American newsmagazines of breakdowns of discipline in the American expeditionary force in Vietnam (nothing similar to that had ever been revealed in the newspapers during World War II); and in June, 1969, *Life* magazine put out a special issue listing—with photographs—all the American soldiers who had died in Vietnam in a single week.

President Nixon had his vice president, Spiro Agnew, publicly denounce the media, and also used threats to make the television networks more sympathetic to the administration's viewpoint. After being criticized by the White House for allowing a television news reporter to speak favorably about a North Vietnamese peace proposal, the networks ended the policy of allowing instant analysis by television newsmen in front of the camera.

Yet the growing division of opinion over Vietnam in Congress had, by the early 1970's, emboldened at least some journalists to risk displeasing the executive branch of the government. In June, 1971, the Nixon administration tried to prevent *The New York Times* from publishing the Pentagon Papers, U.S. government documents on the war's origins that had been stolen by Daniel Ellsberg, a Defense Department bureaucrat who had been involved in planning the war effort. The documents were embarrassing to American officials, but they endangered no American soldier's life; a Supreme Court decision guaranteed the people's right to see them in print.

As the number of American troops in Vietnam dwindled between 1971 and 1973, American media interest in the war also dwindled. American correspondents still in South Vietnam found themselves dealing less and less with American military censorship, and more and more with South Vietnamese government censorship. The Vietnam peace accords were signed in January, 1973. Nixon's resignation in August, 1974, in the wake of the Watergate scandal, ended all presidential attempts to pressure the media into supporting government policy on Vietnam. When Nixon's successor, Gerald Ford, asked for American aid to South Vietnam, a Congress mindful of popular war-weariness flatly rejected the idea. Coverage of the war ended after the North Vietnamese army overran South Vietnam in March-April, 1975.

Television Images and Public Opinion

Those who blamed the press for the U.S. defeat in Vietnam argued that excessively gory television coverage of the war so weakened popular support as to make defeat inevitable. Yet many scholars contend that the television coverage that critics of the medium remember most vividly—the burning of the village of Cam Ne and the police chief's killing of a captured Viet Cong—was atypical of the combat scenes presented on the evening news. Television news broadcasts tried to avoid showing the bodies of dead American soldiers. Most combat footage simply showed American soldiers trudging onward, with enemy fire merely a menacing sound in the distance. Television reporters who tried to get combat footage were handicapped by the elusive nature of guerrilla foes, and by the fact that much combat occurred at night, when it could not be filmed. The most bloody American atrocity, the My Lai massacre of March, 1968, was not captured on film by a television journalist; it was uncovered a year after it happened by a United States-based print journalist. Revulsion against the war, many scholars contend, was caused not by images on the television screen but by high American casualty levels sustained over a long period of time.

Legacy of the War

Although many scholars question whether any conceivable American strategy could have won the Vietnam War, the belief grew in some military and governmental circles that lack of press censorship had doomed the American effort in Vietnam to defeat. To prevent further such debacles, President Ronald Reagan decided that future military expeditions would be accompanied by tight controls over the press. Such strict censorship characterized the American expeditions in Grenada in 1983 (from which all newsmen were excluded) and Panama in 1989, and the Persian Gulf War of January-February, 1991.

Yet it is unlikely that strict censorship, by itself, assured victory. The more decisive role of air power in the Persian Gulf War, the complete absence of guerrilla warfare from that conflict, and Iraq's total diplomatic isolation may all be more important than censorship policy in explaining the difference between failure in Vietnam and success in the Persian Gulf.

Paul D. Mageli

Campaigns, Battles, and Other Events

August, 1964
Gulf of Tonkin Resolution

Date: August 7, 1964
Location: Washington, D.C.
Principal figures: *American*, President Lyndon B. Johnson (1908-1973); Senator J. William Fulbright (1905-1995)
Result: Facts concerning an incident in Vietnam's Gulf of Tonkin that was used to justify empowering the president of the United States to conduct warfare without Senate approval were suppressed by the U.S. government in order to rally popular support for the Vietnam War.

In early August of 1964, when U.S. forces in Vietnam still numbered only 25,000 troops, President Lyndon B. Johnson announced to the American public that two U.S. destroyers had been targets of unprovoked attacks by North Vietnamese torpedo ships. At the president's urging, Congress passed the Gulf of Tonkin Resolution on August 7, giving the president power to send U.S. troops into combat without asking Congress for a formal declaration of war. This resolution, in effect, contributed significantly to the subsequent escalation of the Vietnam War.

The American public was generally supportive of swift and decisive action. However, an inquiry conducted by Senator J. William Fulbright later raised serious doubts about the validity of Johnson's claims. Details of Johnson's account of what had transpired on August 2 and 4 conflicted with those of his own senior officials. When asked about the attacks, Secretary of Defense Robert McNamara often gave conflicting testimony, as did other military officials. Based on all testimony given at this inquiry, Fulbright concluded that the entire incident had been a "misrepresentation" of the facts and that conclusions based on military accounts and by the American press were suspect.

Initially, the American news media saw the incident and Johnson's reaction to the alleged attacks as a sign of American strength and decisiveness. In numerous press conferences reporters avoided asking hard and probing questions. The European press was more skeptical. For example, a Danish paper stated: "To create a pretext for an attack on Poland, Hitler ordered the Germans to put on Polish uniforms and attack a German guard. What the Americans did in Vietnam is not the same. But the story sounds doubtful."

Although historians have continued to debate what actually occurred in that August off of Vietnam's coast, most agree that the Johnson administration misled the public into thinking that American sovereignty had been attacked. The press, although it had not engaged in overt censorship, tacitly suppressed a more factual and detailed accounting of the incident by not following up on the numerous and varied inconsistencies in the accounts of the incident. The Gulf of Tonkin incident and its subsequent impact on international relations set a dangerous precedent; but perhaps the most damaging aspect of this affair was the blow it delivered to the public trust.

Michael Shaw Findlay

November, 1965
Battle of Ia Drang Valley

Date: November 14-16, 1965
Location: Principally landing zones X-Ray (fourteen miles southwest of Plei Me) and Albany (two miles northeast of X-Ray), Pleiku province, South Vietnam
Combatants: 450 Americans vs. 1,600 North Vietnamese at X-Ray; 450 Americans vs. about 1,000 North Vietnamese at Albany
Principal commanders: *American*, Lieutenant Colonel Harold G. Moore at X-Ray, Lieutenant Colonel Robert McDade at Albany; *North Vietnamese*, Lieutenant Colonel Nguyen Huu An
Result: American disruption of a planned North Vietnamese offensive.

In November, 1965, North Vietnamese forces gathered in the Ia Drang Valley in Pleiku province in the central highlands of South Vietnam with the intention of dividing the country in two. On November 14, 1965, Harold G. Moore's First Battalion, Seventh Cavalry, landed by helicopter at landing zone X-Ray, where the North Vietnamese were assembled, and was assaulted by portions of three North Vietnamese army regiments. Moore's troops fought against overwhelming odds for more than forty hours while U.S. air and artillery strikes closed to within fifty yards of U.S. positions.

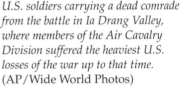

U.S. soldiers carrying a dead comrade from the battle in Ia Drang Valley, where members of the Air Cavalry Division suffered the heaviest U.S. losses of the war up to that time. (AP/Wide World Photos)

Gradually reinforced, Moore's men successfully fought off the final North Vietnamese attacks and were withdrawn on November 16, having lost 79 killed and 121 wounded. On November 17, Robert McDade's battalion was ambushed while marching to landing zone Albany, suffering 155 killed and 124 wounded. North Vietnamese combat deaths from both battles were estimated at 3,561.

The campaign decisively altered the Vietnam War. It convinced U.S. leaders to send more combat troops to Vietnam and to pursue a war of attrition and conclusively proved the combat potential of the helicopter. For the North Vietnamese, the campaign provided confidence they could defeat superior U.S. firepower by fighting at close quarters.

Lance Janda

January-April, 1968
Siege of Khe Sanh

Date: January 21-April 6, 1968
Location: Marine air base at Khe Sanh in northern province of South Vietnam
Combatants: 3,500 Marines and 2,100 South Vietnamese soldiers vs. 22,000 North Vietnamese troops
Principal commanders: *American*, General William Westmoreland (1914-); *North Vietnamese*, General Vo Nguyen Giap (1911-)

Result: Although U.S. firepower clearly overwhelmed the North Vietnamese, General Giap refused to admit defeat, claiming that the battle was a deliberate diversionary tactic.

As part of the Tet Offensive, in January, 1968, North Vietnamese troops directed by General Vo Nguyen Giap attacked the marine air base at Khe Sanh, scoring an early direct hit on the base's main ammunition dump, which detonated more than 1,500 tons of explosives. With little food and a precarious water supply, marines and other soldiers were besieged for seventy-seven days. The United States retaliated with massive round-the-clock air strikes, one of the most concentrated aerial bombardments in the history of warfare.

General William Westmoreland, seeking a decisive set-piece battle, placed the defense of Khe Sanh over all other military operations, with an estimated five tons of artillery and aerial munitions deployed for every North Vietnamese soldier. During the siege, 205 U.S. Marines and an estimated 10,000 to 15,000 North Vietnamese were killed in action. After the battle, Khe Sanh reverted to its previous status as a strategically unimportant site. Although the United States claimed victory, the siege at Khe Sanh brought about serious debate on U.S. military strategy in Vietnam. Soon after, General Westmoreland was relieved of his command.

Margaret Boe Birns

January-February, 1968
Tet Offensive

Date: January 30-February 25, 1968
Location: Throughout South Vietnam
Combatants: Communist guerrilla forces and North Vietnamese troops vs. South Vietnamese and U.S. troops
Principal commanders: *North Vietnamese*, Vo Nguyen Giap (1911-   ); *American*, General William Westmoreland (1914-   )
Result: A North Vietnamese military failure but a political and psychological victory for communist forces.

On January 30, 1968, the Viet Cong and North Vietnam army opened a new phase of the war by launching surprise attacks on most major cities and towns of South Vietnam. The campaign began at the start of Tet, the Vietnamese celebration of the new year in the lunar calendar. The United States had nearly 500,000 troops stationed in Vietnam, and the army of South

Vietnam was not entirely reliable. The Viet Cong guerrilla forces included about 200,000 fighters, and the North Vietnam army had some 100,000 troops in the south. The Americans enjoyed an overwhelming superiority in military technology and air power.

The leadership of North Vietnam began to prepare for the Tet Offensive in July, 1967. Defense Minister Vo Nguyen Giap's goal was to win the war quickly in one master stroke. Influenced by Chinese communist theory, Giap's doctrine of a "general offensive" assumed that a coordinated attack would be followed by a "general uprising" of the Vietnamese people. To surprise the enemy, the timing and objectives of the offensive were withheld from field commanders until the last possible moment.

The Offensive Begins

In the fall of 1967, Viet Cong and North Vietnamese forces began diverting U.S. forces from urban centers by initiating a series of random but bloody attacks in isolated border garrisons. In November, 1967, the 101st Airborne Division captured a communist document suggesting a general offensive, but U.S. intelligence analysts dismissed it as unrealistic. During the Christmas, 1967, cease-fire, the communists started moving their forces into position. Beginning on January 21, 1968, they attacked the marine outpost in Khe Sanh near the demilitarized zone, successfully deceiving most U.S. leaders into expecting a concentrated attack on Khe Sanh. However, one commander, Lieutenant General Frederick Weyand, expecting a possible attack around Saigon, convinced General William Westmoreland to increase the combat battalions in the region from fourteen to twenty-seven.

The massive offensive was actually scheduled to start on January 31. Confused by the new lunar calendar of North Vietnam, however, commanders in the center of South Vietnam began their campaigns twenty-four hours too early, attacking Da Nang, Pleiku, and nine other central cities. As a result, U.S. forces went on alert, minimizing the element of surprise.

On January 31, Viet Cong and North Vietnamese forces attacked 36 of the provincial capitals, 64 of the 245 district capitals, and 5 of the 6 autonomous cities. Initially, the attackers were able to occupy several cities, including much of Saigon. A Viet Cong suicide squad even managed to penetrate the U.S. Embassy compound before they were finally killed by Marine guards. Most cities were retaken within a few days, although the Saigon region was not cleared of Viet Cong guerrillas until March 7.

The communists' greatest success was in the imperial city of Hue. After the North Vietnamese conquered Hue, they executed an estimated 3,000 residents accused of collaboration with the enemy. The U.S. military subjected the city, including its huge citadel, to sustained bombardment. An

U.S. Marines hold a position overlooking a street in Hue during the Tet Offensive in February, 1968. (AP/Wide World Photos)

estimated 10,000 soldiers and civilians died in the battle for Hue. By February 25, U.S. and South Vietnamese forces had regained control of the city.

By the end of the Tet Offensive, more than 58,000 Viet Cong and North Vietnamese troops were dead, with the Americans suffering 3,895 deaths and the South Vietnamese army losing 4,957. Also, some 14,300 South Vietnamese non-combatants died in the fighting.

Significance

The Vietnamese communists suffered a military defeat, and the Viet Cong was destroyed as an effective organization. The Tet Offensive, nevertheless, convinced the majority of the American public that the war in Vietnam could not be won easily or quickly—a perception that greatly encouraged the antiwar movement. Shortly thereafter, President Lyndon B. Johnson refused to agree to General Westmoreland's request for an additional 200,000 soldiers, and on March 31, Johnson announced a halt to the bombing combined with efforts to negotiate a peace settlement.

Thomas T. Lewis

January-February, 1968
Battle of Hue

Date: January 31-February 25, 1968
Location: Hue, Vietnam

Combatants: North Vietnamese and Viet Cong vs. Americans and South Vietnamese
Principal commanders: *South Vietnamese*, Brigadier General Ngo Quang Troung (1929-   )
Result: The battle signaled the beginning of the end of U.S. involvement in the Vietnam War.

On January 31, 1968, the battle for Hue begin with a fierce bombardment and military assault by North Vietnamese army regulars (NVA) of the Fourth and Sixth Regiments and Viet Cong. Hue was overrun in the first hours, except for the U.S. Military Assistance Command, Vietnam (MACV) Advisory compound in southern Hue and the Army of the Republic of Vietnam (ARVN) First Division headquarters in the northern sector of the Citadel. Brigadier General Ngo Quang Troung, the respected commander of the First Division, quickly gave orders for major elements of the division, as well as other U.S./ARVN forces, to converge on Hue.

In the next few days, major U.S. and ARVN military forces fought their way into Hue to reinforce the tottering defenses of the northern sector of the Citadel and the MACV compound, as well as to prepare for military counterattacks. In the days that followed, the allied bombardment of the Citadel and U.S. marine and ARVN airborne attacks slowly began to dislodge North Vietnamese forces from the Citadel. On February 25, the Citadel and Hue was finally secured, and NVA and Viet Cong forces in areas surrounding Hue were defeated. The Battle of Hue indicated North Vietnam's psychological willingness to endure huge military losses to win the war.

Michael J. Siler

March, 1968
My Lai Massacre

Date: March 16, 1968
Location: My Lai Village, South Vietnam
Principal figures: William L. Calley (1943-   ), Frank A. Barker (1928-1968), Steven K. Brooks (1942?-1968), Ernest Medina (1936-   ), William R. Peers (1914-1984), Hugh Thompson (1947?-   ), Samuel W. Koster (1919-   )
Result: Lieutenant William L. Calley was convicted of murdering twenty-two Vietnamese civilians and was the only person convicted of any crime in the aftermath of the My Lai massacre.

The My Lai massacre occurred during the first hours of a March 16, 1968, operation carried out by a battalion-sized unit, code-named Task Force Barker, of the Americal Division of the U.S. Army. This unit, comprising three infantry companies (A, B, and C) supported by artillery, helicopters, and coastal patrol craft, was intended to sweep between two hundred and four hundred Viet Cong from a group of hamlets in the Son My subdistrict of Quang Ngai Province in South Vietnam.

Following the surprise Tet offensive launched by the Viet Cong on January 31, American commanders sought to reestablish control and to destroy known Viet Cong units. The Americal Division, including Task Force Barker, had been searching around Quang Ngai in February and March but encountered few Viet Cong.

On March 15, Lieutenant Colonel Frank A. Barker announced a three-day sweep against the Viet Cong 48th Local Forces battalion operating in and around a large, coastal fishing village. This was the third such operation against this village since February. Barker planned to move his three infantry companies into place by helicopter about 8:00 A.M., following a short artillery barrage. Helicopters were to engage fleeing or fighting Viet Cong. Offshore, small Navy patrol craft blocked any escape through the eastern seaward end of the noose.

Company C landed at 7:30 A.M., just west of another hamlet, My Lai. Lieutenant William L. Calley's platoon of twenty-five men moved first through the hamlet's south section; Lieutenant Stephen Brooks's platoon went through the north. Lieutenant Larry LaCroix's platoon remained in reserve near the landing zone.

The men of Company C expected to encounter two armed Viet Cong companies. Captain Ernest Medina, commander of Company C, had instructed his officers to burn the houses and destroy the livestock, crops, and foodstuffs in My Lai. Several men from Company C later testified that Captain Medina, who stayed at the landing zone, had specifically instructed them to kill civilians found in the hamlets. Medina denied such statements.

Calley's platoon slaughtered two large groups of villagers sometime between 7:50 A.M. and 9:15 A.M. In one instance, more than twenty people were gunned down on a pathway; in another, around 150 were systematically slaughtered with machine gun and small-arms fire in a ditch about one hundred meters east of the hamlet. Soldiers later testified that Calley ordered them to kill their civilian captives. Men from all three platoons of Company C committed murder, rape, and other atrocities that morning.

About 8:30 A.M. Brooks's platoon turned northward on Medina's command to recover the bodies of two Viet Cong killed by a helicopter gunship. Brooks's platoon then entered Binh Tay, a hamlet a few hundred meters away, where they raped and murdered villagers before rejoining Company C around 10:00 A.M.

While this killing was going on, Warrant Officer Hugh Thompson, an experienced combat helicopter pilot, was flying close overhead in an armed observation craft. At various times from 8:00 A.M. to 10:00 A.M., Thompson attempted to aid wounded South Vietnamese civilians in the fields around My Lai, saw Medina kill a wounded Vietnamese woman in a field, and landed his craft near the ditch where so many defenseless people were shot. He urged members of Company C to stop the killing, but killings resumed after he left. Around 10:00 A.M. he landed again to protect a group of women and children who were being herded toward a bunker by men of Company C. Thompson called in one of his gunships to evacuate some of the wounded civilians and then landed his own small helicopter to save one slightly wounded child from the heaps of bodies. In addition to his combat radio transmissions, Thompson made reports upon his return to base to his commander about the slaughter.

Cover-up

The truth of these events was covered up within the Americal Division for a year, until a letter from a Vietnam veteran, Ronald Ridenhour, to Secretary of Defense Melvin Laird in late March, 1969, claimed "something very black indeed" had occurred at My Lai. Laird ordered an investigation. In September, 1969, William Calley was charged with murdering more than one hundred civilians at My Lai. The full dimensions of the massacre became public knowledge in mid-November, 1969, when newspapers carried Seymour Hersh's interviews with men from Company C, the CBS Evening News broadcast other interviews, and photographs of the massacred victims were printed in *Life* magazine.

Lieutenant General William R. Peers was assigned responsibility for conducting the official investigation of the incident. He learned that Hugh Thompson's accusations of a civilian massacre, as well as reports by South Vietnamese officials of more than five hundred civilian deaths, were never properly investigated. Peers's report of March, 1970, contained detailed findings about what happened at My Lai and a recommendation that thirty individuals be held for possible charges.

War Crimes Charges

The Army preferred charges against a total of twenty-five men: twelve for war crimes and thirteen for other military offenses. Four of the five men eventually tried on war crime charges were members of Company C. The fifth was Captain Eugene Kotouc, the staff intelligence officer of Task Force Barker. He was acquitted of torturing a prisoner. There was no evidence of any misdeeds by men from Company A, but Company B had been involved in killings of civilians at the hamlet of My Khe. Captain Earl Michles, in command of Company B, was killed in the same helicopter crash that killed Lieutenant Colonel Barker in June, 1968, so both of those men were beyond the reach of the law. Charges against Lieutenant Willingham of Company B were dismissed in 1970, in spite of evidence of between thirty-eight and ninety civilian deaths caused by his men in My Khe on the morning of March 16.

Charges were brought in 1970 against thirteen officers in the Americal Division for various military offenses that were less than war crimes and did not involve murder or attempted murder. Charges were dismissed against several of the officers, and several had their cases resolved in other manners. Only four men were tried for the war crimes of murdering civilians, all were members of Company C: Captain Medina, the company commander; Lieutenant Calley, in command of one of the company's platoons; Staff Sergeant David Mitchell, a squad leader in Calley's platoon; and Staff Sergeant Charles E. Hutto, a squad leader from Brooks's platoon. Lieutenant Brooks was killed in combat after the incident and so was not charged.

Initially, seven enlisted men from Company C had been charged by the Army with crimes including murder, rape, and assault. Charges against five were dropped and two men were tried.

Courts-Martial

The first court-martial resulting from My Lai was that of David Mitchell, a career soldier; it began in October, 1970, at Fort Hood, Texas. Mitchell was acquitted of all charges. While Calley's trial was still in session, Charles Hutto was tried at Fort McPherson, Georgia, and found innocent. Medina's trial took place at Fort McPherson in August and September, 1971, after Calley's March, 1971, conviction. Medina was found not guilty of murder and assault.

Calley's trial was the most prominent of all the courts-martial. He had been identified from the start as ordering the shooting of women and children and was tried under article 118 of the Uniform Code of Military Justice for premeditated murder of more than one hundred Vietnamese. The trial at Fort Benning, Georgia, lasted about four months. On March 29, 1971, Calley was found guilty of three counts of murder by a panel of six officers. He was sentenced "to be confined at hard labor for the rest of [his] natural life; to be dismissed from the service; to forfeit all pay and allowances." Two days later, President Richard M. Nixon ordered Calley released from the stockade and returned to his quarters to serve his sentence. In August, 1971, the Army reduced Calley's sentence to twenty years, and in April, 1974, further reduced it to ten years. In the Army, prisoners become eligible for parole after one-third of their sentence is served. With Calley's punishment reduced to ten years, he became eligible in the fall of 1974 and parole was granted in November.

Impact

The reactions both to the My Lai massacre and to Lieutenant Calley's conviction cover a tremendous range. Most Americans and many people around the world expressed horror and distress at the massacre itself; yet a great many considered Lieutenant Calley to be a scapegoat. To some, it was not Lieutenant Calley or the others who were tried in courts-martial, but the United States that was on trial for its Vietnam war.

The outcome of the courts-martial reveals that no one—not the Army, the president, Congress, or the American public—relished punishing American fighting men for their conduct in Vietnam. The Army backed away from a joint trial of the accused and did not carry through the stern spirit of justice that pervades the official Peers Report.

American official and popular statements from the time typically express outrage toward the massacre itself but suggest that it would be best to reserve judgment about Calley's or others' guilt. Some veterans and Army members believed that Calley was being punished for one of the inevitable tragedies of war. Still others believed Calley had done only what

Ruined remains of My Lai in late 1969, one and one-half years after the massacre. (AP/ Wide World Photos)

the army had trained him to do: kill communists. Many believed, in contrast, that since the United States was fighting to protect Vietnam from communism, the Army should be saving, or at least protecting, Vietnamese civilians.

Immediately following Calley's conviction for murder, the White House and Congress received a strong wave of popular sympathy for him. It was believed that Calley's conviction condemned, by implication, all Americans who had fought in Vietnam. Others believed that what occurred at My Lai were war crimes and that Calley, and others, should have been punished by death in the same way that German and Japanese war criminals were following World War II.

Beneath these opposing emotional calls for Calley's release or execution, the My Lai massacre and the subsequent courts-martial had a profound impact on the United States and the Army. Knowledge of the massacre came twenty-one months after the Tet Offensive, but it was additional confirmation that hopes for an American victory in Vietnam were unfounded. If U.S. troops were slaughtering the South Vietnamese, how could the people ever be won over to the side of the United States?

People also wondered if My Lai was only the first of many such massacres that would come to light. In fact, evidence of thousands of unnecessary and unwarranted deaths of South Vietnamese civilians caused by U.S. and other allied units have been documented, but nothing quite so horrible as that at My Lai.

Reconsiderations of the War

Simply because of the questions raised about possible American atrocities in Vietnam, the whole discussion of the war itself took on a new color. The massacre gave proof to those antiwar protestors who called the war immoral and unjust. The atrocity marked an end, or at least a profound shock, to trust in American goodness and nobility of purpose.

During the 1970's, evidence of various hidden schemes and deadly plans by the U.S. government came to light, many of them completely unconnected with My Lai. The My Lai massacre remains a key incident that loosed the tide of self-doubt and questioning about the American purpose and moral stature that marked much of national life in the 1970's and 1980's. One of the most profound and lasting impacts of the My Lai massacre and the Calley court-martial was the coldness and distaste Vietnam veterans encountered after 1969 upon return to the United States. Many Americans treated all veterans as if they had joined with Company C to abuse and murder Vietnamese women and children. For those remaining in the military service, the vision of a unit running amok killing civilians in

Vietnam's guerrilla war was one of several powerful forces that led to major reforms in Army military doctrine and the abandonment of the draft in favor of an all-volunteer armed services.

David D. Buck

April-June, 1970
Cambodia Invasion

Date: April 29-June, 1970
Location: Cambodia, adjacent to the border with Vietnam
Principal figures: *American*, Creighton Williams Abrams, Jr. (1914-1975), Henry Kissinger (1923-   ), Richard M. Nixon (1913-1994); *Cambodian*, Lon Nol (1913-1985), Norodom Sihanouk (1922-   )
Result: An abortive effort to hasten the end of U.S. involvement in Vietnam plunged Cambodia into two decades of civil war.

In 1968, when Richard M. Nixon was voted into office, partly on the strength of his promise to bring peace to Vietnam, Cambodia was at peace. Its ruler, Prince Norodom Sihanouk, had successfully maneuvered to keep his country separate from the Vietnam War by allowing the North Vietnamese to use border provinces both as sanctuaries and to channel supplies destined for South Vietnam through Cambodian territory. For Sihanouk, the decision to aid the Vietnamese communists in this manner was one of expediency rather than sympathy. In his eyes, the choices were few; he must either help the communists or accept "American imperialism."

According to the Nixon doctrine, in the future the United States would provide material support to troops of countries resisting communist aggression but refrain from sending U.S. personnel to the battlefield. The key to Nixon's plan for ending the war was "Vietnamization," a program calling for the gradual extrication of U.S. troops and their replacement by Vietnamese. In essence, it was a solution to the U.S. problem of disengaging from the war rather than a solution to the war. In the same way, the prospect of invading Cambodia was viewed only as a means to ease disengagement. That it would actually widen the war and introduce a previously neutral country to the conflict were possibilities that remained secondary considerations.

In April, 1964, U.S. planes, flying from bases in Thailand, strafed two Cambodian villages. Sihanouk soon severed diplomatic relations with the United States. Subsequent border forays by the South Vietnamese army into Cambodia, coordinated with U.S. military advisers, also had little effect on stopping the flow of support from North Vietnam to South Vietnam.

Background

The U.S. military leadership had, for some time, sought permission to invade Cambodia. President Nixon's immediate predecessor, Lyndon B. Johnson, had rejected several requests on the grounds that the impact of such an invasion on the course of the war would be negligible. In February of 1969, however, less than a month after Nixon assumed office, General Creighton W. Abrams, commander of U.S. forces in Vietnam, requested that B-52 bombers be used against sanctuaries and supply routes. Nixon, in concurrence with his national security adviser, Henry A. Kissinger, agreed, and in March, 1969, the bombing of Cambodia began. As the U.S. Constitution specifically holds that only Congress can decide to wage war, this act to widen the war almost certainly was illegal. To prevent the issue of legality from arising, however, Nixon ordered that the bombing be kept secret. To prevent a news leak, he even bypassed the ordinary military chain of command, failing to notify the Pentagon. The domestic outcry over the bombing forced him to order a halt. In this manner, without the knowledge of Congress or the American people, Cambodia was introduced to the war one year prior to the U.S. invasion.

Although the bombing in itself achieved limited success in interdicting North Vietnamese supply routes and storage areas, it killed more Cambodians than North Vietnamese, had a significant impact on the Cambodian political situation, and was primarily responsible for initiating a series of events that would impact Cambodia's future for years. First, it pushed the communists out of the border sanctuary areas and deeper into Cambodia. This irritated rightist elements in Sihanouk's government who, already dissatisfied with his permissiveness in allowing Vietnamese communists access to Cambodian territory, became even more so as they witnessed the communists usurp still more. Sihanouk, aware of the discord, took measures to allay it. He reopened diplomatic relations with the United States. He informed Washington that he would not object to some attacks on Vietnamese sanctuaries inside Cambodia, but he never agreed to indiscriminate bombing. By not protesting the B-52 raids, which he strongly opposed, he felt he was making a significant concession to these same rightist elements who supported them. Fearing eventual annexation by Vietnam, rightist General Lon Nol, Cambodian armed forces commander, ordered all Vietnamese to leave the country, and anti-Vietnamese demonstrations were organized in Phnom Penh and the provinces along the Vietnamese border.

In March, 1970, as tensions continued to mount within his government, Sihanouk departed from Phnom Penh on a diplomatic mission to Moscow and Peking. Again, motivated by the need to settle the unrest among his ministers, he intended to urge both governments to restrain the North Vietnamese from encroaching further into Cambodian territory. However, he had failed to assess accurately how far the crisis in his capital had actually advanced. While still in Moscow, he learned he had been deposed by his pro-U.S. defense minister, Lon Nol. Although there is no evidence that the United States or any other foreign power promoted the coup, it precipitated crucial policy changes on both sides of the Vietnam War. The struggling Cambodian communist movement Khmer Rouge, which previously had been judged by Hanoi to be too small to be effective, was suddenly thrust by Sihanouk's downfall into a position from which it could make a serious attempt at gaining power. As a result, Vietnamese assistance increased dramatically, and the Khmer Rouge received the support it needed eventually to achieve power. For those among the U.S. leadership who supported an invasion plan, Sihanouk's downfall was a fortuitous event, since he alone among Cambodia's leaders had remained strongly opposed. With his removal, all Cambodian government opposition to an invasion attempt ended.

The Invasion

On April 29-30, 1970, an invasion was mounted with thirty thousand U.S. and South Vietnamese troops crossing into Cambodia. Secrecy had so pervaded the operation's planning that no one in Cambodia, including the United States mission and Lon Nol, learned of it until after it occurred. Although Nixon spoke of the invasion as a decisive victory, the military regarded it as having attained a temporary advantage at best. While uncovering enormous stores of supplies, it encountered few enemy troops. In effect, military planners had failed to take into account the communists' move westward under the impact of the bombing. Thus, while temporarily disrupting the communists' logistics, the invasion made little impact on their long-term conduct of the war. Pentagon estimates suggested that North Vietnamese plans for an offensive had been set back by no more than a year; in keeping with this assessment, the North Vietnamese, within two months of the withdrawal of United States invasion forces, had reestablished their supply trails and sanctuaries.

Within the United States, the effect of the invasion was devastating. The antiwar movement reacted with intensified demonstrations and student strikes. The deaths of four students at Kent State University as the result of a confrontation between National Guardsmen and protesters shocked the nation. The extent of the reaction engendered by the invasion surprised President Nixon. Although he defended his action to the American people, his arguments appeared flimsy and misrepresentative. Claiming that the United States had for five years respected Cambodian neutrality, he neglected to mention the bombing. Declaring that the invasion was intended to destroy the headquarters for the entire communist military operation in South Vietnam, he ignored overwhelming evidence offered by the military proving that no such target existed. Depicting the invasion as a necessary step taken against the North Vietnamese to preclude the possibility of attacks on U.S. troops withdrawing from the war, he hid the fact that during the course of negotiations for peace, the North Vietnamese had already offered to refrain from such attacks once a withdrawal date was determined. Finally, asserting that his decision was crucial to the maintenance of U.S. prestige abroad, Nixon contradicted evidence indicating a substantial fall in U.S. prestige following the invasion. Both internationally and domestically, the feeling prevailed that the president had succeeded only in expanding an already wearisome war.

Impact

For Cambodia, the invasion completed the destruction of a tenuous neutrality already severely damaged for more than a year by the bombing campaign. It precipitated an internal war that had not existed before U.S. forces crossed the border and that subsequently enveloped Cambodia in a prolonged conflict between United States-supported anti-communist forces and Vietnam-supported Khmer Rouge insurgents, thereby subjecting the country to still further devastation and eventual communist rule.

In this way, the fate of Cambodia was decided. U.S. policymakers, interested only in exploiting Cambodia's territory as an adjunct to the Vietnam War, held the welfare of Cambodians and their land in small regard. President Nixon made this clear when in December, 1970, he stated that the Cambodians were "tying down forty thousand North Vietnamese regulars [in Cambodia and] if those North Vietnamese weren't in Cambodia they'd be over killing Americans." The Cambodians were thus reduced to acting as surrogate U.S. targets for North Vietnamese guns. The tragedy of the U.S. invasion was that so much was suffered for so little reason.

Cambodia was but a sideshow for Nixon, who failed to take either the subtleties of Indochina or the domestic antiwar movement into account. Sihanouk's assessment of policymakers in Washington was, in characteristic hyperbole, that "They demoralized America, they lost all of Indochina to the communists, and they created the Khmer Rouge."

When U.S. and Vietnamese troops withdrew from Cambodia, civil war ensued. The Khmer Rouge, which came to power in 1975, soon attacked Vietnam to regain lost territory. Hanoi counterattacked in 1978, pushing the Khmer Rouge to the border with Thailand by 1979. In 1989, Vietnamese troops withdrew, and in 1993, the United Nations held elections, resulting in an elected parliament, which restored Sihanouk as king of Cambodia.

Ronald J. Cima
updated by Michael Haas

March, 1973
U.S. Withdrawal from Vietnam

Date: March 29, 1973
Location: South Vietnam and Paris
Principal figures: *American*, Henry Kissinger (1923-   ), Richard M. Nixon (1913-1994); *Vietnamese*, President Nguyen Van Thieu (1923-   ), president of South Vietnam, Le Duc Tho (1911-1990)
Result: The American withdrawal from Vietnam marked the first defeat of the United States in a foreign war.

Throughout the history of the United States, only the Civil War aroused as many conflicting emotions among citizens, officials, and soldiers as did the Vietnam War. Debate in the United States began in the early 1960's over what means should be used to protect the Republic of South Vietnam. Division spread with time to questions of ends: What sort of peace was being sought in Asia? Were the Viet Cong really worse than the South Vietnamese government? Could the United States achieve an honorable withdrawal? The war posed such dilemmas that the government was soon caught up in a charade of truth, obscuring issues and purposes even further.

Nixon's Peace Plan

From the time Richard M. Nixon became president in 1969, he was chiefly dependent upon the negotiating table for bringing the peace he had promised. His bargaining position was weak. With half a million U.S. troops in South Vietnam, the Viet Cong and North Vietnamese forces could not win a direct offensive, but their guerrilla techniques ensured that they could not lose, either. The war was essentially a waiting game, and the stakes were so much higher for the communists that they could afford to wait longer. Nor did the communists need a negotiated peace as much as Nixon did. The massive opposition at home to continued war required Nixon to deescalate, but strong popular support of U.S. intervention made total withdrawal an equally unacceptable policy.

Nevertheless, communist initiatives brought the first real breakthroughs in discussions over peace. From May, 1968, formal negotiations had been carried on in Paris, but these talks produced little more than rhetoric and repeatedly broke down in frustration. In June, 1971, Hanoi backed away from two earlier demands and agreed to discuss an in-place ceasefire and the conduct of internationally supervised elections without prior abolition of the Saigon government. Shortly afterward, the Viet Cong (South Vietnamese communists) made similar concessions, showing a conciliatory attitude toward the West. With these concessions, a second round of negotiations began, held between Le Duc Tho, a prominent North Vietnamese official, and Henry Kissinger, Nixon's national security adviser.

Although a subordinate of Nixon, Kissinger viewed his role in a different light. For Kissinger, the peace settlement would have to reflect the actual power situation, in which the North remained strong, the United States was to leave, and the government of the South lacked popular support and would probably collapse. Domestic political considerations did not matter to him. Nixon, on the other hand, wanted to end the war without alienating his domestic political support and by reassuring allies that the United States would come to their aid if needed in the future.

The United States made several minor concessions in the ensuing discussions, but little real progress was made. President Nixon was feeling the pressure of an election year, and U.S. troop levels in Vietnam dropped rapidly, weakening his leverage at the talks. Although U.S. forces numbered ninety-five thousand, only six thousand were combat-ready. Despite the historic détentes Nixon achieved with China and the Soviet Union during 1972, neither of these two allies of North Vietnam pressured Hanoi to accept a compromise with the United States. Instead, the North launched a major offensive in the spring, overrunning Quang Tri province.

In May, 1972, Nixon retaliated by ordering the bombing of North Vietnam to be stepped up, and the ports of the country mined and blockaded (bringing economic crisis to the communists); but at the same time, Kissinger offered major modifications of the United States bargaining position. For the first time, the United States was willing to permit North Vietnamese troops to remain in South Vietnam after a cease-fire, and to modify the Saigon government before elections. Intensive talks between Kissinger and Le Duc Tho resumed, with special incentives for both sides. The Nixon administration had to prove that its gamble in escalating the war was effective, and the North Vietnamese, watching the increasing likelihood of Nixon's reelection, wanted to reach an agreement before a safer Nixon became tougher.

Negotiated Settlement

In early October, Kissinger and Le Duc Tho agreed to a peace settlement along the lines of a proposal made by Hanoi in 1969, except that the confident North would allow the precarious government in the South to remain in place. The first step in the settlement was a cease-fire that would go into effect on October 24, 1972. When the text was revealed to Nixon, who was confident of reelection, the president insisted that South Vietnamese President Nguyen Van Thieu must also support the peace. Kissinger went to Saigon but was unable to apply pressure on Thieu, who was intransigent. The North expressed its anger by releasing the text of the draft agreement and the history of the hitherto secret negotiations. Kissinger then flew back to Washington, D.C. Hoping to apply pressure on Saigon, he informed the U.S. press upon his arrival that "Peace is at hand," although not "in hand," but South Vietnam soon announced sixty-nine objections to the proposed text of the peace agreement.

In early November, Nixon won reelection in a landslide. In Paris, the North, believing that it had been duped by Kissinger, refused to make any concessions to the South. The talks became bitter and broke down in mid-December. When the talks collapsed, Nixon tried one more bold stroke and ordered the Christmas bombing of North Vietnam. Dozens of B-52 bombers were set upon the largest cities of the country, widely destroying industry. The communist antiaircraft defense was so vigorous, and U.S. anger at the attack so powerful, as to make the success of the bombing questionable. It was stopped in less than two weeks, and war-weary negotiators returned to Paris.

The Peace Accords

On January 31, 1973, peace accords were signed by North Vietnam, the Viet Cong, the United States, and a reluctant South Vietnam. The provisions of the treaty were substantially the same as those of the October agreement. By March 27, the United States was to withdraw its troops from Vietnam; exchanges of prisoners would go on during those two months. All Vietnamese forces would remain in place, and a cease-fire would be supervised by an International Commission of Control and Supervision, comprising representatives from Canada, Hungary, Indonesia, and Poland. All parties concurred on Vietnam's sovereignty and right of self-determination, and a council was established with responsibility for developing and executing plans for an open election. In 1973, Kissinger and Le Duc Tho were awarded the Nobel Peace Prize.

There is room for doubt concerning how seriously the treaty was taken by any of the concerned nations. Cease-fire lines never were clearly established, many of the provisions were vague and invited violation, and both sides broke the treaty almost as soon as it was signed. Kissinger's creative ambiguity in the wording of the peace treaty meant that all sides could interpret the text the way they wished, without being aware of alternative interpretations by others. The United States quickly withdrew, regained its captured prisoners, and could claim "peace with honor." Both President Thieu of South Vietnam and the scattered communist forces seemed to believe that their best prospects lay in renewed fighting. Congress had no intention of providing humanitarian aid to the North, as provided in the treaty, and Hanoi ignored the pledge to stop sending supplies to the Viet Cong. After U.S. troops withdrew on March 29, 1973, the United States sent the South some $2.6 billion in aid, resumed reconnaissance flights over Vietnam, and continued to bomb Cambodia. Upon learning that Kissinger had given secret assurances to Thieu to reenter the war if the South faltered, Congress required all military operations in and over Indochina to cease by August 15, 1973.

By the end of 1973, open war had returned to the nation. U.S. aid continued to flow to South Vietnam, and Thieu controlled a well-trained army of one million men. However, the Viet Cong and North Vietnamese seemed to have gained some critical psychological edge on their enemy, and their successes were self-reinforcing. During 1974, with Nixon distracted by investigations of his effort to cover up the burglary of Democratic Party headquarters at the Watergate apartments, Congress reduced military aid to the South to $907 million and then to $700 million in 1975. Accordingly, the communist positions were generally strengthened, and at the outset of 1975 they launched a last major offensive. After a major direct victory at Hue, communist forces drove rapidly over South Vietnam, pursuing an utterly demoralized army. By the end of April, Saigon was captured; the last U.S. advisers abandoned the country; and the Vietnam era of U.S. history was truly at an end.

Richard H. Sander
updated by Michael Haas

Further Reading

Anderson, David L., ed. *Facing My Lai: Moving Beyond the Massacre.* Lawrence: University Press of Kansas, 1997.

Angers, Trent. *The Forgotten Hero of My Lai: The Hugh Thompson Story.* Lafayette, La.: Acadian House, 1999.

Arnold, James. *Tet Offensive 1968.* Sterling Heights, Mich.: Osprey, 1991.

Barnouw, Erik. *Tube of Plenty: The Evolution of American Television.* New York: Oxford University Press, 1975.

Baskir, Lawrence M., and William A. Strauss. *Chance and Circumstance: The Draft, the War, and the Vietnam Generation.* New York: Alfred A. Knopf, 1978.

Belknap, Michal R. *The Vietnam War on Trial: The My Lai Massacre and the Court-martial of Lieutenant Calley.* Lawrence: University Press of Kansas, 2002.

Bickel, Alexander M. *The Least Dangerous Branch.* Indianapolis, Ind.: Bobbs-Merrill, 1962.

Brown, Robert McAfee, Abraham Heschel, and Michael Novak. *Vietnam: Crisis of Conscience.* New York: Association Press, 1967.

Calley, William. *Lieutenant Calley: His Own Story, as Told to John Sack.* New York: Viking Press, 1971.

Capps, Walter H. *The Unfinished War: Vietnam and the American Conscience.* Boston: Beacon Press, 1982.

Caputo, Philip. *A Rumor of War.* New York: Henry Holt, 1996.

Casey, William Van Etten, and Philip Nobile, eds. *The Berrigans.* New York: Praeger, 1971.

Cash, John A. *Seven Firefights in Vietnam.* New York: Bantam, 1993.

Chomsky, Noam. *For Reasons of State.* 1972. Reprint. Introduction by Arundhati Roy. New York: W. W. Norton & Co., 2003.

Clark, Johnnie M. *Guns Up!* Rev. ed. New York: Ballantine Books, 2002.

Corbett, John. *West Dickens Avenue: A Marine at Khe Sanh.* New York: Ballantine Books, 2003.

Cummings, Dennis J., ed. *The Men Behind the Trident: SEAL Team One in Vietnam.* Annapolis, Md.: Naval Institute Press, 1997.

Daum, Andreas W., Lloyd C. Gardner, and Wilfried Mausbach, eds. *America, the Vietnam War, and the World: Comparative and International Perspectives.* New York: Cambridge University Press, 2003.

Davidson, Phillip B. *Vietnam at War: The History 1946-1975.* New York: Oxford University Press, 1988.

Donovan, Robert J., and Ray Scherer. *Unsilent Revolution: Television News and American Public Life.* Cambridge, England: Cambridge University Press, 1992.

Dunn, Peter M. *The First Vietnam War.* New York: St. Martin's Press, 1985.

Ellsberg, Daniel. *Secrets: A Memoir of Vietnam and the Pentagon Papers.* New York: Viking, 2002.

Frankum, Ronald B., Jr. *Like Rolling Thunder: The Air War in Vietnam, 1964-1975.* Lanham, Md.: Rowman & Littlefield, 2005.

Freedman, Dan, and Jacqueline Rhoads. *Nurses in Vietnam: The Forgotten Veterans.* Austin: Texas Monthly Press, 1987.

Freeman, Gregory A. *Sailors to the End: The Deadly Fire on the USS Forrestal and the Heroes Who Fought It.* New York: William Morrow, 2002.

Friel, Howard. *The Record of the Paper: How the New York Times Misreports US Foreign Policy.* New York: Verso, 2004.

Gates, Gary Paul. *Air Time: The Inside Story of CBS News.* New York: Harper & Row, 1978.

Gilbert, Marc, and William Head, eds. *The Tet Offensive.* Westport, Conn.: Praeger, 1996.

Goldman, Sheldon. *Constitutional Law: Cases and Essays.* New York: Harper-Collins, 1991.

Halberstam, David. *The Powers That Be.* New York: Alfred A. Knopf, 1979.

Hall, Mitchell D. *Because of Their Faith: CALCAV and Religious Opposition to the Vietnam War.* New York: Columbia University Press, 1990.

Hallin, Daniel. *The "Uncensored War": The Media and Vietnam.* New York: Oxford University Press, 1986.

Hammel, Eric. *Fire in the Streets: The Battle for Hue, Tet 1968.* New York: Dell, 1991.

_____. *Khe Sanh: Siege in the Clouds, an Oral History.* Pacifica, Calif.: Pacifica Press, 2000.

Hammer, Richard. *The Court-Martial of Lt. Calley.* New York: Coward, McCann & Geoghegan, 1971.

Hammond, William M. *Public Affairs: The Military and the Media, 1962-1968.* Washington, D.C.: Center for Military History, 1988.

_____. *Reporting Vietnam: Media and Military at War.* Lawrence: University Press of Kansas, 1998.

Herring, George C. *America's Longest War: The United States and Vietnam, 1950-1975.* 2d ed. New York: McGraw-Hill, 1986.

Hersh, Seymour. *My Lai Four: A Report on the Massacre and Its Aftermath.* New York: Random House, 1970.

Holm, Jeanne. *Women in the Military: An Unfinished Revolution.* Novato, Calif.: Presidio Press, 1982.

Karnow, Stanley. *Vietnam: A History.* 2d rev. ed. New York: Penguin Books, 1997.

Kissinger, Henry. *Ending the Vietnam War: A Personal History of America's Involvement in and Extrication from the Vietnam War.* New York: Simon & Schuster, 2003.

Lanning, Michael Lee. *Inside the Crosshairs: Snipers in Vietnam.* New York: Ivy Books, 1998.

Laurence, John. *The Cat from Hue: A Vietnam War Story.* New York: PublicAffairs, 2002.

Levy, David W. *The Debate over Vietnam.* 2d ed. Baltimore: Johns Hopkins University Press, 1995.

Lewy, Guenter. *America in Vietnam.* New York: Oxford University Press, 1978.

Lowe, Peter, ed. *The Vietnam War.* New York: St. Martin's Press, 1998.

McMahon, Robert J., ed. *Major Problems in the History of the Vietnam War.* Lexington, Mass.: D.C. Heath, 1995.

MacPherson, Myra. *Long Time Passing: Vietnam and the Haunted Generation.* Garden City, N.Y.: Doubleday, 1984.

Maraniss, David. *They Marched into Sunlight: War and Peace, Vietnam and America, October 1967.* New York: Simon & Schuster, 2003.

Marolda, Edward J. *The U.S. Navy in the Vietnam War: An Illustrated History.* Washington, D.C.: Brassey's 2001.

Marshall, Kathryn. *In the Combat Zone: An Oral History of American Women in Vietnam, 1966-1975.* Boston: Little, Brown, 1987.

Michel, Marshall L. III. *Clashes: Air Combat over North Vietnam, 1965-1972.* Annapolis, Md.: Naval Institute Press, 1997.

_____. *The Eleven Days of Christmas: America's Last Vietnam Battle.* San Francisco, Calif.: Encounter Books, 2002.

Moise, Edwin E. *Tonkin Gulf and the Escalation of the Vietnam War.* Chapel Hill: University of North Carolina Press, 1996.

Moore, Harold G., and Joseph L. Galloway. *We Were Soldiers Once . . . and Young: Ia Drang, the Battle That Changed the War in Vietnam.* New York: Random House, 1992.

Morden, Bettie J. *The Women's Army Corps, 1945-1978.* Washington, D.C.: Center of Military History, 1990.

Murphy, Edward F. *The Hill Fights: The First Battle of Khe Sanh.* New York: Ballantine Books, 2003.

Nalty, Bernard C. *Air War over South Vietnam, 1968-1975.* Washington, D.C.: Air Force History and Museums Program, 2000.

Nichols, John B., and Barrett Tillman. *On Yankee Station: The Naval Air War over Vietnam.* 1987. Reprint. Annapolis, Md.: Naval Institute Press, 2001.

Nolan, Keith William. *Battle for Hue: Tet, 1968*. Novato, Calif.: Presidio Press, 1996.

_____. *The Magnificent Bastards: The Joint Army-Marine Defense of Dong Ha, 1968*. Novato, Calif.: Presidio, 1994.

Norman, Elizabeth. *Women at War: The Story of Fifty Military Nurses Who Served in Vietnam*. Philadelphia: University of Pennsylvania Press, 1990.

Oberdorfer, Don. *Tet!* New York: Doubleday, 1971.

O'Brien, David M. *Storm Center: The Supreme Court in American Politics*. New York: W. W. Norton, 1990.

Olson, James S., and Randy Roberts. *My Lai: A Brief History with Documents*. New York: St. Martin's Press, 1999.

_____. *Where the Domino Fell: America and Vietnam, 1945-1995*. New York: St. Martin's Press, 1996.

Palmer, Dave Richard. *Summons of the Trumpet: A History of the Vietnam War from a Military Man's Viewpoint*. San Rafael, Calif.: Presidio Press, 1978.

Peers, William R. *The My Lai Inquiry*. New York: W. W. Norton, 1979.

Pisor, Robert. *The End of the Line: The Siege of Khe Sanh*. New York: Ballantine Books, 1982.

Plaster, John L. *Secret Commandos: Behind Enemy Lines with the Elite Warriors of SOG*. New York: Simon & Schuster, 2004.

_____. *SOG: The Secret Wars of America's Commandos in Vietnam*. New York: Simon & Schuster, 1997.

Podhoretz, Norman. *Why We Were in Vietnam*. New York: Simon & Schuster, 1982.

Prados, John, and Ray W. Stubbe. *Valley of Decision: The Siege of Khe Sanh*. Boston: Houghton Mifflin, 1991.

Price, Alfred. *War in the Fourth Dimension: US Electronic Warfare, from the Vietnam War to the Present*. Foreword by Charles A. Horner. Mechanicsburg, Pa.: Stackpole Books, 2001.

Prochnau, William. *Once Upon a Distant War: Young War Correspondents and the Early Vietnam Battles*. New York: Random House, 1995.

Reporting Vietnam: American Journalism, 1959-1975. Introduction by Ward Just. New York: Library of America, 2000.

Rochester, Stuart I., and Frederick T. Kiley. *Honor Bound: American Prisoners of War in Southeast Asia, 1961-1973*. Annapolis, Md.: Naval Institute Press, 1999.

Rosas, Allan. *The Legal Status of Prisoners of War: A Study in International Humanitarian Law Applicable in Armed Conflicts*. Helsinki: Suomalainen Tiedeakatemia, 1976.

Rossum, Ralph A., and G. Alan Taer. *American Constitutional Law*. New York: St. Martin's Press, 1991.

Safer, Morley. *Flashbacks: On Returning to Vietnam.* New York: Random House, 1990.

Sales, Kirkpatrick. *SDS.* New York: Random House, 1973.

Schuck, Peter H. *Agent Orange on Trial: Mass Toxic Disasters in the Courts.* Cambridge, Mass.: Belknap Press of Harvard University Press, 1986.

Sheehan, Neil. *A Bright Shining Lie: John Paul Vann and America in Vietnam.* New York: Vintage Books, 1989.

——————, et al. *The Pentagon Papers.* Toronto: Bantam Books, 1971.

Sim, Kevin, and Michael Bilton. *Four Hours in My Lai.* New York: Viking Press, 1992.

Smith, George W. *The Siege at Hue.* Boulder, Colo.: Lynne Rienner, 1999.

Smith, Jean E. *The Constitution and American Foreign Policy.* St. Paul, Minn.: West Publishing, 1989.

Solis, Gary D. *Son Thang: An American War Crime.* Annapolis, Md.: Naval Institute Press, 1997.

Strum, Philippa. *The Supreme Court and Political Questions.* Tuscaloosa: University of Alabama Press, 1974.

Summers, Harry G., Jr. *On Strategy: A Critical Analysis of the Vietnam War.* Novato, Calif.: Presidio Press, 1995.

Turley, William S. *The Second Indochina War: A Short Political and Military History, 1954-1975.* New York: Mentor/Penguin Books, 1987.

United States Department of the Army. *The My Lai Massacre and Its Cover-up: Beyond the Reach of the Law? The Peers Commission Report: Joseph Goldstein, Burke Marshall and Jack Schwartz.* New York: Free Press, 1976.

Van Devanter, Lynda. *Home Before Morning: The Story of an Army Nurse in Vietnam.* Amherst: University of Massachusetts Press, 2001.

Van Staaveren, Jacob. *The United States Air Force in Southeast Asia: Interdiction in Southern Laos, 1960-1968.* Washington, D.C.: Center for Air Force History, 1993.

Walker, Keith. *A Piece of My Heart: The Stories of Twenty-Six American Women Who Served in Vietnam.* New York: Ballantine Books, 1985.

Walker, Samuel. *In Defense of American Liberties.* New York: Oxford University Press, 1990.

Warr, Nicholas. *Phase Line Green: The Battle for Hue, 1968.* Annapolis, Md.: Naval Institute Press, 1997.

Wetterhahn, Ralph. *The Last Battle: The Mayaguez Incident and the End of the Vietnam War.* New York: Carroll & Graf, 2001.

Willbanks, James H. *Abandoning Vietnam: How America Left and South Vietnam Lost Its War.* Lawrence: University Press of Kansas, 2004.

Windrow, Martin. *The Last Valley: Dien Bien Phu and the French Defeat in Vietnam.* Cambridge, Mass.: De Capo Press, 2005.

Wirtz, James. *The Tet Offensive: Intelligence Failure in War.* Cornell, N.Y.: Cornell University Press, 1994.

Woods, Randall B., ed. *Vietnam and the American Political Tradition: The Politics of Dissent.* New York: Cambridge University Press, 2003.

Woodward, Bob, and Scott Armstrong. *The Brethren.* New York: Simon & Schuster, 1979.

Wyatt, Clarence R. *Paper Soldiers: The American Press and the Vietnam War.* New York: W. W. Norton, 1992.

Young, Marilyn B. *The Vietnam Wars, 1945-1990.* New York: HarperCollins, 1991.

Conflicts in the Caribbean
1961-1989

Conflicts in the Caribbean

At issue: U.S.-Soviet competition for influence in the region
Date: 1961-1989
Location: Caribbean Basin
Combatants: Americans vs. Soviet allies and suspect allies in the Caribbean
Principal conflicts: Bay of Pigs (1961), Cuban Missile Crisis (1962), Dominican Republic occupation (1965), Grenada occupation (1983), Panama occupation (1989)
Result: The dissolution of the Soviet Union in 1991 ended the Cold War and lessened tensions in the Caribbean, but the United States continued to cast a long shadow over the region.

American interests in the Caribbean region go back to the pre-independence era, when Great Britain was developing trade relationships between its Caribbean and North American colonies. After the United States won its Revolutionary War during the early 1780's, it stood as the only independent nation in the Western Hemisphere. In the early nineteenth century, a wave of independence movements swept throughout Latin America. Ironically, although the Caribbean island nation of Haiti became the second country in the Western Hemisphere to assert its independence in 1804, most of the region's islands—including all of Great Britain's colonies—remained colonial dependencies throughout the rest of the century. Some did not become independent until as late as the 1970's and 1980's, and ten territories remained colonial dependencies into the twenty-first century.

The Monroe Doctrine

Meanwhile, virtually all the Spanish and Portuguese colonies on the continental land masses surrounding the Caribbean were becoming independent, and a new era of political disorder began. Most of the new national governments were unstable and appeared vulnerable to foreign intervention. Concerned about the possibility of other European powers moving into the region to fill the power void created by Spain and Brazil's withdrawal, U.S. president James Monroe enunciated four foreign policy points during his 1823 state-of-the-union address to Congress that much later became known as the Monroe Doctrine.

The first point of the Monroe Doctrine was that the United States would not interfere in the affairs of, or conflicts among, European nations. The second point was assurance that the United States would respect the rights

TIME LINE OF CONFLICTS IN THE CARIBBEAN

May 20, 1902	Cuba becomes independent after four-year occupation by U.S. troops.
Nov. 3, 1903	With U.S. backing, Panama declares its independence from Colombia.
Nov. 18, 1903	United States signs agreement with Panama to build Panama Canal and assumes permanent sovereignty over a six-mile-wide zone bordering the canal.
1904	U.S. president Theodore Roosevelt articulates the Roosevelt Corollary to the Monroe Doctrine, asserting that the United States has the right to intervene in the internal affairs of any Western Hemisphere nation guilty of flagrant misconduct.
Aug. 3, 1912-Jan., 1933	U.S. troops occupy Nicaragua to quell political unrest.
Aug. 15, 1914	Panama Canal opens to shipping.
July 28, 1915-1934	U.S. Marines occupy Haiti.
May 15, 1916-1924	U.S. Marines occupy Dominican Republic.
1930	President Herbert Hoover's administration rejects the Roosevelt Corollary and adopts the "Good Neighbor Policy" toward Latin America. Meanwhile, U.S.-trained Dominican army officer Rafael Leónidas Trujillo Molina seizes power in the Dominican Republic.
Dec., 1956	Fidel Castro launches Cuban Revolution.
Jan.-Feb., 1959	Castro's Revolution overthrows Cuban government; Castro takes power as premier.
Mar., 1960	U.S. president Dwight D. Eisenhower authorizes the training of a Cuban exile force to be used against Castro's government.
1961	United States severs diplomatic relations with Cuba.
Apr. 17, 1961	Bay of Pigs Invasion.
Oct. 22-Nov. 3, 1962	Cuban Missile Crisis.
Apr. 24, 1965-June 1, 1966	United States occupies Dominican Republic after coup overthrows President Juan Bosch.
Feb. 7, 1974	Grenada becomes independent.
Mar.-Apr., 1978	United States and Panama sign treaties designed eventually to give Panama full control over the canal.

Oct. 13, 1983	Grenadan army overthrows government of Prime Minister Maurice Bishop, who is killed six days later.
Oct. 25-Dec. 15, 1983	United States occupies Grenada.
1987	Army general Manuel Noriega takes power in Panama.
May 7, 1989	Noriega voids Panama's presidential election after his favored candidates suffer a crushing defeat.
Dec. 20, 1989-Jan. 3, 1990	U.S. troops occupy Panama and arrest President Noriega after he survives a bungled coup attempt.
Apr. 9-July 10, 1992	Noriega is convicted on drug and racketeering charges in a Florida court and is sentenced to forty years in a federal prison.
Dec. 31, 1999	Panama assumes full ownership of the Panama Canal.

of European colonies that remained in the Western Hemisphere—most of which were in the Caribbean. The third point asserted that the Western Hemisphere was closed to further European colonization. The fourth point was an elaboration on the third, stating that the United States would regard any attempt by any European nation to control or threaten any Western Hemisphere nation as a hostile act against the United States itself.

Under the principles of the Monroe Doctrine, the United States saw itself as the protector of the Western Hemisphere—a view that has colored U.S. policy in the region ever since. Through the early nineteenth century, the Monroe Doctrine meant little, as the United States was militarily too weak to pose a serious threat to most European powers and because there was little interest in Europe in recolonizing Latin America. The first true assertion of the doctrine came during the 1860's, when France attempted to install a puppet government in Mexico. Partly in response to U.S. pressure, France withdrew from Mexico in 1867. As the century wore on, and as U.S. military strength increased, succeeding presidential administrations broadened their interpretations of the Monroe Doctrine, and it became a partial justification for the U.S. intervention in Cuba's revolt against Spain that led to the Spanish-American War in 1898.

The Roosevelt Corollary

Theodore Roosevelt won fame from his brief combat experience in Cuba during the Spanish-American War and was elected vice president of the United States in 1900. After President William McKinley was assassinated the following year, he became president. In 1904, he added what be-

CARIBBEAN BASIN

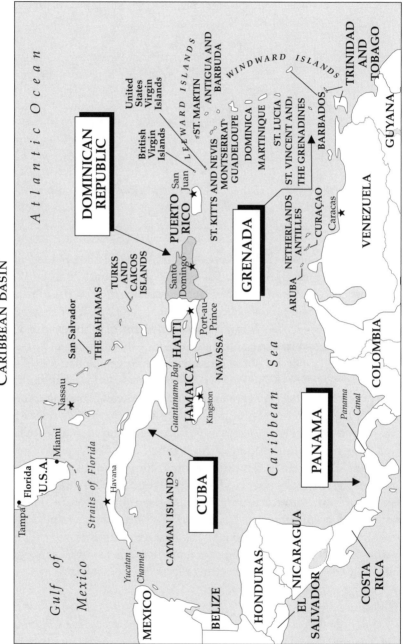

came known as the Roosevelt Corollary to the Monroe Doctrine. Under Roosevelt's doctrine, the United States asserted that it had the right to intervene in the internal affairs of any fellow Western Hemisphere nations guilty of flagrant misconduct. Roosevelt justified the doctrine as an extension of the Monroe Doctrine because U.S. intervention would prevent the intervention of European powers seeking redress against misbehaving Latin American nations; however, the doctrine became a justification for U.S. imperialism against its own neighbors.

During the first half of the twentieth century, the United States repeatedly intervened in the affairs of Latin American nations in the Caribbean and surrounding land masses. In addition to occupying Cuba from late 1898 through mid-1902, the United States sent troops into Mexico on occasion and occupied Nicaragua from 1912 to 1933 and Haiti from 1915 to 1934. From the mid-1930's until the mid-1950's, the United States kept its hands off its neighbors. However, the relatively long period of nonintervention ended when Cold War tensions reached the Caribbean. In 1954, the United States backed an invasion that overthrew the left-leaning government of Guatemala. Five years later, socialist revolutionaries under the leadership of Fidel Castro took power in Cuba, and the U.S. government moved to isolate the new government. This policy pushed Castro closer to the Soviet Union and transformed the Caribbean into a major Cold War arena.

The Cold War

From the mid-1950's until the collapse of the Soviet Union in 1991, all the U.S. military involvements in the Caribbean region had Cold War ramifications. In 1961, the United States severed diplomatic relations with Cuba and imposed a rigid trade embargo on the Caribbean's largest island. That same year, the United States backed an attempt to overthrow Castro's regime in the abortive Bay of Pigs invasion. In October, 1962, the world was poised on the brink of nuclear war when the United States forced the Soviet Union to withdraw missiles that it was installing in Cuba.

The Cold War again flared up in the region in 1965, when the United States occupied the Dominican Republic to suppress a popular movement to restore to power the country's legally elected president, whom the U.S. government regarded as a potentially dangerous ally of Castro. Cold War politics were also behind the U.S. intervention in the tiny island nation of Grenada in 1983, which the U.S. government feared was falling under the influence of Cuba.

The motives behind U.S. intervention in Panama in 1989 had less to do with Cold War politics than with disciplining Panama's President Manuel

The United States sowed seeds for future conflict in the Caribbean Basin during the early twentieth century, when it built the Panama Canal and afterward administered the zone surrounding the canal as if it were sovereign U.S. territory. Panamanian resentment against the U.S. presence erupted in violence during the 1960's that prompted a renegotiation of the U.S.-Panama treaty governing the canal and ultimately led to the United States turning the canal over to Panamanian control on the last day of 1999. (Library of Congress)

Noriega, a former U.S. ally who had gone too far in profiteering from illegal narcotics dealing. However, the occupation itself fell into the same pattern as earlier U.S. interventions in the Caribbean region and set the stage for U.S. military interventions in other parts of the post-Cold War world.

Christopher E. Kent

Campaigns, Battles, and Other Events

1961

Bay of Pigs Invasion

At issue: Legitimacy of Fidel Castro's government in Cuba
Date: April 17-19, 1961
Location: Bay of Pigs, Las Villas province, Cuba
Combatants: U.S.-trained Cuban exiles vs. Cuban military
Principal commanders: *American/Cuban exile*, President John F. Kennedy, Jr., (1917-1963); *Cuban*, Fidel Castro (1926 or 1927-   )
Result: The invasion of Cuba by an American-trained Cuban guerrilla force resulted in a crushing defeat.

In 1959, Fidel Castro and his revolutionary forces overthrew Cuba's government, establishing a revolutionary socialist regime in its place. Lands formerly owned by members of the upper classes and by U.S. companies were seized and redistributed, and many Cubans fled to the United States—primarily Florida—in exile.

In March, 1960, President Dwight D. Eisenhower authorized the Central Intelligence Agency (CIA), headed by Allen Dulles, to train and equip a Cuban exile guerrilla force for the purpose of infiltrating Cuba and joining the anti-Castro underground. With the cooperation of the Guatemalan government, the CIA soon established training camps in that country, and the training of Cuban exile volunteers began. By November, 1960, the CIA operation, under the supervision of Richard Bissell, had changed from the training of guerrillas to the preparation of an invasion force. After that date, guerrilla training ceased, and a small army was trained in conventional assault landing tactics.

Cuban Exiles

Meanwhile, in the Cuban exile community in Miami, Florida, the United Revolutionary Front was formed. Headed by Dr. José Miró Cardona, who would become provisional president of Cuba upon the exiles' return, the group in Miami managed the recruitment of soldiers for the expeditionary force, although the operation was completely directed by the CIA. Volunteers were screened for political acceptability, and leftists were discouraged or rejected. Consequently, the force in training took on a conservative character.

The CIA-directed operation ran into severe problems from the start. Numerous political conflicts that threatened to undermine the entire operation erupted among the exile volunteers. U.S. involvement in the affair was supposed to remain covert, but in Miami the existence of the invasion force and the Guatemalan camps, as well as the CIA direction of the operation, were common knowledge. Increasingly, the American press reported on the preparations in progress for an invasion of Cuba. Castro, the premier of Cuba, also knew of the exile army being trained in Guatemala.

In February, 1961, the invasion plans underwent an important change. Originally, the CIA had specified the city of Trinidad as the landing point for the exile force. The newly elected president, John F. Kennedy, decided that the invasion plans could proceed, however, only if U.S. support troops were better camouflaged. The site at Trinidad was judged too risky. In its place, the Bay of Pigs, one hundred miles to the west of Trinidad on the south-central coast of Cuba, was chosen. Trinidad was the better of the two sites for one simple reason: In the event of failure, the invasion force could retreat into the Escambray Mountains with little difficulty. The beaches at the Bay of Pigs, on the other hand, were surrounded by the Zapata swamps. Escape to the mountains some eighty miles to the east would be extremely difficult, if not impossible. In the event that the exiles could not establish a defensible beachhead at the Bay of Pigs, the only realistic retreat possible for them would be in the direction from which they came: to the sea.

Invasion Plans

By April, 1961, the invasion plans had taken shape. Castro's air force was to be destroyed on the ground by two scheduled air strikes against Cuban air bases. The invasion force of fifteen hundred troops would disembark under the cover of night and acquire the advantage of complete surprise. Meanwhile, paratroopers would be dropped to establish advance positions, from which they could scout approaching Cuban forces and cut off transportation routes. With the skies to themselves, the exile forces initially would be resupplied at the Playa Girón airfield, close to the Bay of Pigs. Simultaneously, a diversionary landing would occur on the eastern coast of Cuba in an attempt to deceive Cuban forces about the exiles' real intentions. The main invasion force then would advance into Matanzas Province with the goal of securing a defensible area of Cuban territory.

President John F. Kennedy examines the combat flag that the 2506th Cuban Landing Brigade carried during the Bay of Pigs invasion. (National Archives)

This accomplished, the leaders of the United Revolutionary Front would be flown to Cuba to establish a provisional government.

It was hoped that the local Cuban population might join the invaders in their fight against the Castro regime. With this possibility in mind, the supply ships accompanying the invasion force were to be stocked with arms and ammunition for a force of four thousand.

The Invasion

From the beginning, Operation Pluto, as the invasion plan was called, went badly. On April 15, 1961, eight B-26 bombers, supplied by the United States and disguised as Cuban air force planes, departed from Puerto Cabezas, Nicaragua, and attacked Cuban airfields in an attempt to destroy the Cuban air force. The bombing raid was unsuccessful. Although considerable damage was done to Cuba's small air force, the attack left unharmed two or three T-33 trainer jets, three Sea Furies, and two B-26's.

At the United Nations, Raúl Roa, Cuba's foreign minister, charged that the attack was a prelude to invasion from the United States. Adlai Stevenson, the U.S. ambassador to the United Nations, replied that the attacking planes were of Cuban origin. Because one of the planes had landed in Florida after the raid, Stevenson was able to produce photographs showing a B-26 bomber displaying the insignia of the Cuban air force. Stevenson actually believed the Cuban pilots to be defectors from Castro's own forces; he was unaware of the deception. The trick was soon discovered, however, when reporters pointed out certain differences in the nose cones of the Cuban B-26's as compared with the one that had landed in Florida. U.S. complicity in the air strike was apparent, and President Kennedy, at the recommendation of Secretary of State Dean Rusk and Special Assistant for National Security McGeorge Bundy, canceled the second air strike, scheduled for dawn on April 17.

In the early-morning hours of Monday, April 17, the invasion force (now named Brigade 2506) began to disembark at two beaches on the Bay of Pigs: Playa Girón and Playa Larga. Contrary to advance intelligence reports that the area was virtually uninhabited and that militia in the area had no communications with Havana, the invaders were spotted almost immediately, and the news of invasion was relayed quickly to Castro's headquarters. Thus, the dangerous night landing was conducted under fire from the very start. The unloading of troops and arms progressed more slowly than planned, and at dawn there were still invasion forces on the ships. The element of surprise had not been achieved, and the force of the undestroyed Cuban planes soon would be felt. Throughout the day on Monday, events continued to go against the invaders.

Cuba's air force, particularly the jets, proved to be the decisive factor in the battle. Two of the exiles' escort ships, the *Rio Escondido* and the *Houston*, were sunk with arms, ammunition, and supplies on board. The exile air force (the Free Cuban Air Squadron), which consisted of sixteen B-26

BAY OF PIGS INVASION, 1961

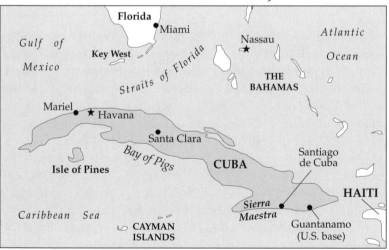

bombers, lost half of its planes. Flying from Nicaragua, the B-26's carried extra fuel and had no tail guns. Unable to maneuver quickly, they made easy targets for the T-33 jet trainers. At sea, the escort vessels that were not sunk by Cuban planes were forced to withdraw from the invasion area. On the ground, the invasion forces fought well but were hampered by wet communication equipment and a scarcity of ammunition. Only one of the paratroop drops succeeded. The other failed because the paratroopers were dropped too close to the invasion area and because their heavy equipment was dropped into the swamps, never to be found again during the remainder of the battle.

Failure

The Bay of Pigs region was politically one of the worst possible sites for a successful counterrevolution in Cuba. What before 1959 had been an exclusively agricultural zone peopled by woodcutters was being developed by the revolutionary government as a future tourist haven. New roads, markets, and schools had won Castro the support of the populace, and few welcomed the invaders, who represented the middle and upper classes of Havana. Once the invasion foundered, the men of Brigade 2506 could not count on the local inhabitants to give them refuge. The U.S. planners of the invasion, through wishful thinking, had misread the mood of the Cuban people in the spring of 1961. Almost all of those dissatisfied with the revolution had already departed for the United States, and the bombing of Cuban airfields by the exile air force rallied public opinion behind Castro.

The national uprising that the CIA was counting on to coincide with the debarkation of the exile force never occurred. The Cuban army and militia remained loyal to the regime, and between April 15 and 17, Castro ordered the arrest of more than one hundred thousand opponents of his government, eliminating dissident elements in the Roman Catholic Church and the Cuban press and destroying the CIA's underground network of agents. With all of these problems at the Bay of Pigs, it probably made no difference in the final result that the diversionary landing on the eastern coast of Cuba never took place.

In Washington, the discouraging news from the Bay of Pigs led President Kennedy to reinstate the second air strike, which earlier had been canceled. The planes of the Free Cuban Air Squadron based in Nicaragua were to strike the San Antonio de los Banos airfield at dawn on Tuesday, April 18. The following morning, six B-26 bombers piloted by Cuban exile pilots were over the designated target, but the bombers were forced to return to Nicaragua without dropping a single bomb because of fog and cloud cover.

On the ground, Castro was moving twenty thousand troops toward the Zapata swamp region as Brigade 2506 was running out of ammunition. Because the Cuban air force still commanded the skies, there was no chance to unload the remaining arms, supplies, and troops aboard the two remaining escort ships at sea.

In the early-morning hours of Wednesday, April 19, President Kennedy authorized an "air-umbrella" at dawn over the invasion area. He gave permission for six unmarked jet fighters from the USS *Essex* in the Caribbean to protect a B-26 attack from Nicaragua and to cover the unloading of the exile escort ships at sea. This final attempt to help the invading forces also proved to be a failure. Probably because of confusion about the difference in time zones between Cuba and Nicaragua, the B-26 bombers from Nicaragua arrived an hour early over Cuba and were shot down by the Cubans; only one escaped. The jets that were to have provided air cover never left the *Essex*.

Later on April 19, 1961, the invasion was crushed. Facing overwhelming opposition and out of ammunition, the leaders destroyed their heavy equipment and ordered a retreat into the swamps. Only a handful of exiles escaped to the sea; the remainder were rounded up by Castro's forces and imprisoned. Of 1,297 brigade members who had come ashore, 1,180 were captured. Cuban losses are difficult to estimate. Although Castro admitted to losing fewer than a hundred men in battle, a more accurate estimate would be 1,250.

Charles E. Cottle
updated by Julio César Pino

1962
Cuban Missile Crisis

At issue: Right of the Soviet Union to install missile bases in the Western Hemisphere

Date: October 22-28, 1962

Location: Washington, D.C., and Cuba

Principal figures: *American*, President John Fitzgerald Kennedy (1917-1963), Secretary of Defense Robert S. McNamara (1916-   ), Secretary of State Dean Rusk (1909-1994), Attorney General Robert Kennedy (1925-1968), McGeorge Bundy (1919-1996); *Cuban*, Fidel Castro (1926 or 1927-   ); *Soviet*, Premier Nikita Khrushchev (1894-1971), Ambassador Anatoly F. Dobrynin (1919-   ), Aleksandr S. Fomin

Result: At the height of the Cold War, the United States and the Soviet Union risked nuclear war but managed to end the confrontation without resorting to combat.

When Fidel Castro's revolutionary July 26 Movement assumed power in Cuba in 1959, it marked the end of U.S. political and economic dominance over the island. Ever since the late nineteenth century, the United States, supported by loyal Cuban politicians, had enjoyed control over all Cuba's commerce and industry. Castro, however, refused to adhere to U.S. interests, and, as a result, the United States attempted to overthrow Castro's government through the use of covert military operations and an economic blockade.

In 1960, President Dwight Eisenhower and the Central Intelligence Agency (CIA) began organizing and training anti-Castro Cuban exiles for a potential invasion. When President John F. Kennedy entered the White House in 1961, he agreed to continue this program, and in April, more than fourteen hundred commandos landed at the Bay of Pigs. U.S. experts believed that the people would rise up and revolt against Castro during this assault, but Castro easily quashed this rebellion. Afterward, Kennedy developed several assassination plots against Castro, and he sanctioned the CIA to conduct sabotage raids upon Cuban sugarcane fields, railroad bridges, and oil tanks through Operation Mongoose.

Cuba and the Soviet Union

All of these attacks, however, backfired. Threatened with continuous military invasions and the loss of trade, Castro turned to the Soviet Union for support. He declared himself a Marxist-Leninist in 1961, and, afterward, Soviet influence substantially increased. By 1962, the Soviet Union had stationed several military advisers in Cuba, and Kennedy feared that communist influence ultimately could undermine U.S. hegemony in Latin America if this relationship continued to grow.

In October, 1962, Senator Kenneth B. Keating of New York startled the United States by alleging that offensive missile bases were under construction in Cuba. Keating did not reveal the source of his information, but a flight by a U.S. U-2 reconnaissance airplane on October 14 substantiated his charges. Long-range nuclear missiles, which had begun arriving in Cuban ports from the Soviet Union in September, were being installed at San Cristobal on the western part of the island. An international crisis of potentially catastrophic proportions threatened the safety of the world.

After President Kennedy viewed the satellite photos on October 16, he called his key military and political advisers to the White House. The ini-

U.S. aerial reconnaissance photography of the Soviet missile installations that precipitated the crisis. (National Archives)

tial discussion centered on the issue of whether the missiles were fully armed and ready to fire. After concluding that the United States still had time before the Soviets attained nuclear readiness on Cuba, the president and his executive committee (Ex Comm) discussed various options. General Maxwell Taylor of the Joint Chiefs of Staff recommended an immediate air strike. Others, including Secretary of Defense Robert McNamara and McGeorge Bundy, the president's special assistant for national security affairs, suggested that the president resort to diplomacy rather than war.

U.S. Blockade

By Thursday, October 18, a consensus had emerged from the discussions, and the next day, the president indicated that he favored a naval blockade as the first step. He also decided that he would announce his decision to the U.S. people on the evening of Monday, October 22. At 5:00 P.M., he briefed congressional leaders. An hour later, Soviet ambassador Anatoly F. Dobrynin was ushered into the office of Secretary of State Dean Rusk, where he was handed a copy of Kennedy's speech. At 7:00 P.M., the president spoke over nationwide television and radio.

"The purpose of these bases," Kennedy said in a calm but firm voice, "can be none other than to provide a nuclear strike capability against the Western Hemisphere." The Soviet action was "a deliberately provocative and unjustified change in the status quo which cannot be accepted by this country, if our courage and commitments are ever to be trusted again by either friend or foe."

The president then outlined the initial steps the United States would take to deal with the situation: a quarantine on offensive military equipment being shipped to Cuba; an assertion that any missile launched from Cuba would be regarded as an attack by the Soviet Union, requiring a total retaliatory response by the United States; emergency meetings of both the Organization of American States and the United Nations to consider this threat to peace; and an appeal to Nikita S. Khrushchev, premier of the Soviet Union, "to abandon this course of world domination, and to join in an historic effort to end the perilous arms race and to transform the history of man." The quarantine was to become effective on October 24 at 10 A.M.

Confrontation

On Wednesday, October 24, the Soviet Union officially rejected the U.S. proclamation of quarantine. Late that day, however, some Soviet ships sailing toward Cuba altered course or stopped in midsea. Yet, a direct confrontation between U.S. and Soviet ships could not long be delayed, as this crisis escalated into an international war of brinkmanship. The American Strategic Air Command went to Defense Condition 2, one step away from actual war; B-52 bombers took off with nuclear arsenals; and soldiers were moved to bases in the southeast and briefed for a potential invasion of Cuba.

The first real thaw in the crisis occurred on Friday afternoon, October 26, when John Scali, diplomatic correspondent of the American Broadcasting Company, received a call from Aleksandr S. Fomin, an official of the Soviet embassy who was also a colonel in the Soviet State Security Committee (KGB) and a personal friend of Khrushchev. At lunch, Fomin proposed a settlement of the crisis and asked Scali if he could find out from contacts

Editorial cartoon published during the crisis showing Soviet premier Nikita Khrushchev blaming the United States for threatening world peace, as he tows an armada of Soviet weapons intended to threaten the United States.
(Library of Congress)

in the Department of State if it would be acceptable. The missile bases in Cuba, Fomin said, would be dismantled and the Soviet Union would promise not to ship any more offensive missiles in exchange for a U.S. pledge not to invade Cuba. Scali immediately took this proposal to Rusk, who felt it was legitimate. At the same time, a personal letter from Khrushchev confirmed Fomin's offer, but it also reminded Kennedy that the Soviet Union's actions were simply a response to his provocative measures toward Castro's government.

The next day, the situation deteriorated when Khrushchev seemed to change the proposal markedly when he demanded that the United States abandon its missile bases in Turkey. This angered Kennedy. Despite the fact that the missiles in Turkey were of little strategic value, he felt that U.S. credibility was at stake. Several members of Ex Comm, including U.S. ambassador to the Soviet Union W. Averell Harriman, suggested that this provided Khrushchev with a face-saving alternative. The president and his advisers decided to proceed on the basis of the meetings with Fomin and to ignore Khrushchev's demand, but at the same time, Kennedy sent his brother, Attorney General Robert Kennedy, to meet with Soviet ambassador Dobrynin and secretly agree to remove the missiles in Turkey if the Cuban crisis were resolved peacefully.

Other news also threatened the peace. The afternoon of October 27, a U.S. U-2 strayed over Soviet air space; it managed to return home safely, but Kennedy feared that the Soviets would view this as the first step in a preemptive strike. On the same day, another U-2 was shot down over Cuba, and as a result, most members of Ex Comm believed that a nuclear exchange was imminent.

Soviets Back Down

On the morning of Sunday, October 28, Moscow radio carried an announcement that had come from Khrushchev: "In order to eliminate as rapidly as possible the conflict which endangers the cause of peace . . . the Soviet Government . . . has given a new order to dismantle the arms which you have described as offensive, and to crate and return them to the Soviet Union." The Cuban missile crisis had passed, and a nuclear holocaust had been averted. The United States removed the missiles from Turkey in 1963, both nations installed a nuclear hotline between Washington, D.C., and Moscow to prevent future misunderstandings over nuclear war, and both nations began to explore talks to curtail the nuclear arms race.

William M. Tuttle
updated by Robert D. Ubriaco, Jr.

1965
Dominican Republic Occupation

At issue: Suppression of a leftist revolt
Date: April 24, 1965-June 1, 1966
Location: Santo Domingo, Dominican Republic
Combatants: Rebels (pro-Bosch) vs. loyalists (anti-Bosch), with the help of 30,000 U.S. troops
Principal commanders: *Rebel,* Francisco Caamaño; *Loyalist,* Elías Wessin y Wessin
Result: In a compromise to settle the hostilities, a new presidential election was held, allowing Bosch to run once more; but he was defeated by Joaquín Balaguer.

The Dominican Republic shares the Caribbean island of Hispaniola with the Republic of Haiti. The history of the Dominican Republic has been a tumultuous one, dating back to the time of its settlement by the Spanish conquistadores at the beginning of the sixteenth century. In 1930, a Dominican army officer trained by the United States, Rafael Leónidas Trujillo Molina, took over the government. He ruled the country as a dictator for the next thirty-one years. His violent excesses finally led to his assassination, and the country again returned to a period of unstable but supposedly democratic government.

Civil War

The civil war that racked the country in 1965 reflected the tumultuous history of the Dominican Republic. The president at this time, Donald Reid Cabral, had been installed as the result of the ouster of the country's legitimately elected president, Juan Bosch, through a military coup. Reid Cabral was not a popular leader. In 1965, a lack of economic progress, coupled with a severe water shortage in the capital itself, had turned the general public against the president.

On April 24, 1965, the revolt broke out. A group of civilians and younger army officers seized the principal radio station in the capital, Santo Domingo, as well as two army bases. They announced that they planned to restore Bosch to power. Bosch, at that time living in exile in nearby Puerto Rico, commenced packing his bags for a return to the Dominican Republic. A militarily powerful opposition group announced that they would not s-accept Bosch's resumption of the presidency. The intense fighting that erupted between these self-described loyalists and the pro-Bosch rebels precluded the former president's return.

The U.S. government, already nervous concerning the Caribbean political situation because of the rise of Fidel Castro in nearby Cuba, regarded Bosch as a potential ally to the Cuban dictator. The U.S. embassy committed itself to backing General Elías Wessin y Wessin, the commander of the loyalist troops. The navy of the Dominican Republic, its air force, and a number of army units also sided with Wessin in his opposition to the coup.

Colonel Francisco Caamaño, who had received training from the U.S. Marines, assumed command of the rebel forces. When he attempted to secure the support of American ambassador W. Tapley Bennett, Jr., to arrange peace negotiations with General Wessin, he was told that the rebels had no choice but to surrender unconditionally. The rebel leadership immediately rejected this suggestion.

U.S. Occupation

U.S. president Lyndon B. Johnson had reached the conclusion that the rebel movement was a communist plot. He agreed initially to send U.S. troops into the country to aid in the evacuation of U.S. citizens. As time went on, and the conflict between the rebels and the loyalists continued,

U.S. troops guarding a food distribution center during the American occupation of the Dominican Republic. (National Archives)

Johnson announced that the rebel movement was in the hands of communist conspirators and authorized the use of American forces to maintain peace. The Americans provided support, if indirectly, to the Wessin loyalists. The U.S. forces set up a cordon around downtown Santo Domingo, the district that contained the bulk of the rebel troops, limiting the ability of that faction to maneuver. Ultimately the number of U.S. Army and Marine troops, both ashore and on support vessels, reached 30,000.

The United States sought international support for its intervention by involving the Organization of American States (OAS), comprising the Western Hemisphere governments, in the peacekeeping effort. The U.S. government worked to find a political solution among the Dominican Republic factions as well. At the urging of the U.S. government, the OAS recommended the establishment of a provisional government until popular elections could be held once more. Under the proposed pact, the Dominican military leaders from both factions were required to leave the country.

Aftermath

The Dominican Republic held presidential elections in 1966. A former Trujillo Molina supporter, Joaquín Balaguer, defeated Bosch convincingly. Balaguer had open U.S. support, for the United States felt that Bosch might ally himself with Fidel Castro. U.S. troops departed Hispaniola after the election.

Carl Henry Marcoux

1983
Grenada Occupation

At issue: Soviet influence in the Caribbean
Date: October 25-December 15, 1983
Location: Republic of Grenada
Combatants: 6,000 American troops vs. Grenada forces and some Cubans
Principal commanders: *American*, Joseph Metcalf; *Grenadian*, Hudson Austin
Principal battles: Pearls Airport, Point Salines Airport, Fort Rupert, Government House, Fort Frederick
Result: A late Cold War confrontation on a Western Hemisphere island nation, aimed at communist containment.

Relations between Grenada, an independent republic within the British Commonwealth of Nations, and the United States began to deteriorate in the late 1970's with the creation of a Grenadian Marxist government, the New Jewel Movement (NJM), led by moderate socialist Maurice Bishop. Beginning in 1979, Bishop established cordial relations with the Soviet Union and Cuba, including an exchange of diplomatic recognition and the beginnings of extensive Cuban-Soviet military and financial aid to Grenada. As a result, the United States government initiated a boycott of the Bishop government, refused to accept the credentials of the Grenadian ambassador in Washington, D.C., and withdrew the United States ambassador to Grenada.

The United States also attempted to block loans to Grenada from Western Europe, the World Bank, and the Caribbean Development Bank. Grenada was excluded from U.S. regional assistance programs available to other Caribbean and Latin American states. Soviet and Cuban assistance for Central American rebellions hostile to the United States strengthened the U.S. resolve to prevent further possible Soviet threats to U.S. interests in Latin America and the Caribbean.

U.S.-Grenada Tensions

The immediate cause of heightened U.S.-Grenadian tensions, however, was the construction of an international airport at Point Salines, southwest of St. George's, Grenada's capital. According to U.S. intelligence sources, the airport was being built with assistance from Cuba, as well as several European nations. Cuban engineers were alleged to be in the process of lengthening and strengthening the airport runways for the possible use of Cuban and Soviet military aircraft. The alleged military application of the new Grenadian airport was used from 1981 to 1983 by President Ronald Reagan, a longtime critic of Soviet influence and a staunch supporter of Cold War diplomacy, to focus attention on the alleged Soviet and Cuban direction of Bishop's NJM. The Reagan administration claimed that the Soviet Union had established a missile base in Grenada's central mountains, and that sophisticated Soviet monitoring equipment might be installed in Grenada to track U.S. submarine movements in the Caribbean.

U.S. Intervention

The Reagan administration's decision to use military force was reinforced by an October, 1983, coup against Bishop, sparked by Bernard Coard, the leader of an extremist revolutionary faction within the New Jewel Movement and an ardent admirer of Cuban communism. Coard also was accused of being responsible for Bishop's murder during the fighting

U.S. soldier poses with American students at a Grenadan medical school. Protecting the safety of U.S. nationals was a primary justification of the U.S. occupation of the minuscule eastern Caribbean nation. (U.S. Department of Defense)

between NJM factions and Grenadian government forces. Coard's extremist revolutionary regime immediately requested increased Cuban and Soviet military assistance and ordered the creation of a people's militia, the jailing of political opponents, and an end to Bishop's pledge of free elections by the beginning of 1984. Following several weeks of ineffective diplomatic negotiations between the Reagan administration and the Coard regime, on October 25, 1983, U.S. Marines and U.S. Army Rangers, plus a small military police force from six Caribbean nations, invaded Grenada. The U.S. military force included nineteen hundred Marines, the helicopter carrier *Saipan*, a sixteen-ship battle group led by the aircraft carrier *Independence*, and the amphibious assault ship *Guam*.

President Reagan's official announcement of the invasion included a statement that the United States was responding to an October 23 request from the Organization of Eastern Caribbean States (OECS) to help restore law and order in Grenada and guarantee political freedom and free elections for the Grenadian population. Reagan also maintained that information from the OECS and reports that U.S. citizens, many of them medical students enrolled at the Medical University of St. George's, were trying to escape the island and could be held hostage by the Coard regime or Cuban military advisers had persuaded him that the United States had no choice but to act decisively. Reagan's assertions were seconded by Prime Minister Eugenia Charles of Dominica, chairwoman of the OECS. Charles asserted that the Coard-led coup against Bishop was inspired and directed by Cuban advisers who feared that free elections in Grenada would result in a repudiation of revolutionary Marxism and the end of Cuban influence on the island.

Resistance to the U.S. Invasion

Armed resistance to the U.S.-led invasion was stronger than anticipated. U.S. military intelligence concluded that between six hundred and eleven hundred Cuban construction workers, military advisers, and militia were in Grenada. U.S. Marines reported that the airport, government buildings, and other strategic areas were heavily defended. By October 26, however, most opposition had been subdued and, once the major U.S. military objectives were attained, three hundred members of a joint eastern Caribbean police force landed on the island to begin security operations. By October 29, all Cuban personnel on the island had been captured, and Coard and other members of his regime had been arrested. Under OECS auspices, a new interim government was announced under British Commonwealth jurisdiction. Sir Paul Scoon, Commonwealth governor general, on November 1 announced plans for elections and revealed his intention to bring to trial those responsible for the murder of Maurice Bishop. Scoon also delivered diplomatic messages to the Soviet Union and Cuba that Grenada was cutting all ties with the two nations, and that approximately 650 captured Cubans would be repatriated.

By early November, the U.S. Department of State had revealed the contents of thousands of secret documents discovered by U.S. and Caribbean security forces. The documents included three Soviet supply agreements with the Bishop regime. U.S. officials also cited evidence that the Soviet Union had agreed to provide military training for the Grenadian militia. Other documents indicated that Cuba had long-range plans to take over the island and initiate a terrorist training camp to be used to foment revolutionary movements in the Caribbean and Central America. The Central Intelligence Agency released captured Cuban communications indicating that Cuba had planned to send 341 additional officers and 4,000 reservists to Grenada by the end of 1983. Reagan administration officials also cited documentary evidence to show that Cuba and the Coard regime planned to hold U.S. citizens hostage in the event of hostile U.S. actions.

International Reactions

International reaction to the U.S. invasion was almost universally negative. British prime minister Margaret Thatcher expressed considerable doubt regarding the invasion and advised Reagan to reconsider using military action as a substitute for economic sanctions against the Coard regime. Thatcher also announced publicly that the Grenada situation should be considered a British Commonwealth affair and therefore outside the interests of the United States. By November 1, however, the Thatcher government announced limited support for Reagan's decision to invade, based on the prime minister's understanding that the United States was entitled to act at the request of the OECS. The French government, on October 25, declared the U.S. invasion a violation of international law. The Canadian government also announced its regret for the invasion in light of the lack of substantial evidence to show that U.S. citizens in Grenada were in danger. The governments of the Soviet Union and Cuba, and the Sandinista regime in Nicaragua issued pro forma condemnations of U.S. actions, which asserted that the Reagan administration was interested solely in subordinating Grenada to U.S. neocolonialist rule. On October 28, the United Nations Security Council approved, by a vote of eleven to one, with three abstentions, a resolution condemning the armed intervention in Grenada. The United States vetoed the resolution.

In the United States, political opinions regarding the invasion split along party lines. Democratic congressmen and senators generally condemned the invasion as unprovoked, hasty, an overreaction, and tantamount to an act of war. Other Democratic Party leaders in Washington ridiculed Reagan as having a "cowboy mentality" and criticized the president for relying too heavily on the military solution to diplomatic problems. Republican political leaders, however, praised Reagan's "decisive actions." Most proinvasion sentiment centered on arguments for enforcement of the Monroe Doctrine, the thwarting of Soviet-inspired terrorism, and the necessity for backing the president and the U.S. Armed Forces during a time of crisis. U.S. public opinion generally favored President Reagan's decision to invade Grenada and eliminate Soviet and Cuban influence.

William G. Ratliff

1983
Censorship During the Grenada Occupation

During this surprise invasion, U.S. military leaders kept the press out of Grenada, thus preventing independent news coverage of initial military operations.

On October 25, 1983, approximately six thousand U.S. Marines and paratroopers invaded the tiny Caribbean island of Grenada on the orders of

President Ronald Reagan. Hostilities ended ten days later, and U.S. combat troops were withdrawn by December 15, 1983. Military commanders, supported by the Reagan administration, kept all news reporters out of Grenada during the first two days of military operations. Not surprisingly, representatives of the news media bitterly accused the president and the Pentagon of denying freedom of the press and encouraging censorship in the name of national security.

The military's contention that the exclusion of press representation during the initial fighting was motivated solely by concerns for the reporters' safety was promptly challenged. Journalists pointed out that they had always accepted the risks of war as part of their profession, citing the 146 war correspondents killed during World War II and the 53 correspondents killed in the Vietnam War. Management of the news by the Department of Defense was described as a military blackout. This implied that unsympathetic coverage of the war against Grenada should not be available to the American public or the U.S. Congress.

A long tradition of war reporting and the First Amendment's protection of the public's right to know dates back to the U.S. Civil War. In Grenada, however, the Pentagon chose to bar independent media access by not arranging transportation, allowing unrestricted movement among the troops, or providing communications facilities on the island until the invasion's success was achieved.

This type of censorship differed from that during the British-Argentine Falkland Islands War seven years earlier. In that conflict the British government provided journalists with access to warships, and gave a limited number of journalists access to the ground fighting, but it subjected their reports to official scrutiny, deletion, and revision. In Grenada the U.S. officials did not overtly censor the press; it simply did not bring reporters along during the initial fighting, thereby creating a news blackout. The important exceptions to the blackout were the Pentagon's official statements on the fighting, White House justifications of the invasion, and statements of other officials, who portrayed the rescue mission of American medical students and removal of Grenada's communist government in the best possible light.

The relationship between the U.S. press and the military establishment had deteriorated so greatly since the Vietnam War that, in the eyes of leading military officers, much of the press was viewed as motivated by malevolent intent and lacking any sympathy for a strong military. An attempt to reconcile the media and the press was made by the Sidle Commission report, August 23, 1984. It recommended that the media should be allowed to cover U.S. military operations to the maximum degree possible in the future. If only a few journalists could be accommodated, then "pool" reporters would be selected by the Pentagon who then would share their information with other journalists.

Christopher E. Kent

1989
Panama Occupation

At issue: Legitimacy of Manuel Noriega's government
Date: December 20, 1989-January, 1990
Location: Republic of Panama
Combatants: Americans vs. Panamanians
Principal figures: *American*, President George Bush (1924-   ), General Maxwell Thurman (1931-   ); *Panamanian*, President Manuel Noriega (1934-   ), President-elect Guillermo Endara (1936-   )
Result: U.S. troops captured Panamanian president Manuel Noriega, permitting a legally elected president to take office; however, the U.S. seizure of a foreign head of state in his own country raised troubling questions about U.S. intervention in the affairs of other nations.

The generally amicable relations between the United States and Panama began to falter after Panamanian general Manuel Noriega came to power in Panama in 1987. Despite his history of involvement in drug trafficking, gun running, and money laundering, Noriega had been receiving support from the Central Intelligence Agency (CIA) as a friendly resource in Panama. However, relations between the two countries deteriorated rapidly after Noriega arranged the ouster of Panama's legally elected president Eric Delvalle and annulled the subsequent election of Guillermo Endara. The U.S. government continued to distance itself from Noriega as both Panamanian domestic unrest and international opprobrium rose against Noriega.

Background

Growing instability in Panama raised American concern about the security of the Panama Canal, which was vital to international shipping. On December 20, 1989, President George Bush ordered U.S. troops into Panama with the ostensible purpose of seizing Noriega on drug-smuggling charges. Code-named Operation Just Cause, the invasion was undertaken with the primary goal of capturing Noriega. General Maxwell Thurman commanded forces that included paratroopers, amphibious assault units, attack helicopters, and jet fighters. Thurman's invasion overwhelmed the Panamanian Defense Forces within a few days. About twenty-five thousand U.S. military personnel were involved, and their weapons included two advanced Stealth fighter-bombers.

In spite of their superior technology, Thurman's forces did come upon some difficulties. Their attack on Noriega's military headquarters was effective, but this multistory building was located in a densely populated part of Panama City. After American attack helicopters and artillery set the building ablaze, the fire spread until almost two thousand surrounding homes were destroyed. Fifteen thousand people were left homeless, and a number of civilians were killed or injured.

For several days Noriega succeeded in hiding from the U.S. forces. Finally, he took refuge in the Papal Nunciature—the office of the pope's representative in the country—where he stayed until January 3, 1990. After officials of the Roman Catholic Church informed the Bush administration where Noriega was hiding, General Thurman decided to use psychologi-

U.S. Drug Enforcement Agency officers taking deposed Panamanian president Manuel Noriega aboard the Air Force transport plane that took him to the United States, where he was tried and convicted of drug dealing. (U.S. Air Force)

cal weapons: He surrounded the Nunciature with large numbers of troops and played rock-and-roll music over powerful loudspeakers.

Noriega finally surrendered to the U.S. military. After an overnight airplane flight to Miami, he found himself in a Florida jail awaiting trial. On April 9, 1992, he was convicted of eight out of ten drug and racketeering charges, and in July he was sentenced to forty years in prison.

U.S. Embarrassments

Several aspects of the invasion held the potential for embarrassing the U.S. government—not least of which was Washington's earlier support for Noriega. Moreover, the military operation itself had a number of embarrassing problems, including civilian deaths, and there were instances of Panamanian civilians protesting the American effort to "liberate" them. Despite these problems, the American news media were unusually supportive of the invasion, portraying it in a positive light—even in comparison with the media's coverage of the following year's Persian Gulf War. More significantly, there was little official effort to restrict or manage news coverage of the Panama invasion. The "press pool" system that would be used in reporting on the later Gulf War was not utilized in the Panama operation. American reporters and photographers were present at the invitation of the invasion force and had relatively free access to cover events. American press coverage might therefore have been partly a product of self-censorship.

Although the U.S. government did not overtly hinder media access, there is some evidence that the Endara government—which the U.S. military returned to power after removing Noriega—worked to limit negative portrayals of the military intervention by its American benefactors. Also, Noriega's numerous moral and political faults may have made portraying the invasion as a morality play almost irresistible. Finally, the relative swiftness of Noriega's defeat provided little time for antiwar sentiment to materialize.

Noriega's capture was a victory over brutal dictatorship and international lawlessness, but it also raised some controversial issues. Using military force to capture a citizen of one country for criminal charges in another country was a dangerous step to take, for in other circumstances it might bring greater bloodshed, even war. A gutted, burned-down area of Panama City remained as a sad illustration of the risks President Bush had taken in ordering the invasion. Also, Latin American countries remembered how the United States had used its military forces to get its way in their countries earlier in the twentieth century. They were unhappy to see the pattern repeated.

Christopher E. Kent

Further Reading

Allison, Graham T. *Essence of Decision: Explaining the Cuban Missile Crisis.* 2d ed. New York: Longman, 1999.

Beck, Robert J. *The Grenada Invasion: Politics, Law, and Foreign Policy Decisionmaking.* Boulder, Colo.: Westview Press, 1993.

Blight, James G., and Peter Kornbluh, eds. *Politics of Illusion: The Bay of Pigs Invasion Reexamined.* Boulder, Colo.: Lynne Rienner, 1998.

Boot, Max. *The Savage Wars of Peace: Small Wars and the Rise of American Power.* New York: Basic Books, 2003.

Brugioni, Dino A. *Eyeball to Eyeball: The Inside Story of the Cuban Missile Crisis.* New York: Random House, 1991.

Buckley, Kevin. *Panama: The Whole Story.* New York: Simon & Schuster, 1991.

Chang, Laurence, and Peter Kornbluh, eds. *The Cuban Missile Crisis, 1962: A National Security Archive Documents Reader.* New York: New Press, 1992.

Dunn, Peter M., and Bruce W. Watson, eds. *American Intervention in Grenada: The Implications of Operation Urgent Fury.* Boulder, Colo.: Westview Press, 1985.

Entman, Robert M. *Projections of Power: Framing News, Public Opinion, and U.S. Foreign Policy.* Chicago: University of Chicago Press, 2004.

Frankel, Max. *High Noon in the Cold War: Kennedy, Khrushchev, and the Cuban Missile Crisis.* New York: Ballantine Books, 2004.

Fursenko, Alexander, and Timothy Naftali. *One Hell of a Gamble: Khrushchev, Castro, and Kennedy, 1958-1964.* New York: Norton, 1997.

George, Alice L. *Awaiting Armageddon: How Americans Faced the Cuban Missile Crisis.* Chapel Hill: University of North Carolina Press, 2003.

Gleijeses, Piero. *The Dominican Crisis.* Baltimore, Md.: Johns Hopkins University Press, 1978.

Hartlyn, Jonathan. *The Struggle for Democratic Politics in the Dominican Republic.* Chapel Hill: University of North Carolina Press, 1998.

Huchthausen, Peter A. *America's Splendid Little Wars: A Short History of U.S. Military Engagements, 1975-2000.* New York: Viking, 2003.

Johns, Christina Jacqueline, and P. Ward Johnson. *State Crime, the Media, and the Invasion of Panama.* Westport, Conn.: Praeger, 1994.

Kornbluh, Peter, ed. *Bay of Pigs Declassified: The Secret CIA Report on the Invasion of Cuba.* New York: New Press, 1998.

Lindsay-Poland, John. *Emperors in the Jungle: The Hidden History of the U.S. in Panama.* Durham, N.C.: Duke University Press, 2003.

Lowenthal, Abraham F. *The Dominican Intervention*. Baltimore: Johns Hopkins University Press, 1995.

Lynch, Grayston L. *Decision for Disaster: Betrayal at the Bay of Pigs*. Washington, D.C.: Brassey's, 1998.

May, Ernest, and Philip Zelikow, eds. *The Kennedy Tapes: Inside the White House During the Cuban Missile Crisis*. New York: Norton, 2002.

Mermin, Jonathan. *Debating War and Peace: Media Coverage of U.S. Intervention in the Post-Vietnam Era*. Princeton, N.J.: Princeton University Press, 1999.

Nathan, James A., ed. *The Cuban Missile Crisis Revisited*. New York: St. Martin's Press, 1992.

O'Shaughnessy, Hugh. *Grenada: An Eyewitness Account of the U.S. Invasion and the Caribbean History That Provoked It*. New York: Dodd, Mead, 1984.

Palmer, Bruce, Jr. *Intervention in the Caribbean: The Dominican Crisis of 1965*. Lexington: University Press of Kentucky, 1989.

Peguero, Valentina. *The Militarization of Culture in the Dominican Republic, from the Captains General to General Trujillo*. Lincoln: University of Nebraska Press, 2004.

Pérez, Orlando J., ed. *Post-invasion Panama: The Challenges of Democratization in the New World Order*. Lanham, Md.: Lexington Books, 2000.

Rodríguez, Juan Carlos. *The Bay of Pigs and the CIA*. Translated by Mary Todd. New York: Ocean Press, 1999.

Salinger, Pierre. "Bay of Pigs." In *John F. Kennedy, Commander in Chief: A Profile in Leadership*. New York: Penguin Studio, 1997.

Stern, Sheldon M. *Averting 'the Final Failure': John F. Kennedy and the Secret Cuban Missile Crisis Meetings*. Stanford, Calif.: Stanford University Press, 2003.

Strober, Gerald S., and Deborah H. Strober. "Let Us Begin Anew." In *An Oral History of the Kennedy Presidency*. New York: HarperCollins, 1993.

Thompson, Robert Smith. *The Missiles of October: The Declassified Story of John F. Kennedy and the Cuban Missile Crisis*. New York: Simon & Schuster, 1992.

Tiwathia, Vijay. *The Grenada War: Anatomy of a Low Intensity Conflict*. New Delhi: Lancer International, 1987.

Triay, Victor Andres. *Bay of Pigs: An Oral History of Brigade 2506*. Gainesville: University Press of Florida, 2001.

White, Mark J. *Missiles in Cuba: Kennedy, Khrushchev, Castro, and the 1962 Crisis*. Chicago: Ivan R. Dee, 1997.

_____, ed. *The Kennedys and Cuba: The Declassified Documentary History*. Chicago: Ivan R. Dee, 2001.

Wyden, Peter. *Bay of Pigs: The Untold Story*. New York: Simon & Schuster, 1980.

Post-Cold War Conflicts
1991-2005

Post-Cold War Conflicts

At issue: Political stability, secular vs. theocratic government, and suppression of world terrorism
Date: 1991-
Location: Middle East, Northeast Africa, and the Balkans
Principal conflicts: Gulf War (1991), Somalia occupation (1992-1994), Bosnia (1994-1995), Afghanistan and Sudan (1998), Terrorist attack on the USS *Cole* (2000), Terrorist attacks on the United States (2001), Invasion of Afghanistan (2001), War on Terrorism (2001-   ), Iraq War (2003-   )
Results: Since the fall of the Soviet Union in 1991, the tensions associated with the Cold War have abated; however, new and potentially more dangerous conflicts have arisen to take their place. By the year 2005, most of these conflicts remained unresolved.

One of the most unexpected developments of the last years of the twentieth century and first years of the twenty-first century has been the failure of the ending of the Cold War to bring peace and stability to the world order. Although there has been a dramatic lessening of tensions between the United States and its former Cold War rivals, new and unexpected conflicts and tensions have arisen to take their place, and many of these have drawn U.S. forces into combat. Moreover, by the year 2005, a majority of Americans believed that the world was an even more dangerous place than it had been during the days of the Cold War. Between 1991 and 2005, U.S. military forces were directly involved in lethal conflicts in three different regions: the Middle East, Northeast Africa, and the Balkans. Several of these conflicts developed into full-scale wars.

Northeast Africa and the Middle East

The Middle East was a center of conflicts throughout the second half of the twentieth century, but much of the region's tension and actual armed conflict arose from the animosity between the Jewish state of Israel, which was founded in 1948, and the predominantly Muslim nations that surround it. The United States generally supported Israel through those years but was never directly involved in any of Israel's wars with its Arab neighbors. What finally drew the United States into major armed conflict in the region was only tangentially related to the Arab-Israeli struggle.

With the collapse of the Soviet Union and the end of the Cold War during the late 1980's and early 1990's, unequivocal U.S. diplomatic support for its long-time ally Israel came to an end. U.S. diplomats began to bring

(continued on page 682)

TIME LINE OF POST-COLD WAR CONFLICTS

June, 1961	Kuwait becomes independent; Iraq begins challenging the new nation's sovereignty.
May, 1988	Somali civil war begins.
Aug. 2, 1990	Iraq occupies Kuwait; United Nations Security Council orders Iraq to pull out.
Nov. 29, 1990	U.N. Security Council gives Iraq January 15, 1991, deadline to withdraw from Iraq.
Jan. 16, 1991	United States launches air strikes on Iraq, while leading international coalition in what becomes known as the Gulf War (or Persian Gulf War).
February 23, 1991	Coalition land offensive vs. Iraq begins.
Feb. 28, 1991	Iraq capitulates and withdraws from Kuwait, but Iraq's President Saddam Hussein stays in power.
May 17, 1991	Northern Somalis declare independent Republic of Somaliland.
Oct., 1991	The Yugoslavian republics of Slovenia, Croatia, and Bosnia-Herzegovina declare their independence.
Jan. 15, 1992	Yugoslavian federation dissolves into constituent parts.
Feb., 1992	Cease-fire is declared in Somali civil war but soon breaks down; national famine worsens.
Mar., 1992	Civil war begins in Bosnia-Herzegovina.
August 11, 1992	U.N. human rights inspector reports that Hussein is killing his own people.
August 27, 1992	To counter Hussein's attacks on Shiite Muslims in southern Iraq, United States, Great Britain, and France establish "no fly" zone for Iraqi aircraft below the 32d parallel.
Dec. 9, 1992-Mar. 31, 1994	U.S. troops occupy Somalia.
Feb. 26, 1993	Terrorist bombing damages lower level of one of the towers of New York City's World Trade Center.
Apr. 10, 1994	U.S. troops intervene in Bosnian civil war.
Dec. 14, 1995	U.S. troops are major part of NATO contingent that enter Bosnia to enforce peace agreement.
Aug. 7, 1998	Terrorist bombs explode at U.S. embassies in Kenya and Tanzania, killing more than 250 people—mostly African nationals.

Aug. 20, 1998	United States launches missile strikes against targets in Afghanistan and the Sudan in retaliation for terrorist bombings.
October 31, 1998	Iraq suspends all cooperation with the U.N. weapons inspectors.
Dec. 16, 1998	United States and Britain bomb five Iraq radar sites.
Oct. 12, 2000	Suicide terrorist attack on USS *Cole* in the port of Aden, Yemen.
Sept. 11, 2001	"9/11" terrorist attacks on the World Trade Center and the Pentagon; U.S. Congress responds by passing the Patriot Act to give president greater power to combat terrorism.
Oct. 7, 2001	United States launches invasion of Afghanistan after Taliban regime refuses to comply with U.S. request to turn over Osama bin Laden and other al-Qaeda leaders. President George W. Bush declares "war on terrorism."
Jan., 2002	In his state of the union address, President Bush alludes to Iraq, Iran, and North Korea as "an axis of evil."
Oct., 2002	Al-Qaeda bombs resort complex in Indonesia.
Oct. 10-11, 2002	U.S. Congress empowers President Bush to invade Iraq if latter fails to dismantle its alleged weapons programs.
Nov., 2002	United Nations approves a resolution calling upon Iraq to disarm.
Jan., 2003	In his state of the union address, President Bush claims that Iraq is attempting to acquire uranium in order to build nuclear weapons. U.S. secretary of state Colin Powell presents evidence to the U.N. Security Council that Iraq is building "weapons of mass destruction" (WMD).
Mar. 15-16, 2003	President Bush and British prime minister Tony Blair hold emergency meeting and issue ultimatum to Iraq to disarm.
Mar. 19, 2003	United States leads a new coalition in a new invasion of Iraq, in what becomes known as the Iraq War, after Hussein fails to meet U.S.-British ultimatum.
May 1, 2003	President Bush proclaims that the Iraq War is won.
December 13, 2003	Saddam Hussein is captured.
Mar., 2004	Al-Qaeda bombs commuter train in Madrid, Spain.

continued

TIME LINE OF POST-COLD WAR CONFLICTS—continued

May, 2004	U.S. soldiers' torture and abuse of Iraqi prisoners is made public.
June 1, 2004	Iraq's Interim Governing Council names Iyad Allawi prime minister.
Sept., 2004	U.N. secretary-general Kofi Annan calls the war in Iraq "illegal" under the U.N. Charter.
Sept. 8, 2004	One thousandth American service person is killed in Iraq.
Jan. 30, 2005	8.4 million Iraqis defy insurgent violence by voting in election for transitional national assembly; Shi'ite candidates win 48 percent of votes; Kurdish candidates place second. Afterward, civilian and military death tolls rise as assassinations and bombings continue.
Mar., 2005	U.S. military death total passes 1,500.
Dec., 2005	Scheduled date for national election on new constitution.

pressure to bear on the Israelis to make concessions to the Palestinians and other Middle Eastern states to achieve a lasting peace in the region. In 1991 war again interrupted the peace process. The Gulf War—or Persian Gulf War as it is also known—resulted from Iraq's invasion of the tiny oil-rich nation of Kuwait, which Iraq claimed as a lost province.

Encouraged by mixed signals from U.S. diplomats, Iraqi armed forces under Saddam Hussein occupied Kuwait, a region Hussein considered to be legally part of Iraq. U.S. trading partners in Europe and Asia received much of their oil from Kuwait. Consequently, U.S. president George Bush secured a United Nations (U.N.) condemnation of Iraqi actions and a Security Council resolution calling for the expulsion of Iraqi forces from Kuwait by force of arms. A military force made up overwhelmingly of American troops landed in Kuwait, while American aircraft bombed Iraqi military targets and cities.

During the brief conflict, the Iraqis launched guided missile attacks on Saudi Arabia and Israel. The American-led U.N. forces quickly overwhelmed the Iraqis and drove them out of Kuwait, forcing Hussein to capitulate. U.S. military forces remained stationed in Saudi Arabia and Kuwait into the next century, to guard against renewed Iraqi attempts to incorporate Kuwait into Iraq. Allied forces continued to monitor Iraq through the 1990's and renewed bombing attacks on Iraqi bases in 1998, but Iraq eventually renounced its claims to Kuwait, and the situation seemed to stabilize. In the early twenty-first century, new—and possibly unrelated—developments would turn U.S. attention back to Iraq. Meanwhile, other disturbing events were commanding American attention and placing new demands on U.S. military forces.

In December, 1992, the United States sent troops into the Northeast African nation of Somalia to help bring order to a country whose central government had literally collapsed. The United Nations-authorized humanitarian mission was doomed from the start, and U.S. troops spent more than one year fighting a no-win war against feuding warlords. Eventually, both U.S. and U.N. forces were withdrawn, after accomplishing almost nothing and leaving Americans skeptical about intervening in the internal conflicts of developing nations.

Bosnia

The end of the Cold War was brought about by the collapse of communist regimes throughout Eastern Europe, the Soviet Union, and the Balkans during the late 1980's and early 1990's. In Eastern Europe, this develop-

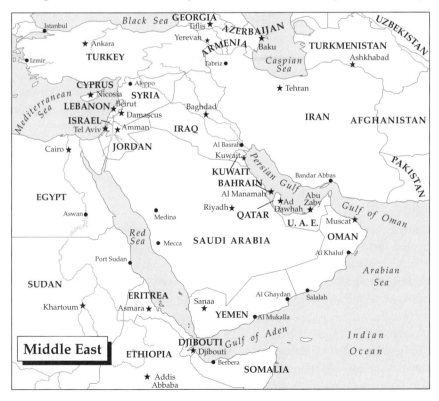

ment led to the democratization and increased prosperity of such nations as Poland, Hungary, the Czech Republic, and Slovakia—all of which later joined the North Atlantic Treaty Organization (NATO). By contrast, the transformation brought mostly chaos to the Balkans. The death in 1980 of Yugoslavia's communist dictator, Tito, revealed the tenuousness of the fabric holding together the diverse and mutually antagonistic ethnic and religious groups that Tito's federation had held together for more than three decades. These tensions were aggravated by the general collapse of communist regimes elsewhere in Europe, and Yugoslavia itself began breaking up in October, 1991, when the former Yugoslav republics of Slovenia, Croatia, and Bosnia-Herzegovina declared their independence.

In March, 1992, a bitter civil war began in Bosnia between Christian Serbs and Bosnian Muslims. Two years later, U.S. troops entered Bosnia, under U.N. auspices, to help restore peace. As was the case in Somalia, U.S. forces could do little to improve the apparently intractable situation, even after more troops entered Bosnia at the end of 1995, under the auspices of NATO. The whole experience merely exasperated Americans and renewed their suspicions that the end of the Cold War was not bringing the stability to world order that they had expected.

World Terrorism

Less than three months after U.S. forces entered Somalia, world terrorism made its presence felt on American shores, when agents of al-Qaeda bombed the lower level of one of New York's World Trade Center towers. The bombing attack did comparatively minor damage to the gigantic structure but made Americans uneasy about the vulnerability of their open society to terrorism. The attacks that came eight years later would replace uneasiness with something akin to widespread panic.

In August, 1998, the United States again became the target of al-Qaeda attacks, but this time on foreign shores, when the U.S. embassies in the capital cities of East Africa's Kenya and Tanzania were both bombed. The United States responded quickly by launching missile strikes against suspected terrorist bases in Afghanistan and the Sudan. Yet another terrorist attack against the United States occurred in October, 2000, when suicide bombers managed to cripple the U.S. destroyer *Cole* while the ship was in the Yemen port of Aden, across the inlet to the Red Sea from Somalia.

Finally, on September 11, 2001, terrorist attacks on the United States mounted by radical Islamic fundamentalists based in the Middle East brought the most serious armed conflict to the U.S. mainland since the U.S. Civil War. Indeed, when the terrorists flew hijacked American airliners into the Pentagon Building and the towers of New York City's World Trade

Iraqi president Saddam Hussein (left) and his oldest son, Uday, shortly before the beginning of the Gulf War. In official portraits, Hussein often posed in military uniforms.
(AP/Wide World Photos)

Center on September 11, more Americans died than had perished during Japan's surprise attack on Pearl Harbor in December, 1941. Thereafter, September 11—or "9/11"—became a patriotic rallying cry for Americans feeling threatened by little-understood enemies from abroad. It would be difficult to overstate the feeling of alarm that the attacks created throughout the United States.

Under the leadership of President George W. Bush, the nation quickly retaliated by launching an invasion of Afghanistan—the nation in which the terrorists were based, and calls for a general "war on terrorism" arose. Much of the alarm was focused on the Middle East, including Iraq. Although no credible evidence has been brought forth to establish a link between the Iraqi regime of Saddam Hussein and the September 11 attacks, the Bush administration fostered the notion that Iraq shared some of the blame and posed a threat to world peace. This notion was reinforced by unresolved questions about the Iraqi regime's building of weapons of mass destruction, and the United States led another invasion of Iraq in early 2003. However, despite the use of overwhelming force that quickly defeated Iraqi's formal military units, the United States and its allies failed to gain complete control of the country even after nearly two years of occupation.

Christopher E. Kent

.

Campaigns, Battles, and Other Events

1991
Gulf War

At issue: Kuwait's sovereignty
Date: January 16-February 28, 1991
Location: Iraq, Kuwait, and the Persian Gulf
Combatants: Iraqis vs. the allied coalition forces
Principal commanders: *Iraqi,* Lieutenant General Sultan Hashem Ahmad, Lieutenant General Saleh Abbud Mahmoud; *Coalition,* U.S. General H. Norman Schwarzkopf (1934-)
Principal battle: Khafji
Result: An allied victory allowed the reestablishment of Kuwaiti sovereignty and began a prolonged and controversial isolation of Iraq that would eventually lead to another war.

In August, 1990, a number of factors contributed to Iraqi president Saddam Hussein's decision to invade and annex neighboring Kuwait. Since Kuwait's independence, in June, 1961, Iraqi leaders had questioned the legitimacy of Kuwait's sovereignty and the border demarcating the two countries. An important oil field straddled the ill-defined frontier, and Kuwait had been tapping it. Iraq also charged Kuwait with exceeding its oil quota set by the Organization of Petroleum Exporting Countries (OPEC), thereby increasing supplies and depressing prices. Iraq had pressed Kuwait unsuccessfully for the latter to make available to Baghdad two islands, Warba and Babiyan, strategically located across from Umm Qasr, Iraq's only outlet on the Persian Gulf proper.

Iraq's Goals

Most important, 1990 was a time of acute financial hardship for Iraq because of the great indebtedness it had incurred following its murderous eight-year war with Iran, which had concluded in 1988. Iraq had to rebuild its devastated economy, especially its crucial oil industry.

Several factors led Saddam Hussein to decide that this was a good time to force Iraq's creditors, especially Kuwait, to relinquish their claims on their wartime "loans": Iranian-Iraqi relations were improving; Iraqi economic problems were becoming more pressing; he had misread the degree of U.S.-Soviet cooperation possible in the post-Cold War era; and he apparently misinterpreted U.S. ambassador April Glaspie's statement to him on July 25, 1990, that the Bush administration was neutral in matters of inter-Arab disputes "like your border disagreement with Kuwait." Hussein also hoped to punish those who had brought down the price of oil by overproduction or had committed other "offenses."

Various meetings of leaders and conferences involving Iraq, Kuwait, and others were fruitless, partly because Kuwait refused to give ground on substantive issues and partly because Saddam Hussein seemed to be determined to invade Kuwait. The invasion occurred at 2:00 A.M. on August 2, 1990. Token resistance by the tiny Kuwaiti army and the escape of most members of the extended al-Sabah ruling family to Saudi Arabia followed within hours. Kuwait was occupied by Iraq and soon declared to be its nineteenth province.

The World Response

Saddam Hussein proved to be wrong in his estimate of the response of the international community, which insisted that his invasion of the neighboring country be rolled back. The United States, the Soviet Union, and

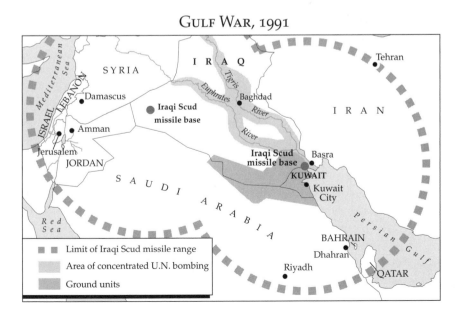

GULF WAR, 1991

United Nations Security Council Resolution 660 called for Iraq's immediate withdrawal from Kuwait. Four days later, on August 6, the Security Council imposed mandatory trade sanctions by members of the international organization, including a ban on Iraqi and Kuwaiti oil (Resolution 661).

Despite Saddam Hussein's reassurances to Joseph Wilson, the U.S. chargé d'affaires in Baghdad, President George Bush ordered the Eighty-second Airborne Division to protect neighboring Saudi Arabia in case Iraq was contemplating monopolizing the bulk of Middle Eastern oil production. Spearheading the emerging international response, Operation Desert Shield became the largest deployment of U.S. troops overseas since the Vietnam War. Iraq's formal annexation of Kuwait brought several Arab and other Muslim countries to side with the U.N.-sponsored, U.S.-led coalition. Westerners in Iraq and Kuwait were moved as human shields to sites that could become potential coalition targets in Iraq.

On November 29, the U.N. Security Council, acknowledging that its Resolution 660 of August 2 ordering Iraq to evacuate Kuwait had not been followed, mandated that all necessary means be used to expel Iraq after January 15, 1991 (Resolution 678). One last meeting between U.S. secretary of state James Baker and Iraqi foreign minister Tariq Aziz in Geneva on January 9, 1991, proved unsuccessful, as Aziz refused to accept Baker's renewed call for Iraq's unconditional withdrawal from Kuwait. The same was true of U.N. Secretary-General Javier Pérez de Cuéllar's visit to Saddam Hussein on January 13.

The War

The Persian Gulf War is usually broken down into four stages. Operation Desert Shield covered the period from the invasion of Kuwait on August 2, 1990, to the unleashing of the U.S.-led U.N. coalition's air war on January 17, 1991. The next phase, Operation Desert Storm, had two components: the air war through February 23 and the ground war from February 24 through February 28. The aftermath following the cease-fire saw the withdrawal of Iraqi forces from Kuwait; the redrawing of the Iraqi-Kuwaiti border by a U.N. commission; the creation of U.N.-sponsored safe zones and no-fly zones in Iraq to protect Kurds and other minorities; U.N. inspection of Iraqi facilities to monitor and force the destruction of any nuclear, biological, or chemical weapons; and the continued imposition of U.N. trade sanctions on Iraq.

The military operations involved more than three-quarters of a million troops on the coalition side (some 541,000 from the United States and about 254,000 from a number of the twenty-nine other countries participating in Desert Storm at its peak) facing some one million Iraqis. The Iraqi numeri-

Antiaircraft fire illuminates the sky over Baghdad during the early hours of January 18, 1991, as U.S. warplanes bombard Iraq's capital city. (AP/Wide World Photos)

cal advantage was not translated into battlefield successes; the technological edge of the coalition greatly offset other factors. As news reporters from CNN broadcast the events of the airwar live, a world audience watched and wondered whether the high-tech advantage of the coalition forces had spawned a new type of "bloodless" war. Such expectations proved illusory: The disproportionate Iraqi casualties not only testified to this fact but also raised the question of a just war among some observers. On March 3, senior military representatives from both sides met to finalize the cease-fire, whose terms the Iraqis accepted unconditionally.

In the aftermath, a protracted controversy continued over the Bush administration's decision to halt the ground war after a hundred hours, allowing Saddam Hussein and his Baathist regime to remain in power and the Iraqi army to suppress the Kurdish and Shiite uprisings soon after the cease-fire. President George Bush was aware that any longer-term entanglement might antagonize his constituency back home, as presidential elections were already on the horizon. He was unable to capitalize on his spectacular victory and soaring postwar popularity in the polls, however, because by November, 1992, economic problems had become the electorate's primary concern.

Questions also were raised as to whether enough time had been given for the economic embargo to take effect before Operation Desert Storm was

As Iraqi troops withdrew from Kuwait, they set fire to most of the oil fields, causing millions of dollars in damages and creating a massive ecological disaster in the Persian Gulf. (U.S. Department of Defense)

initiated. A debate regarding the high cost in Iraqi civilian suffering and lives that the U.N. embargo was exacting also continued. Despite the suspected contraband with its next-door neighbors Jordan and Iran, Iraq, deprived of its major export and foreign currency earner, oil, was becoming impoverished and unable to provide for the needs of the masses. Controversy also continued regarding the degree of encouragement that the earlier tilt toward Iraq of the Reagan and Bush administrations and the ambivalent words of Ambassador April Glaspie had given to Saddam Hussein. United Nations agencies were saddled with additional responsibilities and outlays in their several missions, especially the caring for many internal and external refugees.

As for the overall significance of the Persian Gulf War, there was no consensus on whether it was either the defining moment of President Bush's "New World Order" to uphold international law or the event simply reflecting oil politics as usual, packaged to appear as a stand for what was right with a few Arab members in the coalition providing an appropriate cover.

Peter B. Heller

1991
Censorship During the Gulf War

The war included strict controls on the information allowed to the media.

The Gulf War, which began as Operation Desert Shield to protect Saudi Arabia from Iraqi invasion and became Operation Desert Storm to liberate Iraqi-held Kuwait, involved world access to Persian Gulf oil. The United States fought to keep the mercurial Iraqi leader, Saddam Hussein, from military dominance in a sensitive region. Consequently, the United States began a military buildup in the region in August, 1990, after Iraq overran its small neighbor, Kuwait. United States and allied forces waged a massive air and ground assault on Iraq from January 16, 1991, to February 28, 1991. This assault liberated Kuwait but stopped short of total occupation of Iraq or removal of Saddam Hussein. The campaign involved serious censorship issues.

Military Censorship

Generally, the restriction or manipulation of information in a free society during wartime has been viewed as acceptable when national or military security is at stake. It is viewed as unacceptable when information is restricted or manipulated for political purposes—such as protecting the images of military and civilian leaders. Generally too, the media and the wartime authorities conflict over the manner and degree of censorship.

The Vietnam War prompted American leadership to develop a new model for dealing with the media during subsequent conflicts. Vietnam had been the most open war in U.S. history. It was also the first television war. Brutal images flashed back to the United States the reality of war. Although political and military leadership had tried to influence the type and flow of information, the media were free to roam the war zone and talk to the troops. In a war without fronts, the count of enemy dead became the military yardstick by which success was measured. The media exposed the body count system as fantasy and folly. Some in the military blamed the media for damaging American morale to the extent that the war became unwinnable.

The new model for war coverage in an age of instant communication, based on the British practice during the Falkland Islands War of 1982, involved sanitizing visual images, controlling media access to military operations, censoring information that could upset civilians, and excluding journalists who filed unfavorable stories. True to the British model, during the U.S. invasion of Grenada in 1983 the media were simply held incommunicado until the operation was complete. During the Gulf War, this proved impractical, owing to the duration of the conflict. Not a single journalist, however, accompanied the first American troops to the Persian Gulf in August of 1990 (actual fighting did not begin until January, 1991), as the Department of Defense began to lay the groundwork for censorship. In September, 1990, the Department of Defense claimed that at least 250,000 Iraqi troops were massing in Kuwait to attack Saudi Arabia. President George Bush used this misinformation to "draw a line in the sand." No such buildup existed. Journalists at first accepted the military's word. As journalists arrived in the Persian Gulf, the military implemented the pool system for controlling the flow of information.

The pool system restricted journalists to group meetings with selected military units and accompanied by a military official. The military also instituted a security-review procedure, which constituted a prior restraint on the news. Escort guidelines further dictated that the media were allowed no "unilateral coverage" of events. Finally, all stories and photographs had to be cleared by the Pentagon.

The commanding U.S. field general, Norman Schwarzkopf, deflected all criticism of the system by claiming that he was merely following orders and referring all critics to the assistant secretary of defense for public affairs in the Pentagon. Schwartzkopf's own rules for dealing with the media were "Don't let them intimidate you"; "There's no law that says you have to answer all their questions"; "Don't answer any questions that in your judgment would help the enemy"; and "Don't ever lie to the American people."

As a junior officer in Vietnam, Schwartzkopf had had firsthand experience with the high command's insistence upon a body count. Consequently, as commander in the Persian Gulf, he angrily rejected any talk about body counts. He claimed that he was as forthcoming as he could be, and that he even had to intercede with the Saudis to ensure some media access to the war. Saudi Arabia and Kuwait were without any tradition of a free press. Officially, the Saudis and the Kuwaitis could not understand why censorship could not be complete. Schwartzkopf's command had to handle this situation delicately.

Political Necessities

Politics, rather than military necessity, was the motive for much of the censorship in the Persian Gulf War. Washington insisted that it engaged in "precision bombing" using "smart" bombs during its forty-three day pounding of Baghdad, and doctored its photographic evidence accordingly. In fact, more than 90 percent of the bombs dropped were "dumb" bombs (those without guidance systems). Success was defined as avoiding civilian targets. Peter Arnett, a Cable News Network (CNN) correspondent who was allowed to broadcast from Baghdad, documented damage to civilian targets. He also verified the destruction of a plant that produced powdered milk for infants (the United States had insisted that the plant was used to produce biological weapons). The Iraqi government shadowed Arnett, but likely figured it was getting more propaganda value from his reports than the enemy was getting morale value. This introduced a new technological twist to modern warfare. A correspondent may broadcast live attacks on the enemy from the enemy's position; Arnett did so. Some viewed this, in the heat of war, as treasonous. Arnett was vilified in Washington. Senator Alan Simpson even went so far as to call him a "sympathizer" with the enemy.

War is ugly and any attempt to beautify it—such as showing only attractive videos of perfect hits with smart bombs—must have political implications. Presidential orders barred the media from Dover Air Force Base in Delaware when American caskets returned from the war zone. The military report minimizing the number of Iraqis killed became a sanitized account of how many tanks, planes, and pieces of equipment had been destroyed. Critics have claimed that these attempts to shield a free people from the consequences of their country's actions can have no justification as military security. They see this as a way of shielding political and military leaders from criticism. Clearly, a controversial and delicate balance exists between military security and freedom of information.

Brian G. Tobin

1991
Air War in the Gulf

The 1991 Gulf War demonstrated the overwhelming and decisive role of air power in modern warfare. As the first major international crisis following the Cold War, the war demonstrated that a cooperative effort between the United States and the Soviet Union, along with the support of China, could enable the United Nations to quell a world crisis in a volatile area such as the Middle East.

During the early hours of August 2, 1990, Iraqi military forces occupied the tiny, oil-rich nation of Kuwait, Iraq's Arab neighbor on the Northern Persian Gulf. Ordered by Iraqi president Saddam Hussein, the invasion employed hundreds of tanks and surprised nearly the entire world. Within twenty-four hours, Iraq had taken complete control of Kuwait and moved thousands of Iraqi troops to Kuwait's Saudi Arabian border. Industrialized nations, such as the United States, that depended heavily on Kuwaiti and Saudi petroleum immediately terminated its foreign policies that had previously benefited Iraq. The United States and the United Nations organized a coalition of thirty-nine countries, including Egypt, France, Great Britain, Canada, Australia, Saudi Arabia, and Syria, that expelled Iraq within just six weeks and restored Kuwaiti independence without stripping Hussein of power. The United States made the unusual request that other countries contribute financially to the campaign. More than fifty-three billion dollars was received, with Saudi Arabia and Kuwait the largest donors. Several countries donated resources but not personnel.

Military Buildup

Immediately following the Iraqi occupation of Kuwait, King Fahd of Saudi Arabia invited U.S. troops onto Saudi soil for protection against further aggression. This coalition, termed Operation Desert Shield, deployed 1,800 combat aircraft, 3,500 tanks, and 670,000 troops (425,000 of which were American), into the Gulf region by mid-January. The coalition also had moved 200 warships into the Gulf region, including six U.S. aircraft carriers and two battleships. By contrast, Iraq mobilized between 350,000 and 550,000 troops into Kuwait and southern Iraq, along with 550 aircraft, 4,500 tanks, and a small navy.

Had Hussein taken advantage of his initial military leverage and invaded Saudi Arabia in August, 1990, no military force in the immediate area could have deterred him. Any immediate American retaliation would have been limited to air and missile attacks from the USS *Independence* aircraft carrier in the Gulf and by B-52 bombers stationed on Diego Garcia Island, 2,500 miles away in the Indian Ocean. Hussein's unexplained delay gave U.S. president George Bush time to organize the largest deployment of air power and troops since World War II. Fifty thousand air and ground troops were sent to bases in Saudi Arabia in addition to three aircraft carrier fleets: the *Independence*, the USS *Eisenhower*, and the USS *Saratoga*. The number of American troops in the region had increased to more than 200,000 by November, after which Bush tried to scare Hussein into retreating by doubling the size of the American force.

Operation Desert Storm began with 539,000 American troops in the Gulf, along with 270,000 other coalition troops. There were 545,000 Iraqi troops in and around Kuwait. U.S. general H. Norman Schwarzkopf commanded the non-Arab units and Saudi general Khalid Sultan commanded the Arab units.

Air Power Strategies

The primary goal of the coalition air command was to destroy Iraq's ability to launch either offensive or defensive air campaigns. Secondary goals included the elimination of Iraq's weapons facilities and the disruption of Iraq's ability to gather information about coalition forces and to communicate internally. Coalition aircraft first bombed the Iraqi capital of Baghdad before attacking strategic military targets throughout Iraq and Kuwait. The allies focused their heaviest bombing on Iraqi troops, artillery centers, tanks, transportation routes, and supplies of ammunition, food, fuel, and water, as Hussein attempted to shield his military behind civilians. Iraq then launched crude Scud missiles at populated areas in Israel and Saudi Arabia, enraging many by killing civilians.

Operation Desert Storm

Hussein was given a deadline of January 15, 1991, to exit Kuwait. When he made no attempt to honor this deadline, Operation Desert Shield was upgraded to the military offensive Operation Desert Storm.

On January 16, 1991, at 6:40 P.M. eastern standard time, the White House announced that "the liberation of Kuwait has begun." Intensive air attacks continued for five and one-half weeks, concluding with a ground assault

A Baghdad hotel destroyed by Allied bombing. (Barry W. Barker)

that began on February 23, 1991, at 8:00 P.M. eastern standard time, and lasted for exactly one hundred hours. The United States flew most of the campaign's sorties, and the British, French, and Saudis flew most of the rest. The coalition deployed unprecedented technological weapons systems, such as the unmanned Tomahawk cruise missile, the antimissile version of the Patriot antiaircraft system, and advanced infrared targeting that illuminated Iraqi tanks buried in the sand. Iraqi forces were overwhelmed by the use of new aircraft such as the British Tornado and the U.S. F-117A stealth fighter.

Other new technology included coalition smart bombs, which utilized previously untested laser guidance systems and accounted for 7 percent of all bombs dropped. Modern media coverage enabled the entire world continually to view coalition bombing raids. As Hussein desired, Iraq's longstanding neighbor and enemy, Iran, did not make a stand. As the bombing intensified, Iraq evacuated to Iran 137 aircraft, all of which Iran kept after the war.

For its initial thirty-seven days, Operation Desert Storm was almost exclusively a war of air bombardment. Iraq's military installations, communications facilities, air bases, armed forces in the field, missile launchers, weapons-producing factories, and nuclear production facilities were relentlessly bombed by more than 100,000 sea-launched sorties and missiles from the Persian Gulf. The Iraqi air force had surprisingly been grounded by Hussein after only the one day of bombing. Iraq's only offensive effort after its initial invasion of Kuwait was to launch eighty-five Scud missiles against Israel and Saudi Arabia. They resulted in a relatively minimal loss of life. Some were intercepted by American Patriot antimissile rockets, and others broke up upon reentry or missed their targets.

Operation Desert Saber

The land offensive Operation Desert Saber was launched on February 23, 1991, and lasted for four days. Deployment of ground troops was restrained until nearly the entire Iraqi infrastructure, including bridges, highways, electric power systems, water filtration plants, and airports, had been destroyed. With thousands of Iraqis already dead, surviving troops surrendered by the tens of thousands. The few Iraqi troops, including many of the elite Republican Guard, who continued to fight while retreating, shot their surrendering comrades in the back. When President Bush ordered a cease-fire on February 27, Kuwait was liberated, and the most extensive air bombardment and land offensive since World War II was over. Bush's early termination of the ground war was later criticized, as Baghdad was able to rescue a substantial amount of military equipment, which was later used to suppress postwar Shiite and Kurdish rebellions as Hussein remained in power.

Military Warcraft

Initial air attacks led by the United States included Tomahawk cruise missiles launched from warships in the Persian Gulf, F-117A stealth fighter-bombers armed with smart bombs, and F-4G Wild Weasel aircraft loaded with antiradar missiles. These attacks permitted F-14, F-15, and F-16 fighter-bombers, and F/A-18 Hornet fighters to gain air superiority. Bombing missions were timed to reduce the effectiveness of Iraqi ground radar defenses. The A-10 Thunderbolt, with its Gatling gun and heat-seeking or optically-guided Maverick missiles, effectively provided support for ground units. Other essential coalition support was provided by the AH-64 Apache, Black Hawk, AH-1 Cobra, and Super Cobra helicopters, which fired laser-guided Hellfire missiles, the E-3A airborne warning and control system (AWACS), and a modernized fleet of older B-52G's.

The coalition's 2,250 combat aircraft, including 1,800 U.S. planes, overmatched Iraq's 500 Soviet-built MiG-29's and French-made Mirage F-1's. Coalition combat missions dropped more than 88,000 tons of bombs. Precision-guided missiles, night-vision devices, an infrared navigation and target designation system, and target sensors enabled round-the-clock bombing by the coalition. Coalition ground-based firepower included the multiple-launch rocket system, the M-2 Infantry Fighting Vehicle, the M-60A3 main battle tank, the M-109 self-propelled howitzer tank, the M-1A1 main battle tank, and ninety Patriot missile launchers.

Casualties and Aftermath

Immediately following the Gulf War, the United States Defense Intelligence Agency estimated that 100,000 Iraqi soldiers had been killed, 300,000 wounded, 150,000 deserted, and 60,000 taken prisoner. U.S. representatives later stated these estimates could be off as much as 50 percent following claims by various human rights organizations of significantly different numbers. U.S. casualties included 148 killed in action, 407 wounded, and 121 killed in nonhostile activities, such as friendly fire.

Coalition bombing severely damaged Iraq's transportation systems, communication systems, and petroleum and other industries. Much of Iraq's electric power and clean water were destroyed, resulting in many civilian deaths from lack of food or medical treatment. Severe environmental pollution resulted after Hussein ordered approximately six hundred Kuwaiti oil wells set afire. The blazes took more than twelve months to extinguish and caused severe air pollution. Huge amounts of Kuwaiti oil were dumped into the Persian Gulf as the war ended. Postwar economic sanctions continued to cause great hardship to the civilians of Iraq and neighboring countries, as efforts to strip Hussein of power repeatedly failed. The operation had another, unintended effect: The presence of U.S. troops angered Osama bin Laden and other Islamic fundamentalists. The terrorist attacks of September 11, 2001, that killed almost three thousand people were tied to the Gulf War.

Following Gulf War duty, many veterans complained of physical and psychological ailments, including memory loss, fatigue, and joint pain, collectively known as Gulf War syndrome. In 1996, the Pentagon warned five thousand veterans of the war that these symptoms might have been caused by exposure to nerve gas during an attack on a weapons depot.

Daniel G. Graetzer

1991
Women in the Gulf War

Women's assistance in the Gulf War operations of Desert Shield and Desert Storm led to legislation allowing female pilots to fly combat missions.

Historically, there has been much debate about women serving in military and combat roles. The level of that debate increased when the United States armed forces were mobilized after the invasion of Kuwait by Iraq in August, 1990. As the country watched, 33,000 women were among the 537,000 U.S. troops sent to Saudi Arabia. Women constituted 11 percent of the total active duty military and 13 percent of the reservists of all military personnel. They operated in key combat support positions in the largest U.S. military action since the Vietnam War. The contributions of these soldiers enabled women to gain greater acceptance and to make inroads in the military service.

Duties of Women in the War

Women were responsible for many of the same jobs as men in the Gulf War. Their duties brought them close to combat zones, where they directed artillery, fired Patriot missiles to intercept incoming Scud missiles, constructed buildings, flew airplanes, and refueled tanks. For the first time, American women flew helicopters over battle zones, carrying more than two thousand men and supplies into enemy territory. Women repaired tactical satellite communications systems and battlefield radios and were visible in all phases of the conflict, from operating high-tech equipment to repairing tanks and earth-moving equipment to commanding brigades and platoons.

Each branch of the service interpreted the ban on women in combat in its own way. The Army had the greatest number of military women. Many Army commanders ignored normal procedure and assigned tasks without regard to gender. Others took capable women out of their normal positions, interpreting the Direct Combat Probability Coding (DCPC) system by their own standards. Women were often close to combat areas simply because front lines shifted constantly. In the Air Force, women were in danger of being struck by Iraqi Scud missiles as they serviced and armed combat aircraft. Navy women were kept from combat areas, as they were not given any offshore carrier assignments.

The controversies regarding gender were largely put aside as men and women treated one another with mutual respect amid the hardships of the desert. Critics claimed that there would be sexual tension among men and women, but such fears proved unwarranted as the sexes shared tents and duties without noticeable friction. In addition to the pressures of combat, both male and female soldiers had to adhere to the strict customs of Muslim culture. For women, these customs were more stringent. When leaving their military compounds, they had to be escorted by men, keeping their heads covered and their eyes lowered, and they could not drive vehicles or wear shorts.

Heroines

One of the first American Army helicopter pilots to fly into a combat zone, Major Marie T. Rossi, a commander of B Company, 18th Army Aviation Brigade, appeared on national television shortly before she died when her chopper hit a tower. She had carried troops, supplies, ammunition, and fuel and had encountered hostile fire, but ironically her death came a day after a cease-fire had begun. Rossi became a symbol of heroism for American women.

African American women played an important role in the Gulf War, risking their lives with fellow military personnel. Captain Cynthia Mosley, a commander of Alpha Company, received a bronze star for combat service. Commanding a one hundred-person unit that was close to the front lines, Mosley and her company were responsible for supplying troops with fuel, water, and ammunition.

Lieutenant Phoebe Jeter was another of the thousands of African American women who served with distinction during Desert Storm. In charge of the control center that deployed Patriot missiles, Jeter headed an all-male platoon that destroyed at least two Scud missiles. She became the first and only woman to shoot down a Scud.

A total of thirteen women died during the Gulf War. The war claimed the lives of the first enlisted women to be killed in action during a Scud missile attack. In addition, Major Rhonda Cornum, a flight surgeon, and Army truck driver Melissa Rathbun-Nealy were captured by the Iraqis, and both received purple hearts on their release.

The Continuing Debates

The questions concerning women's role in the military and whether they should be drafted was argued during the ratification drive for the Equal Rights Amendment (ERA). In May, 1991, Representatives Patricia Schroeder and Beverly Bryon introduced a measure to rescind the ban on women flying combat missions. Despite a proposal by the Senate Armed Services Committee to study the measure, it passed both the House and the Senate. The Senate also included an addendum that provided an option for the defense secretary to waive other combat exclusions as well. In 1993, Defense Secretary Les Aspin stated that although women were still excluded from actual ground combat, they would now be allowed to serve as combat pilots and aboard combat ships. The favorable public opinion about the women's role in the Gulf War helped lead to this decision.

Other debates affected women in the Gulf War. Headlines and newspaper photographs depicted mothers leaving behind their children as they were sent to war. Emphasizing such role reversal, the press popularized Operation Desert Storm as the "Mommy War."

Impact on Women in the Military

When President George Bush announced the start of an air war against Iraq in January, 1991, he referred to the military troops that he was sending into Saudi Arabia as "our sons and daughters." The Gulf War narrowed the divisions between men and women in the armed forces, placing them all in the category of service personnel, not servicemen or servicewomen.

Prior to Desert Storm, women had been unable to gain significant ground in their struggle to be accepted as part of the military. Their contributions in the invasions of Grenada and Panama had been downplayed. The performance of women in the Gulf War enabled all female soldiers to gain new respect because it showed that women were as capable as men in the completion of military duties. While the war opened the door for women as combat pilots, however, women in ground troops continued the fight for the right to engage in combat. Without full recognition as members of combat units, women could not hope to break through the military's glass ceiling to advance in rank and position.

Marilyn Elizabeth Perry

1992
"No Fly" Zone in Iraq

Date: August 27, 1992
Location: Iraq
Principal figures: *American,* George Bush (1924-   ); *Iraqi,* Saddam Hussein (1937-   ); *British,* John Major (1943-   ); *French,* François Mitterrand (1916-1996)
Result: To stem Iraqi attacks against rebellious Shiite Muslims in southern Iraq, the United States, Great Britain, and France established a "no fly" zone for Iraqi aircraft below the 32d parallel.

On August 27, 1992, the United States, Great Britain, and France made a joint decision to establish a "no fly" zone in southern Iraq. The decision not to allow Iraqi aircraft south of the 32d parallel was controversial. There were those who doubted the humanitarian motives of the allies. The Iraqis saw the change as a plot designed to break up their country. Iranian leaders wondered about U.S. president George Bush's motives—did he support the "no fly" zone simply to give himself a boost in public opinion polls and improve his chances for reelection? Such doubts were echoed in newspaper editorials within the United States. Egypt, Syria, and several Persian Gulf states worried that Iraq would eventually splinter and leave Iran in control of the area. The Arabs wanted to keep the eastern flank of their world intact, but not necessarily under the control of Iran's fundamentalist Shiite government.

The allied leaders dismissed such concerns about the "no fly" zone. Their stated motives were simple—they were merely responding to the defiance of Saddam Hussein, the political leader of Iraq. Hussein, the allies argued, had repeatedly defied requests of the international community and violated the cease-fire agreements still in effect from the Gulf War of 1991. Hussein, for example, deployed antiaircraft missiles in northern Iraq, refused to accept his postwar border with Kuwait, blocked humanitarian aid convoys throughout the countryside, and interfered with United Na-

A female U.S. Navy aviation electronics technician performs maintenance work on a fighter plane on the deck of the aircraft carrier USS Carl Vinson in the Persian Gulf in early 1999. The carrier's mission was to support coalition enforcement of the no-fly zone over southern Iraq.
(U.S. Department of Defense)

tions (U.N.) weapons inspectors trying to investigate suspected nuclear, biological, and chemical facilities.

As a result of these violations and many others, the United States, Great Britain, and France decided to issue an ultimatum and then strike if Hussein did not comply. The allies' military options were limited by the fact that U.N. representatives remained in Iraq. If his three foes attacked him, Hussein could take hostages from among more than one thousand U.N. representatives. The "no fly" zone policy seemed to be a better option. It would help the Shiites in southern Iraq and possibly inspire the overthrow of Hussein from within the country.

U.N. Resolution 688, which passed in April, 1991, required Iraq to ensure the human and political rights of all of its citizens. Without any legal blessing from the United Nations, the United States and its two allies, Great Britain and France, responded to Hussein's aggression and adopted a "688 strategy" to defend the rights of Iraqi citizens. The strategy went into effect on August 27, 1992, and established an Iraqi "no fly" zone south of the 32d parallel. The zone covered 47,500 square miles, or about one-fourth of Iraq's land area. The goals of the strategy were simple: to protect the Shiites, although not from Iraqi ground forces already in the area; to stir up a mutiny in the south; and possibly to inspire a palace coup in Baghdad against Hussein. The strategy was not immediately successful in achieving its three goals, although allied fighter planes continued to keep the skies clear of Iraqi aircraft below the 32d parallel.

The Politics of the Decision

After the Persian Gulf War, American, French, and British aircraft continued to control the skies over the northernmost portion of Iraq. Their goal was to protect the local Kurdish population from the wrath of Hussein. The Kurds were an ethnic minority that rebelled against the Iraqi dictator after the Gulf War. They tried to establish their own state, but the so-called butcher of Baghdad had other ideas. He wanted to reassert his control over northern Iraq and force the Kurds into submission.

To prevent this from happening and also to prevent the creation of a Kurdish state, the United States, Great Britain, and France established a "no fly" zone north of the 36th parallel. The allies vowed to attack any Iraqi aircraft or ground troops that entered the zone and tried to attack the Kurds. The policy appeared to work. The Kurds remained protected, and the Iraqi regime did not bully its way back into northern Iraq.

In the case of southern Iraq, however, things were different. The allies did not establish a "no fly" zone there after the Gulf War, even though local Shiite Muslims also rebelled against Baghdad. The uprising failed, but rebels continued to operate in the vast marshes where the Tigris and Euphrates Rivers meet. Hussein wanted to crush these rebels once and for all and turn the area into a "dead zone." He deployed 100,000 troops and began a strafing and bombing campaign against the estimated 50,000 Iraqi Shiites living in the marshes.

The Iraqi campaign did not go unnoticed. Max van der Stoel, a U.N. human rights inspector, reported on August 11, 1992, that Hussein was killing his own people. This was a violation of U.N. Resolution 688. The United States and its two allies, Great Britain and France, responded to Hussein's aggression with their "688 strategy."

Consequences

The "no fly" zone policy failed to accomplish its most important goals. Because it did not require Iraqi ground forces to retreat north of the 32d parallel, troops stayed in southern Iraq. They drained wells and defoliated marshlands, and they then used tanks and artillery to wipe out completely the Shiite Muslim rebels. The United States, Great Britain, and France may have controlled the skies of southern Iraq, but there was no real resistance to Hussein on the ground. Further, there were few mutinies and coup attempts against his government. By protecting his supporters from the effects of the U.N. economic blockade, Hussein bought their loyalty and remained firmly in power into the next century.

Peter R. Faber

1992
Somalia Occupation

At issue: Restoration of order in a nation whose central government collapsed
Date: December 9, 1992-March 31, 1994
Location: Somalia
Principal figures: *American*, President George Bush (1924-   ), President Bill Clinton (1946-   ), Special Envoy Robert B. Oakley (1931-   ); *United Nations*, Secretary-General Boutros Boutros-Ghali (1922-   ); *Somali*, Mahammad Farah Aideed, Ali Mahdi Mahammad (1939-   ), former president Mahammad Siad Barré (1921-   )
Result: Under the auspices of the United Nations, U.S. forces entered a northeast Africa nation living in anarchy to secure humanitarian operations.

On December 4, 1992, U.S. president George Bush announced that U.S. forces would be sent to Somalia in order to provide security for the provision of emergency humanitarian assistance. This announcement followed months of civil war and famine in Somalia and many months of international debate about how best to deal with that country's deteriorating situation. On December 3, 1992, the U.N. Security Council authorized a member state to intervene in Somalia, where anarchy reigned. The intervening power was authorized to use all necessary means to provide security for humanitarian relief. The Bush administration, which had been preparing for this eventuality, took formal steps to mount a peacekeeping operation, called Operation Restore Hope, under U.S. command. The first troops landed in Mogadishu, Somalia's capital and largest city, in the early morning hours of December 9. U.S. forces remained in Somalia until March 31, 1994, when President Bill Clinton formally called for the withdrawal of all but a handful of U.S. troops, in the face of ongoing civil strife and discord. Although the operation failed to produce a political resolution to the Somali civil war, it did restore considerable order to the Somali countryside and ended the famine.

Somali Background

Although Somalia is a largely homogeneous country in terms of ethnicity, religion, and language, its people are divided into six major clans and numerous subclans. The majority of Somalis are fiercely independent nomads, with strong loyalty to the family and clan. Traditionally, clans and subclans have engaged in disputes over pasture and water resources, but significant interclan marriage has muted such conflict, as has the mediating authority of clan elders. This traditional capacity for conflict resolution was weakened during the 1980's, as President Mahammad Siad Barré, who had seized power in a coup in 1969, nine years after Somalia's independence, sought to manipulate the clan system to maintain his increasingly unpopular regime.

Siad Barré's policies of reform in his early years were welcomed by most Somalis. After the failure of his attempt to capture the predominantly Somali-inhabited Ogaden region in Ethiopia, his regime gradually became more authoritarian and increasingly brutal. As opposition to Siad Barré grew, he responded by rewarding fellow Marehan clan members with positions of power. Other clans responded with determined resistance. The northwestern part of Somalia fell into open rebellion in May, 1988. Siad Barré re-

During the period of the United Nations occupation, members of rival clans moved freely through the streets of Mogadishu carrying weapons as advanced as the hand-held rocket launcher seen here. The complicated rivalries among factions and generally undisciplined nature of the fighting made Somalia an exceptionally dangerous place for occupation forces. (AP/Wide World Photos)

sponded ruthlessly with aerial bombings of Hargeisa, the regional capital, and hundreds of thousands of Isaq Somali took refuge in nearby Ethiopia.

The civil war in the north continued for three years, culminating in a declaration of independence on May 17, 1991, and the formation of Somaliland Republic. During the latter months of 1990, civil war had spread throughout southern Somalia. Awash in arms from years of military assistance during the Cold War, opposition groups flourished. Mahammad Farah Aideed's well-armed Somali National Army (SNA) gradually gained the upper hand against Siad Barré's forces, which had been reduced by defections to Marehan clan units. Aideed's forces captured Mogadishu in late January, 1991, as Siad Barré fled from the capital city after plundering it and retreated into the southern countryside, where pitched battles were fought with Aideed's forces in fertile agricultural areas, interrupting local farming and precipitating the famine.

If Siad Barré's opposition had been united, Somalia might not have devolved into anarchy. However, disputes over who should govern the country developed immediately after Siad Barré's flight, the principal contest being between Aideed and Ali Mahdi Mahammad, a Mogadishu businessman. Both men were members of the Hawiye clan of the United Somali Congress (USC), but they hailed from different subclans. Ali Mahdi Mahammad had considerable political support, especially among his Agbal subclan, but Aideed had a more effective fighting force. In late 1991, the two sides clashed for several months in the streets of Mogadishu. International relief organizations of the United Nations withdrew from the country because of the complete lack of security, leaving only the International Committee of the Red Cross and some private agencies to cope with the growing famine. Regional diplomatic efforts failed. By February, 1992, a cease-fire was agreed upon and a special coordinator was appointed to reinitiate a U.N. presence. These efforts failed, and U.N. Secretary General Boutros Boutros-Ghali called for a more concerted international effort.

United Nations Intervention

The U.N. Security Council responded by creating the United Nations Operation in Somalia (UNOSOM I), under the direction of Mohamed Sahnoun. This ill-fated effort was underfunded and met with strong Somali resistance. The famine deepened during 1992, and relief supplies could not be delivered, owing to the ongoing civil war. Boutros-Ghali and Sahnoun clashed over how the United Nations should respond, and the latter resigned in September, just before a planned national reconciliation conference.

Matters deteriorated further as death rates from starvation and disease skyrocketed. Facing this grim humanitarian situation, the Bush administration, in its waning months in office, offered to deploy U.S. troops to provide security for relief supplies. Special envoy Robert Oakley was dispatched by Bush to negotiate a smooth entry for U.S. forces with Somali factional leaders, and U.S. forces, designated the Unified Task Force (UNITAF), were on the ground by December 9, 1992, with assistance from military units of Canada, France, Italy, Belgium, and Morocco. The troops initially received a hero's welcome from the Somali people and cautious acquiescence from the Somali factions. Within a month, Mogadishu and key regional cities had been secured, relief supplies were reaching famine-stricken areas, and the emergency situation had been greatly stabilized—but the political situation remained tenuous. Diplomatic efforts to restore the local elders' influence, to establish an interim police force, and quietly to impound the large caches of weapons were initiated.

Initially, public support in the United States for Operation Restore Hope was strong. Most U.S. citizens perceived the operation as being consistent with U.S. humanitarian policies, even though the United States paid for three quarters of the UNITAF expenses. The problems came after the United States handed over authority to a reconstituted UNOSOM II. President Clinton, a newcomer to foreign policy, was eager to reduce the U.S. presence in the region and for the U.N. to take overall operational control. Robert Oakley finished his assignment in March, 1993. Later in the same month, UNITAF functions were transferred formally to UNOSOM II, and the U.S. marines began to withdraw from Somalia, leaving a much smaller U.S. contingent of four thousand to join UNOSOM II.

With the United Nations taking a more direct role, Aideed's forces became bolder in resistance to UNOSOM II. Aideed greatly resented U.N. secretary general Boutros-Ghali and took an early opportunity to challenge him. SNA forces attacked a Pakistani patrol in early June, 1993, killing many. Boutros-Ghali called the action a war crime and Aideed a criminal. U.N. forces began a cat-and-mouse effort to capture Aideed, and UNOSOM II became increasingly unpopular among Somalis.

In early October, 1993, U.S. units of UNOSOM II engaged in a running gun battle with Aideed forces, suffering more than ninety casualties, including eighteen dead. This event stirred outrage in the United States and sparked calls for complete U.S. withdrawal. Bowing to the political pressures, the Clinton administration agreed to withdraw all U.S. forces by March 31, 1994. The vast majority of U.S. forces were withdrawn from Somalia by the summer of 1994, although several thousand U.S. troops were deployed in 1995 to provide security for the complete withdrawal of U.N. forces, leaving Somalis to work out a political solution for themselves.

Robert F. Gorman

1994
U.S. Troops in Bosnia

At issue: Control of Bosnia after the breakup of Yugoslavia
Date: April 10, 1994
Location: Gorazde, Bosnia
Principal figures: *Serbian and Bosnian,* Slobodan Milošević (1941-   ),
Franjo Tudjman (1922-1999), Radovan Karadžić (1945-   ), Alija Izet-
begovic (1925-2003); *American,* Bill Clinton (1946-   )
Result: By United Nations request and under NATO auspices, American
air forces became involved in the protracted war in Bosnia between the
Serbs and Bosnian Muslims.

At dusk on the evening of April 10, 1994, two American F-16 jets from the
American air base in Aviano, Italy, flew over Gorazde, Bosnia. The planes
dropped three five-hundred-pound bombs on Serbian positions used to
bombard the city, which had been designated by the United Nations as a
safe zone for Bosnian Muslims (Bosniaks). The strike, under North Atlantic
Treaty Organization (NATO) auspices, brought the United States military
further into the civil war being waged in the former Yugoslav republic of
Bosnia. In February, 1994, U.S. airplanes had shot down Serbian aircraft violating the "no fly" zone established by the United Nations. The April 10
bombing was the first time in forty-five years that NATO air forces attacked ground targets in Europe.

The attack occurred after repeated warnings from the United Nations,
NATO, and American president Bill Clinton to the Serbs that continued
bombardment of Gorazde would bring retaliation. Gorazde was one of
several regions the United Nations had designated as havens for Muslim
refugees and was garrisoned by U.N. peacekeeping troops.

When the Serbs refused to stop their bombardment, Yasushi Akashi, the
U.N. representative in Bosnia, advised U.N. secretary general Boutros
Boutros-Ghali to call NATO strikes. NATO charged the American command to carry out the task, and Admiral Leighton Smith, Jr., commander of
the NATO southern forces, ordered the strikes.

The bombing at first appeared to stop the Serbian shelling, but the Serb
leader in Bosnia, Radovan Karadžić, claimed that the strikes brought the
United Nations into the war on the Bosniak side, and he threatened retaliation against U.N. forces. President Clinton responded that the air attack was
a clear expression of the will of NATO and the will of the United Nations.
When Serb shelling resumed, a second attack was carried out on April 11.

Centuries of Conflict

The collapse of communism in Eastern Europe in 1989 revealed long-standing national and communal hostilities that dictatorship had hidden for forty-five years. Nowhere was this more evident than in the Federation of Yugoslavia, a collection of six republics that was home to eight major nationalities. Created after World War I, Yugoslavia never came to grips with its nationality problem, a major reason the country fell prey to fascist aggression in World War II. After that conflict, the powerful and charismatic communist leader Tito was able to maintain stability in the country.

After Tito died in 1980, Yugoslavia began to unravel because of national differences. Hostilities that extended back to the Middle Ages appeared in full bloom once more, and the republics declared their independence. The first serious war between the republics erupted in 1991, pitting Serbia, led by Slobodan Milošević, against Croatia, led by Franjo Tudjman. Croats and Serbs are members of the same nationality but differ in religion (the Croats are Roman Catholic, the Serbs Eastern Orthodox) and historical experience. Both republics claimed territory in Bosnia.

Bosnia itself was a republic Tito had created in 1945 for the Bosniaks, descendants of Serbo-Croatian Christians who converted to Islam in the fourteenth and fifteenth centuries. Milošević and Tudjman considered dividing Bosnia between them. In response to this possibility, Bosniak leaders headed by Alija Izetbegovic declared Bosnia's independence from Yugoslavia and appealed to the nations of the world for recognition. This was slow in coming because of the problems the former Yugoslavia presented on the international stage at that time. European nations approached the situation carefully because traditional alliances divided them between the Serbs and the Croats. These peoples, especially the Serbs, reacted to Bosnian independence by launching a war against the Bosniaks. Serbs living in Bosnia soon formed an independent force under Karadžić. Milošević came to his aid with all the resources of the Yugoslav state and military. As violence increased, especially toward civilian populations, the United Nations placed an arms embargo on the area. This worked to the advantage of the Serbs, and attacks against the Bosniaks increased. The nations of the West finally recognized Bosnia, but the civil war continued.

Western nations were forced to act by the pressure of public outrage, fanned by detailed media reports of atrocities, particularly the systematic raping of Bosnian women by Serbian soldiers and the deaths and maiming of hundreds of children. NATO voted to take military action but not to send in ground forces against the Serbs. Pressure was applied on Serbian leaders in Belgrade to stop the support of their conationals in Bosnia.

Numerous plans for a negotiated settlement failed. Serbian military units surrounded Bosniak cities, including the safe zones the United Nations had established, and bombarded them from the surrounding highlands. NATO then decided to attack these Serbian outposts from the air. President Clinton agreed and, when asked, ordered American planes to begin raids.

Consequences

The action had little effect in lessening the war. Serbs continued their onslaught with success, with ground forces increasing the territory they controlled. In December, 1994, former U.S. president Jimmy Carter visited Bosnia to mediate a peace and worked out a cease-fire with Karadžić, only to see it fail within a few weeks. An airplane piloted by American Scott F. O'Grady was shot down in June, 1995, but he was rescued after a six-day ordeal hiding in the mountains. In July, the Serbian forces captured Gorazde and then moved on to the other safe areas. Within the United States, Congress, administration officials, military leaders, and numerous presidential candidates debated the course of action to take—lift the arms embargo, continue existing policies, commit ground troops, or simply ignore the war. NATO forces, with a large U.S. contingent, entered Bosnia in December, 1995, to enforce a peace agreement.

Frederick B. Chary

1995
NATO Troops in Bosnia

Date: December 14, 1995
Location: Bosnia
Principal figures: *Serbian*, Slobodan Milošević (1941-   ), Croatian president Franjo Tudjman (1922-1999), Alija Izetbegovic (1925-2003); *American*, General William Lafayette Nash (1943-   ), Admiral Leighton W. Smith, Jr. (1940?-   )
Result: NATO forces, one-third from the U.S. military, entered Bosnia to enforce the peace agreement drawn up by the warring sides.

On December 14, 1995, after being delayed by foul weather, the first troops of the United States Army crossed the Sava River and entered the Republic of Bosnia. The troops were part of a North Atlantic Treaty Organization (NATO) force charged with implementing the peace treaty agreed to by

Bosnia and its neighbors the previous month. NATO planned a contingent of sixty thousand military personnel, twenty thousand of them from the United States.

The first American soldiers were part of the advance group assigned to prepare the way for the remainder of the American troops. At the same time, forces from the other NATO countries entered at different locations. The NATO forces replaced the failed United Nations (U.N.) mission, which was unable to maintain peace among the communities or secure safe areas for the beleaguered Bosniaks (Bosnian Muslims). NATO sought to provide buffers separating the three ethnic communities and to ensure that the timetable of the negotiations was carried out.

Both Admiral Leighton W. Smith, Jr., the commander of the NATO operation, and General William Nash, the commander of the American contingent, emphasized that any attack on the troops would be met with a suitable response, including force. There was virtually no resistance to the entry by the warring Serbs, Croats, and Bosniaks. On the contrary, the various ethnic armies welcomed the NATO forces and promised full cooperation.

The greatest danger came from land mines strewn along the roads and fields between the points of entry and the staging areas where the troops were to encamp. Winter weather conditions also caused problems. Snow and ice jammed the river, making the crossing extremely difficult, interfering with the operation of the motorized and electronic equipment, and slowing the progress of the entry of troops as well as their travel to their destinations. Over the next days, more troops and supplies entered the country as the various contingents established their bases.

A New Initiative

In the fall of 1995, after more than three years of fighting, there appeared to be no end in sight to the war among the Serbs, Croats, and Bosniaks of Bosnia. Reports of unspeakable atrocities had aroused the moral outrage of the world. Attempts to bring peace through use of U.N. forces and NATO air raids had little effect. Political divisions kept the European nations from taking decisive action.

The final straw was the Serb attack against and conquest of Srebrenica, a Muslim safe area protected by the United Nations. The reported massacre of Muslim men and boys from the area by Serbs and threats to the U.N. forces drove the West to action.

It appeared to U.S. president Bill Clinton's administration that an American initiative was necessary to bring a conclusion to the conflict. Such an initiative would be complicated by divisions in the federal government:

The Democratic president faced a hostile Republican Congress and a difficult election in November of 1996. President Clinton invited the presidents of Serbia, Croatia, and Bosnia to come to Dayton, Ohio, to work out a new peace plan that would establish Serbian and Croatian areas in Bosnia and allow the Bosnian government to function in the rest of the country.

The negotiations were interrupted several times by disagreements among the principals, but all sides had a commitment to see an end to the war. The talks were further complicated by a military campaign in September by the Croatian army that drove Serbian families out of the Krajina region of their country. Furthermore, the leaders of the Bosnian Serbs were not invited to take part in the negotiations, and they continued their attacks on Muslim areas.

The three parties in Dayton agreed to a peace plan including a specific timetable for withdrawal from the front lines, the exchange of prisoners, and the punishment of war criminals. The agreement called for a large NATO force, including a substantial American contingent, to enforce the treaty. The commitment of American troops caused concern in the United States because of fear of becoming embroiled in an endless conflict. The failures associated with the 1993 American operation in Somalia were still fresh in people's memories. Public opinion opposed the venture, and Congress insisted that the president get its approval before the commitment. The president realized this would not come about and insisted that as commander in chief of the U.S. military, he could commit the troops. He ordered them to Bosnia. Congress reluctantly agreed to support the troops but not the decision to send them.

Consequences

Twenty thousand American and forty thousand other troops entered Bosnia with few incidents. NATO forces, unlike those of the United Nations, responded to the occasional attacks against them. The one American casualty in the initial weeks was a soldier who was wounded by a land mine.

After the first month of the peacekeeping mission, despite some friction, the various ethnic armies cooperated with NATO and in general adhered to the timetable. Most of the difficulties concerned the investigation of Serbian war crimes, but even in that situation the Bosnian Serbian army reluctantly went along. An atmosphere of uncertainty and cautiousness nevertheless prevailed.

Many observers thought that it might take generations to sort out what had happened in the Bosnia Herzegovina war, as well as what should be done about the war's legacy. Historians and journalists have come to different conclusions. Some speculate that there is something endemic in the Balkan character that has resulted in civil wars, religious persecution, and war crimes; others dismiss the idea of blood feuds and historic animosities, preferring to analyze how Yugoslavia broke apart after its strong communist leader, Tito, died and a power vacuum opened up that former communists and nationalists of all kinds exploited.

Frederick B. Chary

1998
Missile Attacks on Afghanistan and Sudan

At issue: Retaliation for acts of terrorism
Date: August 20, 1998
Location: Reputed terrorist facilities in Afghanistan and Khartoum, Sudan
Principal figures: *American*, President Bill Clinton (1946-   ), William Cohen (1940-   ), Henry Hugh Shelton (1942-   ); *Arab*, Osama bin Laden (c. 1957-   )
Result: U.S. military forces conducted coordinated cruise missile attacks on what were identified as terrorist facilities in Afghanistan and the Sudan. These facilities belonged to the terrorist group reputed to be behind the earlier bombing of two U.S. embassies in East Africa.

On August 7, 1998, two bombs exploded at the U.S. embassies in Kenya and Tanzania, killing more than 250 people and injuring more than 5,000. An Islamic terrorist group identified as the International Islamic Front for Jihad Against Jews and Crusaders indirectly claimed responsibility for the bombings and threatened additional terrorist attacks on American targets worldwide. This terrorist group was reportedly founded and financed by a renegade Saudi Arabian millionaire, Osama bin Laden, previously linked to other attacks by terrorist groups. U.S. intelligence and military officials, reviewing the available circumstantial evidence, concluded that bin Laden's group was responsible for these two embassy bombings.

Intelligence reports also indicated that this group of terrorists was in the process of developing chemical weapons in the Sudan and concurrently training additional Islamic terrorists in Afghanistan. President Bill Clinton, on advice from Defense Secretary William Cohen and General Henry Hugh Shelton, the chairman of the Joint Chiefs of Staff, determined that an immediate surprise military response would appropriately punish the perpetrators. The president also concluded that such a military strike would delay, and possibly prevent, additional terrorist attacks by this group. Detailed military planning for the strikes commenced immediately and took about one week to complete.

Missile Strikes in Retaliation

To avoid losses, U.S. armed forces used only cruise missiles rather than manned aircraft to attack what had been identified as terrorist-related facilities in Afghanistan and the Sudan. Cruise missiles, fired from U.S. Navy ships in the Red Sea and the Arabian Sea, simultaneously struck the reported terrorist facilities. The missiles hit six individual targets in Afghanistan, most of which were located along the border with Pakistan. Specific targets were in Khost, south of Afghanistan's capital city of Kabul, and Jalalabad, east of the capital. Collectively, these targets constituted a suspected terrorist training complex in which bin Laden's group reportedly trained hundreds of other terrorists.

In the Sudan, the target of the U.S. missiles was the El Shifa Pharmaceutical Industries plant. This factory, located in Khartoum, Sudan's capital, was alleged to be storing chemical weapons for later use by the terrorists. The precise number of casualties in Afghanistan and the Sudan as a direct result of the missile strikes was never established with certainty. No U.S. casualties occurred in any of the attacks.

Consequences

Following the missile strikes, U.S. spokespeople conceded that the strikes would not eliminate the problem of state-sponsored terrorism but said that they would clearly convey that there would be no safe haven for terrorists who chose to attack the United States or its embassies worldwide. Bin Laden and his closest associates were all reported to have survived the attacks unscathed. Damage to the facilities themselves was extensive, however, and military planners labeled both attacks as successful. Already under some international pressure for harboring bin Laden, a fugitive, the government of Afghanistan showed no sign of reconsidering its policy because of the U.S. strike. Instead, Afghan spokespeople interpreted the American missile strike not as an attack on bin Laden or terrorists but instead as an attack on the Afghan people.

The Sudanese government immediately condemned the attack on its nation and disavowed any knowledge of chemical weapons on Sudanese territory, claiming that the plant manufactured pharmaceuticals for civilian use. The Sudanese government also suggested that it might request an inspection by the United Nations (U.N.) Security Council to firmly dis-

Aerial photograph of the Shifa pharmaceutical plant in Sudan that was used by the secretary of defense and chairman of the Joint Chiefs of Staff to brief reporters on the U.S. missile strike on the site. (U.S. Department of Defense)

prove the allegations of chemical weapons at the destroyed plant. No U.N. inspection was subsequently conducted.

American politicians, regardless of political affiliation, almost universally supported the need for the attacks, as well as the manner in which the missile strikes were conducted. China, Japan, Kenya, and several other countries chose neither to condemn nor to support the United States. U.N. secretary-general Kofi Annan, informed of the strikes by American diplomats only moments before they occurred, also maintained a cautious silence. Traditional U.S. allies were generally supportive of the military retaliation against state-sponsored terrorism. The strongest support was offered by Great Britain, but Israel, Germany, and Australia also spoke out in favor of the U.S. measures.

As a general rule, Muslim countries expressed the loudest outrage at the U.S. attacks. Muslim nations that most vehemently condemned the American actions included Iraq, Iran, Libya, and Pakistan. Muted protests came from other Muslim nations such as Turkey, Egypt, and Indonesia. Non-Muslim nations condemning the strikes included the Soviet Union and Cuba. Anti-American public demonstrations took place in many of these countries. U.S. flags were burned in protest in dozens of cities around the globe. Many critics of the unilateral American response, at home and abroad, charged that President Clinton had ordered the missile attacks only to draw attention away from the sex scandal in which he was personally becoming embroiled.

After the terrorist attacks on the Pentagon and the World Trade Center on September 11, 2001, suspicion again fell on bin Laden's organization. With the backing of the world's most powerful nations, the United States issued an ultimatum to Afghanistan's Taliban regime to surrender bin Laden and his followers. After the Taliban refused to comply, the United States led a massive missile and bomber assault on Taliban targets. This assault, in conjunction with a ground-based attack from the regime's Afghan opponents in the north, brought down the government in December of the same year. Many of bin Laden's subordinates were killed in the attacks, but the whereabouts of bin Laden himself remained unknown as late as early 2005.

Michael S. Casey

1998
Bombing of Military Sites in Iraq

Date: December 16, 1998
Location: Iraq
Principal figures: *American*, President Bill Clinton (1946-   ); *British*, Prime Minsiter Tony Blair (1953-   ); *Iraqi*, President Saddam Hussein (1937-   )
Result: U.S. president Bill Clinton and British prime minister Tony Blair authorized the bombing of five Iraqi radar sites on the eve of the impeachment vote against Clinton.

At the conclusion of the Gulf War in early 1991, restrictions imposed on Iraq by the United Nations included an agreement that required United Nations (U.N.) inspectors to visit sites within the country for the purpose of verifying compliance with the treaty terms governing the production of biological, chemical, and nuclear weapons. Over the next several years, Iraq repeatedly violated the agreement and attempted to renegotiate new terms, backing down only when the threat of retaliation appeared imminent.

On October 31, 1998, Iraqi officials suspended all cooperation with the U.N. inspectors, prompting U.S. president Bill Clinton and British prime minister Tony Blair to order additional troops and ships into the region for a possible military response. While the military coordinated the movement of men and matériel into the Persian Gulf area, U.N. secretary-general Kofi Annan contacted Iraqi president Saddam Hussein in an effort to persuade him to reconsider his position. As negotiations continued, Clinton authorized National Security Adviser Sandy Berger to inform the Joint Chiefs of Staff that the strike should commence on the following day.

At 8:00 A.M. eastern standard time on November 14, the Cable News Network (CNN) reported that an Iraqi government announcement would be made shortly, prompting Clinton temporarily to place the strike on hold. Later that morning, a letter arrived from Baghdad in which Iraq agreed to permit the return of U.N. inspectors, but since the dispatch contained what appeared to be conditions, Clinton rejected the offer. The following day, Clinton received a second letter from Iraq, clarifying its position and informing him that the "conditions" were meant as preferences only. A third letter that officially rescinded Iraq's decision to end cooperation with U.N. inspectors arrived later that afternoon. Clinton suspended the U.S. military operation and contacted Blair, who then ordered British troops to follow the lead of the American forces.

On November 17, U.N. inspectors returned to Iraq, but within one week, Iraqi leaders denied their requests for access to specific documents,

Antiaircraft fire again illuminates the sky over Baghdad after British and American aircraft resume bombing attacks during the early hours of December 17, 1998.
(AP/Wide World Photos)

claiming that the demands were provocative and designed to justify a military attack against their country. For the next three weeks, Iraq continually denied U.N. inspectors access to the reports, leading Richard Butler, the chief U.N. inspector, to issue a statement on December 15 stating that Hussein had failed to fulfill the earlier promises and instead had placed additional restrictions on U.N. investigators.

Military Action Begins

On December 16, as the U.N. team left Baghdad, Clinton conferred with his national security advisers regarding the situation. Domestically an attack against Iraq on the eve of the House of Representatives' vote on impeachment articles might be suspicious, but international concerns over initiating an attack during the Muslim holy month of Ramadan, then just days away, required an immediate response. Clinton authorized the deployment of more than two hundred aircraft and twenty warships, including the USS *Enterprise* along with fifteen B-52 bombers carrying more than four hundred cruise missiles and a variety of other arms. Targets included military installations and possible chemical, biological, and nuclear weapons sites as well as the barracks of the Republican Guard. A second attack on the following day knocked out additional military air defense sites for the protection of U.S. and British pilots. Although the U.N. Security Council held an emergency session throughout the day, no course of action was decided upon.

Meanwhile, the U.S. Navy commenced Operation Desert Fox, attacking at 3:10 P.M. eastern standard time, deploying two hundred Tomahawk missiles from ships located in the Persian Gulf. One and one-half hours later, the president informed Congress of the attack. Shortly after 5:00 P.M. eastern standard time, the first missiles landed in Iraq as the White House announced that a "substantial" attack was underway. During prime time, Clinton informed the American public about the strike against Iraq and warned Saddam Hussein that any violation of treaty obligations would be dealt with swiftly and severely. An hour later, Republicans voted to delay the impeachment hearings.

Consequences

Critics of President Clinton questioned the timing of the air strike, raising concerns that Operation Desert Fox was initiated to push the impeachment hearings from the front page of the news. Congressional members, including Representatives Joe L. Barton and Ron Paul of Texas, Senator Paul Coverdell of Georgia, Senator Bill Frist of Tennessee, and Senator Richard Shelby, supported military action against Hussein but argued that

Clinton had already paused the strike before and should not have initiated hostilities while facing the impeachment vote. Others, including both Republicans and Democrats such as Senate Minority Leader Tom Daschle, Senator John Chafee, and Senator Sam Brownback, supported the president's action, arguing that military action was necessary immediately because the Muslim holy month prevented strikes for the next thirty days, during which time, Hussein could have prepared his forces for a confrontation.

During the next year, Iraq rebuilt most of the military sites destroyed in the bombing. The United Nations, concerned with the increasing threat from Iraq, proposed a resolution designed to persuade Iraq into once again accepting U.N. inspectors in exchange for a loosening of restrictions on the country's economy. On December 19, 1999, the United Nations passed a resolution, by a vote of 11-0, with the Soviet Union, China, France, and Malaysia abstaining, calling for the removal of the $5.26 billion limit imposed on the sale of oil for food and the lifting of sanctions against the country for renewable 120-day periods once inspectors verified disarmament. Iraq rejected the resolution and prepared to accept the consequences. Although official sanctions remained in place for most items, the U.N. agreed to gradually increase the total amount of oil that could be sold to pay for food and other humanitarian items such as medical supplies.

Cynthia Clark Northrup

2000
Terrorist Attack on the USS *Cole*

Date: October 12, 2000
Location: Aden, Yemen
Principal figures: *American*, Captain Kirk S. Lippold; *Arab*, Jamal al-Bedawi
Result: Terrorists on a suicide mission aboard a small boat approached the U.S. Navy destroyer *Cole*, setting off an explosion that created a large hole in the hull of the ship.

On October 12, 2000, while the U.S. Navy destroyer *Cole* was refueling in the port of Aden in Yemen, it was attacked by two men who pulled alongside the ship in a small boat and caused an explosion that blew a large hole in the hull of the ship, killing seventeen people. Although Yemen was officially a friend of the United States and had been trying to promote good relations, it also was home to terrorists and Islamic extremists who considered the United States a major enemy.

The *Cole* entered the harbor on the morning of October 12, planning to stay only a few hours. The destroyer was on threat condition bravo, a moderate level of security alert. The mooring of the *Cole* was complete about 9:30 A.M. local time, and refueling began soon thereafter. Shortly after 11:00, a small boat with two men in it approached the ship. No one recognized the small boat that pulled alongside as a danger because it blended in with the boats that were servicing the ship. At 11:18 as the two men in the small boat stood at attention, about 400 to 500 pounds (181 to 226 kilograms) of military type explosives went off, blowing a 40-by-40-foot (12-by-12-meter) hole in the hull of the *Cole*. The attack was a suicide mission; the men on the small boat knew they would die in the explosion but believed it was their duty to do so in order to carry out their mission.

Sailors were thrown into the air, and thick, black smoke was everywhere. Hatches were blown open, doorways bent, and parts of the upper deck buckled. Entire lower compartments were blown upward, trapping some crew members. The floor of the mess galley was pushed up against the ceiling. The *Cole* lost electrical power, and all onboard communication equipment was disabled.

The hole was near engine rooms and eating and living quarters, and if it had come minutes earlier, it might have caught many more crew members in the ship's mess area just above where the explosion took place. The ship listed at a four-degree angle, but the keel was not damaged, no fires started, and the ship did not take on water. It was later found that seventeen crew members had been killed in the blast, and thirty-nine were injured, but the captain, Kirk S. Lippold, was not hurt, and he and the remaining crew acted decisively and quickly to help the injured and keep the ship from sinking.

The Aftermath

The injured were taken to a local hospital, then to a military hospital in Germany, and finally home to the United States. The crew and U.S. investigators had to cut through the wreckage to retrieve all the bodies of the victims, but they tried to disturb as little as possible so as to preserve evidence. It took a week to recover all the bodies.

The crew then worked to make the ship seaworthy enough to be towed into deeper water, where it could be loaded onto a special Norwegian ship built to transport offshore oil rigs. This ship, the *Blue Marlin*, was a floating dock, and once the *Cole* had been towed out of the harbor into deeper water, the *Blue Marlin* took on ballast, or extra water, which sank its upper deck under the sea. The *Cole* was towed onto its deck, and the ballast was removed, lifting the deck back above water. The *Cole* was then secured for the trip home. The ship arrived in the United States on December 13, where it was to be repaired and returned to service.

Consequences

In the United States, two investigations were carried out soon after the incident, one by the U.S. Navy into what happened aboard the ship, and the other by the Pentagon into what could have been done overall to prevent such an attack. Neither investigation cast blame on any individual, although the Navy investigation found that the captain and crew of the *Cole* were lax about following a number of security procedures. The Pentagon report recommended better methods all along the chain of command for preventing terrorist attacks.

In May, 2001, congressional hearings were held regarding the incident, and lawmakers criticized the apparent relaxation of the accountability standards to which the *Cole*'s commander was held. Admiral Vern Clark, chief of naval operations, said the Navy declined to punish Lippold because even if Lippold had carried out the security procedures he ignored, he would have been unable to prevent the attack. William S. Cohen, defense secretary at the time of the attack, supported Clark's decision.

The Federal Bureau of Investigation (FBI) sent investigators to Yemen, but initially, they were not allowed to directly question suspects or witnesses. Later they were given permission to question suspects, but Yemen refused to allow the suspects to be taken to the United States for trial. Finally it was decided that suspects found outside Yemen could be tried in the United States, although those found and charged by the Yemeni government were to be tried in Yemen.

The United States suspected from the beginning that Osama bin Laden was behind the attack. Bin Laden was a fugitive from Saudi Arabia, a millionaire who had fought in the Afghan War against the Soviets in 1980, and who afterward organized a worldwide terrorist network focused on the United States. No direct evidence immediately linked him to the attack, but reports from suspects showed that he could have been behind it.

Six men were arrested and prepared for trial in Yemen; other suspects remained at large. The chief suspect was Jamal al-Bedawi, who said he received his orders from Muhammad Omar al-Hazari, a man who may have links to bin Laden.

Eleanor B. Amico

2001
Terrorist Attacks on the United States

At issue: Security of the United States against terrorist attacks
Date: September 11, 2001
Location: New York City; Washington, D.C.; Somerset County, rural Pennsylvania
Principal figures: *Arab*, Mohammad Atta (1968-2001), Osama bin Laden (c. 1957-   )
Result: The use of hijacked jetliners as flying bombs directed against densely populated civilian targets was the largest-scale act of terrorism on U.S. territory and raised the scale of terrorist violence to an unprecedented level.

Around the beginning of the business day in the eastern United States, two American Airlines jetliners and two United Airlines jetliners were hijacked after taking off from Boston and Washington, D.C. Three of the four planes were deliberately smashed into targets in order to kill as many people and to do as much damage as possible; the fourth plane crashed in a rural area of Somerset County in western Pennsylvania, eighty miles southeast of Pittsburgh. It was later established that the fourth plane went down after passengers, having learned via cell phones that the first planes had been deliberately flown into buildings, attacked the hijackers.

It also became known later that the fourth plane had been assigned to hit the White House, the presidential mansion in Washington, D.C., symbol for many of American democracy. The planes that hit their intended targets were flown into the two towers of the World Trade Center (WTC) in Lower Manhattan, New York City, and the Pentagon, the headquarters of the American military, near Washington, D.C. Both of the World Trade Center towers collapsed, killing almost 2,800 people; the Pentagon attack resulted in 189 deaths; and the crash in rural Pennsylvania killed 44 more persons. Thus almost 3,000 persons lost their lives in the attacks.

Terrorist acts in the public sphere are generally regarded as illegal attempts to kill, physically harm, or intimidate civilians to further a political end. However, international law recognizes no political ends that justify deliberate attacks on civilians. The notion of terrorism concerns the means used in attempts to attain political ends; it does not concern the legitimacy of the ends themselves. Such judgments constitute a separate issue. Just as "just" wars may be fought with unjust means, so may "just" causes be fought with vicious and morally untenable tactics. To believe otherwise is to believe that ends can justify means—a doctrine that sets loose the ill-winds of nihilism, since it destroys the legitimacy of all complaints against limitless tactics.

Because the Pentagon was not, strictly speaking, a civilian target, an attack on it might be characterized as an act of war, rather than a terrorist act. However, the airline passengers and crew who died in the attack were innocent civilians who were deliberately killed, and the plane itself was a civilian plane, making its hijacking itself a terrorist act. Moreover, the Pentagon attack was part of the same plan of attack as the assaults on the Trade Center, which were purely terrorist acts. The Pentagon attack thus also involved terrorism, even if it were to be considered primarily an act of war. Acts of war, however, are generally considered to be those undertaken by politically organized societies, namely national governments, and the participants in the act were not—so far as is known—acting on behalf of a government, but rather for the shadowy network of organizations known as al-Qaeda. Thus characterization of the September 11 attacks as "acts of war" is suggestive, but not precise.

One of the hijacked jetliners crashes into the second tower (left) of New York City's World Trade Center, creating a shower of flames and debris, as the first tower burns from the earlier plane crash. (AP/Wide World Photos)

Impact of the Attacks

The September 11 terrorist attacks were notable for the fact that they were not carried out in retaliation for some unmet concession demanded of the American government or some private entity. Their apparent aim was simply to maximize death and destruction as an end in itself and to terrorize American society at large and, presumably, America's allies. No specific set of demands was ever issued, before or after the attacks. Moreover, no organization openly took responsibility for the attacks, though subsequent videotaped statements by Osama bin Laden left no doubt in the minds of fair-minded observers that he and his organization were behind the carnage.

The military, political, and economic consequences of the attacks were of great significance. The United States, assisted by various allies, led by the British, attacked and subdued Afghanistan, home to al-Qaeda. The Taliban, the radical Islamist political movement that governed that country, was brought down, and a moderate regime was chosen by popular representatives to replace it. Numerous antiterrorist covert and overt operations were set in motion in dozens of countries throughout the world, often—but not always—with the cooperation of the nations involved.

In the months that followed the attacks, U.S. stock markets fared badly. Falling swiftly, they recovered to some degree but then sagged again. Some of this downturn was attributed to the direct economic effects of the attacks, which included temporary suspension of all airline services in the United States, interruptions in mail services, and the destruction of businesses and financial institutions in the World Trade Center itself. Although other factors were at work, investor fears of further attacks also played a role in the markets' decline. Airlines took tremendous financial hits, as many people were reluctant to fly after the airlines resumed operations. With the decline of air travel, the travel and hospitality industries, catering to both business and recreational travel, suffered as well.

At the same time, the attacks elicited a strong upswell of overt American patriotism, as millions of Americans were jolted into the realization of what they owed to their country. Pride in citizenship—which had been out of fashion in many quarters since the Vietnam War—again came into vogue. In important ways American democracy appeared to be a beneficiary of the attacks. Internationally, for a time, solidarity with the American cause was seen throughout nearly the whole of the industrialized world. A notable exception was neighboring Canada, whose government's concern for terrorism on American soil was, at best, tepid and fragmentary.

A few weeks after the September 11, 2001, terrorist attacks on the United States, a video-tape showing al-Qaeda leader Osama bin Laden praising the attacks appeared on world television. The belief that bin Laden taped his message inside Afghanistan fueled U.S. calls for a military invasion of that country. (Associated Press/Wide World Photos)

Aftermath

As weeks turned to months after the attacks, however, traditional, well-ingrained European anti-Americanism began to reemerge. However, the Soviet Union, which had been fence-sitting in its attitude to the West, in light of its having been badly wounded by terrorism itself, now moved decisively into the camp of its one-time historic rival. In Central Asia, America gained several allies, as countries such as Uzbekistan opened their doors to U.S. military installations, but at a price. Elsewhere in Asia, China proclaimed its solidarity with the United States on the terrorism issue, though perhaps with unspoken reservations.

The fact that both governmental and nongovernmental objectives—both civilian and military—were attacked showed that there was no intention to discriminate among those who were to be killed and property that was to be destroyed. The terrorists made no attempt to protect the human rights of any segment of society. No humane value structured any portion of the actions, which may be accordingly described as nihilistic in character.

To understand the attacks at a deeper level, the background to prohibitions against attacking civilians needs exploration. International laws of war, which are recognized by most of the world's nations, require that any combatants planning attacks do everything possible to ensure that no civilian targets are selected. While the terrorists did not act on behalf of a state that had ratified the War Conventions that articulate these international laws, clearly their actions took no heed of civilized requirements for making war.

Although the terrorists' primary intended victims were Americans, those who planned the WTC attack failed to discriminate between American and non-American victims. Consequently, hundreds of non-Americans from dozens of countries around the world were incinerated in the assaults on Lower Manhattan. The planners of the attacks did not investigate the nationalities of those who were likely to die in their attacks either because they were not interested, or because such matters did not occur to them. Either possibility illustrates the perpetrators' stark indifference to the first and most fundamental human right—the right to life, especially of innocents.

International military convention has long prohibited attacks on civilians. Such formal international "conventions" (treaties signed and ratified by states, which become obligated to their terms upon ratification) attempt to protect innocent human life, under the implicit or explicit grounds that human life is valuable for its own sake. Such conventions assume that human beings have a right to life and therefore ought not to be arbitrarily attacked.

Terrorism grew apace in the 1980's, when states such as Libya and Iran began sponsoring terrorist activity. Outstanding among the acts that form a background to the September 11 attacks is the terrorist bombing of a Pan American World Airways jetliner that crashed near Lockerbie, Scotland, killing 259 persons aboard and 11 on the ground in 1988. Two of the worst terrorist incidents aimed at American targets outside the United States were committed on August 7, 1998, when 224 civilians—mostly Africans—were killed by terrorist bombs exploding at the U.S. embassies in Nairobi, Kenya, and Dar es Salaam, Tanzania. These and other incidents of terrorism spelled out the weakening of international human rights norms among those involved in a variety of political struggles.

Another terrorist act on American soil stands as a prelude to September 11 and a warning that terrorists would be as heedless of basic human rights in the United States as they were elsewhere in the world. This was the bombing at the World Trade Center of February 26, 1993, when four Islamic militants detonated a bomb in the Twin Towers' underground parking garage. The explosion killed six people and injured more than 1,000 but failed to threaten the buildings' structure, although it did send smoke into all 112 stories of the WTC's two towers. The incident proved that American landmarks had become the targets of foreign terrorists and that acts posing significant risks to basic human rights could be expected in the future. This fact was underlined when in July, 1993, it was found that some terrorists involved in the February WTC incident were close associates of participants in an aborted plot to blow up a number of New York City targets, including the Holland and Lincoln Tunnels and the United Nations Building.

In the end, the September 11 attacks represented a qualitative change for the worse in terrorist activity. It was generally believed that future terrorists might be expected to consider these attacks as a benchmark to be emulated with respect to numbers killed, dire economic consequences, and the sheer level of terror unleashed within the country attacked and upon its allies and sympathizers around the world.

Charles F. Bahmueller

2001
Invasion of Afghanistan

At issue: Stabilizing Afghanistan's government and removing terrorist bases in the country
Date: October 7, 2001-
Location: Afghanistan and Pakistan
Combatants: United States vs. Afghanistan government troops and al-Qaeda forces
Principal commander: *American*, General Tommy Franks (1945-   )
Result: The U.S. invasion toppled Afghanistan's Taliban regime and made possible free elections; however, the al-Qaeda leader Osama bin Laden remained a fugitive through 2004.

The United States was not the first country to invade Afghanistan in modern times. In 1979, the Soviet Union invaded Afghanistan, took Kabul, its capital city, within one week and then spent the next decade trying to defeat Afghanistan's mujahideen insurgents. The mujahideen received aid from the United States, Saudi Arabia, Pakistan, and a loosely organized group of radical Muslims drawn from more than thirty countries. These Muslims deplored the Soviet invasion and the presence of 100,000 Soviet troops in Afghanistan because they feared the Soviet Union would attempt to impose atheism upon the country.

Osama bin Laden

The mujahideen were ill equipped to fight invaders. The Saudis sought someone prominent to funnel money and military assistance into Afghanistan but had trouble finding anyone willing to accept that responsibility. Then Osama bin Laden, a wealthy Saudi who knew Afghanistan well, emerged to accept the challenge. He established training camps to prepare men to fight in what they regarded as an Afghan holy war, or *jihad*. Under bin Laden's fundamentalist Islamic training, his followers formed al-Qaeda, an organization that would later be responsible for bombing two United States embassies, attacking the U.S. naval vessel *Cole*, and bombing the U.S. Air Force barracks in Khobar, Saudi Arabia.

On September 11, 2001, members of al-Qaeda launched air attacks on prominent American landmarks with four simultaneous suicide missions on hijacked commercial airliners. Two of the hijacked planes were flown into the twin towers of New York City's World Trade Center, causing both buildings to collapse, with a loss of thousands of lives. Another airliner was flown into the Pentagon Building outside Washington, D.C. A fourth crashed in Pennsylvania, while evidently headed toward an attack on the White House or the Capitol Building in Washington, D.C.; it was evidently brought down when its civilian passengers—who had learned of the other attacks through cell-phone calls—rose up against the hijackers. All these incidents claimed approximately three thousand lives—mostly Americans.

The horrendous attacks of September 11 were recognized as the handiwork of Osama bin Laden, whose fingerprints were on earlier acts of terrorism that involved suicide bombers. Immediately after the attacks, the Bush administration demanded that the Taliban, which controlled Afghanistan, turn over bin Laden and other al-Qaeda leaders to the United States and close al-Qaeda training camps inside Afghanistan. On October 7, 2001, after the Taliban refused to comply with the U.S. request, the United States declared war on Afghanistan, designating the campaign Operation Enduring Freedom. The ensuing American victory was swift. The Taliban regime capitulated in December.

The Hunt for bin Laden and New Weaponry

The U.S. Department of Justice made capturing Osama bin Laden its highest priority, offering a $25-million-dollar reward for his capture dead or alive. However, the hunt for bin Laden was made almost unimaginably difficult by Afghanistan's rugged topography. The land is half again the size of California, and its climate is harsh. The country is honeycombed with networks of intersecting caves familiar to bin Laden and his cohorts but not to the Americans.

The search for bin Laden centered on Tora Bora, thirty miles southeast of Jalalabad. The Americans employed advanced weaponry designed to penetrate caverns in an effort to kill bin Laden or flush him from the caves in which he was presumed to be hiding. In March, 2002, a thermobaric bomb, the BLU-118/B, was dropped close to a cavern in which bin Laden was thought to be. However, because its laser guidance system was faulty, it fell short of its target. The BLU-118/B bomb releases a fine mist of combustible fuel that erupts into a fireball when ignited and penetrates deep caves and bunkers. Even with the use of thermobaric bombs and laser guidance systems, the search for bin Laden had not succeeded three years later.

Laser guidance systems require personnel on the ground to direct the the systems' laser beams to their targets. These systems are disrupted by smoke or fog. In the Afghan war, Global Positioning Systems (GPSs), computers embedded in bombs, replaced many laser guidance systems. These so-called "smart bombs" proved accurate and reliable. The war with Afghanistan was also the first to employ unmanned aircraft (UVAs) as attack vehicles. Such aircraft had previously been used for target practice and reconnaissance, but early in the Afghan conflict, the Central Intelligence Agency used a reconfigured UVA to fire a Hellcat missile at a group of three men it identified as al-Qaeda operatives. After the three men were killed, they were found to be innocent bystanders, residents of an Afghan village. A similar error was made when a wedding party was misidentified from the air as a group of al-Qaeda and fired upon, killing nearly one hundred innocent civilians. Overall, American bombs had killed some 3,000 Afghan civilians by early 2005.

The Global Hawk and Predator were the two UVAs used in Afghanistan. Both of these aircraft are vulnerable to enemy fire as well as to bad weather and icing on their wings. They have the advantage, however, of being able to stay aloft unmanned for long periods to accomplish their missions without imperiling crew members. Through 2004, the United States lost one Global Hawk and five Predators in the Afghan war.

The initial Afghan invasion involved more bombing than ground combat. A mere fifteen Americans and five U.S. allies were killed by hostile fire. Another fifty-five Americans and twenty allies died in accidents or from so-called "friendly fire." Meanwhile, innocent Afghan citizens were left wondering what they had done to deserve the punishment the United States and it allies visited upon them.

Logistics of the Afghan War

Because Afghanistan is a landlocked country, waging war upon it has historically always been difficult. The monumental problems involved in

The American commander of a coalition task force talks with Afghan citizens during a routine patrol in the Cehar Cineh area during Operation Outlaw in October, 2004. (U.S. Department of Defense)

supplying troops with necessities in a place that is not accessible by ship have caused many would-be invaders to retreat. By the early twenty-first century, however, the United States possessed the technical wherewithal and financial resources to supply large numbers of troops by air. As the United States was preparing to wage war against Afghanistan, it committed approximately 140 supply aircraft to the war effort. These aircraft included C-5 Galaxy and C-17 Globemaster III transport planes. The C-5 Galaxy can carry more than one hundred tons of cargo but requires airfields almost one mile long on which to land. The C-17 Globemaster, although it cannot carry as much cargo as the C-5 Galaxy, can land on airfields only three thousand feet long, which gives it an advantage in a country such as Afghanistan, whose airfields are small and often in poor condition.

During each of the early months of the U.S. invasion of Afghanistan, American troops consumed 3.6 million gallons of water and the contents of seventy-two eighteen-wheel truckloads of food and other supplies—all delivered by air. However, having the technology to supply the troops is not enough. The cost of supplying troops by air entails colossal expenditures. For this reason, the Pentagon favored waging a massive bombing campaign rather than a ground war in Afghanistan. As a consequence, the United States has conducted much of its offensive in the Afghan conflict from offices in the Pentagon Building, half a world away.

Specialized Military Personnel

In earlier wars, most army personnel were infantrymen and cavalry whose training was not highly specialized. Modern wars, however, have required soldiers trained to use highly complex and expensive equipment whose operation can be entrusted only to those who have had extensive specialized training. In Afghanistan, the logistics of ferreting out the enemy from caves and other hiding places in remote parts of the country have required the development of innovative weapons such as the thermobaric bombs. More than two thousand special forces from the United States, along with troops from other coalition member countries that joined with the United States, have been deployed to help in the Afghan conflict. These special forces usually comprise clusters of military personnel that seldom exceed a dozen members. They specialize in such fields as combat search-and-rescue, counterterrorism, clandestine surveillance, and jungle or desert warfare.

It is essential that highly specialized personnel be as mobile as possible. The MH-533 Pave Low III heavy-lift helicopter is designed specifically to transport specialized personnel, generally under cover of darkness. Equipped with special radar and infrared sensors to detect objects from a distance, this helicopter can fly close to the ground, making it difficult for enemy radar to detect it. It is armed with machine guns and heavy armor so that enemy fire cannot easily penetrate it.

When the United States attacked Iraq in March, 2003, many troops stationed in Afghanistan were redeployed to that country. The search for bin Laden continued, but the United States relied more than before on the aid of Afghans in the search. Some of those employed in the search were Afghan warlords whose loyalty to the U.S. cause was doubtful. Indeed, many of them were directly involved in Afghanistan's illegal drug trade, which thrives because Afghanistan is well suited to growing the poppies from which opium is produced. After March, 2003, a much reduced force of American military personnel remained in Afghanistan, where insurgents constantly threatened them.

Democratic Changes in Afghanistan

On December 22, 2001, Hamid Karzai was inaugurated chairperson of the Afghan Interim Authority. In April, 2002, the former Afghan king, Muhammad Sahir Shah, returned to Kabul from his exile in Paris to attend the *loya jirga*, a grand council of Afghanistan's leaders. During the following June, this council elected—by secret ballot—Karzai president of the Transitional Islamic State of Afghanistan, a post in which he served until a constitution was drafted and nationwide elections scheduled. On October 9, 2004, direct elections were held in Afghanistan. Ten and one-half million Afghans registered to vote, and for the first time, women were eligible to vote. Hamid Karzai won the presidency with 55.9 percent of the votes cast.

Through many decades of the twentieth century, the Afghan people lived in a country lacking central political authority. When the Taliban emerged in the early 1990's, many Afghans eagerly embraced it because it offered an internal security that the country needed. During the mid-1990's, an emerging al-Qaeda capitalized on the political and economic distrust of many Afghan citizens.

The drug trade has long been a thriving enterprise in Afghanistan. The provincial warlords who enrich themselves through this trade have no wish for a strong central government. Since occupying the country at the end of 2001, the United States has introduced representative government but has made minimal progress in controlling Afghanistan's drug traffic. At the beginning of 2005, it remained to be seen whether the Karzai regime, with Washington's continuing support and encouragement, would survive in a political climate rife with insurgents and warlords. The geography of the country provides a daunting impediment to the establishment of a strong central government, and Afghanistan's situation in southwest Asia, which is among the most troubled areas in the world, seemed tenuous at best.

R. Baird Shuman

2001
War on Terrorism

At issue: Elimination of the al-Qaeda terrorist network responsible for the September 11, 2001, attacks in the United States and military action as judged necessary against supporting groups or states
Date: 2001-
Location: Worldwide
Combatants: United States vs. al-Qaeda, Afghanistan, and Iraq
Principal commanders: *American*, General Tommy Franks (1945-   ) (Afghan campaign); Lieutenant General Ricardo Sanchez (Iraq), General Richard Myers; *al-Qaeda*, Osama bin Laden; *Afghanistan*, Mullah Omar; *Iraq*, President Saddam Hussein (1937-   )
Principal battles: Tora Bora (Afghanistan); siege of Baghdad (Iraq)

Result: The first three years of U.S. military effort toppled Afghanistan's Taliban regime and Iraq's Saddam Hussein regime and captured senior al-Qaeda commanders but failed to capture Osama bin Laden himself or suppress violent insurgencies in Afghanistan and Iraq.

The so-called war on terrorism is in some respects typical of other wars that the United States waged after 1917. In other respects, however, it is unique. In common with the two world wars in which the United States fought and the amorphous, quasi-military conflict known as the Cold War, the war on terrorism has been justified on ideological grounds rather than those of territorial, commercial, or imperial aggrandizement. Unlike those earlier conflicts, however, it is not a neatly staged "theater" war against a clearly defined territorial opponent. Instead, it has been represented as a global war against an all-pervasive foe whose most salient defining characteristic is the desire to inflict harm on the United States in particular and on the civilized world in general. The war on terrorism may thus be regarded in part as an outgrowth of wars of the past and in part as a novel extension of them.

Ideological Antecedents

When President Woodrow Wilson asked the Congress for a declaration of war against Imperial Germany and its allies in 1917, he did so on the basis of the right of a neutral America to trade with belligerent (warring) states over the high seas, a right under attack by Germany's resumption of unrestricted warfare against all nations trafficking with its enemies. Wilson subsequently broadened his war aims to include such far-reaching and vaguely defined purposes as the inherent right of peoples to political self-determination and the desire to create a world "safe for democracy."

Similarly, in 1941, President Franklin D. Roosevelt depicted World War II not merely as a war against Germany, Italy, and Japan, but as a war against fascism. Although American entry into World War II was triggered by Japan's surprise attack on Pearl Harbor in December, 1941, the war's ideological foundations had been laid down in the Atlantic Charter issued by Roosevelt and British prime minister Winston S. Churchill during the previous summer.

The Cold War of the second half of the twentieth century focused on the communist Soviet Union, China, and their allies but was represented primarily as an ideological war against communism. That war, although it never involved direct military conflict between the superpower principals—the United States and the Soviet Union—did involve theater actions against the Soviet Union and China's perceived proxies in Korea, Vietnam,

U.S. Marines patrolling in Beirut, Lebanon, during a multinational peacekeeping operation in 1982. (U.S. Navy)

and Afghanistan. Whereas the two world wars had been fought to decisive conclusions capped by unconditional surrenders—which are characteristic of wars of ideology that require total victory—the Cold War did not seem to offer a definitive resolution in the foreseeable future. The U.S. objective in the Cold War was merely containment of the Soviet Union and was coupled with avoidance of a nuclear exchange between the superpowers.

The Post-Cold War World

The unexpected collapse of the Soviet Union during 1989-1991 provided a satisfying conclusion to the Cold War and appeared to vindicate the principles of political democracy, religious freedom, and market capitalism that the United States espoused. As the regimes of the Soviet client states of Eastern Europe fell, and China, Vietnam, and other erstwhile communist states moved away from managed economic systems toward market capitalism, a Western victory in the Cold War seemed complete.

Despite the end of the Cold War, the roots of future war had been sown. Although the United States had come into conflict with the theocratic regime of Iran's Ayatollah Ruhollah Musawi Khomeini in Iran shortly after the latter's assumption of power in 1979, the United States continued to train, equip, and finance Muslim insurgents fighting against the Soviet occupation of Afghanistan. Many of these insurgents were not Afghans. The consequence of this American policy was to lay the basis of the fundamentalist Taliban regime in Kabul after the Soviet withdrawal from Afghanistan.

Meanwhile, the 1991 Gulf War against Iraq, a former U.S. ally that had been encouraged and covertly supplied in its long border war with Iran, weakened a buffer against what was now perceived as a general threat to the region. Partly in response to this, American troops were stationed in Saudi Arabia after the Gulf War.

Until the United States entered the region during the early 1990's, no Western army had occupied a Middle Eastern Muslim state since the departure of French forces from Algeria in 1962. The brief American incursion in Lebanon in 1983 had been swiftly withdrawn in the wake of a terrorist attack that had killed 241 soldiers. The Saudi garrison provoked a similar response, and on June 25, 1996, nineteen Americans were killed by a truck bomb detonated outside the U.S. Air Force compound near Khobar. This attack had been preceded both by another attack on the Riyadh headquarters of the U.S. military mission in November, 1995, and one on the World Trade Center in New York in 1993. These attacks were gradually traced to a shadowy, multinational network of Islamic militants known as al-Qaeda, Arabic for "the base." Its leader, Osama bin Laden, was the heir

U.S. Air Force compound near Khobar after the terrorist bombing of June 29, 1996. (U.S. Department of Defense)

of one of Saudi Arabia's wealthiest families. A former Afghan resistance fighter sponsored by the United States, bin Laden had covert patronage from members of the Saudi elite, including state elements, as well as from the Taliban in Afghanistan, where he trained his agents.

The U.S. military bases in Saudi Arabia were not the only source of resentment against the United States in the Middle East. The Arab-Israeli dispute, in which Israel was widely regarded as an American client, festered despite attempts at a diplomatic resolution by President Bill Clinton during the 1990's. Meanwhile, the Gulf War continued as a low-intensity conflict in which the United States sponsored a commercial embargo and a weapons-inspection regime against Iraq, enforced a no-fly zone over the northern and southern thirds of the country, and bombed suspected military installations at will. As the United States began to disengage its forces from Saudi Arabia in the wake of the Khobar attack, neoconservative commentators in the United States, including former officials of the administration of President George Bush, envisaged Iraq as a possible site for American bases, and urged a war to overthrow Saddam Hussein. At the same time, a Harvard scholar, Samuel P. Huntington, suggested in a widely influential study that the coming century would see a "clash of civilizations" between the Muslim and Western worlds. This, too, helped to lay the ideological foundations for war.

The Bush Administration

As the administration of George W. Bush came to power in 2001, war with Iraq was given high priority. Its long-term planning, however, was primarily concentrated on identifying potential state antagonists, notably China. Warning signs of another al-Qaeda attack on the United States were ignored or lost in the bureaucratic maze of intelligence agencies. As a result, the events of September 11 caught the nation by surprise. Nineteen militants succeeded in hijacking four commercial American airliners. Two of the planes were crashed into the towers of New York City's World Trade Center, resulting in the collapse of both buildings. A third was crashed into the Pentagon near Washington, D.C. A fourth was downed by its passengers in rural Pennsylvania. In all, about three thousand American lives were lost, a number exceeding the total American fatalities at Pearl Harbor in December, 1941, although first reports put the death toll at twice that number. Immediate economic damage was placed in the hundreds of billions of dollars.

As Americans and others reacted to the terrorist attacks of September 11 with shock, horror, and outrage, President Bush responded the next day by proclaiming a generalized war on terrorism. He characterized it in near-biblical terms as "a monumental struggle between good and evil," adding that the enemy was not simply a group or groups but "a frame of mind" that fostered hatred of Christianity, Judaism, and, in a word, "everything that is not them." These comments were all the more extraordinary in that the identity of the hijackers had not been fully established at that time, although the Central Intelligence Agency reported that al-Qaeda had been involved. Several days later, the president declared his intention to bring Osama bin Laden to justice, "dead or alive." Nevertheless, during the interval, members of bin Laden's family had been permitted to leave the United States without even being interrogated.

Both the legal and operational dimensions of the new war were unclear. None of the military actions of the Cold War had been accompanied by a congressional declaration of war, including the major conflicts in Korea and Vietnam. Likewise, certain other long-term military operations of earlier years, such as the U.S. occupations of Nicaragua (1912-1933) and Haiti (1915-1934), had not received congressional sanction. When President Bush consulted congressional leaders on September 12, he asked for a resolution endorsing the use of force under the War Powers Act rather than a declaration of war. His intention, however, was not to limit military action in either scope or duration, but to preserve maximum executive discretion about how, where, and when to use American power.

Launching the War

One evident difficulty in launching the war was knowing precisely whom to attack. Afghanistan's Taliban regime was a logical target; its leaders had harbored al-Qaeda and permitted it to train forces on Afghan soil. In the days after September 11, a consensus developed in the Bush administration that the Taliban and al-Qaeda were to be treated as a single belligerent entity. However, members of the Taliban themselves were to a large extent creatures of Pakistan's intelligence services, and al-Qaeda's chief funding had come from Saudi Arabia. Neither nuclear-armed Pakistan nor oil-rich Saudi Arabia could be attacked with impunity. By contrast, Afghanistan, although difficult to access, had an established guerrilla insurgency, the Northern Alliance. Using Northern Alliance troops, American Special Forces units, and air power, the Taliban could be put to rout, and a symbolic initial victory achieved. Participation of the North Atlantic Treaty Organization (NATO) was also secured. On October 7, 2001, following a last demand that the Taliban surrender Osama bin Laden, the United States commenced bombing attacks.

The Afghan campaign went raggedly. Determined to minimize American casualties, the Bush administration did not insert regular forces in unit strength into the country until March, 2002. Meanwhile, the Northern Alliance, itself divided by factions, ignored American instructions and captured Kabul. In the strategic confusion that ensued, Taliban leaders regrouped in the south, their base of ethnic support, and al-Qaeda commanders, including Osama bin Laden, escaped to sanctuary in Pakistan. Tribal chieftains and warlords asserted their authority in the northern and western parts of Afghanistan, leaving the American-appointed president, Hamid Karzai, effectively confined to Kabul under heavy American guard.

The war had its usual by-products: unknown thousands of civilian deaths and casualties, many caused by high-altitude bombing attacks, and fresh refugees in the millions, many of whom fled to Pakistan. The United States promised, but did not deliver, substantial reconstruction aid. In its absence, opium cultivation, banned by the Taliban, resumed in the north. American and allied forces remained, but with little or no control over large stretches of the country, and subject to guerrilla assault.

In October, 2004, Karzai was formally elected president but remained under American protection. The United States spirited captured fighters and others suspected of collaboration with al-Qaeda out of the country. The captives included an American citizen, John Walker Lindh, who was conspicuously displayed in confinement despite serious injuries. More than six hundred of the captives were imprisoned at the U.S. naval base at Guantanamo Bay, Cuba, while others were "rendered" to third-party countries for interrogation.

The Iraq War

In the meantime, the Bush administration prepared for war on a second front, Iraq. Planning for this war went forward at the highest levels from the first days of the Bush administration, but the September 11 attacks gave them new impetus. Some White House personnel were startled in the immediate aftermath of the attacks to find senior advisors preoccupied with Iraq rather than Afghanistan, and the president himself demanding evidence of links between Saddam Hussein and al-Qaeda. The improvisational response to Afghanistan and the absence of serious logistical commitment at key moments of the war may be explained in part by this preoccupation. Seven hundred million dollars appropriated for the Afghan war were subsequently diverted to prepare for invading Iraq, without notification to Congress.

The U.S. commitment to go to war against Iraq had several sources. Some Bush officials regretted the failure to depose Hussein during the earlier Gulf War, and thereby to reshape the Middle East. They coveted Iraq as a source of secure oil supply and a base of operations to replace the one evacuated in Saudi Arabia. Meanwhile, Hussein had succeeded in interrupting United Nations efforts to monitor his military arsenal. After September 11, it was alleged that Hussein would share his arsenal with terrorist groups.

The road to war was carefully plotted. Under American pressure, Hussein readmitted U.N. weapons inspectors, but the United States insisted that he was concealing so-called weapons of mass destruction prohibited under Gulf War protocols. Vice President Dick Cheney claimed that Hussein was on the verge of achieving nuclear capability, and the president's National Security Advisor, Condoleeza Rice, conjured up visions of mushroom clouds rising up over American cities.

In February, 2003, Secretary of State Colin Powell appeared before the United Nations to display what he claimed to be incontrovertible evidence of Hussein's hidden weapons caches. In the meantime, a legal rationale for attack was prepared. On October 10 and 11, 2002, both houses of Congress gave President Bush authority to invade Iraq should diplomatic efforts to dismantle Hussein's presumed arsenal fail. The vote was 296 to 133 in the House of Representatives and 77 to 23 in the Senate. These congressional resolutions fell short of a declaration of war, and some members of Congress, notably Senator Robert Byrd of West Virginia, warned against ceding constitutional powers to the president. In November, the United Na-

U.S. soldiers cautiously enter a building in Zumrat, Afghanistan, that they believe may be storing illegal weapons, in October, 2004. (U.S. Department of Defense)

tions approved a Resolution 1441 after intense American lobbying, calling upon Hussein to disarm and warning of potential military consequences should he fail to do so.

The War on Terrorism Begins

Despite concessions by Hussein, antiwar protests, and last-minute efforts by the international community to broker a compromise, the United States attacked Iraq on March 19, 2003 in company with a hastily improvised "Coalition of the Willing." The latter numbered some thirty nations, but only Great Britain provided significant support. Some of the other allies supplied token contingents numbering as few as twenty-five troops. Baghdad fell on April 9, and on May 1 President Bush declared "major combat operations" over and Iraq liberated. Hussein and his chief officials went into hiding, but most Iraqi leaders were captured in the succeeding months, and Hussein himself was finally found in December.

Securing Iraq, however, proved elusive. Elements of Hussein's army and Baathist Party organized resistance, and they were joined by native Islamic militants and foreign fighters. The American force, only 140,000 in number, proved grossly inadequate to pacify the country or even to secure military arsenals (which contained no WMDs, much to the embarrassment of the Bush administration). Repeated attempts to take rebel strongholds such as Fallujah resulted in devastation but no lasting success. The insurgency spread, and by the time of President Bush's election to a second term of office in November, 2004, more than 1,100 American troops had been killed. Unnumbered thousands of Iraqi soldiers and insurgents had also died, and civilian deaths, based on projections of ordinary mortality, were estimated as high as 100,000.

Abuse of Iraqi Prisoners

A further complication arose when revelations of widespread torture and abuse in the central Baghdad detention center, Abu Ghraib, were made public in May, 2004. As worldwide condemnation mounted, prisoner deaths not only at Abu Ghraib but at other, sometimes secret, facilities were revealed. Abuses at Guantanamo Bay, where prisoners had been held for two and a half years without charge or review, were brought to light as well. President Bush denounced the abuses, although he had himself signed off on memoranda defining captured terrorists as "enemy combatants" falling outside the protections of the Geneva Conventions against torture. Some notorious offenders were prosecuted by military tribunals, but senior officers and civilian officials were shielded, and the president resisted calls for the resignation of his defense secretary, Donald H. Rumsfeld.

Detainees, many of whom proved to be innocent persons swept up in dragnets or otherwise misidentified, remained in a legal limbo until the U.S. Supreme Court ordered their processing in June, 2004. Among them were two American citizens, Yaser Esam Hamdi and José Padilla, who had been held without charge or access to counsel. Hamdi was subsequently deported to Saudi Arabia. Their cases highlighted concerns about the erosion of basic constitutional safeguards at home. The so-called Patriot Act, hastily passed by Congress in September, 2001, to give the president extraordinary authority in pursuing terrorists, was widely criticized for permitting secret searches and other infringements of civil liberties.

The legal, constitutional, and civil rights issues raised by the war on terrorism were underscored by the uncertainty over its nature, duration, and purposes. Terrorism itself, as the action of organized, nonstate agents to promote political or social change through violence or coercion, has been a feature of modern life since the nineteenth century. The terrorist "problem," like that of crime or narcotics (against which "wars" have also been periodically proclaimed), has proved ineradicable as such, although particular manifestations have been contained or suppressed by police work, such as the Red Brigades faction in Italy or the Baader-Meinhof Gang in Germany.

In proclaiming a war on terrorism, however, and in identifying an "axis of evil" of terrorist-associated or terrorist-sponsoring states (Iraq, Iran, and North Korea), President Bush not only raised the rhetorical stakes of the U.S. response to September 11 but also laid the groundwork for a broad doctrine of intervention, collaborative if possible but unilateralist where necessary. Such an open-ended war against an ever-shifting foe— Secretary Rumsfeld had suggested that it might last a generation or more— conjured up fears of an entrenched national security state, and, among traditional allies as well as potential foes, the perception of the United States as a hyperpower in quest of global hegemony under the guise of a war of self-defense. When, in September, 2004, U.N. Secretary-General Kofi Annan characterized the war in Iraq as "illegal" under the United Nations Charter, he gave voice to the opinion of many that American policy was undermining the international order.

Al-Qaeda itself, reputedly with cells in some sixty countries, remained active despite the capture of some senior operatives. Prominent attacks included bombings of a resort complex in Bali, Indonesia, in October, 2002, and of commuter trains in Madrid, Spain, in March, 2004. Saudi financing continued with little impediment, and in Iran, Pakistan, Thailand, Indonesia, and the Philippines, al-Qaeda operatives and networks appeared to move freely, sometimes with covert assistance from state security forces or in concert with local terrorist groups.

The United States sent Special Forces units to the Philippines to help combat the Abu Sayyaf insurrection in Mindinao, established a new military base in East Africa at Djibouti, and spurred counterterrorist efforts elsewhere in Asia and Africa. Many governments faced a delicate balancing act between placating American demands for access, military or otherwise, and arousing hostility within their own populations, among whom there was frequently sympathy and support for al-Qaeda. Meanwhile, other groups emerged in the shadowy underworld of terror, whether connected to al-Qaeda or claiming independence of it. In this regard, too, the war on terrorism had created its own paradox, spawning new terrorist entities even as it worked to identify and eliminate existing ones.

American Reaction to the War on Terrorism

Within the United States, the war on terrorism had created a new culture of security in which ordinary citizens found their freedom of movement and expression burdened and sometimes curtailed; even Senator Edward M. Kennedy of Massachusetts, the brother of a former president and one of the most conspicuous figures in American public life, was denied air travel when his name mistakenly appeared on a watch list. After initial resistance, the Bush administration embraced the creation of the new cabinet-level Department of Homeland Security, whose first director was Tom Ridge, the former governor of Pennnsylvania. The new department's mandate was to coordinate security activities, but it met with resistance from entrenched military and intelligence bureaucracies, and its color-coded terror alerts soon became the subject of ridicule.

A bipartisan commission to investigate the circumstances of September 11, also initially opposed by President Bush, detailed the grave intelligence failings that lay behind the World Trade Center attacks, but its recommendation that intelligence budgeting and activity be centralized and coordinated was not implemented. The Justice Department launched numerous investigations and prosecutions of suspected terrorist cells in the United States, but achieved few significant convictions. On the other hand. the United States suffered no new terrorist attacks in the three years following September 11, even as the worldwide civilian death toll from further al-Qaeda attacks approached 1,000. Few doubted, however, that al-Qaeda, and perhaps other groups as well, retained the will and the capacity to strike again at American interests—either at home or abroad. In particular, many pointed to the potential havoc of insufficiently secured Soviet arsenals and to nuclear trafficking by North Korea and Pakistan.

Terrorism is a complex reaction to the authority of the modern state and the associated phenomena, real or perceived, of imperialism, neo-colonialism, globalization, and underdevelopment. The war on terrorism was a response, both real and rhetorical, to the trauma of September 11, the most devastating attack ever launched on American soil. By early 2005, it involved major armed conflicts in Afghanistan and Iraq, neither of which was favorably resolved; the threat of action against Syria and Iran; and covert action in other sectors. It has seen as well a major reorientation of American foreign policy in the direction of an aggressive unilateralism.

The case of Iraq is instructive in this regard. The Bush administration had planned a war against Iraq prior to September 11, which served it as a pretext. Although President Bush made the Iraq war the centerpiece of his war on terrorism, this rationale clearly subsumed other, prior purposes. Meanwhile, in 2005, the threat of terror to American security remained real. On the other hand, the response to it by the Bush administration was giving credence to those who feared that the war would be exploited to advance hegemonic American interests. The war on terrorism was, therefore, in the broadest sense a war in progress, whose character and objectives were still being defined, and whose end was nowhere in sight.

Robert Zaller

2003: Iraq War

At issue: Iraq's potential threat to world order
Date: March 19-May 1, 2003
Location: Iraq
Combatants: Iraq vs. United States, Great Britain, and other coalition members
Principal commanders: *American*, Tommy Franks (1945-   )
Principal political leaders: *American*, President George W. Bush (1946-   ), Vice President Dick Cheney (1941-   ), Secretary of Defense Donald Rumsfeld (1932-   ), National Security Adviser Condoleeza Rice (1954-   ), Secretary of State Colin Powell (1937-   ); *Iraqi*, President Saddam Hussein (1937-   ), Foreign Minister Tariq Aziz (1936-   ), Interim Prime Minister Iyad Allawi (1945-   )
Result: The U.S. military victory toppled Saddam Hussein's regime, but disorder and violence continued through the ensuing occupation, and there were allegations of U.S. imperialism.

The Iraq War of 2003 was the second time that a U.S.-led coalition confronted the armed forces of Saddam Hussein. After Iraq's invasion of oil-rich Kuwait in 1990, the Security Council of the United Nations (U.N.) authorized member nations to force Iraq out of Kuwait. In the resulting Gulf War of 1991, the coalition of some two dozen countries easily accomplished that mission. At the time Kuwait was liberated, some observers argued that coalition forces should march into Baghdad in order to force a change in the Iraqi regime. President George Bush, however, refused to pursue such a policy, which had never been endorsed by the United Nations.

In the ensuing cease-fire agreement, Hussein agreed to destroy all Iraqi weapons of mass destruction (WMD), which included biological, chemical, and nuclear weapons. Because of his non-compliance, however, the United Nations applied economic sanctions that resulted in painful shortages of food and medical supplies. In December, 1998, after Hussein rejected requests for U.N. investigations of numerous sites for possible WMD, President Bill Clinton ordered that the sites be bombed. In December, 1999, following much diplomatic controversy, Hussein refused to allow U.N. inspectors to enter his country.

After George W. Bush became president in January, 2001, he and his advisers believed that Hussein posed a threat to American interests. Although Bush often referred to the tyrannical abuses of the Iraqi regime, he emphasized Hussein's expansionist goals combined with his development of WMD. Following the terrorist attacks of September 11, Bush assumed that Hussein had been affiliated with the Islamic militants responsible for the attacks. In his state of the union address of January, 2002, Bush referred to Iraq, Iran, and North Korea as "an axis of evil." Addressing the United Nations in September, Bush warned that the United Nations would become irrelevant if it failed to enforce its resolutions. Shortly thereafter, the U.S. Congress authorized Bush to use force against Hussein's regime. In November, the U.N. Security Council passed Resolution 1441, demanding that U.N. inspectors be given unrestricted access to visit any sites at their discretion.

Diplomatic Disarmament Crisis

Faced with the prospect of another war, Hussein finally allowed Hans Blix and his team of weapons inspectors to enter Iraq. Hussein's government provided the inspectors documentation asserting that the country had destroyed all its weapons of mass destruction. Blix, however, complained about continued limitations on the work of the inspectors. U.S. officials charged that Iraq was in "material breach" and demanded full and immediate compliance. In March, Hussein tried to gain support by recognizing the sovereignty of Kuwait. The Arab leaders at a summit meeting expressed firm opposition to military action against Iraq and called for an end to sanctions.

In his state of the union address in January, 2003, Bush claimed that the Iraqi government was attempting to purchase uranium in Africa in order to develop nuclear weapons (an allegation later found to be mistaken). Bush asked the Security Council to pass a resolution authorizing war on the grounds that Iraq continued to develop illegal WMD. Secretary of State Colin Powell delivered a long speech at the Security Council, presenting a combination of evidence and allegations collected by the Central Intelligence Agency (CIA). Hans Blix and his team, however, were skeptical about the U.S. allegations and asked for additional time for the investigations to continue.

At the Security Council, Bush's proposed resolution met strong opposition. While the British government firmly supported the resolution, France, Germany, the Soviet Union, and China voiced strong disagreement. Opponents to the U.S. plan argued that there was insufficient evidence of "an imminent threat" to justify going to war. President Bush and British prime minister Tony Blair, in contrast, insisted on the need to take preemptive action to eliminate a developing threat. Although Bush and Blair were unable to get the resolution passed, they put together a so-called "coalition of the willing," which included the limited participation of Spain, Poland, Australia, Japan, and more than twenty other countries.

Officials of the Bush administration spoke optimistically about the prospects for a rapid military victory and for a postwar reconstruction of Iraq. They confidently asserted that Iraq's Shia Muslims would rebel against Hussein's regime as soon as an invasion began. Secretary Rumsfeld even suggested that American forces would be greeted by Iraqis dancing in the streets. His deputy secretary Paul Wolfowitz assured a Senate committee that the Iraqis, given their huge oil reserves, would be able to pay for the reconstruction of the country with little or no help from American taxpayers. Moreover, President Bush argued that the establishment of a democratic Iraq would become a model for the Middle East.

Meanwhile, despite the prospects of an imminent U.S.-led invasion, Saddam Hussein maintained a defiant posture. In an interview with CBS-TV anchorman Dan Rather on February 24, he insisted that his country did not possess any illegal weapons. He declared that he would continue to "maintain the honor of nationalism and pan-Arabism." He further said that he would not seek asylum in another country and that he was prepared to die in Iraq for his principles.

Outbreak of Hostilities

During the weekend of March 15-16, Bush and Blair met in the Azores Islands for an "emergency summit." The two leaders agreed that Hussein had no intention of complying with U.N. resolution 1441. The next day, Bush demanded in a nationally televised speech that Hussein and his two sons, Uday and Qusay, must leave Iraq within forty-eight hours or face the consequences. Bush explained that his purpose was "to disarm Iraq, to free its people, and defend the world from grave danger."

When the deadline expired on March 19, 2003, President Bush issued an order to begin firing tomahawk cruise missiles and guided bombs at military targets in Baghdad and other targets within Iraq. He also ordered U.S. forces in Kuwait and the Persian Gulf to launch an attack on Iraq the next day. Under the code name Operation Iraqi Freedom, the invading forces included 250,000 U.S. combat troops, joined by 50,000 British, 2,000 Australian, and 200 Polish troops. Other coalition nations contributed only token numbers of soldiers.

Secretary of Defense Donald Rumsfeld, who supervised the military strategy of the war, emphasized the intensive use of missiles and bombs, with as few troops on the ground as possible. The massive attacks from the air, called a "shock and awe" campaign, did great damage to Iraqi cities, with limited damage to populated areas. From both the Persian Gulf and the eastern Mediterranean Sea, the U.S. launched guided missile cruisers that struck specific targets throughout Iraq. The Air Force dropped "bunker busters," enormous bombs that weighted 4,700 pounds each. Officials said that they were conducting a "decapitation attack" directed at Saddam Hussein.

Despite angry protests in most U.S. cities, the majority of Americans initially supported the military operations against Iraq. In addition to fears of WMD, Americans tended to assume that the Iraqi government had been an ally of radical Islamic terrorists and appeared to think that Hussein's domestic violations of human rights provided added justification for the use of force. In many parts of the world, however, the U.S. attack on Iraq brought forth waves of anti-Americanism, particularly in Arab countries and in Western Europe, Canada, and the Soviet Union. The large number of protests reflected a widespread distrust of American power. Numerous protesters alleged that the Bush administration was attempting to take control of oil in the Middle East.

The Push to Baghdad

On March 20, the land invasion began from Iraq's border in Kuwait. Plans for an invasion from the north were canceled when Turkey refused

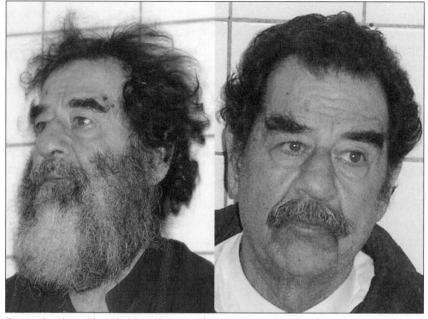

Former Iraqi president Saddam Hussein after his capture in Tikrit by coalition troops in December, 2003. The pictures show him with the beard he had when he was captured and his appearance after being shaved. (AP/Wide World Photos)

the use of its territory. American and British forces quickly took control of the airfields in southwestern Iraq, and they also seized the port city of Umm Qasar on the Persian Gulf. The fighting was brutal in many places. Near the city of An Nasariyah, enemy forces ambushed a supply convoy, which caused many U.S. soldiers to go missing in action. Nevertheless, on March 24, the commander of the invasion, General Tommy Franks, announced that coalition soldiers were only sixty miles from Baghdad, although he acknowledged that casualties were increasing. As U.S. marines fought in the streets of An Nasariyah, British forces shelled Al Basrah, the second largest city of the country.

On March 25, large numbers of U.S. soldiers crossed the Euphrates River by way of the An Nasariyah bridges. They then began to drive northward to Baghdad, located on the Tigris River. By then, the allied supply line stretched from the Persian Gulf to the city of Karbala, only fifty miles southwest of Baghdad. However, the push northward was slower than U.S. military planners had hoped it would be. Aided by blinding sandstorms, Iraqi troops ambushed and harassed the heavily armed column. The resistance was especially fierce in the region between An Najaf and Karbala, where U.S. troops confronted both regular Iraq soldiers and the

Fedayeen Saddam, a paramilitary group that answered directly to Uday Hussein, the oldest son of the dictator. As U.S. forces began to battle the Republican Guard near Baghdad, British troops fought more than a thousand loyalists in the streets of Al Basarah.

Second Front

On March 27, the U.S. military opened a second front in northern Iraq, where the coalition could count on the support of more than 50,000 Kurdish guerrilla fighters. About a thousand parachuters of the 173rd Airborne Brigade landed northeast of Arbil and joined forces with Kurdish fighters. After four days of heavy air strikes in the region, the Iraqi army abandoned the town of Chamchamal, which was northwest of Kirkuk, a city with many loyal supporters of Hussein's Baath Party. Kurdish guerrillas quickly moved into Chamchamal, providing coalition troops with a forward position for attacking Kirkuk.

Resistance to the allied advance northward toward Baghdad was beginning to crumble. On April 2, U.S. Marines defeated Republican Guard forces at Al Kut, a strategic city on the Tigris River one hundred miles southeast of Baghdad. About the same time, the U.S. Army took control of a bridge over the Euphrates at Al Musayyib, thirty miles south of the capital. The next day, the Army's Third Infantry Division seized the Saddam International Airport, located only twelve miles from the capital. Meanwhile, U.S. aircraft conducted about one thousand bombing missions in the regions, most of them aimed at Republican Guard stations.

By April 4, allied forces were advancing rapidly toward Baghdad in three columns—from the south, the southwest, and the southeast. As the conquest of the city appeared inevitable, thousands of its residents attempted to flee in bumper-to-bumper traffic. About 2,500 Republican Guard soldiers surrendered to coalition forces south of Baghdad. Also on April 4, the British Seventh Armored Brigade, called the Desert Rats, entered the center of Al Basrah with thousands of troops and hundreds of tanks. The Shia Muslims of the city enthusiastically greeted the British as liberators.

In the Shia holy city of Karbala, U.S. forces defeated Fedayeen Saddam fighters after a five-day battle that ended on April 6. As the Americans occupied the city, a crowd of 10,000 residents, mostly Shia Muslims who hated Hussein, celebrated in the city's public square. Shouting "Saddam is no more," they pulled down a statue of the dictator. To the American public, the progress of the war appeared to be following the optimistic predictions of Secretary of Defense Rumsfeld and other officials.

Victory in Iraq

U.S. forces pushed into the capital city and occupied a major presidential palace along with other important buildings on April 7. As the Third Infantry Division, supported by air strikes, entered central Baghdad with some seventy tanks and sixty Bradley fighting vehicles, it faced only scattered pockets of resistance. That same day, U.S. intelligence agents reported that Hussein and his two sons were probably located in a private house in an affluent neighborhood of the city. B-1 bombers destroyed the house with four bombs of 2,000 pounds each. However, the dictator and his sons were not present.

The next day, about five hundred of Hussein's loyal soldiers crossed the Tigris and moved into Baghdad to launch a counteroffensive. The U.S. infantry responded with artillery fire, while A-10 attack planes strafed the Iraqi soldiers. The counteroffensive was a complete failure. By April 9, coalition forces had control of the eastern sector of the city. U.S. soldiers were generally greeted with cheering crowds. The Shia Muslims of southeastern neighborhoods were particularly enthusiastic about the fall of the regime. In Firdos Square, U.S. troops helped Iraqi civilians topple an enormous statue of Hussein. The Iraqis then dragged the head of the statue through the streets of the city, while onlookers spat at it and yelled insults at Hussein's memory.

By April 11, Kurdish fighters and U.S. special forces had conquered the northern cities of Kirkuk and Mosul. Two days later, U.S. Marines entered Hussein's hometown of Tikrit, the last remaining city not controlled by the allies. By that date, only 115 U.S. military troops had died in combat. The rapid conclusion of the war and the low rate of casualties delighted the American public. Bush's approval rating soared to 73 percent, which had risen almost 20 percent higher than it had been in polls taken before the war. While visiting the USS *Abraham Lincoln* near San Diego on May 1, President Bush announced that the military phase of the war was essentially over. He described the victory as a battle in "a war on terrorism," necessary to keep WMD out of the hands of such terrorists.

Growing Violence Under the Occupation

Attempts to pacify and reconstruct Iraq turned out to be much more difficult than overthrowing the Hussein regime. The collapse of Iraq's government and army left most of the country without any civil authority. In Baghdad and elsewhere, looters stripped almost everything of value from public buildings, including hospitals and electrical power plants. They even ransacked the National Museum of Iraq, stealing some twelve thousand objects. At the same time, sabotage of oil wells, pipelines, and refineries almost produced a temporary standstill of the country's oil industry. Even though Iraq possessed the second largest oil reserves in the world, it was forced to import gasoline in May.

Critics charged that Bush's postwar reconstruction polices contained three major mistakes: an underestimation of the potential for postwar violence, the sending of too few U.S. soldiers to the war, and the premature disbanding of the Iraqi army. Much of the criticism was directed at Secretary Rumsfeld, who had insisted on keeping the number of soldiers as small as possible. By May 1, the number of troops in Iraq had been reduced to about 160,000—a number that proved inadequate for the multifaceted tasks of hunting for members of Hussein's regime and guerrilla fighters, while also restraining ethnic conflict and trying to maintain public order. Criticism was also directed toward the civilian head of the occupation, Paul Bremer III, who had insisted on disbanding the Iraqi army, with the result of casting loose many thousands of armed men who had no way of legally supporting themselves and their families.

As the majority of Iraq's population failed to see tangible improvements in their daily lives, large numbers of Iraqis blamed the United States for their deplorable conditions. Over the next two years, guerrilla attacks on coalition soldiers grew more frequent and more deadly. Militant insurgents also targeted Iraqis who cooperated with the U.S.-led occupation. Car bombings became increasingly common. By August of 2003, some officials of the Department of Defense were classifying the insurgency as a classic guerrilla war. Between May 1 and October 28, 116 U.S. soldiers died in hostile action. Within a year, the number of American deaths would grow to almost one thousand.

Continuing Controversy About the War

As a rationale for waging the preemptive war, President Bush and Prime Minister Blair had relied almost entirely on the potential threat from Hussein's alleged possession of weapons of mass destruction. After the war, the failure to find any such weapons in Iraq was embarrassing to both leaders—especially to Blair, because of the extreme antipathy for the conflict in Great Britain. Eventually the lack of evidence for WMD forced the Bush administration to admit that it had relied on inadequate information. When Bush continued to try to link Saddam Hussein with international terrorism, critics forced him to concede that the evidence was speculative and uncertain. The Bush administration increasingly defended the war by calling attention to the dictatorial nature of Hussein's regime.

American disillusionment with the war increased as the public learned about its mounting costs. In September, 2003, Bush had to ask Congress for an additional $87 billion. Some respected economists predicted that the combination of war and reconstruction programs would eventually cost U.S. taxpayers more than $200 billion. Even with this expense, the establishment of a democratic and stable Iraq appeared elusive.

Meanwhile, the Bush administration insisted that there were many positive developments. On October 16, the U.N. Security Council passed a resolution endorsing the U.S.-led occupation of Iraq. Later that month, seventy-seven countries meeting in Madrid pledged about $33 billion for the pacification and economic rebuilding of the country. In Iraq, most top leaders of Hussein's government, including his two hated sons, Uday and Qusay, were either captured or killed. Hussein himself was finally captured on December 13, 2003. A provisional government was organized in early 2004, and multiparty elections were held in January, 2005.

Thomas Tandy Lewis

2003
Postwar Occupation of Iraq

At issue: Controlling insurgent activity in Iraq; preparing for nationwide elections in 2005
Date: 2003-2005
Location: Iraq
Combatants: Coalition occupation forces vs. Iraqi insurgents
Principal commanders: *American*, Tommy Franks (1945-   ), John Abizaid (1951-   ), George Casey (1948-   )
Result: No closure in the Iraq War through early 2005.

On May 1, 2003, President George W. Bush boarded the aircraft carrier USS *Abraham Lincoln* that bore a banner, allegedly provided by the White House, proclaiming "Mission Accomplished." The war against Iraq, begun on March 19, 2003, officially ended forty-three days later. Up to that moment, no comprehensive exit plan had been formulated.

President Bush believed that the Iraqis, liberated from Saddam Hussein's despotism, would welcome American and allied soldiers as liberators, as the French had welcomed American troops toward the end of World War II. This assumption underestimated the military sophistication, weaponry, nationalism, and xenophobia of an estimated twelve thousand militant Iraqi insurgents who attacked military occupiers and relief workers. In October, 2004, these insurgents abducted Margaret Hassan, a CARE executive, the wife of an Iraqi and holder of dual citizenship, and thirty-year resident of Iraq who had devoted her life to helping Iraqis. The following month, they executed her.

U.S. forces toppled Saddam Hussein's statue in a Baghdad square on April 9, 2003. Pictures of this symbolic act that were flashed around the world clearly—but falsely—implied that the downfall of the tyrant who had held Iraqis at bay since 1979 was accomplished and that peace was imminent. On December 13, Hussein himself was captured while cowering in a spider-hole near Tikrit, his birthplace.

Meanwhile, in December, 2004, more mass graves were uncovered containing the bodies of Iraqis presmuably slaughtered by Hussein's followers, several of whom were put on trial in mid-December for their involvement in such atrocities. By the beginning of 2005, Hussein was in custody awaiting trial by his fellow Iraqis, and the cost of the conflict with Iraq had exceeded $100 million—twice the figure originally estimated. Moreover, the conflict still appeared to be far from fully resolved.

The Occupation

In 2002, when a war with Iraq seemed to be coming, the U.S. Army's Central Command directed by General Tommy Franks prepared an exit plan titled Operation Desert Crossing. The Bush administration disre-

U.S. Army soldiers move cautiously through a dangerous part of Fallujah during a mission in early November, 2004. (U.S. Department of Defense)

garded this plan. The Pentagon's Central Command requested 380,000 troops for the Iraq War. Secretary of Defense Donald Rumsfeld considered 40,000 troops sufficient. Congress finally approved 250,000 troops, but only 150,000 were actually deployed.

Rumsfeld anticipated the withdrawal of 50,000 troops in June, 2003, another 50,000 in July, and another 50,000 in August. He foresaw transferring day-to-day operation to Iraqis by September, 2003. By January, 2005, however, the 138,000 troops still in Iraq after the formal conclusion of the war had seen their numbers increased to 148,000.

Meanwhile, U.S. troops continued to fight insurgents and discourage dissidents from torching Iraq's oil fields, whose revenues were earmarked for the nation's recovery. By late 2004, Iraq was $122 billion in debt. Thirty billion dollars were to be forgiven by several nations including the United States, France, and the Soviet Union. The American conservators overseeing the distribution of Iraq's oil revenues were accused of mismanagement.

Ahmed Chalabi of the Iraq National Conference provided the administration with intelligence about Iraq. Much of this intelligence proved unreliable. Chalabi's schemes connected with Iraq's rehabilitation often were detrimental to American interests. The Bush administration eventually considered Chalabi *persona non grata*.

On June 1, 2004, the Iraq Interim Governing Council, formed following Hussein's fall, named Iyad Allawi prime minister of Iraq's interim government and the council was, thereupon, dissolved. Although this Iraqi council chose Allawi, his selection was clearly instigated by the Bush administration, with which he had cooperated. At the same time, Ghazi al-Yawar became interim president.

Iraqi Resistance

U.S. forces approaching Baghdad when the war ended met sustained resistance and ambushes from Iraq's second largest city, Basra, to Baghdad, 276 miles to the north. On September 8, 2004, the Iraq War claimed the life of its one thousandth American service person. Of those 1,000 casualties, 818 had died after the "mission-accomplished" ceremony aboard the USS *Abraham Lincoln* in May, 2003. Another 134 American military fatalities occurred during the month of November, 2004, alone.

Insurgents were especially active along the corridor connecting Baghdad's airport to Baghdad proper, a ten-mile thoroughfare that people flying into the city usually traverse. Mortar and small-arms fire became daily occurrences along this vital artery, which was in constant use by both military personnel and civilians. Although the road seemed too dangerous to travel, it was also too important to close. American and British military personnel, however, were ordered to enter the airport via helicopter, also vulnerable to enemy fire.

Life in Baghdad itself also became extremely dangerous. Protective barriers were erected to surround the "green zone," the international section of Baghdad, where most embassies and government offices are located. These barriers, however, could not offer total protection against weapons that lobbed explosives into buildings. Throughout Baghdad and other Iraqi cities, no one was safe from mortar attacks, roadside bombs, small-arms fire, and suicide bombers.

Domestic Problems

The war and subsequent occupation of Iraq were devastating for many Iraqis. In some cities, unemployment approached 90 percent. This was not because workers were not needed but because those working for, or cooperating with, coalition forces faced possible execution by insurgents, who slaughtered Iraqis in training to become law enforcement officers and soldiers. The insurgents also blew up their training facilities and held family members as hostages. Job-placement centers in Iraq's cities were bombed, killing job applicants and office personnel. Nevertheless, on November 24, 2004, a group of 2,500 Iraqis managed to complete military training.

Before and after the war, Sadr City, a Baghdad slum covering about thirteen square miles, was a Shiite stronghold that became a particularly dangerous area. Once named Saddam City, this enclave was renamed to honor Imam Mohammed Sadr, a Shiite religious leader whom Saddam Hussein had had murdered, along with two of his sons. Sadr's surviving son, thirty-year-old Muqtada al-Sadr, a cleric, became Sadr City's charismatic leader; he was adored by followers who stood ready to support him unconditionally. When American troops arrived, they found that the area's lavish municipal building that had been erected years earlier at Saddam Hussein's command, had been stripped of almost everything in it, down to the electrical wiring and water pipes.

In August, 2004, Muqtada solidified his base and increased his influence when Ayatollah Sistani of Najaf, who had brokered a truce that ended two months of fierce fighting in his city, fell ill and sought treatment in England. Muqtada moved in to undo the truce Sistani had achieved in Najaf. Muqtada Sadr's adherents followed him unquestioningly. Sometimes he cooperated with the American forces but more often openly defied them, creating an inflammatory situation in Sadr City and throughout the so-called Sunni triangle region. He expressed his willingness to become a martyr to drive American occupiers from Iraq.

Abu Ghraib Prison Scandal

In the spring of 2004, it was revealed that Iraqi prisoners confined in Baghdad's Abu Ghraib prison had been subjected to torture and humiliation in clear violation of the Geneva Convention and any reasonable standards of human rights. Night guards at Abu Ghraib, including Jeremy Sivits, Charles Graner, and Lynndie England, who were later prosecuted, subjected their prisoners to disgraceful humiliations. Numerous photographs and videotapes showed naked male prisoners chained for long periods to walls and furniture in excruciatingly painful positions. They were smeared with feces and, in some cases, forced to engage in homosexual acts with other naked prisoners. Scores of unclothed prisoners were piled upon each other in human pyramids and forced to remain that way for extended periods.

One videotape showed a naked prisoner with a dog collar around his neck held on a leash by a taunting and laughing Lynndie England. Another naked prisoner was chained to the bars of a cell, while a snarling German shepherd guard dog, with its teeth bared, was brought to within an inch or two of him, making him recoil in terror.

It has been speculated that such treatment was first suggested to guards by senior officers as means of extracting information from prisoners. U.S.

U.S. Army policeman watches over detainees in the Abu Ghraib prison compound in May, 2004. The soldier was part of a new group of military policemen trained to replace the soldiers being investigated for prisoner abuse. (AP/Wide World Photos)

brigadier general Janice Karpinsky, the prison's warden, was relieved of her duties when the Abu Ghraib situation came to light. Commanding general Ricardo Sanchez also came under scrutiny. General William Boykin was reproached for publicly describing the war on terrorism as a battle with Satan, who targeted America because it was a Christian nation. Boykin demonized Iraqis, calling his Christian God superior to Islam's Allah.

Punishment was meted out to some members of the night guard detail at Abu Ghraib shown in the videotape. However, questions remained about how high in the chain of command responsibility reached. It was charged that high officials ignored the scandal as it unfolded.

Battle of Fallujah

In the summer of 2004, it became clear that Fallujah, a Sunni Muslim stronghold thirty-five miles west of Baghdad, was a stronghold for fanatical insurgents. Home to 300,000 Iraqis, Fallujah is an ancient city honeycombed with narrow streets. Its buildings are jammed together, creating the most dangerous environment possible for armed conflict, in which its confines force person-to-person combat.

In October, 2004, the Shiite leader Muqtada al-Sadr announced that he would work with the mujahideen in Fallujah. Several prominent insurgents were hiding there. Chief among them was Jamil Sidqi al-Zarqawi, the Iraqi fugitive wanted for his role in beheading hostages, including several Americans, abducted and marked for death if their countries refused to withdraw from Iraq by stipulated deadlines.

During the week of November 8, 2004, the attack began on Fallujah, where an estimated 1,500 to 3,000 armed insurgents were thought to be hiding in its more than 50,000 buildings. Although many of the most influential insurgents, including al-Zarqawi, had already fled, most remained in the city, whose mosques were used to store weapons and provide sanctuary for insurgents. Americans enraged Iraqis by invading their mosques. They had little choice, however, because at least half the city's 130 mosques were being used to store armaments and hide snipers.

To deal with the situation, some 10,000 American soldiers and marines, accompanied by about 2,000 Iraqis, trained by the Americans in law enforcement, were deployed to attack the city. However, many Iraqi security officers quickly abandoned the Americans and joined the insurgents, who threatened death for them and their families if they supported American or coalition forces. Twenty-two newly commissioned Iraqi security officers in Haditha were ambushed at a checkpoint by insurgents disguised as police and were murdered in a mass execution. Similar actions occurred elsewhere in Iraq. Many police stations were bombed or torched. Under these dangerous conditions, it became difficult to recruit Iraqis into local security forces.

Fighting in Fallujah was almost continuous. Some troops fought for forty-eight hours without sleep and ate only the dry rations they carried with them. About 50 Americans were killed in the first days of the offensive, which claimed an estimated 1,000 insurgents.

Elections

In late 2004, analysts contended that having successful general elections in January, as Iraq's first tentative step toward establishing democracy, would depend upon containing insurgency. The Sunnis and some Kurds, each constituting about 20 percent of Iraq's Muslim population, urged postponement for at least six months. However, The Shi'ites, with their 60-percent majority, pressed for holding the elections on the scheduled date, which the Bush administration supported.

Taking Fallujah did not end insurgent activity, much of which later erupted in Mosul, Ramadi, and Samara. Insurgents threatened to kill political candidates and any Iraqis who registered to vote and carried out their threats with assassinations and devastating bombings in public places. Meanwhile, millions of Iraqis—both at home and abroad—registered to vote.

On January 30, 2005, approximately 8.5 million of the 14 million Iraqis eligible to vote turned out at more than five thousand polling centers throughout Iraq to cast ballots in a nationwide election for an interim national assembly. Under the protection of 100,000 police officers and 60,000 U.S. and Iraqi national guard troops, they elected 275 delegates from a field of 7,700 candidates. Official election results were announced on February 13: Shi'ite candidates of the United Iraqi Alliance won 48 percent of the total vote, and the Kurdish alliance won 25.6 percent. Interim prime minister Aya Allawi's "Iraqi List" candidates won 13.8 percent. Women voted for the first time in Iraqi history, and women candidates won about 30 percent of the contested seats. The immediate mission of the new assembly was to draft a new constitution on which the nation was to vote in December, 2005.

Although the January, 2005, election was generally acclaimed as a success, the level of violence in Iraq did not abate, and political assassinations and public bombings continued. On February 28, more than 100 people were killed by a car bomb in the southern Baghdad suburb of Hilla in the worst such incident since the formal conclusion of the war nearly two years earlier. Attacks on coalition troops also continued. In March, the death toll of U.S. troops topped 1,500, and the total for all coalition troops reached 1,700.

R. Baird Shuman

Further Reading

Alexander, Yonah, and Dan Musch, eds. *Terrorism and Homeland Security.* Madison: University of Wisconsin Press, 2004.

Ali, Tariq. *Bush in Babylon: The Recolonization of Iraq.* New York: Verso, 2003.

Allard, Carl Kenneth. *Somalia Operations: Lessons Learned.* Washington, D.C.: National Defense University Press, 1995.

Anderson, Jon Lee. *The Fall of Baghdad.* New York: Penguin, 2004.

Arnett, Peter. *Live from the Battlefield.* New York: Simon & Schuster, 1994.

Atkinson, Rick. *Crusade: The Untold Story of the Persian Gulf War.* Boston: Houghton Mifflin, 1993.

Bamford, James. *A Pretext for War: 9/11, Iraq, and the Abuse of America's Intelligence Agencies.* New York: Random House, 2004.

Beck, Sara, and Malcolm Downing, eds. *The Battle for Iraq: BBC News Correspondents on the War Against Saddam.* Baltimore: Johns Hopkins University Press, 2003.

Blix, Hans. *Disarming Iraq.* New York: Pantheon Books, 2004.

Boyne, Walter. *Operation Iraqi Freedom: What Went Right, What Went Wrong, and Why.* New York: Tor Books, 2003.

Bresnahan, David M. *9-11 Terror in America.* n.p.: Windsor House, 2001.

Casper, Lawrence E. *Falcon Brigade: Combat and Command in Somalia and Haiti.* Boulder, Colo.: Lynne Rienner, 2001.

Christy, Joe. *American Aviation: An Illustrated History.* Blue Ridge Summit, Pa.: Tab Books, 1987.

Clark, Ramsey. *The Fire This Time: U.S. War Crimes in the Gulf.* New York: Thunder's Mouth Press, 1992.

Clarke, Richard A. *Against All Enemies: Inside America's War on Terror.* New York: Free Press, 2004.

Clarke, Victoria. "The Pentagon and the Press." In *The Media and the War on Terrorism*, edited by Stephen Hess and Marvin Kalb. Washington, D.C.: Brookings Institution Press, 2003.

—————, et al. "Three Months Later." In *The Media and the War on Terrorism*, edited by Stephen Hess and Marvin Kalb.

Cohen, Roger, and Claudio Gatti. *In the Eye of the Storm: The Life of General H. Norman Schwartzkopf.* New York: Farrar, Straus, Giroux, 1991.

Coll, Steve. *Ghost Wars: The Secret History of the CIA, Afghanistan, and bin Laden, from the Soviet Invasion to September 10, 2001.* New York: Penguin Press, 2004.

Cooksley, Peter G., and Bruce Robertson. *Air Warfare: The Encyclopedia of Twentieth Century Conflict*. London: Arms and Armour Press, 1998.

Cordesman, Anthony. *Iraq War: Strategy, Tactics, and Military Lessons*. Washington, D.C.: CSIS Press, 2003.

Cornum, Rhonda, as told to Peter Copeland. *She Went to War: The Rhonda Cornum Story*. Novato, Calif.: Presidio Press, 1992.

Daalder, Ivo H., and Michael E. O'Hanlon. *Winning Ugly: NATO's War to Save Kosovo*. Washington, D.C.: Brookings Institution Press, 2000.

Danchev, Alex, and Dan Keohane, eds. *International Perspectives on the Gulf Conflict, 1990-1991*. New York: St. Martin's Press, 1994.

Davis, John, ed. *The Global War on Terrorism: Assessing the American Response*. Hauppauge, N.Y.: Nova Science Publishers, 2004.

DiPrizio, Robert C. *Armed Humanitarians: U.S. Interventions from Northern Iraq to Kosovo*. Baltimore: Johns Hopkins University Press, 2002.

Donald, David, ed. *The Complete Encyclopedia of World Aircraft*. New York: Barnes & Noble Books, 1997.

Elshtein, Jean Bethke. *Just War Against Terror: The Burden of American Power in a Violent World*. New York: Basic Books, 2004.

Emerson, Gloria, et al. *9/11/01: The Collected "Portraits of Grief" from The New York Times*. New York: New York Times Books, 2002.

Emerson, Steven. *American Jihad: The Terrorists Living Among Us*. New York: Free Press, 2002.

Engel, Richard. *A Fist in the Hornet's Nest: On the Ground Before, During, and After the War*. New York: Hyperion, 2004.

Feldman, Noah. *What We Owe Iraq: War and the Ethics of Nation Building*. Princeton, N.J.: Princeton University Press, 2004.

Francke, Linda Bird. *Ground Zero: The Gender Wars in the Military*. New York: Simon & Schuster, 1997.

Freedman, Lawrence, and Efraim Karsh. *The Gulf Conflict, 1990-1991: Diplomacy and War in the New World Order*. Princeton, N.J.: Princeton University Press, 1993.

Friedman, Thomas L. *Longitudes and Attitudes: Exploring the World After September 11*. New York: Farrar Straus & Giroux, 2002.

Fromkin, David. *Kosovo Crossing: American Ideals Meet Reality on the Balkan Battlefields*. New York: Free Press, 1999.

Gunaratna, Rohan. *Inside Al Qaeda: Global Network of Terror*. New York: Columbia University Press, 2003.

Haass, Richard. *Intervention: The Use of American Military Force in the Post-Cold War World*. Rev. ed. Washington, D.C.: Brookings Institution Press, 1999.

Hamza, Khidhir, with Jeff Stein. *Saddam's Bombmaker: The Terrifying Inside Story of the Iraqi Nuclear and Biological Weapons Agenda.* New York: Scribner, 2000.

Heikal, Mohammed Hassanein. *Illusions of Triumph: An Arab View of the Gulf War.* New York: HarperCollins, 1992.

Hersh, Seymour. *Chain of Command: The Road from 9/11 to Abu Ghraib.* New York: Harper Collins, 2004.

Hilsman, Roger. *George Bush vs. Saddam Hussein: Military Success! Political Failure?* Novato, Calif.: Lyford Books, 1992.

Hiro, Dilip. *Desert Shield to Desert Storm: The Second Gulf War.* New York: Routledge, 1992.

Hirsch, John L. *Somalia and Operation Restore Hope: Reflections on Peacemaking and Peacekeeping.* Washington, D.C.: United States Institute of Peace Press, 1995.

Holden, Henry M., with Lori Griffith. *Ladybirds: The Untold Story of Women Pilots in America.* Freedom, N.J.: Black Hawk, 1991.

Holm, Jeanne. *Women in the Military: An Unfinished Revolution.* Novato, Calif.: Presidio Press, 1982.

Honig, Jan Willem, and Norbert Both. *Srebrenica: Record of a War Crime.* New York: Penguin Books, 1997.

Huntington, Samuel P. *The Clash of Civilizations and the Remaking of World Order.* New York: Simon and Schuster, 2004.

Hutchison, Kevin. *Operation Desert Shield/Desert Storm: Chronology and Factbook.* Westport, Conn.: Greenwood Press, 1995.

Ignatieff, Michael. *Virtual War: Kosovo and Beyond.* New York: Henry Holt, 2000.

Imperial Hubris: Why the West Is Losing the War on Terror. Washington, D.C.: Brassey's, 2004.

Keaney, Thomas A., and Eliot A. Cohen. *Revolution in Warfare? Air Power in the Persian Gulf.* Annapolis, Md.: Naval Institute Press, 1995.

Keegan, John. *The Iraq War.* New York: Alfred Knopf, 2004.

Khadduri, Majid, and Edmund Ghareeb. *War in the Gulf, 1990-1991.* New York: Oxford University Press, 1997.

Lahneman, William J. *Military Intervention: Cases in Context for the Twenty-first Century.* Lanham: Rowman & Littlefield, 2004.

Lyons, Terrence, and Ahmed I. Samatar. *Somalia: State Collapse, Multilateral Intervention, and Strategies for Political Reconstruction.* Washington, D.C.: Brookings Institution Press, 1995.

MacArthur, John R. *Second Front: Censorship and Propaganda in the 1991 Gulf War.* Updated ed. Foreword by Ben H. Bagdikian. Berkeley: University of California Press, 2004.

Mackey, Chris. *The Interrogators: Inside the Secret War Against al Qaeda.* New York: Little Brown, 2004.

Mann, Michael. *Incoherent Empire.* New York: Verso, 2003.

Mermin, Jonathan. *Debating War and Peace: Media Coverage of U.S. Intervention in the Post-Vietnam Era.* Princeton, N.J.: Princeton University Press, 1999.

Mills, Kay. *From Pocahontas to Power Suits: Everything You Need to Know About Women's History in America.* New York: Plume, 1995.

Moore, James. *Bush's War for Reelection: Iraq, the White House, and the People.* New York: John Wiley & Sons, 2004.

Moore, Molly. *A Woman at War: Storming Kuwait with the U.S. Marines.* New York: Charles Scribner's Sons, 1993.

Moore, Robin. *Hunting Down Saddam: The Inside Story of the Search and Capture.* New York: St. Martin's Press, 2004.

Morris, David J. *Storm on the Horizon: Khafji–the Battle That Changed the Course of the Gulf War.* New York: Free Press, 2004.

Murray, Williamson. *Air War in the Persian Gulf.* Baltimore: Nautical & Aviation Publishing Company of America, 1995.

Murray, Williamson, and Robert H. Scales, Jr. *The Iraq War: A Military History.* Cambridge, Mass.: Belknap Press of Harvard University Press, 2003.

National Commission on Terrorist Attacks. *The 9/11 Commission Report.* New York: W. W. Norton, 2004.

Newhouse, John. *Imperial America: The Bush Assault on the World Order.* New York: Knopf, 2003.

Picciotto, Richard, with Daniel Paisner. *Last Man Down: A Firefighter's Story of Survival and Escape from the World Trade Center.* New York: Berkley Books, 2002.

Price, Alfred. *Sky Battles: Dramatic Air Warfare Battles.* Dulles, Va.: Continuum, 1999.

Randolph, Laura B. "The Untold Story of Black Women in the Gulf War." *Ebony* 46 (September, 1991): 100-106.

Robinson, Linda. *Masters of Chaos: The Secret History of the Special Forces.* New York: Public Affairs, 2004.

Schecter, Danny. *Media Wars: News at a Time of Terror.* Lanham, Md.: Rowman and Littlefield, 2003.

Schwartzkopf, H. Norman. *It Doesn't Take a Hero.* New York: Bantam Books, 1993.

Sharkey, Jacqueline. *Under Fire: U.S. Military Restrictions on the Media from Grenada to the Persian Gulf.* Washington, D.C.: Center for Public Integrity, 1991.

Stevenson, Jonathan. *Losing Mogadishu: Testing U.S. Policy in Somalia*. Annapolis, Md.: Naval Institute Press, 1995.

Sudetic, Chuck. *Blood and Vengeance: One Family's Story of the War in Bosnia*. New York: W. W. Norton, 1998.

Swofford, Anthony. *Jarhead: A Marine's Chronicle of the Gulf War and Other Battles*. New York: Scribner, 2003.

U.S. News & World Report. *Triumph Without Victory: The Unreported History of the Persian Gulf War*. New York: Times Books, 1992.

Voices of War: Stories of Service from the Homefront and the Frontlines. Washington, D.C.: National Geographic Society, 2004.

Von Hippel, Karin. *Democracy by Force: U.S. Military Intervention in the Post-Cold War World*. New York: Cambridge University Press, 2000.

West, Bing, and Ray L. Smith. *The March Up: Taking Baghdad with the First Marine Division*. New York: Bantam Books, 2003.

Weiss, Thomas G. *Military-Civilian Interactions: Humanitarian Crises and the Responsibility to Protect*. 2d ed. Lanham: Rowman & Littlefield, 2004.

Woodward, Bob. *Bush at War*. New York: Simon & Schuster, 2002.

_____. *Plan of Attack*. New York: Simon & Schuster, 2004.

Zinsmeister, Karl. *Boots on the Ground: A Month with the Eighty-second Airborne in the Battle for Iraq*. New York: St. Martin's Press, 2003.

Zucchino, David. *Thunder Run: The Armored Strike to Capture Baghdad*. Foreword by Mark Bowden. New York: Atlantic Monthly Press, 2004.

Bibliography

This bibliography contains annotated listings of standard reference works and atlases and categorized listings of books on specific topics in U.S. military history. The latter include titles on each of the major conflicts covered in this set. For additional titles on specific conflicts, see the Further Reading sections at the end of each chapter.

Standard References

Arms, Thomas S. *Encyclopedia of the Cold War*. New York: Facts on File, 1994. Good coverage in a single-volume work.

Beckett, Ian F. W. *Encyclopedia of Guerrilla Warfare*. New York: ABC-CLIO, 1999. An increasingly necessary reference source, as guerrilla warfare becomes more prominent in conflicts throughout the world.

Bercovitch, Jacob, and Richard Jackson. *International Conflict: A Chronological Encyclopedia of Conflicts and Their Management, 1945-1995*. Washington, D.C.: Congressional Quarterly, 1997. Focuses on boundary disputes; numerous cross-references; good bibliography.

Biger, Gideon. *The Encyclopedia of International Boundaries*. New York: Facts on File, 1995. Useful in understanding the details of international disputes, which have often led to war. Arranged geographically. Focuses on contemporary boundaries but includes some historical background.

Black, Jeremy. *War and the World: Military Power and the Fate of Continents, 1450-2000*. New Haven, Conn.: Yale University Press, 1998. A prescient study, which covers both Western and non-Western themes. Brief treatments arranged topically but incorporating the latest scholarship.

Bowyer, Richard. *Dictionary of Military Terms*. Chicago: Fitzroy Dearborn, 1999. Thorough treatment of the basic terminology of warfare.

Brownstone, David, and Irene Franck. *Timelines of War: A Chronology of Warfare from 100,000 B.C. to the Present*. Boston: Little, Brown, 1994. A suggestive chronology, remarkably full and especially useful for the ancient period. Generally reliable, but one wonders where the authors got their information—no bibliography.

Bruce, A. P. C., and William B. Cogar. *An Encyclopedia of Naval History*. New York: Facts on File, 1998. Comprehensive treatment of naval warfare throughout world history.

Burns, Richard Dean, ed. *Encyclopedia of Arms Control and Disarmament*. New York: Charles Scribner's Sons, 1993. A useful adjunct to the the study of military conflict.

Collins, John M. *Military Geography*. Washington, D.C.: Brassey's, 1998. Excellent on the relationships among topography, weather, and culture, and the formation of tactics and strategy.

Cowley, Robert, and Geoffrey Parker. *The Reader's Companion to Military History*. New York: Houghton Mifflin, 1996. Combines coverage of people, battles, weapons, and concepts, expertly edited. Cowley was cofounder and longtime editor of the premier popular military journal, *MHQ: The Quarterly Journal of Military History*. Provides almost six hundred articles, forty maps and several dozen well-chosen illustrations, and a limited bibliography. Gaps in this work reflect its emphasis on modern Western military history; however, what is included is thorough and written by many of the world's best military scholars.

Davis, Paul K. *Encyclopedia of Invasions and Conquests from Ancient Times to the Present*. New York: ABC-CLIO, 1996. Approximately two hundred well-illustrated entries.

Department of Defense Dictionary of Military and Associated Terms. Washington, D.C.: U.S. Department of Defense, 1994. Definitions of terms, including those used by NATO.

Dupuy, R. Ernest, and Trevor N. Dupuy. *The Harper Encyclopedia of Military History: From 3500 B.C. to the Present*. 4th ed. New York: Harper, 1993. The classic one-volume reference. Organized chronologically by region, or by major wars. A narrative introduction provides context, with relatively brief treatments of the battles themselves; excellent discussion of weapons and tactics; extensive index; maps of variable quality. The best source for basic narrative but should be used in conjunction with recent monographs and articles when dealing with controversial points or relatively obscure topics.

Dupuy, Trevor N., Curt Johnson, and David L. Bongard. *The Harper Encyclopedia of Military Biography*. Edison, N.J.: Castle Books, 1995. A good one-volume reference, with three thousand entries from earliest times. Fact-driven, with useful headings listing "principal wars" and "principal battles." The brief bibliographies are sometimes dated but still useful. Not quite comprehensive but close.

Dupuy, Trevor N., Curt Johnson, and Grace P. Hayes. *Dictionary of Military Terms: A Guide to the Language of Warfare and Military Institutions*. New York: H. W. Wilson, 1986.

Eggenberger, David. *An Encyclopedia of Battles*. Rev. ed. New York: Dover, 1985. Covers more than 1,560 battles and wars, including an appendix for battles between 1967 and 1984. Useful maps; lists principal battles under each war.

Featherstone, Donald. *Bridges of Battle: Famous Battlefield Actions at Bridges and River Crossings.* London: Arms & Armour, 1998. Detailed studies of one hundred actions, from ancient times through World War II.

Frankel, Benjamin. *The Cold War, 1945-1991.* 3 vols. Detroit: Gale Research, 1992. Volume 1 includes U.S. and Western figures; volume 2, Soviet, East European and Third World figures; volume 3, articles and appendixes on history, chronology, concepts, archives, and bibliography.

Fregosi, Paul. *Jihad in the West: Muslim Conquests from the Seventh to the Twenty-first Centuries.* New York: Prometheus, 1998. A controversial argument for the unity of Islamic jihads; nevertheless combines a great deal of information on military actions and commanders not found together elsewhere.

Fuller, J. F. C. *A Military History of the Western World.* 1954-1956. Reprint. New York: Da Capo, 1987. A classic work by one of the early theorists and practitioners of mechanized warfare.

Grbasic, Zvonimir, and Velimir Vuksic. *Cavalry: The History of a Fighting Elite, 650 B.C.-A.D. 1914.* New York: Cassell, 1999. A good introduction, including one hundred full-page, full-color plates.

Hart, Kristin, ed. *Americans at War: Society, Culture, and the Home Front.* 4 vols. New York: Macmillan, 2004. Encyclopedic treatment of all aspects of the domestic side of U.S. wars.

Heinl, Robert Debs. *Dictionary of Military and Naval Quotations.* Annapolis, Md.: United States Naval Institute, 1966.

International Military and Defense Encyclopedia. Washington, D.C.: Brassey's, 1993. See both of the Margiotta entries that follow.

Keegan, John. *A History of Warfare.* New York: Vintage Books, 1994. The perfect introduction to the subject, full of both fact and analysis in a stylish narrative.

Keegan, John, and Andrew Wheatcroft. *Who's Who in Military History, from 1453 to the Present Day.* Rev. ed. London: Routledge, 1996. About 725 relatively brief entries. Contains a concise but useful glossary.

Kohn, George C. *Dictionary of Wars.* New York: Facts on File, 1986. Covers about fifteen hundred wars, revolutions, and other conflicts, as well as a few battles. Features an extensive and useful system of cross-referencing. Good index of wars grouped by country or geographical region.

Laffin, John. *Brassey's Dictionary of Battles.* Rev. ed. New York: Barnes & Noble, 1995. Seven thousand battles and campaigns treated concisely but thoroughly. More than ninety maps.

Luttwak, Edward, and Stuart L. Koehl. *The Dictionary of Modern War.* New York: Gramercy Books, 1991. Focuses on technical descriptions of institutions and weapons of international conflict since World War II.

Lynn, John A. *Feeding Mars: Logistics in Western Warfare from the Middle Ages to the Present*. Boulder, Colo.: Westview Press, 1993. Useful work on an often neglected element of military success.

Margiotta, Franklin D. *Brassey's Encyclopedia of Military History and Biography*. Washington, D.C.: Brassey's, 1994. Articles slightly revised from previous publication in *International Military and Defense Encyclopedia*.

Margiotta, Franklin D., and Gordon R. Sullivan. *Brassey's Encyclopedia of Land Forces and Warfare*. Washington, D.C.: Brassey's, 1996. Articles slightly revised from previous publication in *International Military and Defense Encyclopedia*.

Perrett, Bryan. *The Battle Book: Crucial Conflicts in History from 1469 B.C. to the Present*. London: Brockhampton Press, 1992. Contains fewer entries than most battle books (566) but greater uniformity in assessing casualties and in clearly stating objectives. Also includes a useful appendix arranging the battles by the wars of which they were a part.

Powell, John, ed. *Magill's Guide to Military History*. 5 vols. Pasadena, Calif.: Salem Press, 2001. Offers encyclopedic coverage of world military history, from earliest recorded times to the present day. Alphabetically arranged articles on major conflicts, individual battles, military leaders, and nations and societies. In addition to individual bibliographies for every article, the set contains extensive appendices and indexes. See also Powell's companion set, *Weapons and Warfare*.

_____. *Weapons and Warfare*. 2 vols. Pasadena, Calif.: Salem Press, 2002. Companion set to Powell's *Magill's Guide to Military History*. Encyclopedic survey of the weaponry, tactics, and modes of warfare throughout the world, from ancient times to the present day. The first volume covers ancient and medieval warfare through 1500, and the second volume continues the subject up to the present day. Articles range from discussions of individual weapons and modes of fighting to surveys of the military histories of societies and state systems. Well illustrated, with extensive bibliographies, appendices, and indexes.

Purcell, L. Edward, and Sarah J. Purcell. *Encyclopedia of Battles in North America, 1517-1916*. New York: Facts on File, 2000.

Ramsbotham, Oliver, and Tom Woodhouse. *Encyclopedia of International Peacekeeping Operations*. New York: ABC-CLIO, 1999.

Royle, Trevor. *A Dictionary of Military Quotations*. New York: Routledge, 1990.

Shafritz, Jay M., Todd J. A. Shafritz, and David B. Robertson. *The Facts on File Dictionary of Military Science*. New York: Facts on File, 1989.

Spiller, Roger J., Joseph G. Dawson, and T. Harry Williams, eds. *Dictionary of American Military Biography*. 3 vols. Westport, Conn.: Greenwood Press, 1984.

Strait, Newton A. *Alphabetical List of Battles, 1754-1900: War of the Rebellion, Spanish-American War, Philippine Insurrection, and all Old Wars with Dates.* 1905. Reprint. Detroit: Gale Research Company, 1968. Mainly a listing but with some additional information, including casualties. Especially useful in tracking minor engagements seldom treated in encyclopedias or monographs.

United States Joint Chiefs of Staff. *Dictionary of Military Terms*. Rev. ed. London: Greenhill Press, 1999. Comprehensive guide to current use, containing six thousand terms and three thousand abbreviations.

Unsworth, Michael E., ed. *Military Periodicals: United States and Selected International Journals and Newspapers*. New York: Greenwood Press, 1990. A thorough guide to key magazines, journals, and other periodicals, including descriptions, content, and publishing histories.

Wintle, J. *The Dictionary of War Quotations*. London: Hodder and Stoughton, 1989.

Atlases

Anderson, Ewan W., and Don Shewan. *An Atlas of World Political Flashpoints: A Sourcebook of Geopolitical Crisis*. London: Pinter Reference, 1993. The best ready reference to the wars and potential conflicts of the post-Cold War era. Excellent maps.

Banks, Arthur. *A World Atlas of Military History, 1861-1945*. New York: Da Capo Press, 1988.

Barraclough, Geoffrey, and Geoffrey Parker, eds. *The Times Atlas of World History*. 4th ed. Maplewood, N.J.: Hammond, 1996. Pathbreaking maps and perspectives at its first publication in 1978. Still the best general historical atlas, with much of relevance for military historians.

Hartman, Tom, with John Mitchell. *A World Atlas of Military History, 1945-1984*. New York: Da Capo Press, 1985. Provides detailed maps and time lines for more than eighty wars and conflicts worldwide.

Kidron, Michael, and Dan Smith. *The New State of War and Peace, an International Atlas: A Full Color Survey of Arsenals, Armies, and Alliances Throughout the World*. London: Grafton, 1991. Previously published as *The War Atlas: Armed Conflict, Armed Peace*. London: Pan, 1983.

Lloyd, Christopher. *Atlas of Maritime History*. New York: Arco, 1975. Extensive narrative. Most wars and a few key battles are covered.

Murray, Stuart. *Atlas of American Military History*. New York: Facts on File, 2004.

Natkiel, Richard, and Antony Preston. *Atlas of Maritime History*. New York: Facts on File, 1986. Extensive narrative accompanying excellent maps. Many key battles covered.

O'Brien, Patrick K. *Oxford Atlas of World History*. London: Oxford, 1999. An excellent general reference that incorporates much military history.

Pemsel, Helmut. *A History of War at Sea: An Atlas and Chronology of Conflict at Sea from Earliest Times to the Present*. Translated by G. D. G. Smith. Annapolis, Md.: Naval Institute Press, 1977. A superb one-volume treatment, placing key conflicts in the context of both international diplomacy and technological innovation. Excellent maps, action plans, and scale drawings of representative ships.

Pimlott, John, and Richard Holmes, eds. *The Hutchinson Atlas of Battle Plans: Before and After*. Oxford, England: Helicon, 2000.

Smith, Dan. *The State of War and Peace Atlas*. Rev. 3d ed. London: Penguin, 1997.

United States Military Academy: Department of Military Art and Engineering. *West Point Atlas of American War*. 1959. Reprint. New York: Praeger, 1978. Pre-computer but still superb.

Wheatcroft, Andrew. *World Atlas of Revolutions*. London: Hamish Hamilton, 1983.

Woodworth, Steven. *An Atlas of the Civil War*. New York: Oxford University Press, 2004.

Categorized Bibliography
Armies, Navies, and Air Forces

Alexander, Joseph H. *A Fellowship of Honor: The Battle History of the United States Marines*. New York: HarperCollins, 1997.

Beach, Edward L. *The United States Navy: Two Hundred Years*. New York: Henry Holt, 1986.

Boyne, Walter. *Beyond the Wild Blue: A History of the U.S. Air Force*. New York: St. Martin's Press, 1997.

Frisbee, John L., ed. *Makers of the United States Air Force*. Washington, D.C.: Air Force History and Museums Program, 1996.

Fukuyama, Francis, and Abram N. Shulsky. *The "Virtual Corporation" and Army Organization*. Santa Monica, Calif.: Rand, 1997.

Hagan, Kenneth J. *This People's Navy: The Making of American Sea Power*. New York: Free Press, 1991.

Hogan, David W., Jr. *Two Hundred Twenty-five Years of Service: The U.S. Army, 1775-2000*.Washington, D.C.: U.S. Army, 2000.

Howarth, Stephen. *To Shining Sea: A History of the United States Navy, 1775-1991*. New York: Random House, 1991.

Johnson, Robert Erwin. *Guardians of the Sea: History of the United States Coast Guard, 1915 to Present*. Annapolis, Md.: U.S. Naval Institute, 1988.

King, Irving H. *The Coast Guard Expands, 1865-1915: New Roles, New Frontiers*. Annapolis, Md.: U.S. Naval Institute, 1996.

Love, Robert W. *History of the United States Navy*. Harrisburg, Pa.: Stackpole Books, 1992.

Lutz, Norma Jean. *John Paul Jones: Father of the U.S. Navy*. New York: Chelsea House, 1999.

Mackay, James. *"I Have Not Yet Begun to Fight": A Life of John Paul Jones*. Edinburgh, Scotland: Mainstream, 1998.

Mersky, Peter B. *U.S. Marine Corps Aviation, 1912 to the Present*. 3d ed. Baltimore: Nautical and Aviation, 1997.

Miller, Nathan. *The U.S. Navy*. 3d ed. Annapolis, Md.: Naval Institute Press, 1997.

Millett, Allan R. *Semper Fidelis: The History of the United States Marine Corps*. Rev. ed. New York: Free Press, 1991.

Mitchell, Vance. *Air Force Officers*. Washington, D.C.: Air Force History and Museums Program, 1997.

Moskin, J. Robert. *The U.S. Marine Corps Story*. 3d ed. Boston: Little, Brown, 1992.

O'Connor, Raymond G. *Origins of the American Navy: Sea Power in the Colonies and the New Nation*. Lanham, Md.: University Press of America, 1994.

Reynolds, Clark G. *Navies in History*. Annapolis, Md.: Naval Institute Press, 1998.

Simmons, Edwin Howard. *The United States Marine Corps: A History*. 3d ed. Annapolis, Md.: Naval Institute Press, 1997.

Sullivan, Gordon R., ed. *Portrait of an Army*. Washington, D.C.: Center of Military History, U.S. Army, 1991.

Communications and Military Intelligence

Adams, James. *The Next World War: Computers Are the Weapons and the Front Line Is Everywhere*. New York: Simon & Schuster, 1998.

Alexander, Martin S., ed. *Knowing Your Friends: Intelligence Inside Alliances and Coalitions from 1914 to the Cold War*. London: Frank Cass, 1998.

Andrew, Christopher, and Oleg Gordievsky. *KGB: The Inside Story of Its Foreign Operations from Lenin to Gorbachev*. London: Hodder and Stoughton, 1990.

Bateman, Robert L. *Digital War: A View from the Front Lines*. Novato, Calif.: Presidio Press, 1999.

Bauer, Frederich L. *Decrypted Secrets: Methods and Maxims of Cryptology*. New York: Springer-Verlag, 1997.

Bergmeier, Horst J. P., and Rainer E. Lotz. *Hitler's Airwaves: The Inside Story of Nazi Radio Broadcasting and Propaganda Swing*. New Haven, Conn.: Yale University Press, 1997.

Brown, Michael L. *The Revolution in Military Affairs: The Information Dimension*. Fairfax, Va.: AFCEA International Press, 1996.

Browne, John, and Michael Thurbon. *Electronic Warfare*. London: Brassey's, 1998.

Burrows, William. *Deep Black: Space Espionage and National Security*. New York: Random House, 1986.

Campen, Alan D. *The First Information War: The Story of Communications, Computers, and Intelligence Systems in the Persian Gulf War*. Fairfax, Va.: AFCEA International Press, 1992.

Campen, Alan D., Douglas H. Dearth, and R. Thomas Godden. *Cyberwar: Security, Strategy, and Conflict in the Information Age*. Fairfax, Va.: AFCEA International Press, 1996.

Culbert, David E., ed. *Film and Propaganda in America: A Documentary History*. Westport, Conn.: Greenwood Press, 1990-1991.

Devereux, Tony. *Messenger Gods of Battle: Radio, Radar, Sonar, the Story of Electronics in War*. London: Brassey's, 1991.

Dougherty, Thomas. *Projections of War: Hollywood, American Culture, and World War II*. New York: Columbia University Press, 1993.

Fyne, Robert. *The Hollywood Propaganda of World War II*. Metuchen, N.J.: Scarecrow Press, 1994.

Gilbert, James L., and John Finnegan, eds. *U.S. Army Signals Intelligence in World War II: A Documentary History*. Washington D.C.: U.S. Army, 1993.

Herman, M. *Intelligence Power in Peace and War*. Cambridge, England: Cambridge University Press, 1996.

Kahn, David. *Seizing the Enigma: The Race to Break the German U-Boat Codes, 1939-1943*. Boston: Houghton Mifflin, 1991.

Kippenhahn, Rudolph. *Code Breaking: A History and Exploration*. New York: Overlook, 1999.

Kreis, John F., ed. *Piercing the Fog: Intelligence and Army Air Forces Operations in World War II*. Washington, D.C.: Air Force History and Museums Program, 1996.

MacArthur, John R. *Second Front: Censorship and Propaganda in the Gulf War*. New York: Hill and Wang, 1992.

Neilson, Keith, and B. J. C. McKercher, eds. *Go Spy the Land: Military Intelligence in History*. Westport, Conn.: Praeger, 1992.

Page, Caroline. *U.S. Official Propaganda During the Vietnam War, 1965-1973: The Limits of Persuasion*. New York: Leicester University Press, 1996.

Ranelagh, John. *The Agency: The Rise and Decline of the CIA*. New York: Simon & Schuster, 1986.

Reporting Vietnam: American Journalism, 1959-1975. Introduction by Ward Just. New York: Library of America, 2000.

Roeder, George H. *The Censored War: American Visual Experience During World War II*. New Haven, Conn.: Yale University Press, 1993.

Ross, Stewart H. *Propaganda for War: How the United States Was Conditioned to Fight the Great War of 1914-1918*. Jefferson, N.C.: McFarland, 1996.

Sharkey, Jacqueline. *Under Fire: U.S. Military Restrictions on the Media from Grenada to the Persian Gulf*. Washington, D.C.: Center for Public Integrity, 1991.

Taylor, Philip M. *Munitions of the Mind: A History of Propaganda from the Ancient World to the Present Era*. New York: St. Martin's Press, 1995.

Williamson, John, ed. *Jane's Military Communications*. 20th ed. Surrey, England: Jane's Information Group, 1999-2000.

Moral and Legal Issues

Cahill, Lisa S. *Love Your Enemies: Discipleship, Pacifism, and Just-War Theory*. Minneapolis, Minn.: Fortress Press, 1994.

Cole, Leonard A. *The Eleventh Plague: The Politics of Biological and Chemical Warfare*. New York: W. H. Freeman, 1997.

De Lupuis, Ingrid Detter. *The Law of War*. Cambridge, England: Cambridge University Press, 1987.

Feldman, Noah. *What We Owe Iraq: War and the Ethics of Nation Building*. Princeton, N.J.: Princeton University Press, 2004.

Healey, Kaye, ed. *The Nuclear Issue*. Balmain, New South Wales, Australia: Spinney Press, 1996.

Holmes, Robert L. *On War and Morality*. Princeton, N.J.: Princeton University Press, 1989.

Johnson, James Turner. *The Holy War Idea in Western and Islamic Traditions*. University Park: Pennsylvania State University Press, 1997.

Kuper, Jenny. *International Law Concerning Child Civilians in Armed Conflict*. New York: Oxford University Press, 1997.

McCormack, Timothy L. H. *The Law of War Crimes: National and International Approaches*. Boston: Kluwer, 1997.

Miller, Richard B. *Interpretations of Conflict: Ethics, Pacifism, and the Just-War Tradition*. Chicago: University of Chicago Press, 1991.

Morris, Virginia, and Michael P. Scharf. *An Insider's Guide to the International Criminal Tribunal for the Former Yugoslavia*. 2 vols. Irvington-on-Hudson, N.Y.: Transnational, 1995.

Neier, Aryeh. *War Crimes: Brutality, Genocide, Terrors, and the Struggle for Justice*. New York: Times Books, 1999.

Osiel, Mark. *Obeying Orders: Atrocity, Military Discipline, and the Law of War*. New Brunswick, N.J.: Transaction, 1999.

Partner, Peter. *God of Battles: Holy Wars of Christianity and Islam*. Princeton, N.J.: Princeton University Press, 1997.

Reisman, W. Michael, and Chris T. Antoniou, eds. *The Laws of War: A Comprehensive Collection of Primary Documents on International Laws Governing Armed Conflict*. New York: Vintage, 1994.

Roberts, Adam, and Richard Guelff, eds. *Documents on the Laws of War*. Oxford, England: Clarendon Press, 1989.

Schmitt, Michael N., and Leslie C. Green, eds. *The Law of Armed Conflict: Into the Next Millennium*. Newport, R.I.: Naval War College, 1998.

The Tools and Techniques of Waging War

Alexander, David. *Tomorrow's Soldier: The Warriors, Weapons, and Tactics That Will Win America's Wars in the Twenty-first Century*. New York: Avon Books, 1999.

Brice, Martin Hubert. *Forts and Fortresses: From the Hillforts of Prehistory to Modern Times*. New York: Facts on File, 1990.

Brown, George Ingham. *The Big Bang: A History of Explosives*. Stroud, England: Sutton, 1998.

Buckley, John. *Air Power in the Age of Total War*. Bloomington: Indiana University Press, 1999.

Chumble, Stephen, ed. *Conway's All the World's Fighting Ships 1947-1995*. London: Conway Maritime, 1995.

Cooper, Paul W. *Introduction to the Technology of Explosives*. New York: VCH, 1996.

Dunnigan, James F. *Digital Soldiers: The Evolution of High-Tech Weaponry and Tomorrow's Brave New Battlefield*. New York: St. Martin's Press, 1996.

Foss, Christopher, ed. *Jane's Armour and Artillery*. London: Jane's, 1999.

Fowle, Barry W., ed. *Builders and Fighters: U.S. Army Engineers in World War II*. Fort Belvoir, Va.: U.S. Army Corps of Engineers, 1992.

Franks, Norman. *Aircraft Versus Aircraft*. New York: Macmillan, 1986.

Friedman, Norman. *Naval Institute Guide to World Naval Weapons Systems*. 2d ed. Annapolis, Md.: Naval Institute Press, 1992.

Fuller, J. F. C. *Armament and History: The Influence of Armament on History from the Dawn of Classical Warfare to the End of the Second World War*. New York: Da Capo Press, 1998.

Gander, Terry J., and Charles Q. Cutshaw, eds. *Jane's Infantry Weapons, 1999-2000*. Coulsdon, Surrey, England: Jane's Information Group, 1999.

Gardiner, Robert, and Arne Emil Christensen, eds. *The Earliest Ships: The Evolution of Boats into Ships*. Annapolis, Md.: Naval Institute Press, 1996.

George, James L. *History of Warships: From Ancient Times to the Twenty-first Century*. Annapolis, Md.: Naval Institute Press, 1998.

Gray, Colin S., and Roger W. Barnett, eds. *Seapower and Strategy*. Annapolis, Md.: Naval Institute Press, 1989.

Grbasic, Zvonimir, and Velimir Vuksic. *The History of Cavalry*. New York: Facts on File, 1989.

Greene, Jack, and Allessandro Massignani. *Ironclads at War: The Origin and Development of the Armored Warship, 1854-1891*. Pennsylvania: Combined Publishing, 1998.

Hartcup, Guy. *The Silent Revolution: The Development of Conventional Weapons, 1945-1985*. London: Brassey's, 1993.

Hersh, Seymour M. *Chemical and Biological Warfare: America's Hidden Arsenal*. Indianapolis, Ind.: Bobbs-Merrill, 1988.

Hogg, Ian V. *Artillery 2000*. New York: Sterling, 1990.

––––––––––. *The Story of the Gun*. New York: St. Martin's Press, 1996.

––––––––––. *Tank Killing*. New York: Sarpedon, 1996.

Hughes, Wayne P. *Fleet Tactics*. Annapolis, Md.: Naval Institute Press, 1986.

Ireland, Bernard. *Jane's Battleships of the Twentieth Century*. New York: HarperCollins, 1996.

Ireland, Bernard, Eric Grove, and Ian Drury. *Jane's War at Sea, 1897-1997*. New York: HarperCollins, 1997.

Isby, David. *Fighter Combat in the Jet Age*. London: HarperCollins, 1997.

Köhler, Josef. *Explosives*. 4th ed. New York: VCH, 1993.

Laquer, Walter. *Guerrilla Warfare: A Historical and Critical Study*. New Brunswick, N.J.: Transaction, 1998.

Larsen, Jeffery A., et al., eds. *Weapons of Mass Destruction: An Encyclopedia of Worldwide Policy, Technology, and History*. 4 vols. Santa Barbara, Calif.: ABC-Clio, 2004.

Lemish, Michael G. *War Dogs: A History of Loyalty and Heroism*. Washington, D.C.: Brassey's, 1999.

Levy, Beth, and Brian Solomon, eds. *Chemical and Biological Warfare*. New York: H. W. Wilson, 1999.

Macksey, Kenneth. *Tank Versus Tank*. New York: Crescent Books, 1991.

Massie, Robert K. *Dreadnought: Britain, Germany, and the Coming of the Great War*. New York: Ballantine Books, 1992.

Newman, Bob. *Guerrillas in the Mist: A Battlefield Guide to Guerrilla Warfare*. Boulder, Colo.: Paladin Press, 1997.

Norris, John. *Artillery: An Illustrated History*. New York: Sutton, 2000.

O'Malley, T. J., and Ray Hutchins. *Artillery: Guns and Rocket Systems.* Greenhill Military Manuals. Mechanicsburg, Pa.: Stackpole Books, 1994.

Paret, Peter, ed. *Makers of Modern Strategy: From Machiavelli to the Nuclear Age.* Princeton, N.J.: Princeton University Press, 1986.

Pringle, Laurence P. *Chemical and Biological Warfare: The Cruelest Weapons.* Springfield, N.J.: Enslow, 1991.

Rhodes, Richard. *Dark Sun: The Making of the Hydrogen Bomb.* New York: Simon & Schuster, 1995.

——————. *The Making of the Atomic Bomb.* New York: Simon & Schuster, 1986.

Rotblat, Joseph. *Nuclear Weapons: The Road to Zero.* Boulder, Colo.: Westview Press, 1998.

Sharpe, Richard, ed. *Jane's Fighting Ships 1999-2000.* 102d ed. Coulsdon, Surrey, England: Jane's Information Group, 1999.

Sherrow, Victoria. *The Making of the Atom Bomb.* San Diego, Calif.: Lucent Books, 2000.

Shukman, David. *Tomorrow's War: The Threat of High-Technology Weapons.* San Diego, Calif.: Harcourt Brace, 1996.

Swanborough, Gordon, and Peter Bowers. *United States Military Aircraft Since 1909.* Washington, D.C.: Smithsonian Institution Press, 1989.

Tunstall, Brian. *Naval Warfare in the Age of Sail: The Evolution of Fighting Tactics.* Annapolis, Md.: Naval Institute Press, 1990.

Walter, John. *The Modern Machine Gun.* New York: Greenhill Books/Lionel Leventhal, 2000.

Waltz, Kenneth, and Scott Sagan. *The Spread of Nuclear Weapons: A Debate.* New York: W. W. Norton, 1995.

Watson, Bruce A. *Sieges: A Comparative Study.* Westport, Conn.: Praeger, 1993.

Yinon, Jehuda. *Forensic and Environmental Detection of Explosives.* Chichester, England: Wiley, 1999.

Time Line of U.S. Wars and Battles

Dates assigned to each conflict are those that are generally regarded as the formal start and finish of each war. It should be noted that the United States did not enter the two world wars of the twentieth century until several years after those wars began. In order to provide fuller perspectives, this time line includes events that preceded U.S. involvement in several conflicts and thus includes some battles and other developments in which the United States was not directly involved.

Date	Event
Revolutionary War, 1775-1783	
Mar. 5, 1770	Boston Massacre.
Dec. 16, 1773	Boston Tea Party.
Apr. 19, 1775	Battles of Lexington and Concord begin Revolutionary War.
May 10-11, 1775	Battle of Fort Ticonderoga.
June 17, 1775	Battle of Bunker Hill.
Dec. 31, 1775	Battle of Quebec.
Aug. 27-30, 1776	Battle of Long Island.
Sept. 6-7, 1776	Submarine experiments.
Oct. 28, 1776	Battle of White Plains.
Dec. 26, 1776	Battle of Trenton.
Jan. 3, 1777	Battle of Princeton.
Aug. 6, 1777	Battle of Oriskany Creek.
Sept. 11, 1777	Battle of Brandywine.
Oct. 4, 1777	Battle of Germantown.
Oct. 8-17, 1777	Battle of Saratoga.
Feb. 6, 1778	Franco-American Treaties are signed.
June 28, 1778	Battle of Monmouth.
June 21, 1779-Feb. 7, 1783	Siege of Gibraltar.
Sept. 23-Oct. 18, 1779	Siege of Savannah.
Apr. 1-May 12, 1780	Siege of Charleston.
Aug. 16, 1780	Battle of Camden.
Oct. 7, 1780	Battle of King's Mountain.
Jan. 17, 1781	Battle of Cowpens.

Sept.-Oct., 1781	Battle of Yorktown and Virginia Capes.
Oct. 19, 1781	British surrender at Yorktown.
Sept. 3, 1783	Treaty of Paris formally ends the war.

War of 1812, 1812-1814

June 18, 1812	United States declares war on Great Britain.
Sept. 10, 1813	Battle of Lake Erie.
Oct. 5, 1813	Battle of Thames.
Sept. 11, 1814	Battle of Lake Champlain.
Sept. 12-14, 1814	Battle of Baltimore.
Dec. 24, 1814	United States and Britain sign Treaty of Ghent.
Jan. 8, 1815	Battle of New Orleans.
Feb. 17, 1815	Full terms of the Treaty of Ghent go into effect.

Texas Revolution, 1835-1836, and Mexican War, 1846-1848

June 30, 1835	Texans seize Anahuac Garrison and Texas Revolution begins.
Feb. 23-Mar. 6, 1836	Battle of the Alamo.
Apr. 21, 1836	Battle of San Jacinto.
Oct. 22, 1836	Texans declare independence and elect Sam Houston president.
May 6, 1846	Mexican War begins.
Sept. 21-24, 1846	Battle of Monterrey.
Feb. 22-23, 1847	Battle of Buena Vista.
Apr. 17-18, 1847	Battle of Cerro Gordo.
Sept. 12-13, 1847	Siege of Chapultepec.
Feb. 2, 1848	Treaty of Guadalupe Hidalgo ends the war.

Civil War, 1861-1865

Oct. 16-18, 1859	John Brown leads raid on Harpers Ferry.
Apr. 12-14, 1861	Confederate assault on Fort Sumter opens the Civil War.
July 21, 1861	First Battle of Bull Run.
Feb. 11-16, 1862	Battle of Fort Donelson.
Mar. 9, 1862	Battle of *Monitor* vs. *Virginia* (*Merrimack*).
Apr. 6-7, 1862	Battle of Shiloh.
June 25-July 1, 1862	Seven Days' Battles.
Aug. 29-30, 1862	Second Battle of Bull Run.
Sept. 13-15, 1862	Battle of Harpers Ferry.

Sept. 17, 1862	Battle of Antietam.
Oct. 3-4, 1862	Battle of Corinth.
Dec. 13, 1862	Battle of Fredericksburg.
May 1-4, 1863	Battle of Chancellorsville.
May 18-July 4, 1863	Siege of Vicksburg.
July 1-3, 1863	Battle of Gettysburg.
July 13-15, 1863	Draft riots in New York City.
Sept. 19-20, 1863	Battle of Chickamauga.
Nov. 23-25, 1863	Battle of Chattanooga.
May 5-7, 1864	Battle of the Wilderness.
May 8-20, 1864	Battle of Spotsylvania Court House.
June 3-12, 1864	Battle of Cold Harbor.
June 15, 1864-Apr. 3, 1865	Siege of Petersburg.
July 20-Sept. 2, 1864	Battle of Atlanta.
Nov. 15, 1864-Apr. 18, 1865	Sherman's March to the Sea.
Dec. 9-21, 1864	Battle of Savannah.
Dec. 15-16, 1864	Battle of Nashville.
Apr. 9, 1865	Confederate general Robert E. Lee surrenders to General Ulysses S. Grant at Appomattox.

Spanish-American War, 1898

Feb. 24, 1895-Apr. 13, 1898	Cuban war of independence.
Apr. 24, 1898	Spain declares war on the United States.
May 1, 1898	Battle of Manila Bay.
July 1, 1898	Battle of San Juan/El Caney.
Dec. 10. 1898	Treaty of Paris formally ends the war.
Feb. 4, 1899	Philippine insurrection begins.

World War I, 1914-1918

June 28, 1914	Serbian nationalist assassinates Austrian archduke Francis Ferdinand at Sarajevo.
Aug. 1, 3 1914	Germany declares war on Russia and France
Aug. 4, 1914	Great Britain's declaration of war on Germany opens World War I.
Aug. 14-25, 1914	Battle of the Frontiers.
Aug. 26-31, 1914	Battle of Tannenberg.
Sept. 5-9, 1914	Battle of Marne.
Sept. 9-14, 1914	Battle of Masurian Lakes.
Oct. 30-Nov. 24, 1914	First Battle of Ypres.

Dec. 8, 1914	Battle of the Falkland Islands.
Feb. 19, 1915-Jan. 9, 1916	Gallipoli Campaign.
Apr. 22-May 25, 1915	Second Battle of Ypres.
May 2-June 27, 1915	Battle of Gorlice-Tarnow.
June 23, 1915-Sept. 12, 1917	Eleven Battles of the Isonzo.
Dec. 8, 1915-Apr. 29, 1916	Siege of Kut-al-Amara.
Feb. 19-Dec. 18, 1916	Battle of Verdun.
May 31-June 1, 1916	Battle of Jutland.
June 4-Sept. 30, 1916	Brusilov Offensive.
June 24-Nov. 13, 1916	Battle of Somme.
Mar. 11, 1917	Battle of Baghdad.
Apr. 9-15, 1917	Battle of Vimy Ridge.
July 31-Nov. 10, 1917	Third Battle of Ypres.
Oct. 24-Nov. 12, 1917	Battle of Caporetto.
Oct. 31, 1917	Battle of Beersheba.
Nov. 20-Dec. 7, 1917	Battle of Cambrai.
May 27-July 1, 1918	Battle of Chateau-Thierry/Belleau Wood.
Aug. 8-Sept. 4, 1918	Battle of Amiens.
Sept. 12-16, 1918	Battle of St. Mihiel.
Sept. 20, 1918	Battle of Megiddo.
Sept. 26-Nov. 11, 1918	Battle of Meuse-Argonne.
Nov. 11, 1918	Armistice ends the war.
Jan. 18, 1919	Peace conference opens in Paris.
June 28, 1919	Germany signs Treaty of Versailles.
July 2, 1921	Joint resolution of U.S. Congress recognizes formal end to the war.

World War II, 1939-1945

Dec., 1937-Jan., 1938	Japanese troops invade China, beginning World War II in East Asia.
Sept. 15-29, 1938	British and German leaders meet in Munich.
Sept. 1, 1939	Germany invades Poland, beginning World War II in Europe.
Oct., 1939-Dec. 7, 1941	Polish Campaign.
May-June, 1940	Germany occupies France.
July 10-Oct. 31, 1940	Battle of Britain.
Nov. 11, 1940	Battle of Taranto.
Dec. 9-13, 1940	Battle of Sīdī Barrāni.
1941-1942	Battle of Moscow.

1941-1944	Siege of Leningrad.
May 20-31, 1941	Crete campaign.
July, 1941-Sept., 1941	Battle of Smolensk.
Sept. 16-26, 1941	Battle of Kiev.
Nov. 18, 1941-June 21, 1942	Battles of Tobruk.
Dec., 1941-Apr., 1942	Battle of Bataan.
Dec. 7, 1941	Japan's attack on Pearl Harbor brings the United States into the war.
Dec. 10, 1941-Feb. 15, 1942	Battle of Singapore.
Dec. 11, 1941	Axis nations declare war on the United States.
1942-1943	Battles of Kharkov.
Feb. 19, 1942	U.S. government begins relocating persons of Japanese descent on the Pacific Coast.
May 3-8, 1942	Battle of the Coral Sea.
June 3-5, 1942	Battle of Midway.
June 17, 1942	President Franklin D. Roosevelt approves the Manhattan Project.
Aug. 7, 1942-Feb. 9, 1943	Battle of Guadalcanal.
Aug. 19, 1942	Raid on Dieppe.
Aug. 23, 1942-Feb. 2, 1943	Battle of Stalingrad.
Oct. 23-Nov. 4, 1942	Battle of El Alamein.
Feb., 1943	Casablanca Conference.
July 5-15, 1943	Battle of Kursk.
Sept. 9-Oct. 1, 1943	Battle of Salerno.
Nov., 1943-June, 1944	Battle of Monte Cassino.
Nov. 20-23, 1943	Battle of Tarawa.
Jan. 22-May 25, 1944	Battle of Anzio.
June 6, 1944	D Day: Operation Overlord's Normandy invasion begins.
June 15-July 9, 1944	Battle of Saipan.
June 15, 1944	Superfortress bombing of Japan begins.
June 22-July 11, 1944	Operation Bagration.
July 20-Aug. 10, 1944	Battle of Guam.
July 24-Aug. 1, 1944	Battle of Tinian.
Sept. 17-26, 1944	Battle of Arnhem.
Oct. 23-26, 1944	Battle of Leyte Gulf.
Dec. 16, 1944-Jan. 25, 1945	Battle of the Bulge.
Feb. 4-11, 1945	Yalta Conference.

Feb. 19-Mar. 26, 1945	Battle of Iwo Jima.
Mar., 1945	Battle of Mandalay.
Mar. 7-May 8, 1945	Rhine Crossings.
Apr. 1-July 2, 1945	Battle of Okinawa.
Apr. 19-May 2, 1945	Battle of Berlin.
May 7, 1945	Germany signs surrender documents.
May 8, 1945	V-E Day: President Harry S. Truman declares victory in Europe.
July 17-Aug. 2, 1945	Potsdam Conference.
Aug. 6 & 9, 1945	United States drops atomic bombs on Hiroshima and Nagasaki, Japan.
Aug. 14, 1945	V-J Day: Japan accepts terms of surrender and occasion is declared "Victory in Japan" day.

Korean War, 1950-1953

June 25, 1950	Korean War begins when North Korean troops cross the thirty-eighth parallel.
July 29-Sept. 19, 1950	Battle of the Pusan Perimeter.
Sept. 15-25, 1950	Inchon Landing.
Apr. 22-30, 1951	Battle of Imjin River.
Spring, 1953	Battle of Pork Chop Hill.
July 27, 1953	Armistice ends the fighting.

Vietnam War

Aug. 18, 1945	Vietnam nationalists declare Vietnam an independent republic, beginning Indochina War with France.
Mar. 13-May 7, 1954	Battle of Dien Bien Phu.
Aug. 11, 1954	Formal peace treaty partitions the country into North and South Vietnam.
1961	North Vietnam begins struggle to absorb South Vietnam; United States gradually becomes involved.
Aug., 1964	Gulf of Tonkin incident.
Nov. 14-16, 1965	Battle of Ia Drang Valley.
Jan. 21-Apr. 6, 1968	Siege of Khe Sanh.
Jan. 30-Feb. 25, 1968	Tet Offensive.
Jan. 31-Feb. 25, 1968	Battle of Hue.
Mar. 16, 1968	My Lai Massacre.
April 29-June, 1970	U.S. troops invade Cambodia

Jan. 31, 1973	Peace accord is signed; North Vietnam begins releasing U.S. prisoners.
Mar. 29, 1973	Last U.S. troops leave Vietnam.
Apr. 30, 1975	North Vietnam occupies Saigon, ending civil war, and last U.S. advisers leave the country.
July 2, 1976	North and South Vietnam are formally united.

Caribbean Conflicts

Dec., 1956	Fidel Castro launches Cuban Revolution.
Feb., 1959	Revolution overthrows Cuban government; Castro takes power.
Apr. 17, 1961	Bay of Pigs Invasion.
Oct. 22-Nov. 3, 1962	Cuban Missile Crisis.
Apr., 1965-June, 1966	United States occupies Dominican Republic.
Oct.-Dec., 1983	United States occupies Grenada.
Dec., 1989-Jan., 1990	United States occupies Panama.

Post-Cold War Conflicts

Jan. 16-Feb. 28, 1991	Gulf War.
Dec., 1992-Mar., 1994	U.S. troops occupy Somalia.
Feb. 26, 1993	Terrorist bombing of New York City's World Trade Center.
Apr., 1994 and Dec., 1995	U.S. troops intervene in Bosnia.
Aug. 20, 1998	United States launches missile strikes against targets in Afghanistan and the Sudan.
Dec. 16, 1998	United States bombs military sites in Iraq.
Oct. 12, 2000	Terrorist attack on USS *Cole*.
Sept. 11, 2001	"9/11" terrorist attacks on the World Trade Center and the Pentagon.
Oct. 7, 2001	United States launches invasion of Afghanistan.
Mar. 19-May 1, 2003	Iraq War.

Biographical Directory

The brief sketches in this appendix offer highlights of the careers of American military and political leaders who played significant roles in the history of U.S. warfare. For fuller information on these figures and others, consult the pages referenced in the Index of Personages.

Abrams, Creighton Williams, Jr. (1914-1974): A graduate of West Point, Abrams distinguished himself as a tank commander during World War II. He emerged from the war as a leading authority on armored combat and rose steadily in the Army's adminstrative ranks until 1968, when he was appointed to replace General William Westmoreland as commander of all American forces in Vietnam. In October, 1972, Abrams was promoted to chief of staff of the U.S. Army. In that position, he laid the groundwork for post-Vietnam Army reforms.

Allen, Ethan (1738-1789): Allen led Vermont settlers' fight for land rights and secured the first American military victory of the Revolutionary War at Fort Ticonderoga.

Arnold, Benedict (1741-1801): Arnold was one of the most outstanding tactical leaders of the Revolutionary War. However, his mercurial, resentful disposition culminated in the most notorious episode of treason in U.S. history. Despite his skillful leadership of forces in that war, his betrayal of his country has made his name a synonym for treason. During the Revolutionary War, he served in the battles at Fort Ticonderoga, Quebec, Valcour Island, and Saratoga.

Arnold, H. H. (1886-1950): Before and during World War II, Arnold was an ardent advocate of air power. He was in charge of all flight training conducted overseas during World War I. During World War II, Arnold was the principal adviser to the Joint Chiefs of Staff for the employment of aviation in both theaters of operations. He is also known as the father of the U.S. Air Force. President Harry S. Truman named him general of the Air Force in May, 1949.

Attucks, Crispus (1723-1770): Attucks was the first person killed in the Boston Massacre in 1770. A literate former slave, he was among a group of colonists who confronted British troops in Boston. As the first of five colonists to die when the British fired into the crowd, Attucks is often regarded as the first American casualty of the Revolutionary War.

Austin, Stephen Fuller (1793-1836): Austin established the first Anglo-American colony in Texas and played a significant role in the Texas Revolution, which resulted in Texas's securing its independence from Mexico.

Beauregard, P. G. T. (1818-1893): Beauregard served in the Mexican War under General Winfield Scott but is best remembered for his later service during the Civil War. One of only eight full generals in the Confederacy, Beauregard was involved in virtually every major theater during the Civil War. His principal battles included Fort Sumter, First Battle of Bull Run, and Shiloh.

Bowie, Jim (1796-1836): A colonel in the Texas revolutionary army that fought for independence, Bowie shared command at the Alamo with Colonel William Barret Travis when both officers, along with about other 150 men, were trapped in the abandoned mission grounds in early 1836. When the Mexican army overwhelmed the defenders, Bowie was killed while lying sick in his cot.

Bradley, Omar N. (1893-1981): Bradley served during World War I but saw his most notable service during World War II. He led American troops to victories in North Africa and Sicily, commanded the U.S. First Army during the Normandy invasion, and repulsed the German counteroffensive known as the Battle of the Bulge. Bradley provided stability and continuity within the American military establishment during the critical period following the end of World War II and the onset of the Cold War. He was also the first chairman of the Joint Chiefs of Staff and was involved in the creation of the North Atlantic Treaty Organization.

Brown, John (1800-1859): As the leader of the 1859 raid on Harpers Ferry, Brown has come to symbolize the struggle over the abolition of slavery in the United States. He was the catalyst for change from polite debate and parliamentary maneuvering aimed at modification of the institution to physical violence and a direct onslaught on Southern territory and the supporters of slavery.

Burnside, Ambrose E. (1824-1881): Burnside's military record was marked by high and low points. Shortly after assuming command of the Army of the Potomac during the Civil War, he faced a crushing defeat at Fredericksburg. His principal battles included First Battle of Bull Run, Antietam, Fredericksburg, and Petersburg.

Burr, Aaron (1756-1836): During the Revolutionary War, Burr served with distinction at the battles of Quebec, New York, and Monmouth and commanded American forces in Westchester. After his health forced him to resign, he returned to the study of the law. Burr developed the political organization that assured the presidential victory of Thomas Jefferson in 1800 and was the force behind the liberalization of New York's penal codes and political process.

Bush, George (1924-   ): During World War II, Bush flew fifty-eight combat missions in the Pacific and was considered a hero for his conduct at

Chichi Jima. As the forty-first president (1989-1993), he presided over the end of the Cold War, the occupation of Panama in 1989, and the 1991 Gulf War.

Bush, George W. (1946-   ): As forty-third president of the United States (2001-   ), Bush presided over the response to the September 11, 2001, terrorist attacks against the United States, the subsequent invasion of Afghanistan, and the Iraq War in 2003.

Calley, William L. (1943-   ): An army lieutenant during the Vietnam War, Calley was convicted of murdering twenty-two Vietnamese civilians in the My Lai Massacre and was the only person convicted of any crime in that affair. However, his sentence was reduced and he served only three and one-half years under house arrest before receiving parole in 1974.

Carson, Kit (1809-1868): As a trapper, guide, Indian agent, and soldier, Carson helped open the American West to settlement. Although he is better known as a frontiersman than as a soldier, Carson fought in California during the Mexican War and saw action in battles at San Pasqual, Los Angeles, and Valverde. He also served as colonel in the First New Mexico Volunteer Infantry during the Civil War and in that position forced thousands of Navajo to abandon their homes.

Clark, George Rogers (1752-1818): Clark's successful attack against the British forts at Kaskaskia, Cahokia, and Vincennes in 1778-1779 served as the basis for the American claim to the Northwest Territory during negotiation of the Treaty of Paris at the end of the Revolutionary War. His leadership of the Northwest campaign led in turn to the founding of Louisville, Kentucky, and Clarksville, Indiana.

Clark, Mark W. (1896-1984): Clark began his military service as an infantry officer during World War I. During World War II, he commanded Allied forces in Italy from 1943 to 1945, and he commanded United Nations troops in Korea from 1952 to 1953. Clark's principal battles included Salerno, Anzio, and Monte Cassino.

Clinton, Bill (1946-   ): As the forty-second president of the United States (1993-2001), Clinton presided over the nation during the Somalia occupation, U.S. involvement in the Bosnian war, the 1998 missile attacks on Afghanistan and Sudan, and the bombing of military sites in Iraq. The terrorist attack on the USS *Cole* also occurred during his presidency.

Crockett, David (1786-1836): A U.S. congressman from western Tennessee and the author of a best-selling autobiography, Crockett became the most celebrated backwoodsman in the United States. His death at the battle of the Alamo in 1836 turned him into one of America's legendary frontier heroes.

Custer, George A. (1839-1876): Although obscured by the events surrounding his death at the hands of American Indians at the Battle of the Little Bighorn, Custer's Civil War exploits made him one of the nation's most respected military figures and a national idol. After the war, his expeditions into the Yellowstone region and the Black Hills earned him renown as an explorer and compiler of scientific information. His principal Civil War battles included Gettysburg and Appomattox Court House.

Davis, Jefferson (1808-1889): Davis saw military service in the Mexican War and was later a U.S. senator and the secretary of war. However, his commitment to the South at the start of the Civil War led him to accept the presidency of the Confederacy and to attempt to preserve Southern independence against bitter opposition and overwhelming odds.

Decatur, Stephen (1779-1820): Decatur was the most colorful and successful open-sea naval commander and hero of the Barbary Wars and the War of 1812.

Dewey, George (1837-1917): A naval admiral, Dewey defeated the Spanish fleet in the Battle of Manila Bay during the Spanish-American War and afterward served as senior officer of the U.S. Navy until his death.

Eisenhower, Dwight D. (1890-1969): A master organizer, Eisenhower received the Distinguished Service Medal for his organization of the Army Tank Corps during World War I. During World War II, he served with distinction as Allied Commander for the invasions of North Africa, Italy, and France. He won the presidential elections of 1952 and 1956 and guided the country through the beginning of the Cold War.

Farragut, David G. (1801-1870): The first admiral in the U.S. Navy, Farragut is most noted for his victory over Confederate forces in the Battle of Mobile Bay during the Civil War. He earlier served in minor capacities during the War of 1812 and the Mexican War.

Franks, Tommy (1945-   ): Franks served in the Vietnam War and in June, 2000, was appointed commander-in-chief of United States Central Command. He led the attack on the Taliban in Afghanistan and the invasion of Iraq until his retirement in July, 2003.

Frémont, John C. (1813-1890): Frémont's exploits as an explorer helped to propel the American people westward toward Oregon and California. When the nation faced civil war, he fought to maintain the Union and

end slavery. He served as a major general in the Civil War but was relieved of his command in the West after a disagreement with Abraham
Lincoln and received another post in the East, from which he resigned
after losing several battles.

Gadsden, James (1788-1858): Although Gadsden was an accomplished
soldier, engineer, and railroad executive, his lasting fame came as the
U.S. minister to Mexico during the mid-1850's. While in Mexico City, he
negotiated the Gadsden Purchase, the U.S. acquisition of a strip of territory that became the southern portions of Arizona and New Mexico.

Gates, Horatio (c. 1728-1806): As an army general, Gates presided over the
first strategic victory over the British at Saratoga in 1777. At Camden,
three years later, he was responsible for one of the worst defeats ever
suffered by American forces.

Grant, Ulysses S. (1822-1885): Grant became the preeminent Union general during the Civil War, demonstrating the persistence and strategic
genius that brought about victory. His principal battles included Fort
Henry, Fort Donelson, Shiloh, Vicksburg, Chattanooga, Wilderness,
Spotsylvania Court House, Cold Harbor, Petersburg, and Appomattox
Court House. Grant earlier served during the Mexican War, in which he
excelled as a field officer at the battles of Molino del Rey and Chapultepec.

Greene, Nathanael (1742-1786): Greene was one of George Washington's
most trusted subordinates throughout the Revolutionary War, playing a
significant role both as a field commander and as the Continental
army's quartermaster general. His principal battles included Trenton,
Brandywine, Germantown, Guilford Courthouse, Hobkirk's Hill, and
Eutaw Springs.

Haig, Alexander M. (1924-   ): Haig fought in the Korean War, in which
he won a Bronze Star for valor, and participated in the 1950 Inchon
Landing and the march to the Yalu River. He was a successful battalion
commander in Vietnam who later influenced military policy as an aide
to President Richard Nixon before serving as commander of the North
Atlantic Treaty Organization.

Halleck, Henry W. (1815-1872): During the Civil War, Halleck, who was famous as the author of a work on military theory, was named commanding general of all Union armies in July, 1862. In March, 1864, he became
the first chief of staff.

Halsey, William F. (1882-1959): "Bull" Halsey was a colorful and offensive-
minded fighter who went by the slogan "hit hard, hit fast, hit often." A

proponent of naval aviation and an avowed risk taker, he epitomized the aggressive spirit of the U.S. Navy during World War II.

Hancock, Winfield S. (1824-1886): Hancock is probably best known for defending Cemetery Ridge at Gettysburg during the Civil War, avoiding a Confederate victory, and possibly saving the Union.

Harrison, William Henry (1773-1841): Harrison became one of the nation's most popular military heroes because of his victory over the Indian forces of Tecumseh and the Prophet at the Battle of Tippecanoe in 1811. As a soldier and later governor of the Old Northwest Territory, he became identified with the ideas and desires of the West. His military reputation got him elected president in 1840, but he died only one month after he was inaugurated. His principal battles during the War of 1812 were Fallen Timbers, Tippecanoe, Fort Meigs, and Thames.

Higginson, Thomas Wentworth (1823-1911): Higginson wrote prolifically but is best known in the literary world as the discoverer of Emily Dickinson's poetry. He is also noted for commanding a regiment of black enlisted men during the Civil War and for laboring in social causes such as the abolition of slavery and women's rights.

Hood, John Bell (1831-1879): A rash commander for the South during the Civil War, Hood lost Atlanta and the Confederacy's last chance for independence. Hood's principal battles included Antietam, Gettysburg, Chickamauga, Atlanta, Franklin, and Nashville.

Hooker, Joseph (1814-1879): At the Civil War's Battle of Chancellorsville in May, 1863, Hooker was badly outgeneraled and ultimately relieved of army command. He rehabilitated his reputation somewhat in the western theater in late 1863 and 1864. He earlier served in the Mexican War.

Houston, Sam (1793-1863): During the Texas Revolution, Houston served as commanding general of the Texan army and guided the Mexican province to independence in 1836. Afterward, he served as first president of the Republic of Texas, first governor of the state of Texas, and as one of the state's first U.S. senators.

Jackson, Andrew (1767-1845): Possessing the characteristics of the roughly hewn Western frontiersman as opposed to aristocratic propensities of the eastern and Virginia "establishment," Jackson came to symbolize the common man in America and the rise of democracy. In 1815, Jackson prevented the British from seizing New Orleans in the last major battle of the War of 1812. The reputation he won during that war helped lift him to the presidency in 1829.

Jackson, Stonewall (1824-1863): The ablest and most renowned of General Robert E. Lee's lieutenants, Jackson led daring marches and employed do-or-die battle tactics that resulted in key victories that helped sustain the Confederacy during the first two years of the Civil War. His career might have been even more distinguished, had he not died after being accidentally shot by one of his own men. Jackson also served earlier during the Mexican War as an artillery officer.

Johnson, Lyndon B. (1908-1973): Johnson served briefly in the U.S. Navy during World War II as a lieutenant commander, winning a Silver Star in the South Pacific. Johnson went on to become majority leader in the U.S. Senate and was elected vice president in 1960. After President John Kennedy's assassination in 1963, Johnson became president of the United States and approved the escalation of U.S. involvement in the Vietnamese civil war by ordering the first large-scale ground troops to the embattled nation and authorized the beginning of an air-bombing campaign. In 1965, Johnson sent a U.S. occupation force into the Dominican Republic. Johnson's handling of the Vietnam War ultimately doomed his presidency and he chose not to run for reelection in 1968.

Johnston, Albert Sidney (1803-1862): In 1861, Jefferson Davis appointed Johnston to command Confederate Department No. 2, encompassing the entire region west of the Appalachian Mountains. Earlier, Johnston served in the Texan War of Independence and the Mexican War. His principal battles included Monterrey in the Mexican War and Shiloh in the Civil War.

Johnston, Joseph Eggleston (1807-1891): Johnston was one of the most able practitioners of defensive tactics on either side of the Civil War but was limited as a Confederate army commander by his lack of strategic planning and his poor communication skills. His principal battles included First Battle of Bull Run, Seven Pines, and Bentonville.

Jones, John Paul (1747-1792): A naval captain known during his own time for his daring raids on British territory and spectacular engagements with British vessels during the Revolutionary War, Jones is now widely regarded as the symbolic founder of the U.S. Navy.

Kearny, Stephen W. (1794-1848): Kearny joined the U.S. Army as a lieutenant and fought in the War of 1812. Afterward, he held several commands in the West and fought in the Mexican War. He was instrumental in creating the territories of New Mexico and California.

Kennedy, John F. (1917-1963): During World War II, Kennedy served as a lieutenant in the U.S. Navy, for which he commanded a PT boat in the

Pacific, and earned several decorations, including a Purple Heart for his heroism during the war. After serving in the U.S. Senate during the 1950's, Kennedy was elected president in 1960. During the following year, he put into operation the Bay of Pigs invasion that had been planned by the Eisenhower administration and the Central Intelligence Agency. That attempt to overthrow Fidel Castro's government in Cuba was a humiliating failure for Kennedy's administration, but in October, 1962, Kennedy recovered his prestige with his successful management of the Cuban Missile Crisis.

Kimmel, Husband Edward (1882-1968): Admiral Kimmel was commander in chief of the Pacific Fleet when the Japanese attacked Pearl Harbor in 1941. He was blamed for the disaster and relieved of his command but was never officially found at fault for the U.S. Navy's lack of preparedness.

King, Ernest (1878-1956): Admiral King directed all U.S. Navy strategy during World War II. Under his leadership, the U.S. Navy helped win the Allied Battle of the North Atlantic against the German submarine force. Other major battles against Germany included the invasions of North Africa and of Normandy. In the Pacific, King's fleet fought the Japanese at Coral Sea, Midway, and Leyte Gulf.

Lee, Henry (1756-1818): An accomplished horseman and fearless cavalryman, Lee successfully commanded a legion of cavalry and infantry during the Revolutionary War. His victory at Paulus Hook was one of the most impressive feats of the war. He was also the father of future Confederate general Robert E. Lee.

Lee, Robert E. (1807-1870): Perhaps the finest army tactician of his generation, Lee so brilliantly commanded the Confederacy's Army of Northern Virginia that he prolonged the life of the Confederacy during the Civil War. His principal battles included Chancellorsville and Gettysburg. Earlier, he served in the Mexican War.

Lincoln, Abraham (1809-1865): As the sixteenth president of the United States (1861-1865), Lincoln directed the Northern war effort during the Civil War. His abilities and unshakable commitment to preserving the Union mark him as one of the nation's greatest leaders.

Longstreet, James (1821-1904): Longstreet served in the U.S. Army during the Mexican War. As Robert E. Lee's second in command in the Confederate army during the Civil War, Longstreet obeyed Lee and ordered a charge on Cemetery Ridge at Gettysburg that was driven back at great cost to the Confederates and ended the battle.

MacArthur, Douglas (1880-1964): MacArthur may have had a greater impact on American military history than any other officer of the twentieth century. Variously gifted, he was a hero to much of the American public but a center of controversy on several occasions. He commanded Allied forces in the Southwest Pacific during World War II and was instrumental in defeating Japan. After commanding the occupation of Japan, he led United Nations forces in the Korean War until relieved of his command for disobeying President Harry S. Truman's orders. His principal battles in the Korean War included Pusan Perimeter and Inchon Landing.

McClellan, George B. (1826-1885): Although Union general McClellan was unsuccessful in destroying Confederate armies or capturing Richmond during the Civil War, his victory at Antietam permitted President Abraham Lincoln's issuance of the Emancipation Proclamation in 1863, and he helped make the Army of the Potomac a potent fighting force.

Marshall, George C. (1880-1959): As a general, Marshall helped create the U.S. Army of World War II, picked the commanders who led it to victory, and exemplified the best in the American military tradition: civilian control, integrity, and competence. Marshall was also involved in World War I, in which he served as a staff officer in France working on training and planning. He also served as secretary of defense for one year during the Korean War. In 1953, he was awarded the Nobel Prize for Peace for his work in postwar economic relief in Europe, where he was the author the Marshall Plan, which was named after him.

Meade, George G. (1815-1872): Meade first saw combat as an army engineer during the Mexican War. He began the Civil War as a brigadier general, and his courage and aggressive leadership in several early battles marked him as a valuable commander. In July, 1863, he became commander of the Army of the Potomac only a few days before the decisive Battle of Gettysburg. Afterward, he was criticized for not taking advantage of Robert E. Lee's retreat from Gettysburg to counterattack and perhaps hasten the end of the Civil War.

Mitchell, William (1879-1936): An advocate of air power in the armed forces, Mitchell worked to create an air force separate from the U.S. Army and to develop strategic doctrines that would utilize the full potential of air power in the conduct of modern war. During World War I, at the battle of St. Mihiel, Mitchell organized the largest Allied air effort of the conflict, involving 1,481 planes.

Monroe, James (1758-1831): The fifth president of the United States, Monroe served in the Revolutionary War, fighting alongside George Washington in the Continental army, in which he achieved the rank of major.

He later went on to be appointed the military commissioner of Virginia. During his presidency (1817-1825), he presided over the nation during the Missouri Compromise and is perhaps best known for the Monroe Doctrine, which articulated American foreign policy regarding the Western Hemisphere.

Nimitz, Chester W. (1885-1966): Admiral Nimitz commanded American naval forces in the Pacific during World War II and played a crucial role in winning the important and difficult Battle of Midway. After the war, he became Chief of Naval Operations. His other principal battles included Coral Sea, Leyte Gulf, Iwo Jima, and Okinawa.

Nixon, Richard M. (1913-1994): During World War II, Nixon served in the U.S. Navy as a lieutenant commander and was praised as an excellent officer and leader by his own commanders. After becoming the thirty-seventh president of the United States in 1969, he continued the unpopular war in Vietnam. He also ordered a massive bombing campaign in Cambodia in 1970 that was kept secret from the American public and the Congress. The campaign was ineffective and resulted in the death of hundreds of thousands of Cambodian civilians.

Patton, George S. (1885-1945): Though never a theoretician, the U.S. Army's General Patton was a masterful tactician who demonstrated the advantages of mobility and aggressive offensive action as essential elements of modern warfare. During World War II, his principal battles included Sicily, where he captured Palermo in a well-organized armored attack. His other principal battles included Normandy and the Bulge. Patton also organized a French center for training U.S. tank crews during World War I, in which his principal battles included St. Mihiel and Meuse-Argonne.

Perry, Matthew C. (1794-1858): In a naval career spanning almost half a century, Perry, besides commanding ships and fleets with distinction in peace and in war, proposed and accomplished reforms in naval architecture, ordnance, and organization, and through skillful negotiation introduced Japan into the modern community of nations. Perry was also involved in both the War of 1812 and the Mexican War. He was the younger brother of Oliver Hazard Perry.

Perry, Oliver Hazard (1785-1819): Perry's skillful seamanship and tactical tenacity in the War of 1812 provided an example of leadership and courage to the officers and crews of the young republic's fledgling navy. Perry's actions during the battle of Lake Erie earned him the status of hero and a promotion to captain.

Pershing, John J. (1860-1948): A career U.S. Army soldier, Pershing was ready when called upon to lead the American Expeditionary Force to Europe in World War I, helping to preserve democracy in the first global conflict. He also served during the Spanish-American War, in which he fought at San Juan Hill and in the Philippine Insurrection. During World War II, he served as an unofficial military adviser to President Franklin D. Roosevelt

Pickett, George E. (1825-1875): Pickett fought for the United States during the Mexican War and for the Confederacy during the Civil War. Under orders from General Robert E. Lee, General Pickett led 15,000 troops in a charge against the Union stronghold on Cemetery Ridge during the Battle of Gettysburg, losing more than half his forces. Although Pickett served admirably through the remainder of the war, his failed charge at Gettysburg defined his reputation.

Pierce, Franklin (1804-1869): After service in his state's legislature and in both houses of Congress and military service in the Mexican War, Pierce became the nation's fourteenth president in 1853, serving as president during the four politically challenging years leading up to the crisis that brought the Civil War.

Pope, John (1822-1892): Pope served during the Mexican War and the Civil War. During the Civil War he commanded the Confederate Army of Virginia, which was defeated at the Second Battle of Bull Run.

Powell, Colin L. (1937-   ): Career army officer who was the first African American to become chairman of the Joint Chiefs of Staff. He successfully organized and supervised U.S. military operations during the Gulf War of 1991. He was later appointed secretary of state by president George W. Bush and served in that capacity through the September 11, 2001, terrorist attacks, the Iraq War, and the start of the administration's war on terrorism.

Reagan, Ronald (1911-2004): As the fortieth president of the United States (1981-1989), Reagan authorized an increase in the defense budget, increased the size of the U.S. Navy, and supported the creation and development of new and more sophisticated military weaponry. In 1983, after Grenada's government had been overthrown in a leftist coup, Reagan, in conjunction with the Organization of Eastern Caribbean Nations agreed to restore law and order on Grenada through military intervention.

Revere, Paul (1735-1818): A Revolutionary War patriot and propagandist, Revere was a prominent silversmith, engraver, and industrialist. Notable for his famous midnight ride to warn Samuel Adams and John Hancock of the impending arrival of British troops, Revere later served as lieutenant colonel in the Massachusetts State Train of Artillery and as commander of Castle Island in Boston Harbor. Revere and his troops did not see much action, however, and his military career ended without distinction.

Ridgway, Matthew B. (1895-1993): Ridgway commanded the first airborne division in U.S. history, led troops in World War II and Korea, and replaced both General Douglas MacArthur and General Dwight D. Eisenhower. As the commander of the Eighty-second Airborne Division, he invaded Sicily in July, 1943, landed at Salerno in September, and parachuted into Normandy in June, 1944.

Roosevelt, Franklin D. (1882-1945): President of the United States through the Great Depression and most of World War II, Roosevelt served as commander in chief of the armed forces and planned with Great Britain and the Soviet Union strategies for the military defeat of Germany and Japan and for postwar collective security.

Roosevelt, Theodore (1858-1919): During the Spanish-American War, Roosevelt led a volunteer regiment against Spanish positions on Kettle Hill outside Santiago de Cuba. His successful charge secured fortifications on the heights overlooking the city, and he returned a military hero. Afterward, he was elected governor of New York and then vice president of the United States. After President William McKinley was assassinated in 1901, Roosevelt became president (1901-1909). In that capacity, he promoted American imperial designs on the Pacific and advocated a strong army and navy.

Root, Elihu (1845-1937): As secretary of war under William McKinley and Theodore Roosevelt, Root administered territories gained at the end of the Spanish-American War and initiated reforms in army administration. He pursued a conservative line as secretary of state under Roosevelt and later as U.S. senator from New York, and argued for the value of international law as a political instrument.

Rosecrans, William S. (1819-1898): A gifted strategist while serving as a Union army general during the Civil War, Rosecrans was noted for his brilliance at getting his troops into advantageous positions, but he was considered less capable of executing his plans on the battlefield. His defeat at Chickamauga ended his combat career.

Schwarzkopf, H. Norman (1934-   ): As commander of coalition ground forces during the 1991 Gulf War, General Schwarzkopf was credited with liberating Kuwait from its Iraqi occupiers in only one hundred hours of fighting. His lightning moves on the battlefield and diplomatic finesse in handling a diverse multicultural force established him as one of the great coalition leaders. Schwarzkopf earlier served in the Vietnam War—in which he earned two Purple Hearts and three Silver Stars—and in the occupation of Grenada.

Scott, Winfield (1786-1866): In a military career spanning more than fifty years, Scott emphasized offensive warfare and influenced the military tactics employed by Union and Confederate officers during the Civil War. Scott earlier served in both the War of 1812 and the Mexican War, in which he commanded the army's first major amphibious landing operation in 1847. During the latter war, he defeated Mexican forces at Cerro Gordo and at Contreras, Churubusco, and Molino del Rey, before storming the fortress at Chapultepec and capturing Mexico City.

Sheridan, Philip H. (1831-1888): Recognized as a great fighting general, Sheridan experienced a meteoric rise to become the overall commander of Union cavalry in the eastern theater of the Civil War.

Sherman, William Tecumseh (1820-1891): One of the architects of the Union victory in the Civil War and an inventor of modern forms of warfare, Sherman was also a leader in the nation's late nineteenth century Indian wars in the West. His principal battles during the Civil War included Shiloh, Atlanta, and his March to the Sea.

Spruance, Raymond A. (1886-1969): Quiet and unassuming, Admiral Spruance was a highly effective fleet commander during World War II, in which he participated in the raids on the Marshall and Gilbert Islands. He also participated in the Battle of Midway, the turning point in the war in the Pacific. Spruance had overall command of the invasion of the Marianas and the Battle of the Philippine Sea that effectively destroyed Japan's naval aviation.

Stanton, Edwin M. (1814-1869): Combining excellent administrative skills with attention to detail, Stanton served as President Abraham Lincoln's secretary of war during the Civil War and made major contributions to Union victory.

Stimson, Henry L. (1867-1950): Serving as secretary of war during the years 1909 to 1913 and again during World War II, and serving as secretary of state from 1929 to 1933, Stimson helped to define the United States' transition from isolationism to world responsibility.

Taylor, Zachary (1784-1850): Climaxing a military career of nearly forty years with major victories in the Mexican War, Taylor used his popularity as a war hero to win office as twelfth president of the United States in 1848.

Tecumseh (c. 1768-1813): Leading Indians of the Old Northwest in a united defense against the intrusion of white settlers, the Shawnee Tecumseh contributed significantly to the development of pan-Indianism in North American history. During the War of 1812, he and many of his followers joined the British, believing the former colonial ruler offered Indians the best hope for retaining their homelands. Tecumseh fought in a number of battles until he was killed at the Battle of the Thames.

Thayer, Sylvanus (1785-1872): Known as the "Father of West Point," Thayer is remembered for reorganizing the administration and curriculum of the U.S. Military Academy at West Point and for firmly establishing a scientific and theory-based system of engineering education in the United States.

Thomas, George H. (1816-1870): Thomas's victory at the Battle of Nashville during the Civil War effectively ended the war in the western theater. His other principal battles during the Civil War included Mill Springs, Corinth, Perryville, Stones River, Chickamauga, and Chattanooga. Thomas also saw action earlier in the Mexican War at the battles of Monterrey and Buena Vista.

Truman, Harry S. (1884-1972): Truman saw combat service in World War I fighting in the St. Mihiel and Meuse-Argonne campaigns. After the war he served in the reserves, rising to the rank of colonel. Meanwhile, he was elected to the U.S. Senate and chaired a defense committee that came to be called the Truman Committee. After President Franklin D. Roosevelt died in office, Truman became the thirty-third president of the United States. He participated in the conference at Potsdam and prepared for the final stage of World War II. He approved the dropping of the two atomic bombs on Japan in 1945. Truman also presided over the Korean War until Dwight D. Eisenhower succeeded him as president in 1953.

Wainright, Jonathan (1883-1953): During World War I, Wainright served as a staff officer in France. In March, 1942, after the United States entered World War II, he was promoted to lieutenant general and given command of all U.S. forces in the Philippines. Overwhelmed by more numerous Japanese forces, Wainright and his men surrendered at Corregidor in May, 1942.

Washington, George (1732-1799): As commander in chief of the Continental army during the Revolutionary War, as president of the Constitutional Convention of 1787, and as first president of the United States (1789-1797), Washington was the principal architect of the nation's independence and its federal political system. Washington made notable contributions to military strategy—his retreat and counterattack approach and his understanding of the role of naval forces. As president, Washington established the Department of War and he became the only former U.S. president to be renamed commander in chief of American forces in 1798.

Watie, Stand (1806-1871): Among the many Native Americans who fought in the Civil War, Stand Watie may have served with the greatest distinction. As a Confederate brigadier general, he commanded Cherokee, Creek, and Seminole cavalry and was the last fighting general to surrender to the Union.

Wayne, Anthony (1745-1796): Appointed a colonel in the Continental army in January, 1776, Wayne was one of George Washington's most reliable commanders during the Revolutionary War. He was nicknamed "Mad Anthony" for his daring and served with distinction and cunning throughout the war.

Westmoreland, William (1914-   ): Westmoreland led battalions in North Africa and Europe during World War II and saw combat in the Korean War. As a general, Westmoreland was the commander of all U.S. forces in Vietnam from 1964 to 1968.

Wilson, Woodrow (1856-1924): As twenty-eighth president of the United States (1913-1921), Wilson was responsible for America's entry into World War I, and he played a key role in insisting that the Allies refuse to negotiate with William II of Germany. Wilson was also one of the formulators of the Paris peace settlement and was the principal architect of the League of Nations, although the U.S. Senate refused to ratify U.S. membership in that world body.

Index of Personages

Subject Index

Armored vehicles, 402, 585; World War I, 321; World War II, 402
Army Air Corps, U.S., 401, 495
Army of Northern Virginia, 259
Army of Tennessee, 259
Army of the Potomac, 245
Army of the West, 141
Arnett, Peter, 615, 693
Arnold, Benedict, 10, 39, 41, 52, 54, 58, 782
Arnold, Henry Harley "Hap," 494, 782
Arnold, Samuel, 267
Artillery; Civil War, 165, 168, 181, 185, 188, 229, 234, 236, 244, 246-247, 250, 253; Gulf War, 698, 703; Indochina War, 583; Korean War, 543, 545, 567, 584; Mexican War, 125-126, 149; naval, 491; Revolutionary War, 10, 39, 49-50, 58; Vietnam War, 620, 622, 626; War of 1812, 113; World War I, 301, 306, 309, 320-321, 359, 361-362, 364; World War II, 401, 491
Arver et al. v. United States, 342
Atlanta campaign, Sherman's. *See* Sherman, William T., march to the sea
Atlantic Charter, 454, 733
Atomic bomb, 420; development of, 402-403, 468-472, 512, 523, 528; and Germany, 469; and Japan, 523, 525-529; and Korean War, 548, 550, 563; and Yalta Conference, 515
Atta, Mohammad, 722
Attlee, Clement, 522-525
Attucks, Crispus, 27, 29, 782
Atzerodt, George A., 267
Austin, Hudson, 665
Austin, Moses, 134
Austin, Stephen Fuller, 782
Australia, 715; and Gulf War, 694; and Korean War, 548; and Iraq War, 745-746; and World War I, 305; and World War II, 404, 463-464, 473, 476, 501
Austria; annexation by Germany, 398, 410; and Bosnia-Herzegovina, 302; and Serbia, 314; World War I, 313-314, 316, 318

"Axis of evil," 741, 744
Axis Powers, World War I, 312, 314, 315; and Italy, 314
Axis Powers, World War II, 381, 393; and Atlantic Charter, 454; and Italy, 451; and Japan, 447
Aziz, Tariq, 688

Badoglio, Pietro, 482-484
Baker, Newton, 348
Balaguer, Joaquín, 663, 665
Balkans, NATO incursion, 710-713
Baltimore, Battle of, 99, 109-110
Baltimore Massacre, 102
Bao Dai, Emperor, 581
Barclay, Robert H., 104
Barker, Frank A., 625
Barnes v. Glen Theatre, 603
Barras, comte de, 77
Barton, Clara, 218
Barton, Joe L., 718
Baruch, Bernard Mannes, 354
Bataan, Battle of, 455-456
Bataan Death March, 456
Battles. *See under names of individual battles*
Bay of Pigs invasion, 653-658; and Kennedy, John F., 789
Bayard, James A., 116
Bear Flag Revolt, 143
Beauregard, P. G. T., 200, 224, 234-235, 783
Bedawi, Jamal al-, 719
BEF. *See* British Expeditionary Forces
Belgium; Battle of the Bulge, 507-512; U.S. troops in, 368
Bennett, W. Tapley, Jr., 664
Bennington, Battle of, 60
Berlin, post-World War II partition of, 520, 523-524
Berlin Decree of 1806, 96
Berrigan, Daniel, 609
Berrigan, Philip, 609
Bethmann-Hollweg, Theobald von, 313
Biddle, Francis, 458
Bin Laden, Osama, 698, 713, 722, 732; search for, 728; and Taliban, 735-736
Bishop, Maurice, 666, 668

Subject Index

Panama, 671; in Vietnam, 573, 581,
635-636, 638
Ellis, Earl H., 405
Ellsberg, Daniel, 617
Emancipation Proclamation, 170, 177,
202, 216, 240
Emergency Powers (Defence) Bill,
432
Endara, Guillermo, 671
Endo, Ex parte, 426
England. *See* Great Britain
Enola Gay, 420, 525-526, 529
Equal Rights Amendment, 700
ERA. *See* Equal Rights Amendment
Ericsson, John, 182, 231
Eschwege, Rudolf von, 331
Espionage, and conscription, 339
Espionage Act of 1917, 336, 339-340,
342, 351-354, 431
Ethics of Vietnam War, 609-612
Ethiopia; Italian invasion, 387, 398,
435, 443, 451; and Somalia, 705
Ex parte . . . See under key word
Executive Order 9066, 458

Fair Oaks, Battle of, 182
Falbo v. United States, 423
Falkenhayn, Erich von, 306, 314
Falkland Islands, Battle of (1914), 304
Falkland Islands War (1982), 670, 691
Fannin, James W., 138
Farragut, David G., 785
Fascism, 381, 387, 396-397
FBI. *See* Federal Bureau of
Investigation
Federal Bureau of Investigation, 592;
and *Cole* bombing, 721
Federal Republican, 102
Federalist Party, 115
Ferguson, Patrick, 72
Fermi, Enrico, 469
Fighter planes; Gulf War, 703; Vietnam
War, 583; World War I, 327; World
War II, 403
Five-Power Treaty, 409
Flagg, James Montgomery, 339
Flanders, Battle of, 307
Fletcher, Frank, 464-465, 472

Floridablanca, conde de (José Moñino
y Redondo), 62
Flower v. United States, 602
Floyd, John, 230
Foch, Ferdinand, 310, 316, 360-361
Fokker, Anthony, 321, 328
Fomin, Aleksandr S., 658
Foote, Andrew, 230
Ford, Gerald R., 580, 617
Forrest, Nathan Bedford, 230
Fort Donelson, Battle of, 167, 230
Fort Erie, Siege of, 99
Fort George, Battle of, 98
Fort Henry, Battle of, 167, 230
Fort Sumter, Battle of, 165, 177, 191,
224-226
Fort Ticonderoga, Battle of, 10, 38-39,
54
Fourteen Points, Wilson's, 311, 316,
369-370, 372
France; and American Revolution, 12,
62-63, 65, 67, 79; German invasion
of (1940), 390; Gulf War, 694, 701;
and Triple Entente, 312; Vichy
government, 381, 390, 433, 479;
World War I, 327; World War II, 381,
398, 420
Francis Ferdinand, 302, 313
Franco, Francisco, 387, 398
Franco-American Alliance (1778), 77, 79
Franco-American Treaties, 62-63, 65, 67
Franco-Prussian War, 312, 332
Franklin, Benjamin; and Franco-
American treaties, 62-63, 65, 67; and
submarines, 45; and Treaty of Paris,
78-82
Franks, Tommy, 727, 732, 747, 751-752,
785
Fredericksburg, Battle of, 170, 241-243,
245
Fredonian Uprising of 1826, 135
Free French, 381, 404; and Gaulle,
Charles de, 391
Free-Soil Party, 221
Free State Party, 220
Freeborn v. the "Protector," 208
Frémont, John C., 128, 785
French, John, 305